The Uses of Variety

THOMAS J. WILSON PRIZE

The Board of Syndics of Harvard University Press has selected this book as co-winner of the thirtieth annual Thomas J. Wilson Prize, honoring the late director of the Press. The Prize is awarded to books chosen by the Syndics as best first books accepted by the Press during the calendar year.

The Uses of Variety

Modern Americanism and the Quest for National Distinctiveness

Carrie Tirado Bramen

HARVARD UNIVERSITY PRESS
Cambridge, Massachusetts, and London, England
2000

Copyright © 2000 by the President and Fellows of Harvard College
All rights reserved
Printed in the United States of America

Library of Congress Cataloging-in-Publication Data

Bramen, Carrie Tirado, 1964–
   The uses of variety : modern Americanism and the quest for national distinctiveness / Carrie Tirado Bramen.
      p. cm.
   Includes bibliographical references and index.
   ISBN 0-674-00308-X (alk. paper)
   1. American fiction—History and criticism.   2. Difference (Psychology) in literature.   3. Literature and society—United States—History—20th century.   4. American fiction—Minority authors—History and criticism.   5. United States—Intellectual life—20th century.   6. National characterisctics, American, in literature.   7. Pluralism (Social sciences) in literature.   8. Multiculturalism in literature.   9. Ethnic relations in literature.   10. Minorities in literature.   I. Title
PS374.D45 B73 2000
813. 009'355–dc21   00-056703

For David

CONTENTS

	List of Illustrations	ix
	Abbreviations	x
	Introduction: Americanizing Variety	1
I	**THE IDEOLOGICAL FORMATION OF PLURALISM**	
	1 William James and the Modern Federal Republic	29
	2 Identity Culture and Cosmopolitanism	67
II	**THE AESTHETICS OF DIVERSITY**	
	3 The Uneven Development of American Regionalism	115
	4 The Urban Picturesque and Americanization	156
III	**HETEROGENEOUS UNIONS**	
	5 Biracial Fictions and the Mendelist Allegory	201
	6 East Meets West at the World's Parliament of Religions	250
	Afterword: In Defense of Partiality	293
	Notes	307
	Works Cited	337
	Acknowledgments	361
	Index	365

ILLUSTRATIONS

Figure 1. "The Rag Picker," by Alfred Stieglitz.   168
: New York, 1893; titled "Prosperity" in *Scribner's,* March 1903.

Figure 2. "A Political Discussion at the 'Independent Café' on Grand Street," by Jacob Epstein.   180
: In Hutchins Hapgood, "The Picturesque Ghetto," *Century Magazine* 94 (July 1917): 472.

Figure 3. "A Chinese Kitchen," by J. Durkin.   189
: In Wong Chin Foo, "The Chinese in New York," *The Cosmopolitan* 5 (1888): 303.

Figure 4. Delegates during a session at the World's Parliament of Religions.   253
: In *The World's Parliament of Religions,* ed. John Henry Barrows (Chicago, 1893), I:ii.

Figure 5. Eastern delegates on the platform at the World's Parliament of Religions, 15 September 1893.   270
: By permission of the Ramakrishna-Vivekananda Center, New York.

Figure 6. Anagarika Dharmapala at the World's Parliament of Religions, September 1893.   283
: In *The World's Parliament of Religions,* ed. John Henry Barrows (Chicago, 1893), II:861.

ABBREVIATIONS

C&D Horace Kallen, *Culture and Democracy in the United States*
DB *The Oxford W. E. B. Du Bois Reader*, ed. Eric J. Sundquist
P William James, *Pragmatism: A New Name for Some Old Ways of Thinking*
PU William James, *A Pluralistic Universe: Hibbert Lectures at Manchester College on the Present Situation in Philosophy*
WPR John Henry Barrows, ed., *The World's Parliament of Religions*, 2 vols.

Philosophy has often been defined as the quest or the vision of the world's unity. Few persons ever challenge this definition, which is true as far as it goes, for philosophy has indeed manifested above all things its interest in unity. But how about the *variety* in things? Is that such an irrelevant matter?

William James, Pragmatism (1907)

Introduction

Americanizing Variety

> The United States, by its very nature, by its very development, is the essence of diversity. It is diverse in its geography, population, institutions, technology; its social, cultural, and intellectual modes. It is a society that at its best does not consider quality to be monolithic in form or finite in quantity, or to be inherent in class.
> *Arturo Madrid, "Diversity and Its Discontents" (1990)*

> We are a part and a product of Western civilization. That our society was founded upon such principles as justice, liberty, government with the consent of the governed, and equality under the law is the result of ideas descended directly from great epochs of Western civilization . . . These ideas, so revolutionary in their times yet so taken for granted now, are the glue that binds together our pluralistic nation. The fact that we as Americans—whether black or white, Asian or Hispanic, rich or poor—share these beliefs aligns us with other cultures of the Western tradition.
> *William Bennett, "To Reclaim a Legacy" (1984)*

The benefits of American diversity, that inviolable sign of national exceptionalism, are taken to be self-evident. The phrase "cultural diversity" can be used by both Arturo Madrid, a progressive Chicano educator, and William Bennett, the conservative former chair of the National Endowment for the Humanities, to celebrate national uniqueness. Their celebratory rhetoric, however, supports two mutually exclusive models of national unity, demonstrating that American diversity is not loyal to any political persuasion. For Madrid, the United States represents a loosely unified nation, defined according to multiple traditions that reflect its different cultures and institutions. Diversity is a sign of national health rather than a pathological symptom of cultural degeneration; it promises a dynamic mode of national development that is flexible and accommodating, antithetical to the "monolithic."

While Madrid is the romantic celebrating diversity as the "natural order of things," Bennett, who stylistically favors the singularity of "America" over the plurality of the "United States," imagines a national union that is tightly centered around a clearly identifiable Western tradition. Diversity signals a far different social and political agenda for Bennett than it does for Madrid, one that must be domesticated within a seemingly stable conception of the nation. Bennett ultimately manages to turn the diversity of the nation into a strength by arguing that "Western civilization" can appeal to an increasingly diverse student body ("black or white, Asian or Hispanic, rich or poor") through its "universality" and its "uniqueness." Such a tradition, based on the thought of Enlightenment Europe, provides "the glue that binds together our pluralistic nation" (14–15). That a progressive Chicano educator and a conservative government spokesman should agree that diversity is a national attribute illustrates the elasticity and instability of this concept. Its use-value, in other words, is not restricted to a particular political vantage point.

But is diversity as fickle as it seems? Despite their radically different attitudes toward multiculturalism, Madrid and Bennett share the belief that diversity provides the distinguishing mark of national uniqueness, which not only differentiates the United States from other nations but implicitly (and not so implicitly) makes "us" superior to "them." "What makes us a unique, dynamic, and extraordinary nation," continues Madrid, "is the power and creativity of our diversity" (582). Bennett similarly lauds "our pluralistic nation" and claims that "respect for diversity" is a "good thing" (14). Both praise diversity as quintessentially American and inherently democratic. Its "goodness" is uncontested.

One reason diversity is such a powerful source of national exceptionalism is that it appears to be natural, organic, and self-evident. It is reflected, as Madrid suggests, in the landscape, the faces, and the institutions of the nation; its veracity is manifested in the body politic. Compared with uniformity, which connotes scarcity and stagnation, diversity implies abundance and plenitude, terms that have historically been associated with national development and progress. In contrast to multiculturalism, which is a political minefield of contestation and debate, diversity is easily invoked. Its virtues are obvious.

Since the "culture wars" of the 1980s, American exceptionalism has been increasingly recast according to the terms of globalization, heterogeneity, and transnationalism. As Frederick Buell has pointed out in "Nationalist Postnationalism," President Clinton's 1992 campaign invoked the phrase "global economy," not as a sign of cultural and national degeneration, but as part of a "recovery narrative" that blended conservative nationalist and radical-postnationalist positions into a new form of Americanism for the new global order (553). The eighties discourse of multiculturalism has become increasingly internationalized to promote a "new postnational nationalism" in which the United States is at the cutting edge of global development. Roger Rouse refers to this phenomenon as "corporate liberal multiculturalism," in which neoliberal, free-market financial structures are celebrated in terms of diversity and Americanism. He cites a 1993 advertisement in *Business Week* for the French bank Crédit Lyonnais, which describes itself as "An American Success Story": "Our strength is no longer simply the power of a global bank. It is diversity. It is adaptability. Qualities that are truly American" (qtd. Rouse 380). In the same year, a special issue of *Time* extols diversity as the "fuel that runs today's America," which "puts America in the forefront of a new international order" (qtd. Rouse 380).

From the "culture wars" of the eighties to the new globalization of the nineties, American diversity still has its uses. It has provided the conceptual means for refashioning the dominant narrative of American exceptionalism for a new century: the United States is at the forefront of a new global order precisely because it is able to adapt to the perceived fluidity and heterogeneity of a postnational world system.

This connection between cultural diversity and U.S. exceptionalism has been challenged on at least two fronts. First, scholarship on Mexican *"mestizaje"* and the Canadian "mosaic" has offered pan-American versions of exceptionalist tropes that convert internal divisions into a source of national uniqueness.[1] Such work demonstrates that the United States has not been the only nation in the Americas to turn the effects of globalization, combined with the historical consequences of colonial encounter, into a sign of national strength. Second, the very notion of U.S. diversity has recently come under scrutiny. In "The Multicultural Misunderstanding," Anthony Appiah questions "one of the most pious of the pieties of our age," namely that the United States is a "society of enormous cultural diversity" (30). "Coming as I do from Ghana, I find the broad cultural homogeneity of America more striking than its much vaunted variety. Take language. When I was a child, we lived in a household where there were always at least three mother tongues in daily use" (English, Twi, Navrongo). "So why, in this society, which has less diversity of culture than most others, are we so preoccupied with diversity and so inclined to conceive of it as cultural?" American diversity, he concludes, is a "cozy truism" (31).

Appiah's conclusions were substantiated by a 1995 study sponsored by Harvard University, the *Washington Post,* and the Kaiser Family Foundation. This study found that white Americans as well as minorities substantially underestimated the proportion of whites in the United States, which is 74 percent.[2] Americans, regardless of ethnic or racial background, believe that the United States is far more diverse than it statistically is. This belief also informs forecasts of the U.S. population into the twenty-first century. According to one oft-cited prediction, "minorities" will make up 40 percent of the nation's population by 2040. But such forecasts, as Michael Fix and Jeffrey Passel of the Urban Institute have pointed out, are based on the unrealistic assumption that people represent a single ethnic or racial group and that they will continue to marry within their group. Intermarriage and changes in self-definition, Fix and Passel argue, are important factors that have to be included in such forecasts. Latinos, for example, have the highest rate of marrying outside their own group. If the offspring of Latino/non-Latino unions identify themselves to the census as non-Latino, then the Latino population may be as low as 14 percent of the population by 2040; if all identify as Latinos, then this ethnic group may be as high as 22 percent of the total population (42). For Asians, the projections range from 8 to 11 percent of the population depending on how the children of interracial marriages identify themselves. African Americans, who have low rates of intermarriage, will constitute less than one-third of the minority population in 2040.[3]

Besides this demographic evidence, there has also been a critique of American diversity on the grounds that multinational capital has standardized cultural distinctions. Regardless of the ethnic and racial composition of the nation, the argument goes, all Americans are homogenized according to the consumer habits of shopping. Like Appiah, Russell Jacoby asks "why America is obsessed with cultural diversity" (125). Though Jacoby assumes that the United States is ethnically and racially diverse, particularly when referring to his daughter's girlfriends in Los Angeles ("We joke that they look like a little United Nations when they go out together"), he concludes that "distinct cultures" in U.S. society have actually decreased. "For better or worse," he writes, "only one culture thrives in the United States, the culture of business, work and consuming" (122). Mall culture has ironed out the cultural differences of distinct groups, producing a nation of consumers rather than citizens, united by their common pecuniary desires.

With the exception of Appiah, even the critics of multiculturalism, such as Jacoby, leave unscathed the image of the nation as ethnically and racially diverse. American diversity is treated as a *fact*, which can be confirmed through a brief walk (preferably in a major city). My task in this book is to interrogate rather than invoke "American diversity": to examine how this exceptionalist rhetoric has been employed to promote conflicting and mutually exclusive notions of national identity. In general terms, I will explore how this shibboleth has been used rather than attempting to prove or disprove its veracity. The phrase "cultural diversity" designates not merely a descriptive category but constitutive and evaluative terms, whose parameters often change according to context.

Throughout the book I will address two audiences: those interested primarily in the contemporary debates on multiculturalism and those focused more on the historical substance of my argument. These two audiences frequently intersect. My premise is that we cannot understand the self-evidential nature of American diversity in contemporary multiculturalism without turning to the end of the nineteenth century, when "Americanism" and diversity were becoming increasingly fused. During the heyday of immigration and internal migration, certain writers and thinkers sought to redefine or modernize a national identity, in which diversity was not cast as a barrier to modernization but as its fullest expression. The celebration of American diversity needs to be historicized if we are to understand the variety of ways in which it has circulated. Who has invoked this concept as a national ideal and for what ends?

Before shifting temporal registers to answer this question from a historical perspective, I want to clarify our contemporary context by focusing on a predominant pattern of multiculturalism, specifically the celebration of diversity as a benign and democratic force that is expressive of the cosmopolitanism of the nation. After framing this contemporary debate, I will turn to the past to trace the genealogy of American diversity as the *sine qua non* of national modernity.

* * *

Theoretical work on multiculturalism often exhibits the same tendencies and assumptions that characterize colloquial celebrations of American diversity, as seen in Madrid and Bennett. Multicultural theorists frequently assume that diversity is good in itself, an assumption that results in portrayals of the United States as the expression of a postmodern *mélange* or a carnivalesque utopia. In "The Ideal of Community and the Politics of Difference," Iris Marion Young defends her pluralistic ideal of an "unoppressive city" on the grounds that cosmopolitan variety provides occasions for novel and pleasurable cross-cultural encounters: "The city consists in a great diversity of people and groups, with a multitude of subcultures and differentiated activities and functions, whose lives and movements mingle and overlap in public spaces . . . The appreciation of ethnic foods or professional musicians, for example, consists in the recognition that these transcend the familiar everyday world of my life" (319).

Diversity is valuable, according to this argument, because it gives pleasure to the middle-class, "non-ethnic" urbanite; it allows her to "transcend" the familiar daytime world of work in order to explore the night-time world of the "other half," where she can munch on burritos while listening to jazz. Diversity has no value apart from the *flâneuse;* its importance is predicated on her curiosity. To speak of the city as an ideal chronotope, as a utopic union of space and time, allows Young to avoid situating diversity within the context of urban decay, homelessness, and unemployment.[4] Instead, she portrays the ideal city exclusively as a consumerist odyssey, a culinary and visual spectacle of difference.

A similarly naive celebration of diversity is also seen in more recent scholarship, particularly in work that claims to interrogate the basic assumptions of multiculturalism. Judith Stiehm in "Diversity's Diversity" begins by promising to analyze "diversity" as a "symbol" that is often used with the "purpose of avoiding the complex and the sensitive." But in this essay she ultimately does precisely what she initially criticizes. Rather than addressing the complexities that diversity is supposedly avoiding, Stiehm reproduces diversity's problematic of evasion by taking refuge in a Los Angeles taco stand. Like Young in the "unoppressive city," Stiehm ends her essay with ethnic food, which signifies a common ground bringing diverse people together: "One day in a Los Angeles neighborhood which had signs in every other shop in Russian (with Cyrillic alphabet), I stopped at a taco stand where a number of Asian-

American students were also eating. The African-American waiter wore dreadlocks. No one seemed to notice" (Striehm 154). This eclectic montage of images—Cyrillic alphabet, tacos, Asian Americans, and dreadlocks—is supposed to function metonymically as a heterogeneous sign of American democracy. Only in the United States, and more specifically within its cosmopolitan centers, can one experience fully the true diversity of the age. The juxtaposition of styles has a leveling effect, which produces a certain degree of social and economic parity.

But this postmodern pastiche of an LA taco stand neglects to ask more fundamental questions about this gastronomic "contact zone": to what extent is the invisibility of the dreadlocks emblematic of a larger invisibility in Stiehm's argument, namely the invisibility of labor? Diversity is located in the eating rather than the cooking (or the serving) of food. Both examples of American diversity—Young's "unoppressive city" and Stiehm's taco stand—are premised on the pleasures of consumerism, including the consumption of images that no one else, except of course the author, seems to notice.

A final and somewhat less conspicuous example of how contemporary multiculturalism tends to celebrate diversity in the process of analyzing it is seen in David Theo Goldberg's introduction to his important volume *Multiculturalism: A Critical Reader*. He acknowledges that the term "heterogeneity" has been undertheorized in multicultural debates, which has allowed cultural conservatives to seize on "homogeneity"—the bugbear of multicultural discourse—as preferable: "Homogeneity," argues Goldberg, "is claimed as a necessary condition for community, for civility and perhaps even for civilization" (20). To challenge this equation of homogeneity and civilization, which Goldberg associates with the canon of the "monocultural, Eurocentric tradition," he reverses the value of the terms by appropriating the "naturalist argument" to claim that heterogeneity—and *not* homogeneity—is a "natural condition of human social existence." Homogeneity has now been demoted to an "artifice" (21). To say that heterogeneity is more "natural" to the human condition than homogeneity is to stay within the same conceptual conundrum.

Concepts such as diversity and heterogeneity have indeed been undertheorized, but recent attempts to theorize them have also suffered from undertheorization. This reveals the extent to which these terms have become so firmly embedded in a national structure of feeling that their innocence, benevolence, and inclusivity are taken to be self-evident. The discourse of heterogeneity has already been deemed essential and natural to American identity. Rather than naturalizing this discourse, as Goldberg suggests, what is needed is precisely the opposite: a denaturalization of the heterogeneous as intrinsically "good."

In this book I intervene in the contemporary debates on multiculturalism by stepping back from them. I offer a historical and critical analysis of the fundamental terms of this debate, namely diversity and its late Victorian equivalent, variety. I am interested in how the equation of Americanism and diversity/variety became naturalized as common sense. How and for what purposes did the seemingly benign discourse of variety come to signify national exceptionalism? I argue that neither homogeneity nor heterogeneity can claim a privileged relation to the natural, since both are social constructions that signify differently according to context. This is why the title of my book foregrounds the *uses* of variety, as a way to underscore my fundamental critical project: to examine how the essentializing of heterogeneity has been historically constructed in order to serve conflicting social and political ends. It is by de-essentializing variety that we can become aware of the processes of its construction, how its "essential" benevolence has been historically produced and manufactured. This will, I hope, contribute to a left cultural politics that continues to confront rather than evade the ambiguities of multiculturalism's charged language.

There is a sense in which the rhetoric of diversity provides a conceptual crutch, a *deus ex machina* that saves us from having to grapple with complicated and partisan stances. More specifically, diversity, with its connotations of plenitude and abundance, tends to suppress rather than address the uncomfortable issue of limits. Jackson Lears has suggested that in "an age that is obsessed with diversity," a useful antidote is the recognition of limits: "To acknowledge limits is not to remain imprisoned in the status quo: indeed much status quo thinking involves denial of limits" (*Fables* 13). In a different context, Chantal Mouffe has made a similar point: "To acknowledge the limits of pluralism also means that all differences cannot be accepted and that a radical-democratic project has also to be distinguished from other forms of 'postmodern' politics which emphasize heterogeneity, dissemination and incommensurability" (13). One must be able to discriminate, according to Mouffe, between "differences that exist but should not exist, and differences that do not exist but should exist" (13). A politics of difference needs to be reformulated as a politics of emphasis, which addresses honestly and directly the contested process of boundary-making. Not all forms of diversity, in other words, should be championed, such as the rich diversity of neo-fascist groups or the variety of hate crimes. Distinguishing among different kinds of diversity is integral to a system of ethics and a principle of social justice.

I approach the relation between diversity and limits through the historical framework of the late nineteenth and early twentieth centuries, because this transitional period between Victorianism and modernism was a time when variety and Americanism were becoming increasingly linked in ways that prefigure as well as differ from our contemporary age. In forgetting that concepts have histories, even concepts that appear "contemporary," we also forget the strengths and weaknesses of their earlier formulations. To study the uses of variety in the modern period is to approach the now hackneyed phrase "American diversity" in its prehegemonic stage. That is to say, the equation of modern Americanism and diversity was by no means as naturalized at the turn of the century as it is today. In this earlier period, terms such as "diversity" were highly unsettling, destabilizing, and contested. For some, these words suggested entropic chaos, the disintegration of community from the family to the nation; for others, they signaled the immigrant invasion when swarthier hues populated the trolley cars and subways of the American metropolis. For a cosmopolitan few, they offered a way to refashion modern Americanism according to the premise that diversity was a national asset rather than a threat.

The story that I tell highlights this alternative formulation of modern Americanism, in the vein of William James's praise of the "undisciplinables," where the peculiar, the marginal, and the distinct became emblematic of the nation. In *The Uses of Variety* I explore how the rhetoric of diversity operated within U.S. culture to alleviate two apparently contradictory sources of anxiety: first, concerns about the crisis of individuality due to the encroaching homogeneity of modernity; and second, concerns about the excessive heterogeneity of the metropolitan centers. The language of variety reassured Americans on both counts, since national unity would neither turn into dull uniformity nor disintegrate into disorderly chaos.

To tell the story of modern variety, I rely on an interdisciplinary approach that not only connects the past with the present but also traces turn-of-the-century conversations about diversity and modern Americanism across multiple cultural spheres. A study of the category of "variety" requires a definition of culture that is broad and expansive, one that shifts easily from the philosophy department at Harvard to metropolitan walking tours published in popular magazines. The celebration of variety as distinctively American did not emerge within a single institutional or cultural milieu but occurred simultaneously in the fields of philosophy, popular culture, literature, religion, and science. My interdisciplinary approach is comparative without being relativist, which is to say that I have integrated William James's duality of "connection" and "autonomy" in making comparisons and contrasts between the two periods. The earlier period is neither identical nor "other" to our contemporary times. Instead, to quote James, it is in "some ways connected, in some other ways not connected" (*PU* 666).

When I began research on this topic, I was primarily interested in how turn-of-the-century pluralism, specifically as it was formulated in the work of William James, could shed light on present-day multiculturalism. In pursuing this line of inquiry, I became increasingly engaged with primary materials from the period, developing a serious interest in the years between 1880 and World War I on their own terms, independent of the contemporary plea for relevance. The result was an eclectic method that fuses theoretical interests with historical scholarship, a combination that allows me to appreciate the late Victorian period for what it can and cannot teach us about our contemporary times.

The historian Michael Kammen has argued that "American heterogeneity" has prevented a "singular mode or pattern of exceptionalism" (3). Let me suggest instead that it is precisely because of "American heterogeneity" that there has been a common pattern, though by no means the only pattern, of American exceptionalism. At the turn of the nineteenth century, the rhetoric of variety (and domesticated heterogeneity) provided an important means of refashioning Americanism in modern terms, as the incorporation of global (primarily European) cultures within what Randolph Bourne called a "world-federation in miniature."[5] In claiming, however, that American variety was a specifically modern phenomenon, which coincided with the rising international prominence of the United States as a receiving nation for immigrants and an imperial nation with colonies, I do not want to slip into the temporal equivalent of American exceptionalism, or what could be called "epochal exceptionalism."

The celebration of American variety did not suddenly begin in the late nineteenth century. Variety was an inherited term as much as it was a "modern" one. To demonstrate this point, I turn briefly to this earlier period to chart a genealogy of American diversity, a genealogy that rests on the polemical assumption that origins, as inevitably contrived and constructed historical markers, are necessary. They humble us by suggesting that our contemporary debates and even late Victorian ones are not entirely novel or unique. Origins also serve as points of emphasis that define and circumscribe particular traditions.

The tradition that I want to trace includes three seminal events from the late eighteenth century to the antebellum period, when the language of variety was naturalized as distinctively "American." These precursory moments include: (1) Crèvecoeur's "New American" (1782); (2) Madison's *The Federalist No. 10* (1787); and (3) the Lincoln-Douglas Debates (1858). I have chosen these three examples because they contribute to the formation of a "selective tradition," which, according to Raymond Williams, involves the "continual selection and re-selection of ancestors," creating a "historical record of a particular society" and rejecting a considerable amount of what was once a living culture (*Long Revolution* 68–69). These historical antecedents do not create a complete genealogy of American diversity, nor do they simply anticipate late-nineteenth-century variations. They will provide important points of contrast and comparison, which will, in turn, help delineate the historical parameters of modern variety.

In 1782, J. Hector St. John Crèvecoeur, an immigrant from Normandy who would eventually return to Europe, published a series of essays in London entitled *Letters from an American Farmer*. In the third letter, "What is an American," Crèvecoeur prefigures Israel Zangwill's "melting-pot" by describing the formation of the "new man" in terms of melting: "Here individuals of all nations are melted into a new race of men, whose labours and posterity will one day cause great changes in the world" (659–660). Although Crèvecoeur confidently uses the internationalist language of "all nations" and "the world," the actual ingredients of this "new race of men" consist of a selective range of Northern European ethnicities: "They are a mixture of English, Scotch, Irish,

French, Dutch, Germans and Swedes" (658). To demonstrate the extent of such mixture, he refers to a local example: "I could point out to you a family whose grandfather was an Englishman, whose wife was Dutch, whose son married a French woman, and whose present four sons have now four wives of different nations" (659). Although Dutch-English mixtures would not be all that shocking for late Victorians, the significance of Crèvecoeur's "melting" mixture is that it inscribes American variety within a limited Eurocentric framework, whose Protestant core does not significantly change in the next century despite the late-nineteenth-century surge of Catholic and Jewish immigrants from Eastern and Southern Europe.

The second antecedent to modern formulations of variety is James Madison's *The Federalist No. 10,* a paper that aimed to persuade reluctant New Yorkers to adopt the proposed new Constitution, which would sacrifice a degree of local and state power in order to strengthen the national government. A strong federal government, it was argued, would be able to consolidate and protect the interests of the land-owning class, which was geographically scattered throughout the former thirteen colonies. Madison feared that most Americans, who were suffering from considerable inequities, would "secretly sigh for a more equal distribution of [life's] blessings" (qtd. Chomsky 7). Madison made his case for a strong federal government through an alarmist vision of a nation internally torn by faction. Prefiguring William James's "pluralistic universe," the subject of my first chapter, Madison's "Union" exists within a gothic world full of rival parties, conflicting interests, and competing sectors of the population. "The instability, injustice and confusion introduced into the public councils have in truth been the mortal diseases under which popular governments have everywhere perished" (759). In contrast to popular democracy, republicanism, with its central form of government, can withstand the threat of faction because republics do not seek to remove the "causes of faction" but only to seek "relief" in "controlling its effects" (761).

Defined as a "destructive agency," a faction is, according to Madison, a collection of citizens, "amounting to a majority or minority of the whole, who are united and actuated by some common impulse of passion or of interest, adverse to the rights of other citizens, or to the permanent and aggregate interests of the community" (759). The most "common" and the most dangerous factions are produced from "the various and unequal distribution of property," from the disparity between those who possess and those who are without property (760). The republic has two ways of combating the "mischiefs of faction": (1) through the "scheme of representation"; (2) through geographic expansion. A "scheme of representation," in which the few represent the many, would protect the "public weal" only when the number of representatives was large enough to "guard against the cabals of a few" and small enough to "guard against the confusion of a multitude" (762). A representative must remain "acquainted" with the local but not "unduly attached" to it. Increasing the parameters of the nation would further diffuse local attachments: "Extend the sphere, and you take in a greater variety of parties and interests; you make it less probable that a majority of the whole will have a common motive to invade the rights of other citizens" (763).

What is striking about Madison's rhetoric is the dramatic shift from "faction" to "variety." In the first part of *The Federalist No. 10*, when describing the threat to the property holder or "landed interest," he uses the language of "faction" in relation to "mischiefs," "mortal diseases," and "violence." However, in the latter half of the same piece, when underscoring the ability of a strong federal government to contain the destructive potential of faction, he switches to the far more benign language of variety. The "mischiefs of faction," for instance, becomes a "variety of sects." He speaks of the "greater variety of parties" and the "increased variety of parties" as essential to the "security" of the "Union" (763). The language of variety constitutes the "republican remedy" for internal dissent: its positive connotations, associated with abundance and plenitude, provide a way of rhetorically diffusing the threat of domestic strife within a strong federal government. Variety is a residual term of popular democracy, linked to organic tropes of difference and individuality, which Madison transplants to the Constitution as a way of naturalizing a political artifice.

The significance of Madison for my purposes in this book is that he underscores the curative effects of variety; it can operate as a rhetorical anodyne, diffusing the "mischiefs of faction" without having to address the cause. This same strategy is seen at the turn into the twentieth century, when the rhetoric of variety becomes a way of presenting modern America not as a place of social and labor unrest, a republic divided by class, race, and regional factions, but instead as a land of spatial and material abundance.[6]

The historical symbiosis of variety and nationhood finds its third epochal moment in 1858. The Illinois senatorial campaign between Stephen Douglas and Abraham Lincoln had, according to President McKinley in 1899, "as much to do with shaping and molding public opinion as any other event I can now recall" (McKinley 25). In these debates, which primarily consisted of a series of speeches in the summer of 1858, the antinomy of variety and uniformity played a central role. Variety, for Douglas, was synonymous with states' rights and individual liberty. A healthy, democratic Union depended on the full expression of each state's individual character, reflected in the "laws and institutions," which ought to be "as diversified and as dissimilar as the States would be numerous" (Johannsen 30). "I am driven irresistibly," argued Douglas, "to the conclusion that diversity, dissimilarity, variety in all our local and domestic institutions, is the great safeguard of our liberties" (Johannsen 31). Variety functioned euphemistically, as a defense of slavery that did not explicitly claim to be so. Speaking in terms of "variety" also allowed Douglas to convert slavery from a moral issue into an aesthetic one, where variety was more appealing to an American sensibility than uniformity.

The language of variety through its antithesis—uniformity—created a political drama between the forces of democracy and the forces of tyranny. In wanting to rid the nation of slavery, according to Douglas, Lincoln was upholding "uniformity," which would obliterate individuality through despotism: "Uniformity in local and domestic affairs would be destructive of State rights, of State sovereignty, of personal liberty and personal freedom. Uniformity is the parent of despotism the world over" (Johannsen 30). Uniformity, Douglas warned, would convert "these thirty-two sovereign, independent States into one consolidated empire" (Johannsen 30–31). In a speech the following day, Lincoln addressed Douglas's accusations: "He says I am in favor of making all the States of this Union uniform in all their internal regulations; that in all their domestic concerns I am in favor of making them entirely uniform" (Lincoln 491).

Lincoln challenged Douglas by replacing the language of "variety" and "uniformity" with an explicit discussion of slavery: he uttered the word that Douglas refrained from using. In reducing slavery to an issue of states' rights, argued Lincoln, Douglas viewed "this matter of slavery as an exceedingly little thing—this matter of keeping one-sixth of the population of the whole nation in a state of oppression and tyranny unequalled in the world. He looks upon it as being an exceedingly little thing—only equal to the question of the cranberry laws of Indiana—as something having no moral question in it—as something on a par with the question of whether a man shall pasture his land with cattle, or plant it with tobacco" (Lincoln 494). For Lincoln, the language of variety actually trivialized slavery, resulting in the eradication of ethical concerns from the debate.

Douglas's use of variety not only removed the question of morality from the debate about human enslavement; it also defended white supremacy. Though Douglas saved the pejorative term "uniformity" for Lincoln, he nonetheless ended his Chicago speech by praising racial homogeneity. "I repeat that this nation is a white people—a people composed of European descendants—a people that have established this government for themselves and their posterity, and I am in favor of preserving not only the purity of the blood, but the purity of the government from any mixture or amalgamation with inferior races" (Johannsen 34). There was no inconsistency between being pro-variety and being a white supremacist.

By the 1850s, Crèvecoeur's European "melting" mixture had become consolidated and homogenized as "white." The task now was to preserve "the purity of the blood." This example reveals two important features about antebellum uses of variety. First, it demonstrates how this apparently innocent term could be used to defend anti-democratic and racist viewpoints. Although variety was perceived as inherently benevolent, its "goodness" was in fact used to support a range of morally abject practices such as slavery. Second, Douglas's use of variety illustrates that the term's benevolence was already well in place on the eve of the Civil War and that it was seen as a complement to national unity rather than a threat to it. This complementary relation further naturalized the belief that slavery was an extension of personal (white) liberty and state sovereignty. The Lincoln-Douglas debates also point to the fact that "uniformity" had become unsavory and disagreeable. In contrast to Crèvecoeur, who spoke of the "pleasing uniformity" of American domiciles, there was little for Douglas that was redeemable about the word, except in terms of the "good" uniformity of "race purity" or "white blood."[7]

These three precursory examples reveal that the term "variety" already had a complicated and contentious history prior to the turn into the twentieth century. The term surfaced at two critical junctures of national unity: in the late eighteenth century during the debates leading to the acceptance of the Constitution, and on the eve of the Civil War during the senatorial campaign debates on slavery. That the term should have reemerged at the end of the nineteenth century is not surprising. This period marked another significant transition in the nation's history, a transition that historians have described in various ways, as a "crisis of authority" (Lears), a "crisis of abundance" (Kern), a "crisis of incorporation" (Trachtenberg), and a "crisis of community" (Wiebe).

It was a time of unprecedented immigration. "Everyday is moving day," wrote the Norwegian novelist Knut Hamsun, "the population is only half-settled" (qtd. Schlereth 7). Between 1883 and 1907, 81 percent of European immigrants to the United States came from Southern and Central Europe, and most were Catholics, Jews, or members of other non-Protestant groups. The sociologist Edward Ross described the new European arrivals as a "Caliban type," who were "hirsute, low-browed, big-faced persons of obviously low mentality" (*Old World* 286). "Even aside from the pouring in of the ill-favored," augured Ross, "the crossing of the heterogeneous is bound to lessen good looks among us" (*Old World* 288). During this same period, 100,000 immigrants also arrived from the Caribbean. African Americans started to move from the rural South and from New South cities to northern cities. As early as 1903, W. E. B. Du Bois concluded that "the most significant economic change among Negroes in the last ten or twenty years has been their influx into northern cities" (qtd. Meier 274). Internal migrations were catalyzed, in part, by the economic depressions of 1893–1897 and 1907–1908, when industrial unemployment rates soared to 30 percent.[8] The period between 1880 and World War I also witnessed the peak and nadir of the Chinese population in the United States. With the onset of the Chinese Exclusion Act of 1882, the numbers dropped from 107,000 in the early 1880s to a low of 61,639 in 1920.[9]

What unites "modern" variety with its historical antecedents is the acknowledgment of crisis and the attempt to manage it. Variety was both a product of an age of excessive abundance and dire scarcity and its moral antidote. Van Wyck Brooks, for instance, considered surplus a "problem," writing in 1915 that a "familiar distinction between the nineteenth century and the twentieth is that the problem of civilization is no longer the problem of want but the problem of surplus."[10] Variety was a way to negotiate the extremes of an expanding capitalist economy through a principle of moderation. For the genteel liberal as well as for the middle classes, the discourse of variety provided a way to save unity from uniformity while also redeeming it from chaos. It signified social equilibrium, a modern version of Young's "unoppressive city," in representing a unified space that also had a sufficient amount of difference to make it interesting. William James's colleague at Harvard, George Santayana, theorized the term according to a similar moral imperative: "'variety' is good only if a unity can still be secured embracing that variety" (155).

The final point of convergence between modern variety and its earlier incarnations is the intersection of variety, whiteness, and nationhood. When taken together, Crèvecoeur and Douglas represent two stages in the racial consolidation of Americanism as variegated whiteness. At the early stage, Crèvecoeur described the process of European fusion as one of "melting," but the particular ethnicities were still identifiable as "Dutch" or "English." By the time Douglas was writing, the "melting" process was much further along, as is evident in Douglas's phrase "European descendants," which was used interchangeably with "white people" and "purity of the blood." Douglas no longer particularized the component parts of the "new American," since his emphasis was far more on constructing "whiteness" as a homogeneous front against African Americans. By the late nineteenth century, however, the category of whiteness expanded to include a greater variety of European hues so as to incorporate the new immigrants from Southern and Eastern Europe.

In "Are We a People?" (1908), Franklin Giddings, the renowned Columbia sociologist, attempted to break with his late-nineteenth-century preoccupation with the benefits of social and cultural sameness in order to discuss the attributes of immigration. He spoke not in terms of "melting" but of "smelting," which would create "one nation," a common ground through immigrant diversity (37). But the parameters of difference surfaced when he outlined the individual ingredients: "we are injecting Italians, Hungarians, and Slavs; but these can not possibly submerge the Celtic-Teutonic blood already here" (38). In contrast to Israel Zangwill's "melting-pot," which fused "black and yellow, Jew and Gentile," Giddings's "smelting" was a far more restricted process that expanded the category of whiteness to include the swarthier hues of Europe, while excluding people of color as well as Jews. This use of variety was motivated not so much by anti-nativist sentiments as by a revised nativism, which was genteel, confident, and discriminating. Giddings's "smelting process," for instance, maintained an intraracial hierarchy, privileging Northern over Southern Europeans, where the parts still retained their particularity so as not to blend completely. One wonders then if Giddings's more liberal version of "smelting" is actually more inclusive than Crèvecoeur's "melting." In Chapter 2 I broaden the debate between ethnic particularity and blending to include Horace Kallen's "orchestra," but at this point let me suggest that, by the turn of the century, Crèvecoeur's notion of "melting" was both expanded and contested. The debate now centered on whether individual cultures could and indeed should retain their particularity, or what was referred to as "group-individuality."

Although "modern" variety developed fundamental tendencies from its historical antecedents, in that pre-Victorian and Victorian models were forms of crisis management, there were two important differences. First, the rhetoric of variety was now inscribed within a Spencerian trajectory of progress as the "advance from homogeneity to heterogeneity," which privileged industrial society as the height of human civilization. Long after Herbert Spencer's views on Social Darwinism became unpopular among liberal intellectuals such as William James, Spencer's notion of modernity as heterogeneous and urban still held sway.[11] This reveals at one level that the rhetoric of variety was becoming dislodged from its rural roots, from Crèvecoeur's "American farmer," and moving to the city, where it would become the privileged term of the cosmopolitan *flâneur*. This terminological migration also had its critics. Regionalism, as I argue in Chapter 3, was an attempt to reclaim variety as the organic and authentic discourse of the geographical margins. It demonstrated that rural localities were the exceptional spaces of an otherwise uniform nation because they could still maintain their unique character in the midst of incorporation.

Second, the rhetoric of variety was no longer an expression primarily of dominant interests, as in Madison's federalist plan and the antebellum defense of states' rights. It was now used to articulate a far greater spectrum of positions, ranging from prominent intellectuals such as Giddings to lesser-known figures such as the African-American writer and educator Anna Julia Cooper. In a strategy that I elaborate in relation to Du Bois in Chapter 2 and in relation to black women's anti-passing fiction in Chapter 5, Cooper uses the phrase "American diversity" to place the "race problem" at the center of modern Americanism. She modifies the Madisonian tenet that conflict is vital for a republic—a sign of democratic health—and applies it to the exigencies of racial antagonism in the era of Jim Crow. The "Race Problem," argues Cooper in *A Voice from the South* (1892), is a "guaranty of the perpetuity and progress of her [the nation's] institutions, and insures the breadth of her culture and the symmetry of her development" (173). Without a "Race Problem," she warns, there would be "a sameness, a monotonous dullness which means stagnation,—death" (152). Whereas the rhetoric of "variety" allows Giddings and others to bracket off race in order to discuss European ethnicities, Cooper uses the same principle—that difference makes the United States more interesting than it otherwise would be—to foreground racial conflict as part and parcel of the nation's development.

Variety is a way to make the racial margins definitive of Americanism, to put black-white relations at the center of the nation's understanding of itself as an "imagined community." That Cooper frames her intervention in terms of saving the nation from "monotonous dullness" conveys the extent to which late Victorians disliked the standardizing pressures of modernization. Cooper modifies the platitude "variety is the spice of life" by racializing it, and thus makes use of Anglo-American ennui to introduce African-American claims to cultural and political citizenship. Whereas Stephen Douglas accentuates the trivializing aspects of variety as a way to evade the moral question of slavery, Cooper uses this same rhetoric a half-century later to place an ostracized population at the center of the national agenda.

To analyze the productive uses of national variety, the ways in which it could be used to support mutually exclusive definitions of modern Americanism, requires a critical emphasis that is frequently lacking in standard interpretations of the period. The standard story assumes that late Victorians feared the modern, greeting it with neurasthenic disorders and a range of other anxieties in order to escape into a realm of unreality and weightlessness. For Jackson Lears, antimoderns understood the modern social world as "evasive banality," a pattern that allowed them to avoid conflict at every opportunity (*No Place* 7). Genteel New England liberals came to terms with modernity by denying its disturbing underside, by escaping into a therapeutic mode of unreality that yearned for mind-cures and other panaceas. Interestingly, Lears conveys this sense of disorientation and diffuseness through the language of heterogeneity, and its variation "eclecticism." Lears's assumption is that city life, in particular, assaulted the senses with a jumble of multiple styles that produced a "riot of eclecticism." Lears pathologizes "eclecticism" as a "symptom" of degeneration and bewilderment: "Uprooting once-sacred symbols from their appropriate time, place, and purpose, the eclectic approach trivialized them—reduced them to commodities in the marketplace of taste. Eclecticism signified the impoverishment of a culture which lacked resources for creating its own symbols" (*No Place* 33). What Lears cannot acknowledge are genteel interventions such as that of Giddings, who used eclecticism or "smelting" as the distinguishing feature of the new nation, as a necessary stage toward modernization.

Amy Kaplan also characterizes late Victorian culture as hetero-phobic, a trait most clearly seen in the realist fiction of the period. Kaplan notes that in W. D. Howells's realist novels there is a "sense of the city as a shared, or common, reality," a sense that is dependent upon "continually banishing the 'other half,' the common people, into a tamed cityscape" (*Social* 53). This point informs Kaplan's general theory of realism as a counterforce against "foreign tongues and social fragmentation" (*Social* 23). For the late-nineteenth-century realist reader and writer, social difference, argues Kaplan, becomes inseparable from social conflict. As a therapeutic response to a world in which social diversity and difference were considered threatening, realism "does not jar readers with the shock of otherness, it provides a recognizable mirror of their own world" (*Social* 23). Both Lears's anti-modernism and Kaplan's realism operate as ways of configuring the turn of the century as a period fraught with fears of otherness, ranging from "foreign tongues" to a "riot" of eclectic styles. According to this argument, heterogeneity, eclecticism, and variety were the very qualities that had to be suppressed; they signified threats to the late Victorians' understanding of social reality as ordered, stable, and homogeneous.

In this book I emphasize a competing cultural "pattern," one that foregrounds the emergent late Victorian belief that social diversity "loosened up" unity, to borrow William James's phrase, while at the same time ensuring a sense of boundedness. Variegated unions were accommodating and therefore durable amidst the vicissitudes of the modern age.[12] Rather than read the discourse of heterogeneity pathologically as a menace to the social order, I want to interpret it productively, as a creative response to modernization, which was at times full of radical potential and at other times deeply reactionary. "Patterns of culture," as Raymond Williams has argued, do not produce seamless narratives, a consistent understanding of a general historical formation; they demonstrate the continuities and correspondences of separately considered activities while also revealing discontinuities and contradictions (*Long Revolution* 63). To reveal the complex uses of variety at the turn of the century within this cultural pattern of emergent modernism, I discuss a wide range of historical texts, from intra-urban periodical sketches to speeches at the 1893 World's Parliament of Religions. Each chapter captures a separate activity, whether it is intellectual history, regionalism, the urban picturesque, African-American women's anti-passing fiction, or religious debates about a "universal faith."

What unites these various cultural, literary, and intellectual moments is the appropriation of social diversity as central and emblematic of "modern Americanism." In 1907 Brander Matthews, a professor of literature at Columbia, wrote: "New York is quite as American to-day as it ever has been in any of its three centuries. Diversity of blood has always been its dominant characteristic" (475). In his famous Fourth of July speech of 1915, "True Americanism," Louis Brandeis expanded this theme to include the nation as a whole: "America has believed that in differentiation, not in uniformity, lies the path of progress" (10). This point also appears in one of William James's final essays, "A Pluralistic Mystic," where he quotes the poet and philosopher Benjamin Paul Blood: "Variety, not uniformity, is more likely to be the key to progress" (*Writings* 1310). This neglected pattern, in which variety is embraced rather than feared, will serve as the locus of my historical reinterpretation.

Modern variety was not a proto-postmodern version of the notion of "endless variety," but a more restrained concept connected to a larger cultural politics of moderation. In the midst of the excesses of the Gilded Age, when social and economic disparities continued to grow, modern variety emerged, in part, as an antidote that fused nineteenth-century liberalism with twentieth-century modernity. This sense of moderation is most clearly seen in attempts to define the particularity of variety by contrasting it with its anarchic variation—heterogeneity (which was the modern antecedent of Lyotard's postmodern notion of boundless plurality). For late Victorians, the discourse of multiplicity was highly differentiated; its nuances were conveyed through the choice or the type of plurality.[13] For most architects of modern Americanism, variety rather than heterogeneity was the preferred term, because it implied a measure of plenitude that was considered temperate rather than excessive.

By contrast, heterogeneity was a far more loaded and unstable term. For William James, it threatened the equilibrium of the mind. In *The Varieties of Religious Experience,* he warns that a "heterogeneous personality" is on the verge of insanity: "a stronger degree of heterogeneity may make havoc of the subject's life. There are persons whose existence is little more than a series of zigzags, as now one tendency and now another gets the upper hand. Their spirit wars with their flesh, they wish for incompatibles, wayward impulses interrupt their most deliberate plans, and their lives are one long drama of repentance and of effort to repair misdemeanors and mistakes" (154). That James did not decide to entitle his book "The Heterogeneity of Religious Experience" suggests that "variety" signifies the cure whereas "heterogeneity" represents the pathology. Heterogeneity implies a loss of control, a surrender to forces greater than one's self, forces that James internalized as impulses and desires.

Heterogeneity was also a highly racialized term at the turn of the century, referring primarily to the colonized world in the aftermath of the Spanish-American War of 1898. In delineating the limits of U.S. citizenship, Woodrow Wilson in "The Ideals of America" (1902) argued that the ethnic and racial diversity of the Filipinos precluded a communitarian spirit and prevented them from becoming future U.S. citizens: "No people can form a community or be wisely subjected to common forms of government who are as diverse and as heterogeneous as the people of the Philippine Islands" (732). Christian missionaries of the period also considered China and India excessively heterogeneous. At the 1893 World's Parliament of Religions, a supplementary two-week event held during the Columbian Exposition, which is the subject of my final chapter, a Presbyterian missionary described Chinese religion as a "heterogeneous cult" (*WPR* II:1140).

Unlike William James and Woodrow Wilson, who dismissed heterogeneity for its excessiveness, Giddings tried to recuperate the term and reform its recalcitrant ways by domesticating it. Giddings's intervention was one of conversion, an attempt to redeem heterogeneity by assimilating it to a standard of variety. At the turn of the century, his sociological work was undergoing a paradigmatic shift. His critical focus altered from a concern about establishing social connections through sameness or what he called "consciousness of kind" to a principle of heterogeneity-in-moderation. He was now interested in what made society "modern" and "complex." In 1903 Giddings wrote: "Somewhere between excessive heterogeneity and complete homogeneity will be found that precise composition of a people which ensures progress and is yet compatible with personal freedom and a liberal social organization" ("Sociological" 253). Incorporating a Spencerian trajectory of progress as the "advancement from the homogeneous to the heterogeneous," Giddings argued that excessively heterogeneous societies do not have a common ground, while a "really homogeneous people" does not encourage progress ("Sociological" 253).

This distinction between heterogeneity and homogeneity also constitutes an allegory of national development and underdevelopment. Whereas "bountiful environments normally have heterogeneous populations," homogeneous countries tend to "dwell in the relatively poor and isolated environments" ("Sociological" 248). This allegory of modernization reinforces American exceptionalism by linking an economy of abundance with a principle of heterogeneity-in-moderation. What makes the United States unique, according to this argument, is its ability to bypass the extremes of heterogeneity and uniformity by finding a middle ground where cultural variety creates a sense of relative stability without monotony.

I trace the development of this liberal philosophy of the middle ground, where variety "loosens up" unity without sacrificing boundaries, through a diverse range of texts, cultural milieus, and political and social perspectives. I explore the variability of variety—its dynamic and flexible character—by examining its uses in a range of different contexts. Within religious debates, for instance, theologians attempt to resolve the need to preserve sectarian distinctions with the ideals of a "universal faith." For urban journalists, the discourse of variety works to incorporate the particularities of the ghetto into a cosmopolitan vision. For African-American writers, such as Du Bois and Frances Harper, it helps connect "subcultures of criticism" (Cornel West's phrase) with modern Americanism. The discourse of American variety also has limits: it links subcultures with national cultures and international communities, not through a model of fusion or blending, but rather through a strategy of resilient particularity. It seeks to retain the individuality of the component parts, not through a residual move to provincialism or a defensive tactic of protectionism, but rather through modern formulations of contact. Particularity is produced through connection. In this book, therefore, I dramatize eclectic scenes of cross-cultural encounter, in which the challenge of plurality intersects with the necessity of boundaries. I explore the various ways in which a national community could be reconciled with (sub)cultural distinctions.

The book is divided into three parts, each locating the rhetoric of variety within a different locus of debate. In Part I, I establish a genealogy of the term "pluralism" in the work of William James and two of his Harvard students, Horace Kallen and W. E. B. Du Bois. Like contemporary multiculturalism, Gilded Age pluralism originated in a university culture but quickly moved beyond the ivory tower to address the major social and political issues of the day. I begin with James because he believed that the one and the many could be resolved, at least in a limited and temporary manner—a project that his contemporaries such as Henry Adams considered futile. James had a far less cynical and deterministic view of modernity, one that possessed the pragmatic spirit of possibility in believing that one could realize one's potential as an individual while belonging to a larger community. For James, pluralism was a crisis-management guide to modernity; he offered in highly allegorical prose a way to maintain unity at a time of flux and change. The most durable forms of modern collectives, according to James, were modest and flexible ones, those which were able to withstand sudden "jolts."

I then examine how James's allegory of modernity was modified in the work of Kallen and Du Bois. Addressing not "monism" in an abstract sense but 100 percent Americanism and what Kallen aptly called "Kukluxitis," Kallen "Judaized" and Du Bois "Africanized" the Jamesian "each-form" as a sign of subcultural resilience at a time of standardization. While James defended the sacredness of the individual, Du Bois and Kallen defended the right to be different in relation to individuals and ethno-racial subcultures. This different emphasis illustrates larger changes within liberalism, a shift from the classical focus on individual liberty to collective forms of sovereignty. I conclude Part I by exploring the directions in which Kallen and Du Bois took their mentor's pluralism, competing directions that disclose wider tensions between the conservative and radical possibilities of Progressive liberalism.

In Part II, I chart the travels of the Jamesian "each-form" as it ventured beyond intellectual subcultures to marginal geographies, where particularity was understood in terms of the region or the immigrant ghetto. Jamesian pluralism was appropriated by regionalists and cosmopolitan journalists alike, who drew on the language of variety to locate modern Americanism in the country and the city, respectively. Variety was now a way to validate those on the geographical margins, ranging from Dougherty County, Georgia, to Hell's Kitchen, New York. From local color to the urban picturesque, the aesthetic was a way to retain the character and individuality of distinct places in the midst of spatial incorporation, where the persistence of local variety became an emblem of American exceptionalism. Modernization did not necessarily mean standardization. Progress and particularity could be complementary processes. I then explore the variations of variety within the regional and the urban contexts: how different authors invoked the local in conflictual and irreconcilable ways. For some, it was a critique of uneven development, where certain localities were made subordinate to others. For others, local variety was a sign of democratic health in that even new immigrants have the moral right to remain "different."

Part III moves from the national to the transnational, from race relations between the northern and southern United States to international relations among theologians from Asia, Europe, and the United States. In this section I pair black women's anti-passing fiction, a genre I call the "Mendelist allegory" for its hereditarian defense of black exceptionalism, with the 1893 World's Parliament of Religion, a two-week auxiliary event held during the Columbian Exposition in Chicago. In moving from literature to oratory, and from models of racial harmony to models of religious comity, I explore the similar tensions that underlie cross-racial and cross-religious contact, tensions that include minority versus majority communities, discreteness versus fusion, particularity versus universalism, and limited variety versus boundless plenitude. The final chapter also witnesses the return of William James, as I describe personal encounters between James and some of the Buddhist and Hindu representatives, and more broadly, demonstrate how the parliament dramatizes the characteristic tensions and spirit of the Jamesian "pluralistic universe."

Only by looking at a diverse range of contexts will we be able to understand how "variety" circulated at the turn of the century. Its romantic connotations of innocence, plenitude, and benevolence helped construct modern modalities of unity in which the individuality of the Jamesian "each-form" could persist and even become representative of the new age. While variety became essentialized as intrinsically good, its uses remained politically contingent. Therefore, rather than uniformly praise American diversity, I interrogate the formation of this concept as an overdetermined process, one that served mutually exclusive ideological ends. I explore how intellectuals from different regions, races, and religions defined the parameters of variety, a contested domain that determined, in part, the limits of national inclusion.

I

The Ideological Formation of Pluralism

1

William James and the Modern Federal Republic

William James did not invent pluralism; he modernized it. He took a term that had been traditionally associated with church corruption and turned it into a positive sign of modern republicanism. In converting pluralism from an ecclesiastical term to a secular one, James helped purge the concept of its negative connotations. Beginning in the seventeenth century and continuing throughout the nineteenth, "pluralist" referred to a clerk or clergyman who held more than one benefice at the same time. A well-connected member of the clergy could, for instance, earn a church living (and perhaps receive multiple endowments) in addition to land grants. Pluralism suggested abundance and excess but concentrated in the hands of the theocratic elite. By the late nineteenth century, James had liberated the term by making abundance more accessible. Pluralism now referred to individual freedoms, eccentricities, and choices. Culminating in 1909 with the publication of *A Pluralistic Universe*, James created a blueprint for modern pluralism, a blueprint that the next generation of young intellectuals would apply to their contemporary world, in which the term "pluralism" would become synonymous with democracy, liberalism, and Americanism.[1]

This connection between pluralism and Americanism has characterized James's public image as an intellectual populist. From the beginning of the twentieth century to the beginning of the twenty-first, William James has been understood as an all-American philosopher, whose image has been synonymous with democracy, the underdog, and a love of variety. In 1910 Walter Lippmann found James "so very much of a democrat," a point reiterated by James's student Horace Kallen, who declared his mentor "the first democrat in metaphysics." Kallen added that James was a "pioneer" who fled his patrician roots to conquer the American wilderness: "to the west and south was the wilderness untamed and calling for domestication. James himself celebrates the inward beauty of the pioneer's visible ugly triumphs over that wilderness" (*Philosophy* 41).

The image of James as a pioneer, who in domesticating the wilderness discovered pragmatism and pluralism, persists today during what Cornel West has called an "intellectual renascence" of pragmatism. Central to this "renascence" is the image of James as an "authentic American intellectual frontiersman" who, according to West, rejected the political left and right and instead embraced "democratic sentiments" and a "deep moral sensitivity" (*American Evasion* 60). Similarly, Frank Lentricchia, in championing James as the founder of a home-grown left intellectual tradition, remarks that "his pragmatism is emancipatory—it would lead us out of suffocating and tyrannous theorizations" (9). Lentricchia then moves from the philosophy to the philosopher, a familiar trajectory in work about James, to claim that the "man" was "dedicated to the local, the underdog, the heterogeneous—as opposed to oppressive wholes and stifling totalities" (9).

The recent revival of pragmatism, reflected in the work of West and Lentricchia, carries on a century-long tradition that associates James with the image of the frontiersman who liberates the American intellect from totalizing theories and oppressive wholes through an identification with the heterogeneous. Embedded in this image of James is a moral allegory that conflates heterogeneity and variety with democracy and Americanism, terms whose positive meanings rely implicitly and explicitly on the demonization of "wholes" and "totalities."

The contemporary revival of William James, which celebrates his pragmatism for its recuperation of the "local," the "heterogeneous," and the "underdog," tends to invoke his pluralism as an example of his democratic spirit rather than engage with it as a serious theoretical intervention. His pluralism is considered an accompaniment to pragmatism rather than a body of knowledge worthy of separate study.[2] This chapter focuses on James's work on pluralism, specifically his critically neglected book *A Pluralistic Universe,* the final major work published during his lifetime.[3] In placing this text at the center of my analysis, I argue that James's pluralism is fundamental to an understanding of his work as a whole, ranging from his pragmatism and psychology to his study of ethics. His pluralism is also crucial for understanding his social and political writings, ranging from the "undisciplinables" of Harvard to "national self-development" in the Philippines.

A Pluralistic Universe marks the culmination not only of his pluralist theory but also of a lifetime of inquiry into the relations between unity and multiplicity, connectedness and autonomy, reflection and action. Pluralism is James's final attempt to argue for the need for moral and ethical certainty despite empirical doubt, a certainty of belief that can be attained not by banishing the world's plurality but by engaging it. Like his pragmatism, Jamesian pluralism underscores human agency as the foundation of ethics; it also supports the problem-solving capabilities of philosophy. James's work on pluralism diverges from his pragmatism not so much in content as in scope. In *Pragmatism,* James is primarily interested in defining a "pragmatic method," which "unstiffens all our theories, limbers them up and sets each one at work" (*P* 53). From a pragmatic perspective, theories become "instruments" that move ideas forward rather than a search for permanent solutions, since such closure is ultimately impossible. To paraphrase James, one can never reach the end of a metaphysical quest.

A Pluralistic Universe is a continuation of the concerns and debates that appear in *Pragmatism,* but it represents a more self-conscious and formal attempt to produce a comprehensive and systematic theory of incomplete unity. It is a paradoxical text that aims to bring closure to the philosophical position of non-closure. As James said shortly before his death, "All that *my* pluralism contends for is that there is nowhere extant a *complete* gathering up of the universe in *one* focus, either of knowledge, power or purpose."[4] Compared with *Pragmatism,* James's final work is bolder and more ambitious. It intervenes in the metaphysical question of the one and the many in order to return to the pragmatic world of action. It is less a method than a synthesizing theory, which defends the right to remain partial in the double sense, as incomplete and as partisan.

Modern Pluralism versus Postmodern Multiculturalism

James's pluralism, to use his own word, is highly "muddled." This is partly due to the fact that James wanted to have it both ways: he wanted to combine an emergent love of modern variety with a residual Victorian appreciation of a shared moral and cultural code. James's desire to resolve these conflicting objectives is precisely the source of pluralism's confusion, or what Louise Marcil-Lacoste has more generally called the "ethical ambiguity of pluralism" (133). I explore the ethical and conceptual ambiguities of Jamesian pluralism because it is in this "muddled" space that the term "variety" can be de-naturalized as inherently benevolent and innocent. This space also reveals the term's pliability, how its meanings are produced within specific situations that are politically variable.

This approach, which attempts to dislodge variety from automatic and uncritical "goodness," goes against the philosophical grain. In doing so, it is able to draw on pluralism's internal contradictions as a strength rather than a problem. Jamesian pluralism merits critical study, in part, because it anticipates as well as diverges from common patterns of contemporary multiculturalism. In terms of convergences between the past and the present, James prefigures what has become commonplace in contemporary multiculturalism, namely a fundamental trust in the benevolence of variety. For James, pluralism is a way to systematize philosophically the liberal embrace of variety as the expression of individual liberty and autonomy. Variety is a sign of democratic health, because it recognizes and respects particularities and differences.

But Jamesian pluralism does not stop here, as a mere celebration of the different and autonomous; it goes a step further to inscribe variety within a revised notion of unity, which he describes as a "strung-along" type that allows the component parts to retain a large degree of autonomy. "This world *may*, in the last resort, be a block-universe," opines James in *A Pluralistic Universe*, "but on the other hand it *may* be a universe only strung-along, not rounded in and closed" (*PU* 779). This negotiation of local autonomy with commonality, or what James refers to as "independence" and "connectedness," anticipates a similar tension in contemporary multiculturalism, which Avery Gordon and Christopher Newfield have characterized as the conflict between "cultural autonomy" and a "common culture" (4). Both modern pluralism and postmodern multiculturalism are attempts to answer the questions: How should the United States respond to cultural diversity? How can local or subcultural autonomy be reconciled with larger scales of unity? The task of modern pluralism is to articulate a "totality," the term James uses to describe the synthesis of variety and unity. This would resolve what James calls the "bergsonian point of view," which is how something can be "both distinct and connected" (*PU* 749).

Another reason Jamesian pluralism deserves serious study is for what it can offer us today as we grapple with postmodern notions of heterogeneity, which commonly embrace all-inclusivity as the fullest expression of a democratic ideal. The differences between modern and postmodern notions of multiplicity, moreover, can be instructive.[5] In contemporary multiculturalism, the language of diversity is associated with boundlessness and the transgression of borders, where unity is understood as a barrier rather than a means toward democracy. The philosopher Judith Green, for instance, defines "deep democracy" as a "preference for variety, multiplicity, dynamism, and jazz-like fusions instead of purity, unity, simplicity, and stability" (436). Her binary logic casts variety and unity as antithetical terms, which are implicitly and not-so-implicitly racialized as a Manichean allegory of good and evil. While variety is on the side of "jazz-like fusions," unity is associated with a much less appealing array of terms such as "purity." Variety is progressive and dynamic, whereas unity is dangerously retrograde and deeply conservative. Which side would you choose? For someone who is promoting variety as a democratic value, Green ironically offers her liberal-left readers a single set of options, namely support variety at the expense of unity or identify with the other side.

To illustrate the prevalence of such either-or thinking in contemporary multiculturalism, consider two more examples. In defining his notion of "insurgent multiculturalism," which is a subversive alternative to the hegemonic variety, Henry Giroux has invoked a similar moral allegory that links "radical democracy" with that which is "open" and "fluid" rather than that which is "exclusionary" and "fixed" ("Insurgent" 326). Likewise, David Theo Goldberg celebrates "multicultural heterogeneity" in a fashion that even James Madison would approve of. Heterogeneity "sets a limit on intragroup tyranny as it delimits intergroup oppression" (32). In both cases, "multicultural heterogeneity" opposes "exclusion" (33). The contemporary embrace of heterogeneity and variety depends on the vilification of certain terms, specifically those terms which imply limits, whether in the name of "unity" or in the form of "exclusion." That this vilification should occur in the name of insurgency and radicalism is particularly disturbing, because it replays a quintessentially hegemonic liberal gesture (reminiscent of the consensus thinkers of the Cold War) of dismissing a position because it excludes, which is itself an exclusionary gesture.

A predominant strain of contemporary multiculturalism views acts of exclusion as *ipso facto* reactionary. Consequently, unity has become identified with conservatism and variety with a liberal-left progressive agenda. Within such an inflexible binary (which is, ironically, defended on the grounds of "fluidity" and "openness"), a certain brand of "insurgent multiculturalism" must commit the act that it vilifies: in defense of inclusiveness, it must banish those forms of "conservative multiculturalism" that are considered exclusive.[6]

In contrast to its postmodern variation, modern pluralism has a significantly different relation to unity and exclusivity. James would see the contemporary reliance on an "either-or" logic, in which variety and unity are perceived as antithetical terms, as reductive and yet predictable. "The commonest vice of the human mind," he writes, "is its disposition to see everything as yes or no, as black or white, its incapacity for discrimination of intermediate shades" (*PU* 665). Like contemporary multiculturalists, James views variety as beneficial and benevolent, as an extension of Mill's dictum: "diversity is not an evil, but a good." James does not, however, understand variety to be all-inclusive. Just as Jamesian pragmatism renders truth a "half-way station" between extremes, so his pluralism, I will argue, attempts to establish a notion of heterogeneity *via media,* as a pragmatic middle ground opposed to excess.[7]

James's "pluralistic universe," which formally appeared in his book of that title in 1909 but which also informs much of his earlier work, represents an important strain of American philosophical modernism. It designates a third way in which thinkers of the period conceptualized the contradictions and dialectics of modernity, other than through the familiar binary of uniformity versus heterogeneity. Jamesian pluralism rejects this dualistic logic to pose an alternative model based on a dynamic relation between independence and connection, between variety-in-discreteness and what he terms "inextricable interfusion": "each part hangs together with its very next neighbors in inextricable interfusion" (*PU* 778). The world is "neither a universe pure and simple nor a multiverse pure and simple" (*P* 148).

For James, variety and unity are not mutually exclusive terms, but they can be combined in order to produce variegated unions, which would be neither uniform nor entropic. He is interested in capturing the simultaneity of unity and variety semantically through a few hyphenated neologisms, such as "manyness-in-oneness," "much-at-once" and "self-of-selves." Jamesian pluralism is fundamentally dialectic: it concerns the relation between unity and variety rather than being exclusively a meditation on the latter. As he notes in 1910, "Where our intellect really aims at is neither variety nor unity taken singly, but *totality*" (P 130).

James's notion of totality, however, is always incomplete. His pluralism attempts to make modernity less terrifying without taking refuge in a monistic utopia of all-inclusivity. The best way to cope with the indeterminacy and insecurity of the modern age is to confront these qualities rather than flee from them. Accept unity, James argues, even if it is partial, contingent, and dynamic. He admits that such a world view is not for the "tender-hearted" but only for the "tough-minded." In 1906 he declares that the pluralistic universe "is always vulnerable, for some part may go astray; and having no 'eternal' edition of it to draw comfort from, its partisans must always feel to some degree insecure" (*Writings* 940–941). He replaces a Whitmanian celebration of holistic diversity ("I contain multitudes") with a more restrained approach qualified by the word "some" (his version: "I include some multitudes and exclude others"). In one of his earliest introductions to pluralism, James anecdotally refers to its grotesque character: "A friend with such a mind once told me that the thought of my universe made him sick, like the sight of the horrible motion of a mass of maggots in their carrion bed" ("Dilemma" 177).

In contrast to contemporary postmodern pluralism, which is defined according to a highly appealing and positive ideal of social harmony, James's modern version was considered aesthetically offensive and physically repulsive. It describes a world without guarantees, where chance predominates over determinism, and the "each-form" over the "all-form." There are "jolts," discontinuities, and "*dis* unions," making all forms of unity contingent and incomplete. The therapeutic dimension of Jamesian pluralism is in its sobriety: his realist epistemology refuses to take refuge in the philosophical kingdom of heaven.

What contemporary multiculturalism can learn from its modernist counterpart is the importance of confronting exclusions rather than evading them through an idealistic rhetoric of all-inclusivity. Because it prefers modest unions to all-inclusive ones, Jamesian pluralism foregrounds *interests* (or partisanship) as inevitable and necessary.[8] Exclusions are, to quote the literary critic Ellen Rooney, "determinate and determining" (51). James understands that limits are not only inevitable but also important in defining a position, a philosophical system, as well as an ethics. Pluralism, moreover, is defined as much by what it excludes as by what it includes. As James wrote in "The Moral Philosopher and Moral Life" (1891), "Every end of desire that presents itself appears exclusive of some other end of desire. Shall a man drink and smoke, *or keep his nerves in condition?*—he cannot do both" (*Will to Believe* 202–203).[9] In contrast to the "either-or" formulation of "insurgent multiculturalism," which privileges all-inclusivity as the basis for excluding those who exclude, James underscores the partial as constitutive of his "pluralistic universe."

More than contemporary postmodern multiculturalists, Jamesian pluralism demonstrates Roland Barthes's notion of "taking sides," which emphasizes the inevitability of the partisan. Barthes, like James before him, admits that "each time men speak about the world, they enter into a relation of exclusion, even when they speak in order to denounce it" (170). In this chapter I explore how Jamesian pluralism professes as well as resists the inevitability of exclusions. Unlike Barthes, James is still ambivalent about the inescapability of limits; he realizes that exclusion is necessary in theory but difficult in practice.[10] James's ambivalence surfaces when he begins to write *A Pluralistic Universe* as a series of lectures to be given at Oxford University. Will his lectures inevitably please some and disappoint others? In practicing what he preaches, is James willing to accept the inevitability of limits in terms of audience? Or does he believe that he can convert all to his way of thinking?

The Pluralistic Universe and the Limits of Persuasion

Toward the end of his life, James wanted to systematize his pluralistic ideas as a formal philosophical tradition. When he was invited to deliver the Hibbert Lectures at Oxford in 1908, he considered this occasion a mixed blessing. On the one hand, it would give him the opportunity to present his ideas in a formal and coherent manner, yet it would also pressure him to popularize his style at a time when he wanted to make it more specialized for an audience of academic philosophers. Just a few months before leaving for England, James wrote to his friend F. C. S.

Schiller, a fellow pragmatist and pluralist at Oxford: "I accepted because I was ashamed to refuse a professional challenge of that importance . . . I actually *hate* lecturing: and this job condemns me to publish another book written in picturesque and popular style when I was settling down to something whose manner would be more streng [sic] '*wissenshaftlich*,' i.e. concise, dry, and impersonal" (qtd. Perry 583).

James's anxieties about audiences are symptomatic of the professionalization of the turn-of-the-century academy and the subsequent fissure between public and professional knowledges. Never attending graduate school, James personified the Victorian "rhetoric and oratory" professor in the belletrist tradition of Henry Wadsworth Longfellow and James Russell Lowell, who represented "men of letters" in the Arnoldian sense of believers in the moral and spiritual force of education. By the early twentieth century, however, a new generation of scholars returned from graduate schools in Germany and elsewhere, equipped to discuss the complexities of Hegelian dialectics with a finely tuned scientific discourse in a manner that James called "*wissenshaftlich.*" He actually incorporated these anxieties about academic overspecialization into *A Pluralistic Universe,* remarking in the second lecture on the "over technicality and consequent dreariness" of the philosophy of the young (*PU* 637). He imagined "the gray-plaster temperament of our baldheaded young Ph.D.'s boring each other in seminars, and writing those direful reports of the literature in the 'Philosophical Review'" (Kuklick 249). Their presence on the faculty confirmed to him the homogenizing tendencies of the professional graduate schools or what he termed the "Ph.D. Octopus."

Although James was considered the nation's foremost psychologist and preeminent philosopher, with his lectures on pragmatism (1906–1907) attracting over a thousand people in Boston and New York, he was not taken seriously as a systematic thinker, as a theoretically sophisticated professional academic in the manner of the younger generation. Aware of the nascent distinction between professional ("tight") and nonprofessional ("loose") scholarship, James saw in the Hibbert Lectures a way to legitimate himself as a serious figure within a more specialized discipline, rather than as an antiquated remnant of the Harvard Golden Age (1869–1889). To Schiller, he wrote: "My free and easy style in 'Pragmatism' has made me so many enemies in academic & pedantic circles that I hate to go on increasing their number, and want to become tighter instead of looser" (qtd. Perry 583). But James also realized that by impressing his "enemies in academic & pedantic circles" he risked alienating the majority of others, the public audience, whose members were educated but not necessarily university-affiliated. In this sense, the "pluralistic universe" was indeed an irreconcilable multiverse, where the question of public and professional audiences could not be resolved in terms of a single, universal community.[11]

Inevitably, James's lectures on pluralism satisfied some and disappointed others. His series of eight lectures consistently attracted several hundred people, a point that attests to their popular success. James's wife, Alice, described the audience as "simply spellbound" (Allen 462). Many of his colleagues, however, commented that "too much concession was made to his audience and that James was once again diverted from the task of systematically developing his mature philosophical views" (Bernstein xii). James himself believed the lectures to be a failure, describing them as "poor," "rambling and inconclusive" (*PU* 780). What is significant is the inevitability of pluralism's failure, that is, the impossibility of pleasing both the professional and public audiences. The reception of his lectures on pluralism ironically dramatizes James's fundamental argument, namely the limits of persuasion. There will always remain "residual resistance" to a given point of view.

Just as a lecture could not satisfy all segments of an audience, neither can a philosophical practice claim to represent all perspectives. In challenging the universalist claims of most philosophical traditions, James insists that each philosophy can provide only a limited and partial view. "No philosophy can ever be anything but a summary sketch, a picture of the world in abridgment, a foreshortened bird's-eye view of the perspective of events" (*PU* 633). As points of view emerging from "experience-able reality," all philosophies are subjective and particular. There are only "partial knowers," not all knowers. According to James, a "philosophy is the expression of a man's intimate character, and all definitions of the universe are but the deliberately adopted reactions of human characters upon it" (*PU* 639).

What differentiates pluralism then from prior traditions is its insistence on partiality. It flaunts its own limits. To underscore this point, James invokes the category of the "residuum," that space of excess, which differentiates the pluralistic universe from its all-inclusive, monistic other. In his later work, he refers to this concept of incompleteness through a range of phrases such as "ever not quite." He writes,

"Things are 'with' one another in many ways, but nothing includes everything, or dominates over everything. The word 'and' trails along after every sentence. Something always escapes. 'Ever not quite' has to be said of the best attempts made anywhere in the universe at attaining all-inclusiveness" (*PU* 776). This example of a sentence in which a conjunction supplants the period, in which contingency replaces finitude, is the grammatical corollary of the pluralistic universe. Like the ever trailing "and," the pluralistic universe contains "no complete generalisation, no total point of view, no all-pervasive unity, but everywhere some residual resistance to verbalisation, formulation, and discursification, some genius of reality that escapes from the pressure of the logical finger, that says 'hands off,' and claims its privacy, and means to be left to its own life" (*Writings* 1312–13).

One of the most important aspects of pluralism is the refashioning of unity from all-inclusivity to that which is "incompletely unified." The category of the "some" never disappears in James's theory of pluralism; it is James's way of reminding rationalists, monists, and the like that nothing can contain everything, since there is always "residual resistance" to every position. "Something always escapes." Phrases such as "some" and "ever not quite" are reminders that his pluralism contains a notion of limits, which prevents it from inhabiting a permanent state of either atomism or fusion. "The whole question," writes James, "revolves in very truth about the word 'some.' Radical empiricism and pluralism stand out for the legitimacy of the notion of *some*" (*PU* 666). Furthermore, the category of the "some," so integral to James's theory of pluralism, enables a dialectical maneuver that recognizes "inextricable interfusion," while preserving the relative autonomy of the "each-form" in the midst of such fusion: "each part of the world is in some ways connected, in some other ways not connected with its other parts" (*PU* 666).

In pragmatic fashion, James theorizes plurality through the confines of conditions, which is a far more difficult prospect than celebrating boundlessness as a transcendent term of all-inclusivity. In *The American Scene,* Henry James applies the category of the "some" to the social sphere, noting that "even the most inclusive social scheme must in a large community always stop somewhere" (240). William James invokes a similar imperative in his contemporaneous writing on the university, when he insists that professionalism and corporatizing must stop somewhere. Within a university culture, limits are necessary to protect intellectual autonomy, where eccentricities and dissenting points of view can be cultivated and encouraged.

The Pluralistic University and the Elective System

Like multiculturalism, pluralism (at least its Jamesian version) had its origins within educational institutions. More specifically, pluralism emerged within the university as a paradigmatic challenge within the discipline of philosophy. By 1902 the fundamental epistemological division within the discipline was whether the world was singular or multiple (Wahl 114). Students remember seeing James and his close friend and colleague Josiah Royce engaging in vociferous debates on this topic during their afternoon walks in Cambridge (N. Hapgood 60).

In the 1904–1905 academic year the philosophy department at Harvard announced a two-semester sequence, in which "one of the philosophical professors will develop a theory of pluralism on the basis of experience, and in the next term his colleague will develop a speculative theory of the absolute" (Wahl 113). James and Royce's perambulatory debates appear to have become formalized as a course. This departmental history underscores the fact that James's pluralism did not occur within a vacuum; it was not a theory, as Jean Wahl rightly points out, "created by one philosopher and developed by others" (273). Instead, it was part of a highly dialogic set of concerns that emerged within a specific academic milieu at the turn of the century and developed into a transatlantic conversation with intellectuals from Britain to Poland.

James's interest in pluralism coincided with his arrival at the Harvard philosophy department during its Golden Age. In the 1880s James moved from physiology to philosophy, as the discipline of psychology migrated from its traditional institutional base in medicine to the expanding field of the humanities. During this period James's departmental affiliation at Harvard also changed: appointed assistant professor of physiology in 1879, he became a full professor of philosophy in 1885. Owing in part to his eclectic training as an artist, a doctor, a naturalist, and a psychologist, James brought to the discipline of philosophy a fundamental skepticism toward taxonomies of knowledge, which led him to unsettle paradigms rather than to corroborate them.

In *Pragmatism,* James outlines his intervention as one that reverses the dominant disciplinary emphasis from a search for unity to one for variety: "Philosophy has often been defined as the quest or the vision of the world's unity. Few persons ever challenge this definition, which is true as far as it goes, for philosophy has indeed manifested above all things its interest in unity. But how about the *variety* in things? Is that such an irrelevant matter?" (P 129–130). By opening the discipline to various modes of methodological inquiry, philosophy would become, or so James claimed, better equipped to adjust to the contradictions and tensions of the modern age.

This same assumption, that the study of variety would prepare the modern subject for the vicissitudes of life, also informed contemporaneous changes in the undergraduate curriculum at Harvard. James's pluralist intervention emerged in the aftermath of the elective system, which reflected the values of nineteenth-century liberalism in training the future leadership class. The new curriculum privileged individual choice over prescription, and cultivated decisiveness over submission. Under the bold leadership of President Charles W. Eliot, who was a long-time friend of James's, Harvard began to switch to an elective system soon after the Civil War. The "Classics" were demoted from their near-sacred stature as a fixed and required curriculum and put on equal footing with courses in science and modern literature, so that every course was voluntary.[12] As a retired professor of Greek noted, "Now, with an inclusive tolerance, every course in any subject, general or technical, weighed equally in the official scale. The doctrine of democratic equality had invaded the domain of education" (qtd. Morison 35). Some professors feared that such a program would result in a "patternless multiversity."

In 1885, the same year in which James joined the philosophy department, Eliot tried to allay such fears in defending the elective system as the extension of individual liberty: "To fetter this spontaneous diversity of choice . . . by insisting that studies shall be taken in certain mixtures or groups . . . is as unnatural as it is unnecessary . . . Groups are like ready-made clothing, cut in regular sizes: they never fit any concrete individual" (qtd. Morison xlii). At a time when the U.S. economy was becoming increasingly standardized, Harvard resisted by embracing diversity as a sign of individualism. A liberal arts education would become the final bulwark against commodification: it alone would be responsible for the cultivation of character—that mark of individuality—among its students.

Despite the objectives of the elective system, James observed at the turn of the century that standardization was taking its toll on university life. The ivory tower had increasingly yielded to the pressures of professionalism, with Harvard changing from a teaching-based college to a research-oriented university. This was seen in James's own department with philosophy issuing its first doctoral degrees in the 1890s. In 1903 James conveyed his concerns about the "Doctor-Monopoly" in an article in the *Harvard Monthly* entitled "The Ph.D. Octopus." In this article he criticized the anti-intellectualism of a system that reduced the pursuit of knowledge to the task of passing examinations. Understanding this phenomenon in Veblenian terms as a form of conspicuous consumption, James called this "grotesque tendency" a "sham, a bauble, a dodge whereby to decorate the catalogues of schools and colleges" (*Writings* 1115). Despite this trend toward "manufacturing" intellectuals, universities must try to maintain their historical function "as the jealous custodians of personal and spiritual spontaneity" (1117). Such institutions were, for James, the final refuge of individuality in the modern age; and it was precisely this quality that was at greatest risk with the new system of standardized intelligence: "is individuality with us also going to count for nothing unless stamped and licensed and authenticated by some title-giving machine?" (1118).

James reiterated these concerns in a speech delivered in the same year at the Harvard Commencement Dinner. Entitled "The True Harvard," his speech commented on the modern-day paradox that the crisis of individuality had occurred within the very institution designed to protect it. At an occasion typically dedicated to the platitudes and cheers of college fealty, James praised the "solitary sons" of Harvard, its intellectual outcasts and eccentrics, for refusing to assimilate to the club image of the "Harvard man." "Our undisciplinables," he declared, "are our proudest product" (*Writings* 1120). The "lonely thinker" who arrives at Harvard is not attracted to social clubs, but to its "atomistic constitution, of her tolerance of exceptionality and eccentricity, of her devotion to the principles of individual vocation and choice" (1128). The "inner spiritual Harvard" represents an ideal intellectual community, one that respects the autonomy of the individual to pursue a course of knowledge, free from requirements and other restrictions. Harvard offers an ideal equilibrium of independence and connection, and it is precisely this notion of a "concatenated" community that James uses as his model of a "pluralistic universe."

James's pluralism appropriates for the nation an ideal community based on an elite liberal arts college. In good empirical fashion, he begins with the particular (Harvard) and expands it to the general (nation) as a way of modernizing a liberal notion of community, in which intellectual autonomy can exist within a "loose" and "concatenated" union.[13] Written in the highly abstract and metaphoric language of "each-forms" and "all-forms," Jamesian pluralism represents a model of modern individualism, narrated as a heroic saga of individual survival in an age of standardization, where the "each-form" struggles to resist incorporation into the "all-form." Published at a time when trusts and corporations dominated the national scene, his pluralism is an allegory of anti-assimilation and non-incorporation, in which individual integrity is sustained in the age of Standard Oil and U.S. Steel. During a period when mergers increased from 303 in 1898 to 1,208 in 1899 and U.S. Steel absorbed over 200 manufacturing and transportation companies and won control of two-thirds of the steel market (Bailyn 830), James spoke of unity in modest terms, as limited points of connection.

Intellectual Autonomy in an Age of Monopoly

James defines pluralism against its corrupt, monopolistic counterpart, monism. This type of philosophical thinking, known at the time as "post-Kantian" "neo-Hegelianism" or "absolute idealism," was the dominant theoretical paradigm at Oxford by the late nineteenth century, led by such figures as Thomas H. Green and Francis H. Bradley. It was also on the rise at Harvard (*PU* 641). Monism includes any form of idealistic thought, whether religious or rationalist, that promises a conflict-free world with no exclusions. "Philosophers," writes James, "have always aimed at cleaning up the litter with which the world apparently is filled" (*PU* 650). In presenting an "aesthetically pure" view of the world, monists privilege such terms as the "absolute," "complete union," and "perfection," which ignore the contradictions and dynamics of actual contexts. For James, absolute idealism represents the metaphysical embodiment of "bigness," operating according to the same logic of monopoly capital as an "all-devouring" merger that ingests all of its excess. Monism claims that "everything is present to *everything* else in one vast instantaneous complicated completeness—nothing can in *any* sense, functional or substantial, be really absent" (*PU* 776). Monism dramatizes at the level of ideas the expansionist gestures of corporate practices and imperialist policy, which James rejects for their boundlessness as well as for their avarice.

In 1899, the peak year of corporate mergings, he wrote: "I am against bigness and greatness in all their forms . . . The bigger the unit you deal with, the hollower, the more brutal, the more mendacious is the life displayed. So I am against all big organizations as such, national ones first and foremost."[14] James similarly wrote to his friend William Dean Howells, "I am becoming more and more an individualist and anarchist and believer in *small systems* of things exclusively. Small things can be veracious & innocent."[15] Jamesian pluralism theorizes "small systems" and "small things" in the form of modest unions that are incomplete and limited.

Jamesian pluralism can be read as a crisis-management guide to modernity: smaller unions are more secure because they can better withstand the "flux" and "jolts" of turbulent times (*PU* 650). Democracy, like "mother nature," must be "various and flexible" (*P* 81). Jamesian pluralism is both a response to and a reaction against the conflictual dynamics of his age, a period of centralization and fragmentation, of homogenization and heterogeneity, of standardization and multiplicity. Rather than reify this external world as irrelevant to the workings of philosophy, "pluralistic empiricism knows that everything is in an environment, a surrounding world of other things" (*PU* 670). Jamesian pluralism negotiates these conflicting energies in ways that do not completely fuse one element into its opposite, but maintain a (sub)space of non-assimilation. Dialectics is precisely what generates the motion and flux of his pluralistic philosophy: "There *is* a dialectic movement in things" (*PU* 670). James uses dialectics not to promote what he refers to as a "so-called 'higher synthesis,'" in which opposing factors "harmoniously combine," but rather to underscore the limits of synthesis and to claim a space of non-negotiation. Not everything can be reconciled within a common union; there remain opposing positions that ultimately cannot fuse. This is the moral parable of Jamesian pluralism, namely that limits are at times necessary for ethical beliefs.

A Pluralistic Universe prescribes not just unity but a specific type—hierarchical unity—as the antidote for modern angst. Modest unions need to exercise a process of selection. As James writes at the start of *A Pluralistic Universe,* "it is we who project order into the world by selecting objects and tracing relations . . . We *carve out* order by leaving the disorderly parts out" (*PU* 634). Unity depends on human agency for its construction, a process that he likens to the sculptor's production of a statue out of a block of marble by "eliminating irrelevant . . . chips of stone" (*PU* 634). To show how his pluralistic universe possesses limits in contrast to the imperialist proclivities of monism, James does not stop with the necessity of selection, but develops his argument further to claim that any principle of selection requires a notion of hierarchy: "An order must be made; and in that order the higher side of things must dominate" (*PU* 645). His pluralism does not signify a relativist unity, a heterogeneous collection of discrete and distinct parts. There is a principle of organization that privileges certain parts over others.

Hierarchy is a necessary process that ensures a degree of unity: it saves pluralism from chaos, which is precisely what Henry Adams fears is the future direction of modernity. By the end of *A Pluralistic Universe*, James insists that "we still have a coherent world, and not an incarnate incoherence, as is charged by so many absolutists" (*PU* 778). Uttered in the final paragraphs of his final philosophical work, this is not a new remedy for solving the problem of the one and the many. Six years earlier in "The True Harvard," he confides that the key to Harvard's success, as a refuge for the eccentric and the "truth-seeking," can be found in its notion of unity: "It is because she ["inner spiritual Harvard"] cherishes so many vital ideals, yet makes a scale of value among them" (*Writings* 1128). What James appreciates about "true Harvard," defined as a distinct subculture of intellectual outcasts and eccentrics, is not only that it embraces multiple ideals but that it structures these ideals according to an ethical standard. By privileging intellectuals over athletes and the "solitary sons" over club members, James reverses the dominant value system and offers an alternative criterion by which to define the institution. His defense of an intellectual subculture is not made in the name of anti-hierarchy, since that would mean sacrificing a position of discernment. He instead appropriates and reverses the dominant values in redefining "true Harvard."

The therapeutics of hierarchy are also seen in his psychological work. Emotional and mental well-being rely on the internalization of a "scale of values," so that these values become naturalized as "habits." In *The Principles of Psychology* (1890), James describes the process of exclusion in terms of "accentuation" and "emphasis," which "are present in every perception we have. We find it quite impossible to disperse our attention impartially over a number of impressions . . . But we do far more than emphasize things, and unite some, and keep others apart. We actually ignore most of the things before us" (273). Mental illness, according to his theory, is the result of being too democratic, in paying equal attention to each impression without discriminating among them. As a psychologist, James describes the necessity of forming hierarchies and privileging some impressions over others in the formation of what he would later call "healthy-mindedness." The human subject requires a customs house official of the mind who can sort through the plethora of daily impressions, arranging and discarding information. This point is underlined by James's students, such as Horace Kallen, who defines his mentor's notion of the modern "personality" as a "matter of decision, a matter of constant selection and rejection, of conclusion and cutting off" (*Philosophy* 46).

The fundamental thesis of Jamesian psychology is that a mind without borders is literally insane. This emphasis on limits connects his psychology with his pluralism, a connection that he made a decade before the publication of *Principles*. In "Great Men and Their Environment" (1880), he notes that "the human mind is essentially partial. It can be efficient at all only by *picking out* what to attend to, and ignoring everything else,—by narrowing its point of view. Otherwise, what little strength it has is dispersed, and it loses its way altogether" (219). Whether in the mind or in the "pluralistic universe," harmony depends on exclusion.

This was not a particularly novel idea at the turn of the century. James was applying to the new science of psychology nineteenth-century conventions of good and genteel character. Hamilton Wright Mabie, a literary critic of James's generation, similarly discloses to his readers the key to cultivating a "rounded personality": "If one wishes to have a complete and rounded personality and to avoid being a heterogeneous collection of unrelated and inharmonious parts, one must understand his own type and appropriate those things which are vitally related to it. The artist, the man who strives after perfection, is revealed, as Schiller says, quite as much by what he discards as by what he accepts. Rejection is quite as important as selection, in a fully developed and productive life" (206). Like James, Mabie uses an artistic metaphor to describe the process of selection, perhaps as a way to defend exclusion by making it aesthetically pleasing. Like a work of art, the self is consciously made: one must play an active role in transforming a "heterogeneous collection of unrelated and inharmonious parts" into a "rounded personality." It is the imposition of values that transforms a collection of parts into a coherent sense of self. Selection creates character and hierarchy leads to self-realization.[16]

If a self is made, then where does one acquire the tools? To answer this question, we need to go beyond *A Pluralistic Universe* to a speech that James delivered a year before the Hibbert Lectures. In a 1907 address at Radcliffe College entitled "The Social Value of the College-Bred," James answers this question by defining the goal of a college education: "that it should *help you to know a good man when you see him*" (*Writings* 1242). Then, taking into consideration his Radcliffe audience, he adds: "This is as true of women's as of men's colleges." In contrast to industrial schools, where one acquires a "narrow practical skill," a liberal arts college offers a superior product, namely "liberal culture," which is a broader, historical and philosophical knowledge not limited to practical skills. Whereas schools produce a good worker, colleges produce good character: "They redeem you, make you well-bred; they make 'good company' of you mentally" (*Writings* 1242). Written four years apart, "The True Harvard" and "The Social Value of the College-Bred" define the common purpose of a liberal arts education: the college can still be counted on to produce individuals rather than automatons. To apply Mabie's terms, a student enters as a "heterogeneous collection" of experiences and graduates with a "rounded personality."

In underscoring the value of a liberal arts education, James's "College-Bred" lecture betrays a certain anxiety and defensiveness about the modern relevance of the "humanities" at a time of moral crisis. Not only is the value of a liberal arts education in question, but so is the value of democracy: "Democracy is on its trial, and no one knows how it will stand the ordeal" (*Writings* 1245). To describe this crisis, he employs a gothic world view, which he would use again the following year to describe his pluralistic universe: "Nothing future is quite secure; states enough have inwardly rotted; and democracy as a whole may undergo self-poisoning" (*Writings* 1245).

In a world where individual agency seems to be waning, the act of selection actually resuscitates agency by foregrounding the constructed nature of unity. For modern pluralists, democracy and hierarchy, two terms which seem mutually exclusive to the postmodern mindset, were perceived as compatible and inextricably intertwined. Democracy requires a system of ethics, in which certain terms are privileged over others according to a "scale of values." Democracy depends not on an anything-goes moral relativism but on beliefs that are considered non-negotiable. In "The Moral Philosopher and Moral Life," James defines the core of his pluralistic ethics: "the ethical philosopher's demand for the right scale of subordination in ideals is the fruit of an altogether practical need. Some part of the ideal must be butchered, and he needs to know which part" (Will 203).

Jamesian pluralism is a call for philosophical realism, an acceptance of the fact that exclusions are not only inevitable but also necessary whether in making daily decisions or in forming ethical values. As Terry Eagleton has remarked, no one can convincingly claim not to be exclusionary: "everyone is a hierarchist, whereas not everyone is an elitist" (Illusions 94). All "human practices, from storming the Bastille to brushing one's teeth," writes Eagleton, "work by exclusion, negation, suppression; it is just that one should try to avoid excluding the wrong things or suppressing the wrong people" (95). Similarly, the question is not whether or not boundaries should exist, but rather what kinds of boundaries should be maintained, and which should be opposed and dismantled.

Jamesian pluralism offers an important realist antidote to our own idealistic constructions of a diverse community. In contrast to postmodern definitions of multiculturalism, which are defined against power, hierarchy, and a principle of subordination, James argues for its opposite: a pluralism structured in dominance, in which certain values prevail over others through a "right scale of subordination."[17] What is refreshing about modern pluralism is the way it unabashedly incorporates a rhetoric of power—of partiality, exclusion, and limits—to challenge philosophical and material monopolies. It does not, in other words, object to corporate hierarchies through a celebration of boundless inclusivity; it offers instead an alternative hierarchy, a counter-scale of values, which privileges the very terms that corporate America defines itself against, namely the marginal, the undisciplinable, and the eccentric.

My recuperation of Jamesian pluralism, however, is not without reservations. In accentuating the strengths of modern pluralism, I do not want to overlook its problematic aspects, which become apparent when we shift from the abstract prose of *A Pluralistic Universe* to its application in James's social and political speeches of the early twentieth century. James's call for hierarchy as a way to sustain an ethical spirit is also a call for leadership. But James's brand of leadership, which entails a scale of values for saving democracy, betrays his own class moorings. Underneath the coonskin cap and leather boots of the intellectual frontiersman is a gentleman reformer, whose call for hierarchy turns into cultural elitism, which reveals patrician biases that are so deeply entrenched that James hardly seems to notice them.

A Federal Republic or an Imperial Republic?

Cornel West describes American pragmatism as "a continuous cultural commentary or set of interpretations that attempt to explain America to itself at a particular historical moment" (*American Evasion* 5). The same is true of American pluralism. Both are modes of crisis management that depend on an intellectual calling to articulate and sustain shared beliefs during times of political and social upheaval, to constitute communities of like-minded individuals cohered around a collective moral imperative and political aim. Despite the abstract prose of *A Pluralistic Universe,* it nonetheless addresses the crisis of national community and the need for leadership at the turn into the twentieth century. Besides "each-forms" and "all-forms," there is one trope that stands out for its concreteness, namely the "federal republic." This metaphor, with its political connotations, is used interchangeably with a "pluralistic universe," suggesting that James's pluralism is in large part a theory of the nation, and specifically about the different forms of "modern Americanism." In *A Pluralistic Universe,* James returns to a theme that characterizes much of his later work, namely the role of the intellectuals in defining a democratic national community at a time of increased state bureaucracy and standardization. One goal of his final treatise is to modernize the "federal republic," so that intellectuals still matter in an age of professionalism when technicians and engineers seem to reign.

To describe the modern nation, James invokes an antiquated term. Gottfried von Herder, the romantic, considered the republic the source of the "most sublime ideas of the human spirit," but James, the pragmatist, valued the republic less for its sublime qualities than for its economy. "The pluralistic world is thus more like a federal republic than like an empire or a kingdom. However much may be collected, however much may report itself as present at any effective centre of consciousness or action, something else is self-governed and absent and unreduced to unity" (*PU* 776). James also compares the "pluralistic universe" with the "best commonwealth," which "will always be the one that most cherishes the men who represent the residual interests, the one that leaves the largest scope to their peculiarities" (*Memories* 103). His democratic model exemplifies a distinctly "modern" notion of community, defined by Marshall Berman as an "ideal community in which individuality will not be subsumed and sacrificed, but fully developed and expressed" (*Authenticity* ix). James combines Mill's notion of individual liberty with a romantic communitarian ethos, in trying to imagine democratic models of collectivity that would allow the most autonomy for individual expression, while circumscribing individual liberty within a civic community. But James's interest in the federal republic is ultimately expedient. As a pragmatist, he is convinced that the pluralistic universe, when conceived as a federal republic, would be able to maneuver successfully through the "jolts" of the modern world. By contrast, the absolute world of monism could easily "shatter" given the slightest movement.

The choice of the "federal republic" as the predominant trope of the "pluralistic universe" was not arbitrary. It was part of an exceptionalist discourse that resurfaced at the turn of the century, when the guardians of the American republic were no longer seen as the gentry class of antebellum days, but now the "college-bred," and specifically the university intellectuals who could place the old principles of American exceptionalism on modern ground. Republicanism, according to the historian Dorothy Ross, created for the United States an "exceptional place in history" and provided a teleological narrative of American triumphalism in understanding the character and fate of the modern nation. The ideology of American exceptionalism, as Ross argues in her seminal study of the origins of the social sciences, underwent a change at the end of the nineteenth century. It was revised to claim that "the realization of American liberal and republican ideals depended on the same forces that were creating liberal modernity in Europe, on the development of capitalism, democratic politics, and science. America's unique condition did not block the full effects of modernity . . . but rather supported it" (Ross xv).

Rooted in the trope of the "federal republic," Jamesian pluralism is part of this broader project to recast the terms of American exceptionalism as consistent with the effects of modernity rather than resistant to them. The flexibility and pliability of the "pluralistic universe" underscore the ability of the republic (read: the United States) to negotiate the "jolts" of modernity by adjusting to them. The "federal republic" also links modern Americanism with the "germ" of Jamesian pluralism, namely "inner spiritual Harvard." The critic and historian Bernard de Voto defined Harvard as a "republic within the Republic," which was precisely the connection that James was making between the university and the nation, where his intellectual cohort would become the moral and cultural guardians of the American Republic.

James's use of the "federal republic" was not only a modern reworking of a residual term of American exceptionalism; it was also a highly charged term at the turn of the century owing in part to its resurgence among Progressive reformers who wanted a modified version of Madisonian federalism, in which a strong central government would ensure national security and stability at a time of tremendous growth and expansion. The same year that saw the publication of *A Pluralistic Universe* also witnessed Herbert Croly's *The Promise of American Life*. A former student of James and the primary architect of Theodore Roosevelt's "New Nationalism," Croly laid the groundwork for a managerial approach to leadership, in which a nation requires an intellectual elite who will direct it toward democratic goals. Jeffersonian ends (social justice) can be realized only through a centralized and nationalist (Hamiltonian) state. In theorizing liberty for the modern nation-state, Croly appropriates for the early twentieth century what John Stuart Mill proclaimed in the mid-nineteenth, namely that "liberty of the individual must be thus far limited; he must not make himself a nuisance to other people" (Mill 184). In an increasingly complex and "modern" world, local and individual liberties, according to Croly, will be more fully attained through a national formation. James's use of the "federal republic," therefore, was a highly loaded metaphor in the prewar period. It signaled the "new liberalism," which sought to unite federalism with republicanism in claiming that marginal interests would be guaranteed through a national intelligentsia.

Whereas Croly was more willing to trust the powers of the state, James remained fundamentally suspicious. Through the metaphor of the "federal republic," which is a nostalgic and idealistic counterpart to the modern nation-state, James's pluralism is a way to work out the conflictual relationship between the intellectual class and the increasingly bureaucratic state apparatus. James wants intellectuals to have it both ways: to have a space of relative autonomy where ideas still matter, while at the same time to have the authority to intervene at the national level to steer the country through the ebbs and flows of modernity. The intellectual class, according to Christopher Lasch, is a "distinctively modern phenomenon, the product of the cultural fragmentation that seems to characterize industrial and postindustrial societies" (*New Radicalism* xi). James, who is credited with importing the term "*les intellectuels*" from its radical usage during the Dreyfus craze in France, observed the waning authority of his intellectual class as it became confined to the university, as a subculture whose national presence was diminishing.[18]

In the aftermath of the Spanish-American War of 1898 and the Dreyfus Affair (1894–1899), genteel progressives such as James realized that they were now without the authority and influence that his mentor and friend E. L. Godkin, the Boston Brahmin and editor of *The Nation*, had possessed a generation earlier. The intellectuals signified James's "minorities," who were, to borrow Pierre Bourdieu's phrase, the "dominated among the dominant."

A Pluralistic Universe is not a text of mourning and loss but one of recovery, a way of reconsolidating an intellectual class composed of what Bourdieu has called "bidimensional beings": those belonging to an autonomous intellectual world not dictated by commercial pressures, religious dogma, or political partisanship; and involved in the realm of public action beyond the ivory towers (Bourdieu 656). Jamesian pluralism is shaped by a fundamental ambiguity about the role of the intellectual. On the one hand, his pluralism operates as a defensive strategy, protecting a space of relative autonomy, where intellectuals are not persecuted or punished for their positions (as his colleague Charles Eliot Norton was for opposing the Spanish-American War).[19] On the other hand, his pluralism also functions as an aggressive call to arms, by arguing that the crisis of national and subcultural unity can be resolved only if intellectuals become the agents of cohesion. It provides a way of empowering the disenfranchised intellectuals by making an academic subculture of "solitary thinkers" leaders of the "federal republic." Intellectuals, rather than professional bureaucrats, must provide direction for the coming age.

Pluralism is sometimes modest and other times bold; it is attracted to the "innocence" of "small things," but it wants to usurp the power and authority of "bigness."

The fundamental tension of Jamesian pluralism is between its desire to remain "small" and its desire to expand, between being a "federal republic" and being an "imperial republic." A "federal republic" is content to remain small but unified, priding itself on its non-expansionist sentiments, whereas an "imperial republic" is a paradoxical polity in which republican modesty conflicts with expansionist ambitions. The phrase "imperial republic" captures the contradictions between the American Republic as a late-eighteenth-century liberated colony, defined against the British empire, and the Republic after 1898, when the former colony now had colonies of its own. This tension between boundedness and boundlessness, between modest unities and expansionist ones raises questions about the parameters of the "pluralistic universe."

James's pluralism attempts to make the university, and specifically its intellectuals, valued citizens of the federal republic. The university represents the silent center of James's universe, the site of pluralism's genesis and the agent of its dissemination. His academic subculture frames the origins and the conclusions of his philosophy: intellectuals inspired pluralism and now they must practice it. At the end of *A Pluralistic Universe,* he notes that "philosophy and reality, theory and action, work in the same circle indefinitely" (*PU* 780). To complete this circle in my own analysis, it is important to situate *A Pluralistic Universe* in the context of James's writings on the "college-bred" and on the U.S. invasion of the Philippines to see how his pluralist ethics is manifested in the field of "action."

The Therapeutics of "Good" Culture

As a philosopher and a doctor, James was interested in diagnosing social and psychological ills as well as in prescribing remedies. In "The Social Value of the College-Bred" and *A Pluralistic Universe,* the cure for an ailing republic is the proliferation of "good" culture, which depends on human initiative, primarily that of the "college-bred." In "The Social Value of the College-Bred," James focuses on the importance of education, and particularly the humanities, in perpetuating the production of conscientious citizens. Not unlike the more recent jeremiads of E. D. Hirsch,

Harold Bloom, and William Bennett on cultural illiteracy and the threat to democracy, James offers a plan of curricular reform that would be centered around literature and specifically "masterpieces": "Literature keeps the primacy; for it not only *consists* of masterpieces, but is largely *about* masterpieces" (*Writings* 1243). Informed in large part by Matthew Arnold, whose work William and Henry avidly read, James extends Arnold's definition of good culture, as the best that has been thought, to include the biographies of "geniuses" and "great men." For James and Arnold, culture offers a middle ground between "violent extremes," opposed to the materialism of the *nouveaux riches* as well as the threatening "vulgarity" of the working classes.

James sees in Arnold what Lionel Trilling would later develop, namely the power of "good" culture to revitalize a degenerating liberalism through the consolidation of the educated middle classes. Lawrence Levine has noted that the Arnold important to America was not "Arnold the critic, Arnold the poet, Arnold the religious thinker, but Arnold the Apostle of Culture" (223). In 1884 Henry James wrote, "I shall not go so far as to say of Mr. Arnold that he invented the concept of culture, but he made it more definite than it had been before—he vivified and lighted it up" (qtd. Levine 223). William James intended to do the same for liberalism. As his Harvard colleague George Santayana observed, "Culture requires liberalism for its foundation, and liberalism requires culture for its crown" (22).

Culture, for James, provides constancy and continuity at a time of flux and uncertainty. It also reinforces, in Arnoldian fashion, the values of liberalism, which Lionel Trilling has described as "a sense of variousness and possibility," two elements that are an "intellectual and political necessity." Similar to Mill's recommendation that liberals should read poetry, James finds in culture and especially in literary "masterpieces" a way to communicate the republican ideals of a "common culture" and "civic virtue" in terms of sentiment and feeling. Culture is the medium, as Lisa Lowe has argued, through which "the individual invents [a] lived relationship with the national collective" (2). It is through culture, moreover, that the subject becomes American, and it is through "liberal culture" that the American becomes a "good" citizen.

Reading "masterpieces," however, is not enough. Culture as a form of pedagogy and curricular reform cannot fully remedy the crisis of liberalism. To benefit fully from the stabilizing influences of "good" culture, the ailing republic requires culture workers, those among the educated middle class who will depart from the elite college upon graduation and work as missionaries in the battle against philistinism. In his speech to a primarily female audience at Radcliffe College, James declares that such workers must be *"les intellectuels,"* who have internalized a "scale of values" so that it is now "habit." "In our democracy, where everything else is so shifting, we alumni and alumnae of the colleges are the only permanent presence that corresponds to the aristocracy in older countries. We have continuous traditions, as they have; our motto, too, is *noblesse oblige*; and, unlike them, we stand for ideal interests solely, for we have no corporate selfishness and wield no powers of corruption. We ought to have our own class-consciousness. *'Les intellectuels'!"* (*Writings* 1246). What is significant about this passage is precisely how James empowers intellectuals as a class to intervene in the political sphere to weld the nation together.[20] The college-bred, like the sculptor, can transform a block of marble into art: they can turn a "mob-spirit" into "rounded" citizens. That this point is announced primarily to a group of college-educated women assumes, in republican fashion, that women are the guardians of good culture, the ones who will create a new generation of moral citizens.

By the end of *A Pluralistic Universe,* the intellectuals return, not as the victims of James's bleak and morose world, but as its saviors. His final book provides a tale of crisis and redemption, in which the universe, though on the brink of disunion and fragmentation, contains the seeds of its own regeneration. In the concluding chapter of *A Pluralistic Universe,* he writes, "Our 'multiverse' still makes a 'universe'" (*PU* 778). While monism calls on the *deus ex machina* to mend its unity mysteriously (and implausibly) through external forces, pluralism, in good Protestant fashion, must rely on its own agency (*PU* 663). In the last instance, we are told, the pluralistic universe is "self-reparative." There are enemies within the borders of the federal republic, but there are also potential healers. Yet who is to do the healing? At this point, James's tone changes and he addresses his readers directly: "through us, [the pluralistic universe] get[s] its disconnections remedied in part by our behavior" (*PU* 780). The "our" of the passage refers to the citizens of the federal republic. Human agency will ultimately mediate the contradictory impulses of modernity and thus save the republic. As he says in a different context, "civic virtues of the people save the State in time" (*Memories*

59). Civic duty, or what the pragmatist calls "action," will mend the ailing body politic internally. Active citizenship, led by the "college-bred," will repair the federal republic through a spirit of volunteerism in the public sphere.

Cornel West has found the elitism of James's intellectual vanguardism "peculiar" and at odds with his "democratic sentiments." But James's elitism becomes less "peculiar" when situated in the context of genteel reform at the turn of the century. As the historian John Sproat has noted in his study of intellectual reformers of the Gilded Age, "Liberal reform was pre-eminently the instrument of the 'best men' in American society after the Civil War—the men of breeding and intelligence, of taste and substance" (7). James's faith in the college-bred as the moral guides for the future was also indicative of the social democracy movement of the day, which blurred the lines between socialism and liberalism in configuring what the British Fabian Beatrice Webb would later describe as a "socialist commonwealth."

By conceiving of socialism as an ethical ideal rather than the result of class exploitation, the genteel socialists in both Britain and the United States saw the agents of change among genteel intellectuals rather than the working class. Disinterested elites would safeguard the public good by becoming teachers who would profess a moral order that would bind and cohere all classes. According to John Kloppenberg, "Democracy required a new method of promoting the common good, and these American and British social democrats nominated their elite corps of experts to do that job" (272). Pedagogy rather than guns signified the catalyst for social change. As James's friend H. G. Wells said in 1908: "Ultimately, the Socialist movement *is* teaching" (*New* 265). Similarly, James's friend and political guru E. L. Godkin contended that in order to make people more moral, "you must not legislate, but *teach*" (Sproat 213).

Although James in preparing the Hibbert Lectures recognized the limits of persuasion, in practice he attempted to transcend limits by advocating a pedagogy of democratic conversion. The college-bred must become teachers with the task of persuading the public at large that the tune of the intelligentsia is the "higher, healthier tune":

> If democracy is to be saved it must catch the higher, healthier tune. If we are to impress it with our preferences, we ourselves must use the proper tune, which we, in turn, must have caught from our own teach-

ers. It all reverts in the end to the action of innumerable imitative individuals upon each other and to the question of whose tune has the highest spreading power. As a class, we college graduates should look to it that *ours* has the spreading power. It ought to have the highest spreading power. (*Writings* 1248)

James advocates a policy of trickle-down culture, in which the work of the "best and the brightest" becomes the secular religion of the expanding republic. The leadership for this policy will not come from the working classes, whom James sentimentally reveres as the iconic individual laborer (who should figure in public statues dedicated to the modern age) but fears as the masses. Similar to a fellow anti-imperialist, Andrew Carnegie, who argues that the working classes lack the leisure time to produce culture, James remarks: "the barrenness and ignobleness of the more usual laborer's life consist in the fact that it is moved by no such ideal inner springs." For this reason, "individuals of genius" must lead the way, "which common people [will] then adopt and follow" (*Writings* 1246).

This sense of leadership as a form of cultural consolidation is consistent with Gramsci's distinction between leadership and domination:

> The supremacy of a social group manifests itself in two ways, as "domination" and as "intellectual and moral leadership" . . . It leads the classes which are its allies, and dominates those which are its enemies. Therefore, even before attaining power a class can (and must) "lead" as well . . . there can and must be a "political hegemony" even before the attainment of governmental power, and one should not count solely on the power and material force which such a position gives in order to exercise political leadership or hegemony.[21]

A class must lead even before it attains governmental power; it must achieve "political hegemony," that is, an existence that is truly total, which is lived at such a depth that it saturates the consciousness of a social formation and determines the parameters and nature of common sense. While domination depends on coercion, leadership is primarily concerned with the winning of consent, which has to take into account subordinate interests to make itself popular. Like Gramsci, James recognizes that hegemony requires multiple fronts, which include moral leadership, culture, and the educational role of the state. Since hegemony is not singular but highly complex, involving variation and contradiction, it must continually be renewed, re-created, and defended. James metaphorically describes this process of hegemonic consolidation and renewal as the "spreading power [of] the higher, healthier tune." Democracy, especially an expanding and increasingly heterogeneous one, can be saved only through the internalization of the "best culture" naturalized as common sense. Culture, once it saturates the structures of popular thought, will ensure the moral elevation of all citizens.

Although James as an American icon has been cast as a "pioneer," a "democrat," and a "frontiersman," he was ultimately loyal to his patrician roots and his New England genteel culture. Ross Posnock has noted the depth of James's connection to his class, as he "upheld the patrician Victorian ethic of class responsibility" (*Trial* 6). Even his colleague and fellow patrician George Santayana recognized in him someone who did not break from his Brahmin background: "William James has played havoc with the genteel tradition, while ostensibly defending it" (101). James gave this tradition a good dose of internal critique, a "rude shock," to use Santayana's phrase, which challenged genteel liberalism while simultaneously strengthening it. James arguably did the same thing for monism. Just as he wreaked havoc with the genteel tradition without ceasing to be genteel, so he gave monism a "rude shock" only to revise it.

Rethinking James's Anti-Imperialism

The structural tensions of James's pluralism, tensions that surface at the start of *A Pluralistic Universe* with his concerns about audience, also inform his anti-imperialism. Just as his pluralism oscillates between autonomy and connectedness, modest unions and incorporative ones, so his anti-imperialism wavers between a *laissez-faire* approach toward the Philippines, in which he calls for their "national self-development," and a far more ambivalent relation to the colonial "other" that recommends a form of cultural uplift. His conflictual response toward the U.S. involvement in the Philippines contains two clashing "scales of value," with one professing limits to U.S. involvement while the other suggests the export of "good" culture.

In the "intellectual renascence" of pragmatism, however, critics have commonly understood James's anti-imperialism at face value, seeing it as an extension of his pluralistic views of tolerance and openness. Cornel

West, for instance, has claimed that the foundations of James's anti-imperialism are "moral and patriotic" (*American Evasion* 62). Frank Lentricchia explicitly links James's "American anti-imperialism" to his "pluralism" in claiming that both are modernist forms of resistance to imperialism (21). This is certainly true, as I will argue, of James's position in such articles as "The Philippine Tangle" (March 1899), but it does not apply to his later anti-imperialist tracts, such as "Address on the Philippine Question" (December 1903). Critics seem to have forgotten Christopher Lasch's caveat from over forty years ago: that most scholars have in fact "assumed that anti-imperialism was genuinely liberal in inspiration and that the anti-imperialists were voicing objections to colonialism now commonly accepted" ("Anti-Imperialist" 111).

Anti-imperialists could also be racist, nativist, and elitist, sentiments that David Starr Jordan expressed in recommending that the United States remain modest in size: "Every alien race within our borders to-day, is an element of danger . . . Democracy demands likeness of aims and purposes in its units" (*Imperial Democracy* 171). James's brand of anti-imperialism is not as explicitly racist as Jordan's, but neither is it entirely innocent. He remains torn between honoring the autonomy of the Philippines and recommending a "protectorate," in which missionaries of "good" culture would "reform" the natives on a temporary basis.

"The Philippine Tangle," written in February 1899, the same month in which the United States invaded the Philippines, is James's clearest and most unequivocal expression of what we would today consider anti-imperialism, namely a critique of any U.S. involvement and the support of national sovereignty. He calls for "home rule," in which the "Filipinos learn from each other, not from us, how to govern themselves" (5). Just as James argues for the autonomy of intellectuals, so he makes a similar case for colonized peoples. "The Philippine Tangle" represents a direct extension of James's pluralistic ethics from individual independence to national sovereignty, from a celebration of the "undisciplinables" to a defense of Third World self-development: "We are now openly engaged in crushing out the sacredest thing in this great human world—the attempt of a people long enslaved to attain to the possession of itself, to organize its laws and government, to be free to follow its internal destinies according to its own ideals" (3). As the historian Deborah Coon has pointed out, James connected his pluralistic philosophy with political consequences: "an essential characteristic of pluralistic philosophy was its democratic respect for individuality, and this implied a policy of noninterference in the Philippines" (Coon 79).

James's opposition to the U.S. military policy is also seen in his highly emotive response to the capture of the Filipino republican leader Aguinaldo. James recalled that he "cried *hard,* when the hostilities broke out & General Otis refused Aguinaldo's demand for a conference,—the only time I've cried in many a long year" (Cotkin 130). What appalls James most about the military occupation of the Philippines is that it violates his pluralist commandment: "thou shalt not steal individuality."[22] Throughout the next ten years James defended national sovereignty, signing in 1910 a petition calling for Philippine independence.

James's anti-imperialism becomes far more complicated in his later tract "Address on the Philippine Question," when he tries to resolve this international crisis. He suggests that the anti-imperialists "forget" 1899, the year when the United States initially occupied the Philippines, in order to "attend to the practical possibilities of today" (*Writings* 1132). In good pragmatic fashion, James is primarily concerned with problem-solving, shifting his anti-imperialism from a critique of U.S. interference to practical solutions to meliorate the foreign policy blunder. Whereas "The Philippine Tangle" imagines an independent republic based on Filipino ideals, the "Address on the Philippine Question" recommends a dependent "protectorate," as an extension of the "imperial republic," in which the Filipino is cast as a potential convert to an "ethical" culture.

In this later piece James tries to envision a kinder and gentler form of colonial encounter, one based on culture rather than on guns. One must therefore distinguish between his opposition to the military presence in the Philippines and his far more complicated response to the U.S. cultural presence. To put it in Gramscian terms, James wants to switch from "a war of maneuver" to a "war of position," in preferring a protracted war of ideological conversion or persuasion that approaches the Filipinos as "individuals" and seizes upon the "psychological moment" of encounter.[23] "When we landed at Manila we found a passionate native cordiality, which would have met us half way in almost any scheme of protectorate and co-operation which we might have proposed. But, 'like the base Indian,' we threw that pearl of a psychological moment away, and embarked, callous and cold, and business-like, as we flattered ourselves, upon our sinister plan of a preliminary military deglutition of them, just to show them what 'Old Glory' meant" (*Writings* 1131). Similar to his pluralism, which is described as a "halfway station" between "violent extremes," James's anti-imperialism occupies the middle ground between military intervention and non-involvement. This passage also highlights a second attribute of his pluralism. James's liberal anti-imperialism seems to advocate a more "intimate" form of colonial encounter, one involving ideological persuasion rather than brute force.

A year before he presented his "Address on the Philippine Question" to the Anti-Imperialist League, James delivered the Gifford Lectures in Edinburgh, entitled *The Varieties of Religious Experience,* which began as a study of spiritual conversion. In the 1900s James's interest in conversion expanded from the spiritual to the cultural, in that "civilization" required what Henry James called "the conversion of the alien." According to his student Horace Kallen, William James was also interested in the conversion of the foreign into the familiar: "Civilization is such a reformation, such a harmonization of an alien nature with human nature, such a conversion of the foreignness of being into intimacy and ease" (*James and Bergson* 232). James's version of anti-imperialism recommends for the Filipino and the American Indian a less "calloused" and "cold" program of incorporation, one that relies on cultural conversion or "civilization" rather than on "military deglutition."

In another piece about the Philippines (which was quoted at length by David Starr Jordan in *An Imperial Democracy*), James again offers conversion as an alternative to militarism in his critique of President McKinley's policy on psychological grounds.

"If ever," says Dr. William James, "there was a situation to be handled psychologically, it was this one. The first thing that any European government would have done would have been to approach it from the psychological side: Ascertain the sentiments of the natives and the ideals they might be led by, get into touch immediately with Aguinaldo, contract some partnership, buy his help by giving ours, etc. . . .

"But it is obvious that for our rulers at Washington the Filipinos have not existed as psychological quantities at all, except so far as they might be moved by President McKinley's proclamation . . . there is no clear sign of its ever having occurred to anyone at Washington that the Filipinos could have any feelings or insides of their own whatever, that might possibly need to be considered in our arrangements. It was merely a big material corporation against a small one, the 'soul' of the big one consisting in a stock of moral phrases, the little one owning no soul at all.

"In short we have treated the Filipinos as if they were a painted picture, an amount of mere matter in our way. They are too remote from us ever to be realized as they exist in their inwardness. They are too far away; and they will remain too far away to the end of the chapter. If the first step is such a criminal blunder, what shall we expect of the last?"[24]

Understanding the colonial moment as a struggle between the "big" and the "little," James's anti-imperialism intersects with *A Pluralistic Universe* and "The Social Value of the College-Bred" in designing an alternative form of imperialism, one based on "psychological" methods. This passage also dramatizes "repressive tolerance" at the point when the federal republic becomes an imperial republic: the best way to grapple with crisis is to invite Aguinaldo inside the fortress.[25]

The persuasive power of "liberal culture" would come from a friendly and accommodating approach toward cultural difference. Such an approach, which conquers through persuasion, is based on the assumption that the colonial subject possesses an interiority, a depth that can be converted. The problem with McKinley's approach to the colonial subject is that he perceives the Filipinos to be "flat" representations, "a painted picture," rather than subjects with "inwardness." To recognize the interiority of the Filipinos is to admit that they can be reacculturated, that they can catch the "higher, healthier tune" of genteel culture through the trickle-down effects of cultural imperialism. Like the university undergraduate, the "Philippine soul" can acquire a "rounded personality." James's anti-imperialism encouraged rather than shunned contact with the colonial other as long as contact was inscribed within a pedagogical mission of cultural conversion.

James's observation that the Filipino possesses "inwardness" is a recognition of individual autonomy. Although James celebrates the "undisciplinables" at Harvard, he is far less certain about *cultural* autonomy for the Philippines. One reason for this is that the autonomy of the colonizer (the pacifist imperialist) would potentially conflict with the autonomy of the colonized subject. Individual autonomy of the "college-bred" depends on the colonial heteronomy of the Filipino subject. Even in "The Philippine Tangle," which is his strongest defense of Filipino national self-development, there is a paragraph that seems at odds with the main argument: "It is safe to say that one Christian missionary, whether primitive, Protestant or Catholic, of the original missionary type, one Buddhist or Mohammedan of a genuine saintly sort, one ethical reformer or philanthropist, or one disciple of Tolstoi would do more real good in these islands than our whole army and navy can possibly effect with our whole civilization at their back" (4). He imagines the arrival of a single missionary of "good" culture, religion, or ethics. Whether a Christian or a disciple of Tolstoy or Buddha, the missionary would convert the natives to an "ethical" way of life. Referring to the Filipinos as "these benighted brown people," James articulates an anti-imperialist position that is an uncomfortable blend of progressive and reactionary attributes: it recognizes the importance of political autonomy while recommending cultural dependency (4).

To celebrate James's anti-imperialism as a sign of his democratic zeal assumes that his pluralism is politically benign and denies the tensions and contradictions that structure his thought. Foregrounding the contradictions of James's pluralism and examining how they inform other aspects of his work, as I have done in this chapter, tarnishes the image of James as a populist and unequivocal democrat. His pluralism has lost its innocence. What remains is a far more nuanced and dimensional understanding of James's work, which can no longer be simply associated with the "underdog" and the "heterogeneous."

To end the chapter with this point, however, would be to perform a rather familiar gesture in cultural criticism about the nineteenth century, namely to emphasize that the great masters are not as politically correct as we once thought they were. Such observations are critically necessary, especially in regard to James, whose democratic image remained relatively unscathed throughout the twentieth century, but they are not sufficient. I underscore the tensions of Jamesian pluralism not only to challenge the prevalent image of James but also to question contemporary multiculturalism's own sense of innocence in regard to the language of diversity. The tensions that structure Jamesian pluralism are not grounds for its dismissal but the means to strengthen and revitalize our own contemporary formulations of pluralism.

Cosmopolitan Humanism

The "Address on the Philippine Question," James's most problematic tract on the crisis, ends on a far different note than it begins. It shifts from a critique of the military occupation to a meditation on the role of intellectuals. The invasion of the Philippines signifies a crisis of foreign policy as well as a crisis of patriotism. By the end of this tract, pluralist ethics are no longer associated with the "federal republic" and a spirit of Americanism when James acknowledges that "political virtue does not follow geographical divisions" (*Writings* 1135). Observing that there is now "an eternal division inside of each country between the more animal and the more intellectual kind of men," James recommends an internationalist organization that would address global crises as an autonomous body free from the impediments of nation-states. He transfers his earlier defense of intellectual autonomy within the professionalized university to a program of intellectual cosmopolitanism within an international context. He concludes his anti-imperialist tract on the Philippines by imagining a "great international and cosmopolitan party, the party of conscience and intelligence the world over" (*Writings* 1135). The imperialist fervor in the United States in the aftermath of the Spanish-American War disillusioned James as the Haymarket Affair had earlier disillusioned William Dean Howells. In 1900 James suggested to Howells that "'*les intellectuals*' [sic] of every country ought to bond themselves into a league for the purpose of fighting the curse of savagery that is pouring over the world" (qtd. Cotkin 124).

James claimed at the start of the twentieth century what Pierre Bourdieu argued at its end: the need to imagine a *"great collective intellectual,"* composed of scientists, artists, and writers from all over the world, who will counter "cultural imperialism" with "cultural internationalism" (667). Admittedly, the distinction between cultural imperialism and internationalism is disturbingly small in James's case, but what does surface in his critique of U.S. foreign policy is the germ of what he calls a "cosmopolitan liberal party," which is a precursor to Bourdieu's "*Internationale* of Intellectuals." In criticizing James's elitist and imperialist proclivities, I do not want to reject entirely his desire to imagine an international collective of intellectuals who would lay claim to the universal beyond the authority of nation-states. One must have a selective relation to the past, which neither appropriates nor dismisses traditions or genealogies wholeheartedly.

The most valuable conceptual element of Jamesian pluralism is its "scale of values," which surfaces when he describes an intellectual *internationale*. In contrast to Bourdieu's late-twentieth-century call for intellectual solidarity, James took on what are today considered highly controversial topics by delineating a system of values, defining the parameters of "culture" and the "federal republic," and theorizing what he meant by intellectual autonomy. The problem was not that he addressed these topics but how he addressed them. By contrast, Bourdieu advocates "cultural internationalism" but shies away from actually describing his definition of "culture." He professes an "*Internationale* of Intellectuals," but refrains from specifying what values (and whose values) they will uphold.

What is admirable about James is also what is most problematic. He wrestles with difficult issues in highly inconsistent ways, issues such as the inevitability of exclusion, the challenge of limits, and the necessity of moral hierarchies. Asserting a "scale of values" can be imperialist and culturally elitist as well as anti-imperialist and culturally democratic. There is nothing essential about establishing moral hierarchies that makes it either reactionary or radical. His anti-imperialist tracts, in fact, demonstrate the range of its uses. The quality of James's work that would be most instructive in today's critical climate is its combination of boldness and specificity. He offers a situated universalism, a "pluralistic universe," which developed from a specific location, namely Harvard and *fin-de-siècle* debates about intellectuals, liberal culture, and the necessity of variety. His brand of universalism did not exclude particularity but emerged from it, which, as Terry Eagleton has argued, is the only way in which universals can be constructed: "we have access to universals only because we are situated within a specific culture, a point which both rationalists and relativists might do well to ponder" ("Enjoy!" 9). Not only is universalism always already particular, but it is also "dirty," a point that Bruce Robbins has made in defending universalism as inevitably particular and partisan. Robbins adds that "it is only dirty universalisms that will help us against the powers and agents of still dirtier ones" ("Weird Heights" 180).

The most refreshing quality of Jamesian pluralism is its unabashed dirtiness. Likened to carrion and described as "muddled" and "turbid," the pluralistic universe revels in rather than conceals its contradictions and inconsistencies. In defining universalism, perhaps theorists of cosmopolitanism need to get dirty again. We need to grapple with the challenge of partisanism in order to address the question of how a position can be both biased and democratic, selective and progressive.

Although it was "muddled" and problematic, Jamesian pluralism began to address these issues. In the next chapter, I examine what happens to pluralism when James's students and other young intellectuals of the next generation appropriate it. More specifically, how do the difficult issues of universalism, ethics, and intellectual leadership change when "ethnic" and African-American intellectuals participate in the debate? As David Palumbo-Liu has pointed out, minority cultures have a strained relation to the universal, since they typically signify intrinsic particularity, difference, and localism. But what is appealing about modernist pluralism is that it valorizes the particular by universalizing it. W. E. B. Du Bois and Horace Kallen, among others, claim the universal (and the national) by remaining resolutely particular. They explicitly and implicitly apply Jamesian pluralism to African Americans and Jewish Americans, respectively. In the next chapter I explore how "modern Americanism," as a sign of ethno-racial variety, complicates and expands Jamesian pluralism in ways that still inform contemporary multiculturalism and the politics of identity.

2

Identity Culture and Cosmopolitanism

I have argued that William James's pluralism is a theory of minority rights, in which minorities signify an intellectual subculture, the "dominated dominants" to borrow Bourdieu's phrase, within an increasingly standardized and commercial society. Through the category of the "some," James's pluralism saves unity from uniformity and particularity from atomism; it establishes a philosophical middle ground between isolation and fusion, where "each-forms" can experience "interfusion" with others as well as "indifference" and "independence." Jamesian pluralism is a plea for intellectual autonomy in the vein of "inner spiritual Harvard" as well as a call to action: that the crisis of the "federal republic," which is under siege by avaricious neighbors and internal enemies, can be remedied only through the leadership of the "college-bred."

James's pluralistic allegory about "each-forms" and "all-forms" depicts a world in which intellectuals still matter. They become the missionaries of "good" culture and the guardians of humanitarian values nationally and internationally from the "federal republic" to the "cosmopolitan liberal party." Despite the social and political undercurrents of James's philosophy, which are disclosed through his speeches on the "college-bred" and the Philippines, much of his writing on pluralism remains abstract and featureless. Through its vague language of "forms," "parts," and "things," it reproduces rhetorically the "foggy" and "turbid" qualities that James associates with his pluralistic universe.

Despite its abstract and "foggy" character, James's philosophical work provided an invaluable blueprint for the new generation of intellectuals. In an introduction to a popular edition of James's work, his student Horace Kallen called James's philosophy a "map of life for us modern men, a lamp to light our steps upon the hillroad of freedom, courage, and creative endeavor" (*Philosophy* 55). Although James epitomized the Victorian professor who never felt comfortable with the technological and industrial advances of the modern age, his work would teach a new generation of intellectuals how to "build a home for ourselves in this heedless and antagonistic world" (*Philosophy* 48).

This new generation included Kallen, a Jewish immigrant from Silesia (now Poland), and W. E. B. Du Bois, an African American from Massachusetts. They found in James a personal friend and an intellectual mentor, a genteel patrician who opened his home and his intellectual circle to ethnic and racial outsiders. Kallen has been described as James's most loyal student, a point that Kallen himself underscores in the preface of his first book, *William James and Henri Bergson* (1914): "I acquired my own theory of life at his feet, and . . . in five years of close and intimate personal contact with him I attained to a definite perception of what he regarded as central and what tangential to his *Weltanschauung*" (x). Given the lasting impression that James made on Kallen, it seems appropriate that Kallen's first book was about James and dedicated to him. After James's death in 1910, Kallen co-edited his posthumous book, *Some Problems in Philosophy,* before editing a popular edition of his work for Random House in 1925.

Du Bois was equally appreciative and admiring of his former professor. After completing two years at Fisk University, Du Bois transferred to Harvard as a junior, received his B.A. degree in 1890, and took his M.A. the following year. After studying for two years in Germany, he returned to Harvard and received his Ph.D. in history in 1895. "God be praised," he wrote, for "land[ing] me squarely in the arms of William James" (*Dusk* 33). James repeatedly dined with Du Bois, invited him to become a member of the exclusive Harvard Philosophical Club, and even requested his company on a visit to Helen Keller. After taking a position at Atlanta University, Du Bois continued to write to James, sending him a copy of *The Souls of Black Folk,* which James read enthusiastically and sent on to his brother Henry. Du Bois found in his Harvard mentor, whom he described as his "friend and guide to clear thinking," a nascent cosmopolitanism that sought to create alliances across national lines (*Dusk* 38). Not long before James's death, Du Bois persuaded his former professor to join the board of advisers of his proposed compendium on the African diaspora, *The Encyclopaedia Africana.*

Kallen and Du Bois applied Jamesian pluralism to the concrete realities of their day. They situated the highly abstract and allegorical prose of their former professor within the context of nativism, 100 percent Americanism, and immigrant restriction movements. Kallen and Du Bois spoke not of abstract "each-forms" but of Jewish Americans and African Americans, respectively. They spoke not of "foreignness" but of anti-semitism and racism. They challenged not the absolutism of philosophical monism but the homogenizing forces of Americanization and Anglo-Saxonism. As John Higham has pointed out, "pluralism provided minorities with a means of resisting absorption" (*Send* 203).

Kallen and Du Bois saw pluralism as a doctrine of anti-assimilation but also of national incorporation, in which the resilient "each-form," in its refusal to fuse completely with the "all-form," established a model for how ethnic and racial subcultures could maintain their particularity in the name of modern Americanism. Like the "federal republic," modern America was "incompletely unified," a place where "residual resistance" prevented the formation of a closed and secure union. Even within the nation, subcultural borders resisted assimilation, reflected in Kallen's claim that "diversities persist." This understanding of the nation as "loosely connected," to borrow James's phrase, is rhetorically reinforced in Kallen's decision to pluralize the predicate when referring to the United States. "The United States are an English-speaking country," writes Kallen, "but in no intimate and utter way, as in New Zealand or Australia or even Canada" (*C&D* 101). Like Latin in imperial Rome, English signifies a *lingua franca,* a language of business, as well as of privilege and culture. American democracy, therefore, is not a "voice" but a "chorus of many voices each singing a rather different tune" (*C&D* 104).

Jamesian pluralism came to fruition among his students, a development that James, the pragmatist, would have welcomed in his insistence that beliefs become "matter" for the "next day's funding operations" (*Essays* 171). James's students not only situated the abstract prose of *A Pluralistic Universe* within concrete realities, they also embodied the ideals of the "college-bred" as intellectuals who combined scholarship with responsibility, theory with action. In 1919 Kallen and Du Bois appeared at an NAACP rally at Carnegie Hall supporting Pan-Africanism and condemning the European colonization of Africa. In his speech, Kallen called for an end to the European exploitation of Africa, insisting that the German colonies of central Africa, which had been lost during the war, should be turned over to the League of Free Nations in order to encourage their self-development.[1] James's opposition to the imperialist policies of the Spanish-American War of 1898 found new meaning in the aftermath of World War I, when his students publicly criticized the European seizure of the African continent. But in contrast to their mentor, whose anti-imperialism was fraught with ambivalence and an underlying skepticism toward colonial self-development, Du Bois's and Kallen's stances were unequivocal.

Taking public stances *as intellectuals* also included domestic issues. In the 1920s Du Bois debated Lothrop Stoddard, a white supremacist, New England lawyer, and author of *The Revolt against Civilization: The Menace of the Under Man* (1922) and *Re-Forging America: The Story of Our Nationhood* (1927). At the height of nativism and the Ku Klux Klan revival, Du Bois defended the humanity of African Americans and challenged the racism of Stoddard's views in a number of major U.S. cities, including Chicago, where over five thousand people attended (Aptheker 184). Debating the meaning of Americanism, Du Bois did not surrender the term to the conservatives but reclaimed and redefined it for a radical humanism. Kallen similarly opposed the Ku Klux Klan, which was experiencing a revival in the 1920s under the leadership of the Imperial Wizard Edward Clarke Young. By defining Americanism as "native, white and Protestant," the Ku Klux Klan extended hate toward "minorities," which included "Jew, Catholic or negro" (*C&D* 34). "Kukluxitis," according to Kallen, was itself a variety-in-unity in combining "diverse classes" from various regions into one "active" and "thoroughly organized" group. Kallen's appropriation of Jamesian pluralism was explicitly meant to be a humanist alternative, which embraced "manyness, variety, differentiation" as the defining qualities of a democratic nation (*C&D* 43). In contesting the racist meanings of modern Americanism, Kallen and Du Bois exemplified the Jamesian notion of "residual resistance" in wresting important terms away from white supremacists.

Kallen and Du Bois appropriated Jamesian pluralism in similar ways but ultimately toward different ends. They both used the Jamesian "each-form" to defend subcultural autonomy and ethno-racial distinctiveness at a time of increased standardization. The highly philosophical discourse of *A Pluralistic Universe* became an unequivocal public discourse in defense of what Charles Taylor has called "the politics of recognition."[2] Jewishness and blackness, according to this argument, deserve to be recognized because they represent distinct identities. Kallen and Du Bois used Jamesian pluralism to empower minority groups of the early twentieth century, not only in terms of consolidating ethno-racial subcultures as a united and distinct culture battling the forces of "Kukluxitis," but also as a definitive force in the nation at large. This contrasts with Ross Posnock's argument that Jamesian pluralism was explicitly opposed to identitarian claims, including essentialism. In James's world of "inextricable interfusion," according to Posnock, there cannot be fixed and irreducible differences.

But Jamesian pluralism, as I argued in Chapter 1, is as much about "independence" as it is about "inextricable interfusion." Given this dialectical tension in Jamesian pluralism, I consider James's "each-form" as sufficiently vague and "muddled" to allow for an early form of identity politics, but a form that significantly differs from its postmodern counterpart. The Jamesian "each-form" is ethnicized and racialized as an identity culture that is both connected to and independent from the dominant culture.[3]

Like their mentor, neither Kallen nor Du Bois wanted the "each-form" to remain "unconnected" to other parts, to exist as an isolated and local entity. In contrast to our contemporary postmodern mindset, in which identitarian claims are perceived to be inextricably tied to the local, modern pluralists wanted it both ways: to be a member of a specific culture and to be integral to the formation of a modern nation in the spirit of cosmopolitan humanism. As David Palumbo-Liu has argued, "to be derogatorily named 'ethnic' and to have one's cultural products deemed 'ethnic,' is tantamount to being named 'particular' and thereby situated beyond the bounds of the universal" (190). To break out of the confines of particularism, Kallen and Du Bois universalized the minority position as quintessentially American, so that subcultural uniqueness became a source of national exceptionalism.

Second-generation pluralists were not exclusively concerned with making a plea for tolerance, nor were they consumed with a subcultural strategy of recognition; theirs was a much bolder strategy, which sought to lay claim to the dominant culture by transforming definitions of Americanism through the particular. The cosmopolitan and the universal, therefore, were not opposed to minority culture. Instead, identity culture was the means toward cosmopolitanism and universality; it gave cosmopolitanism a content and universality a sense of rootedness.

My reading of Kallen and Du Bois as modern cosmopolitans goes against the contemporary tendency to define cosmopolitanism as a transnational movement opposed to the provincialism of identity politics and essentialism. Despite the current revival of interest in both Kallen and Du Bois, there is little discussion about how they combine essentialist strategies of race politics with nationalism and internationalism. This is partly due to the fact that contemporary cosmopolitanism tends to configure the local, the national, and the international as distinct and, in many respects, as mutually exclusive tiers of identification. Paul Gilroy, in *The Black Atlantic,* which includes a chapter on Du Bois, explicitly defines the "black Atlantic" as a "desire to *transcend* both the structures of the nation state and the constraints of ethnicity and national particularity" (19; emphasis added). This approach to transnationalism as a mode of transcending the particular overlooks the dialectical qualities of Du Boisean thought, specifically the extent to which Du Bois productively theorizes his version of internationalism through black exceptionalism and modern Americanism.

The recent interest in Kallen can be characterized by a similar reluctance to engage with Kallen's strategy of defending particularity in the name of cosmopolitanism. Critics either champion Kallen for being non-particularist (and therefore cosmopolitan) or criticize him for being too particularist (and therefore not sufficiently cosmopolitan). Christopher Newfield and Avery Gordon view Kallen as an anti-essentialist and anti-determinist and applaud him for claiming that ethnic groups "overlap, move and mix" (85).[4] They present Kallen's fluid approach to cultural identity, which opposes "cultural supremacism," as a "rigorously democratic model of multigroup negotiations" (86). Not all critics agree with this depiction of Kallen. David Hollinger, for instance, argues just the opposite: that Kallen represents "the protoseparatist extreme of cultural pluralism" (*Postethnic America* 93). Rather than being an advocate of mixture, Kallen is now cast as a cultural segregationist, who rigidly attaches people to cultures in a reductive and deterministic way. Despite these different interpretations of Kallen, critics tend to agree on the meaning of cosmopolitanism as a healthy detachment from particular identities, as the ability to transcend the local to promote multiple affiliations.

In this chapter I seek to recover the specificity of Kallen's and Du Bois's cosmopolitanism. In my view, neither Kallen nor Du Bois can figure in a genealogy of postmodern cosmopolitanism: they do not transcend partiality and the dilemmas of identity politics and essentialism, nor do they remain mired in the local and the particular. Their modern versions of cosmopolitanism do not rely on debunking smaller scales of unity ranging from an ethno-racial subculture to the nation, but the converse: their versions of a transnational community are partial to the particularity of subcultures and nations. Their universalisms emerge from their loyalty to the particular. Their transnationalism incorporates rather than transcends.

I will first explore Du Bois's and Kallen's defense of subcultural autonomy, as a way to save African Americanness and Jewishness from commercialism as well as to maintain "group consciousness" or what Du Bois calls "race pride" in the face of discrimination. Then I will examine their shared interest in universalizing or nationalizing the subculture, to make the particular representative of the nation through a shared logic of subcultural exceptionalism. Despite their common strategy of maintaining a dialogic relation between autonomy and nationality, Kallen and Du Bois part ways when specifying the content and objectives of their cosmopolitanism. Du Bois, more than Kallen, maintains the dialectical tensions of his mentor's work in imagining a world without guarantees, where various parties conflict for a hegemonic position within a national and global social order. Du Bois captures the partisanship of his mentor's liberalism, the moral and political imperative to choose sides.

When taken together, Kallen and Du Bois accentuate different aspects of Jamesian pluralism. Whereas Kallen develops the nationalist trajectory along the lines of the "federal republic," Du Bois highlights the internationalist proclivities of James as the Dreyfusard intellectual, who combines nationalist with transnational concerns, which in *Darkwater* lead him back to the United States and specifically to Harlem. These different emphases also result in different understandings of liberal culture. While Kallen operates more within the genteel tradition, working within a traditional understanding of culture as that which harmonizes, Du Bois ultimately forsakes such an Arnoldian understanding of culture and instead develops the radical possibilities of James's "unharmonizable variety," the conflictual world of James's gothic universe in which warring parties struggle to sustain a degree of equilibrium in an unbalanced world.[5] Here, as in Chapter 1, I begin with the theorization of the local and trace its development to the national and finally to a cosmopolitan humanism.

In demonstrating that the flexibility of Jamesian pluralism can result in different appropriations of liberalism, I have the added aim of challenging a critical tendency to view identity culture or identity politics as irredeemably nativist, conservative, and racist. In *Our America*, Walter Benn Michaels has, for instance, argued that "nativist pluralism" (there seems to be no other type of pluralism) is antithetical to universalism: "For pluralism's programmatic hostility to universalism—its hostility to the idea that cultural practices be justified by appeals to what seems universally good or true—requires that such practices be justified instead by appeals to what seems locally good or true" (14). In criticizing the essentialism of identity politics in the modern period, critics risk reproducing the same essentialist gesture in dismissing identitarian claims altogether because they are inherently local and particular. Identity politics of this earlier period were not as monolithic as critics suggest. James serves as a reminder of the importance of "loosening up" our theories as well as our critiques. Identitarian claims, in other words, are not "all" irreducibly localist and nativist. I highlight "all" because it was a word that James detested; he preferred the more modest "some."

Second-generation pluralists illustrate that the politics of difference can be put to a variety of uses, which run the political spectrum from left to right. Du Bois and Kallen also demonstrate that theorizing about subcultures is not a strictly particularist project but can be tied to larger forms of community ranging from the "federal republic" to cosmopolitanism. Let me suggest that we need to bring back James's category of the "some" in order to add a more dynamic and nuanced perspective to the analysis of modern identity politics. To contribute toward such a practice, I make two fundamental claims: first, identity culture does not guarantee a specific political or social programmatic; and second, the rhetoric of variety is not irrevocably tied to the local but can be used to link subcultures with nationalism and cosmopolitan humanism.

Before elaborating on how Kallen and Du Bois appropriate Jamesian pluralism, I want to address the purpose of uniting Kallen and Du Bois under the general rubric of minority intellectuals. I use "minority" in a double sense: in its early-twentieth-century incarnation, as synonymous with an intellectual subculture; and in its contemporary usage as a racialized category of subordination. Regarding the first meaning, I refer to Emma Goldman's definition of the term in "Minorities versus Majorities" (1910), a definition that would have been more familiar to James, Kallen, and Du Bois than today's racially inflected meaning. For Goldman, "minority" was synonymous with intellectuals—James's "undisciplinables"—at a time when the majority or the masses were becoming increasingly uniform in thought. Minorities were those in the society who believed in "independence of thought," in the sovereignty of the individual, in moral courage. "As to individualism, at no time in human history did it have less chance of expression, less opportunity to assert itself in a normal, healthy manner" (Goldman 71).

Kallen and Du Bois understood this belief in the autonomy of the individual as an ethical principle of public convictions, and they applied it to ethno-racial cultures, or what Kallen called the "group-individual." Now, as minority intellectuals—sovereign individuals and representative subjects—they must counter the homogenizing forces of assimilation and the violence of discrimination by insisting on the distinctiveness and independence of Jewish Americans and African Americans. But "minorities" were also considered part and parcel of the "majorities." Along the lines of James's "college-bred," they must transform the majority by saving the masses from their "uniform, gray, and monotonous" life (Goldman 78).

The second use of "minority" refers to its significance as a racial category. Discussing Kallen and Du Bois under the general rubric of "minority intellectuals" threatens to collapse the category of ethnicity into race, thus implying that Jewishness and blackness are equivalent identities. Although I do not want to fuse these two categories completely, neither do I want to render them entirely separate, since there were, no doubt, important points of confluence. Kallen, in fact, explicitly identified Jews with African Americans and Asians as a "conspicuous racial minority" (C&D 236). Du Bois similarly called for a coalition between the two groups in challenging the Anglo-Saxonism of "Americanization," which threatened to make the "country one great homogenous whole" and extend the "world rule of Nordic white" (DB 384).

Any attempt, however, to theorize the relationship between identity, culture, and nation during the early twentieth century has to recognize the sharp divisions between race and ethnicity. In relation to Jewishness, the distinction between blackness, on the one hand, and white ethnicity, on the other, is complicated by the fact that at the turn of the century Jews were cast as both white and Other, or what the historian Matthew Frye Jacobson has called "probationary whiteness" (176).[6] Both Jews and non-Jews articulated racial distinctions within the category of Jewishness, between the assimilated German Jews, who were frequently referred to as the "better" Jews, and their Eastern European counterparts, the "darkened Hebrews" (Jacobson 175).

By being both white and Other, Jews occupied a liminal space between ethnicity and race, which at times converged with the African-American experience of racial violence and at other times diverged from it. Charles Chesnutt differentiates between Jewishness and blackness briefly in *The Marrow of Tradition* (1901). In the midst of a race riot, the protagonist, Dr. Miller, an African-American doctor in Wellington, North Carolina, is stopped and searched at several points in town. At one point, the man who stops him is a "well-known Jewish merchant": "A Jew—God Moses!—had so far forgotten twenty centuries of history as to join in the persecution of another oppressed race!" (289–290). This scene of recognition suggests a diasporic connection between Jews and blacks: that their common history of suffering and discrimination should have established a common bond of sympathy. But this scene also conveys a sense of disappointment that such a bond does not exist. The significance of this moment is what it says about Jewish racial liminality, as white and Other, from an African-American viewpoint: at a time of racial crisis, the Jewish subject must take sides.

To be black in Jim Crow America, ultimately, was not the same as being Jewish. Although both groups were targets of abuse, discrimination, and violence, ranging from the northern cities to the rural South, the extent of violence differed. As Michael Omi and Howard Winant have argued, racial inequality and ethnic inequality are not identical. To address racial dynamics in the United States, and specifically within the "racial state" of Jim Crow, one still needs to retain an "exceptionalist" perspective (rather than a relativist framework, which subsumes all cultural differences under the rubric of "ethnicity") in distinguishing between the experiences of white and nonwhite groups.[7]

To illustrate the difference between being Jewish and being black, I want to turn to 1915, the year in which Kallen first coined the term "cultural pluralism." In that year, the modern Klan, which directed threats at both blacks and Jews, received its charter from a court in Georgia. In the same year and in the same state, Leo Frank, a northern Jewish businessman who ran a pencil factory in Atlanta, was lynched for allegedly raping and murdering a thirteen-year-old female employee, an accusation based in part on the testimony of an African-American janitor. Considered to be an "American Dreyfus Affair in the making," the Frank case was cut short when a mob, riled up by the populist leader Tom Watson, lynched Frank outside Atlanta just a few days after the governor commuted his death sentence (Lewis 490). The Frank case, which Higham has called "an exceptional incident," has to be seen in relation to the far less publicized lynchings of fifty-six African Americans during that same year. In 1915 Du Bois published an article in *The Crisis* called "The Lynching Industry," in which he tabulated by year the 2,732 African Americans lynched between 1885 and 1914, including the names, dates, and states of those most recently murdered. I take 1915 as an exemplary year because it illustrates the connection between blacks and Jews as victims of white hate-groups ranging from the Klan to mob rule. But it also highlights a fundamental difference: the scale of violence was far greater toward African Americans than toward Jewish Americans.

Kallen's and Du Bois's different locations within the U.S. racial formation affected their rhetorical strategies, especially in regard to the term "pluralism." Unlike Kallen, Du Bois during this period never explicitly used the term. Du Bois's biographer David Levering Lewis explains this omission by arguing that at the turn of the century Du Bois did not have the language to express a pluralistic world view. The historian William Toll, however, has claimed that after 1915 Du Bois did read Kallen's work and was familiar with the concept of "cultural pluralism" (172). John Higham explains that it was not so much an issue of terminology than one of different racial positioning. In an era of white terror, how could Du Bois visualize "a genuinely multiethnic complex, in which a variety of groups could enjoy an equal status and maintain their cultural autonomy indefinitely" (*Send* 212)?

Given their different experiences within a racial order, black and white intellectuals could not have imagined a common pluralistic vision. "Could anyone," asks Higham, "have designed a pluralism that would have suited blacks as well as Jews, the minorities that were left behind as well as those that were thriving?" (*Send* 210). In contrast to Jewish immigrants, African Americans were considered "voteless citizens," to borrow T. Thomas Fortune's phrase, a distinction that underlines the fact that what was at stake was not exclusively a politics of difference but a critique of disenfranchisement. Whereas Higham describes Du Bois as solely concerned with challenging discrimination and violence with little time for idealism, I see Du Bois as a pragmatist and an idealist. He battled Jim Crow as well as imagined an ideal nation and world-order. Both Kallen's "cultural pluralism" and Du Bois's "genuine democracy" offer multicultural visions that configure variety and unity in ways that converge and diverge. First I want to focus on the convergences, how Kallen and Du Bois redefine modern Americanism through subcultural autonomy.

From Each-Forms to Identity Cultures

What differentiates James from his students is the shift from a defense of individual autonomy to the conservation of subcultural sovereignty. As pluralism developed in the early twentieth century from its philosophical roots to sociological concerns, it became increasingly interested in transposing nineteenth-century ideals of individual liberty onto collective formations. The second generation extended John Stuart Mill's definition of liberty as that which gives "free scope" to "varieties of character" and "different modes of life" to what Kallen called "group-individuals." The genteel liberal embrace of individual eccentricity was translated into post-Victorian liberalism as subcultural distinctiveness, in which the cult of genius became a belief in cultural exceptionalism. Furthermore, the Victorian notion of "character," as an expression of a person's "own nature" as it has been developed in his "own culture," was expanded in the modern era in defense of the autonomy of subordinated peoples.[8]

Modern pluralism did not represent a dramatic break with nineteenth-century liberal traditions of individualism and autonomy, but rather a development according to new modalities of identification. The "most eagerly American of the immigrant groups," wrote Kallen, "are also the most autonomous and self-conscious in spirit and culture" (C&D 114). The same qualities that James praised in "The True Harvard," individuality and independence, became the desirable attributes of ethno-racial groups. Like Kallen, Du Bois applied the ideals of "good" character to collective formations: "Have we in America a distinct mission as a race—a distinct sphere of action and an opportunity for race development, or is self-obliteration the highest end to which Negro blood dare aspire?" (DB 26). For Du Bois, development depended on racial autonomy, on the assertion of difference from the dominant white culture, because Negro ideals, like "inner spiritual Harvard," rested on a spirit of nonconformity.

This emphasis on persistent particularity was in part a response to fears about standardization, fears that the homogenizing influences of a commercial age would minimize subcultural distinctions. Kallen shared such concerns: "Railroads and tractors, telephones and movies, phonographs and radios, school systems and political establishments, lay upon the continental ranges of the American state a uniformity without precedent and without parallel" (C&D 178). In particular, Kallen blamed the nascent mass media for becoming the most powerful force of Americanization: The "prospective American learns from the yellow press, the movies, and similar engines [about] the wealth, the luxuries, the extravagances and the immoralities of specific rich persons. He learns to want to be like them" (C&D 96). Like the "good" American, the "good" immigrant internalizes what Thorstein Veblen calls "emulation" and "conspicuous consumption," and thus assimilates into an economy of consumer desire based on "social imitation." Such imitation would inevitably lead to the assimilation of subcultures. They, too, would become uniform, bringing into crisis group distinctiveness, that sign of American democracy. In 1902 Robert Hutcheson, in his defense of Chinese immigration, remarked that the "Jews are among our best and most useful citizens, thoroughly assimilated with our civilization" (61). Randolph Bourne similarly observed in 1916 that the "Jews have lost their distinction of being a peculiar people" ("The Jew" 127).

Kallen's pluralism was an attempt to recover ethnic particularity at a time of assimilation. If being a white ethnic had one drawback for Kallen, it was the ease with which some could cross over into an Anglo-American norm. In "Democracy versus the Melting Pot," Kallen berated the Jewish writers Mary Antin and Edward Steiner because they had "intermarried" and thus "assimilated" into a standardized image of Americanism: they had become "more excessively, self-consciously flatteringly American than the Americans" (C&D 86).[9]

From its beginning, cultural pluralism was a "modern" theory, committed to imagining a version of Americanism that would conserve immigrant distinctiveness in the midst of standardization and assimilation. Pluralism saved Americanism as well as modernity from cultural insipidity. In his review of Kallen's book *Culture and Democracy,* Bertrand Russell summarized cultural pluralism as a model of democracy, based on "group-autonomy, not a dead-level uniformity" (158). The task before modern intellectuals was how to configure and develop this notion of national unity based on diversity. Culture, for Kallen, was to become the vehicle that would conserve particularities while also creating a common ground. Just as James juxtaposed his pluralism against monism, so Kallen defined the plurality of "culture" against the uniformity of Kultur.

On the eve of World War I, Kallen felt that the United States was at a crossroads, where it had to choose between a monistic Kultur based on "unison, singing the old British theme 'America'—the America of the New England School" and a pluralistic culture that embraced "harmony, in which that theme shall be dominant, perhaps, among others, but one among many, not the only one" (118). A "truly democratic commonwealth" would be based on the "conservation of differences." It would allow "each nationality" to have "its emotional and involuntary life, its own peculiar dialect or speech, its own individual and inevitable aesthetic and intellectual forms" (C&D 124). An ideal democracy would encourage individuality at the level of the "ethnic and cultural" group, so that an American democracy would consist of variety-in-discreteness, in which each ethnic group could maintain its own distinctive character.

From "The Conservation of Races" (1897) to *The Souls of Black Folk* (1903), Du Bois was also concerned with preserving and producing a distinct cultural and collective consciousness as a way to resist the assimilating forces of an encroaching consumer economy. Du Bois was particularly worried about the black intelligentsia, who showed "symptoms of following in the footsteps of western acquisitive society," which would mark the "natural end" not only of African-American culture but of "human culture" (qtd. Boxhill 81). In "Conservation," he stresses "race unity" as a means to "stop the ravages of consumption among the Negro people" (DB 44). The "warring selves" of the black psyche could be interpreted at one level as a culture war between black folk practices rooted in the traditions of the rural South and a homogeneous Kultur emerging out of the commercial urban centers. Du Bois saw African-American culture, with its "gift of story and song," as a corrective to the monotonizing pressures of Kultur, a therapeutic that could save a national culture from crass materialism: "we black men seem the sole oasis of simple faith and reverence in a dusty desert of dollars and smartness" (DB 106).

This view that the nation needs its African Americans to save it from commercial degeneration had been expressed earlier by Alexander Crummell, the founder of the American Negro Academy, whom Du Bois calls his "seer." African Americans, according to Crummell, would rescue the nation from its own demise: "I know no people coming to this land which can confer the gifts the Negro has to offer to save this nation . . . What other people amid its heterogeneous population can arise and help to neutralize the insanity of her political frenzy."[10] Negro culture, and especially its "black men," would bring patience, quiet, and religion to the "great American republic." Through one of its marginalized groups, the nation, disturbingly defined as a female hysteric, would find peace of mind.[11]

Crummell also influenced Du Bois's early work in articulating the double use-value of subcultural autonomy. Not only would it save the republic from demise, it would also consolidate a culture within the Veil, a distinctive subculture that would foster "race pride" and "race organization." Anti-assimilation was not only a matter of keeping American nationalism interesting and variegated, it was also the means of conserving a sense of cultural identity to battle against internalized inferiority: "While any sensitiveness or repulsion discovers itself at your approach or presence, hold on to your own self-respect, keep up, *and be satisfied with,* your own distinctive circles!" (Crummell 263). In "Conservation," which reads as an anti-assimilationist manifesto and is the piece most heavily influenced by Crummell, Du Bois urges his African-American readers to realize that "their destiny is *not* absorption by the white Americans . . . their destiny is not a servile imitation of Anglo-American culture, but a stalwart originality which shall unswervingly follow Negro ideals" (DB 43).

Subcultural autonomy is the key to race development: "to attain our place in the world, he must be himself, and not another." Identity culture signifies a way to establish an affirmative culture, a mode of living and thinking, which according to Frantz Fanon, justifies "the action though which that people has created itself and keeps itself in existence" (*Wretched* 233). Black autonomy is a process of "decolonizing the mind," of asserting freedom and independence at the psychological and national levels. The idea of African autonomy, according to the historian Sterling Stuckey, played a long-standing role in the free black community of the United States dating back to the early decades of the nineteenth century and continued to inform late-nineteenth-century configurations of black nationalism (274).

Besides Judaizing and Africanizing the Jamesian "each-form," Kallen and Du Bois also share a strategy of rooting their respective subcultures in biological and ancestral permanence in which ethno-racial variety is inherited. Essentialism is seen as a way to protect the integrity and existence of the each-form at a time of rampant assimilation into the dominant commercial culture. In "Democracy versus the Melting Pot," Kallen acknowledges the problem of trying to retain cultural distinctiveness in the modern age of perpetual mobility and migration: "Hardly anybody seems to have been born where he lives, or to live where he has been born. The teetering of demand and supply in industry and commerce keep large masses of population constantly mobile: so that many people no longer can be said to have homes" (C&D 84–85). Modernity, for Kallen, represents a perpetual state of homelessness, which has the liberatory effect of releasing people from the burden of orthodox traditions (exemplified in Kallen's rejection of his father's orthodox Judaism), but which also has the negative cost of diffusing cultural specificity.

Essentialism provides Kallen with the rationale for imagining the permanence of identity culture at a time when the boundaries of cultures are highly insecure. "Men may change their clothes; their politics, their wives, their religions, their philosophies, to a greater or lesser extent: they cannot change their grandfathers" (C&D 122). In "Americanization," published nine years after "Democracy versus the Melting-Pot," Kallen is even more relaxed about intermarriage, because the hereditarian character of Jewishness cannot be diluted: "Intermarriage or no intermarriage, racial quality persists, and is identifiable" (C&D 176). Like the neo-Mendelians of the period who do not believe in "blends" but in the discrete character of heredity, Kallen insists that the "older types persist, and there is nothing to keep them from so continuing on any principle of the relation of heredity to environment that may be applied to them" (C&D 177). Like the Jamesian "each-form," racial and ethnic traits have a degree of autonomy, separate from the environment; their distinctiveness cannot be entirely nullified or neutralized even through cross-racial or cross-ethnic unions. No "environmental influence," Kallen claims, can take "different races" and "remold them into an indifferent sameness" (C&D 177). In Chapter 5 I will explore how this same logic informs African-American women's anti-passing fiction in the 1890s, but at this point let it suffice to say that Kallen's nativist pluralism is a form of cultural protectionism, a way to limit the pliability of minority cultures through the permanence of biology. It guarantees against assimilation, since biology was considered more resistant than culture to environmental influences.

Du Bois similarly invokes biology as a defense of racial particularity and a sign of black resilience against Anglo-American standardization. In "Conservation," he defines race as a "vast family of human beings, generally of common blood and language, always of common history" (40). Like Kallen, Du Bois refers to the figure of the grandfather as a sign of racial authenticity. As late as 1928, in his novel *Dark Princess,* Du Bois uses a logic of descent when the protagonist Matthew Towns, who is a fair-skinned African American, defends his blackness to a skeptical group of diasporic intellectuals in Europe: "My grandfather was, and my soul is. Black blood with us in America is a matter of spirit and not simply of flesh" (*Dark Princess* 19).

But Du Bois's use of "common blood" or "Black blood" differs from Kallen's biologism in two respects. First, Du Bois is far more uncomfortable with scientific claims of black particularity; and second, this awkwardness stems from Du Bois's serious engagement with the Jamesian dialectic of autonomy and connection. In "Conservation," Du Bois's discomfort with scientific essentialism is seen in his qualifying language. He claims in prose riddled with doubt that the "essential difference of race" is a matter of "natural law," which translates into scientific fact: "The final word of science, so far, is that we have at least two, perhaps three, great families of human beings—the whites and Negroes, possibly the yellow race" (DB 39). The words "so far," "perhaps," and "possibly" underscore the insecure basis of scientific assertion in that science both legitimates and undermines the stability of racial difference. Physical differences are both apparent and various: the scientific "criteria of race are most exasperatingly intermingled" (DB 39). Du Bois is far more ambivalent than Kallen about using scientific claims to defend racial essentialism, a biologism that he finds at once reassuring and problematic.[12]

One reason Du Bois finds biological essentialism problematic is that it is too permanent and certain. This concern leads to the second distinction between Du Bois's and Kallen's invocations of biological essentialism, namely the use of the dialectic. Du Bois asserts "Black blood" to sustain a productive tension between particularity and connection, or in Jamesian terms between "independence" and "inextricable interfusion." By contrast, Kallen uses ethnic essentialism to obliterate the dialectic, to render cultures static and permanent. As Posnock has argued, Kallen was "a less than careful student of the philosopher. Had he been careful, he would not have linked James to a notion of cultural pluralism as an array of irreducible differences" (*Color* 23). A far more loyal student of James's and a better reader of his work, Du Bois sustains James's notion of the category of the "some," in which racial identity matters some times and at other times does not matter. This dialectic is played out in culture, which is a site of particularity and universality. On the one hand, "Black blood" brings the "gifts of story and song," and black particularity becomes the source of American uniqueness. On the other hand, Du Bois imagines himself sitting alongside Shakespeare in a deracialized "kingdom of culture."

Du Bois, however, never completely forgoes the rhetoric of racial distinctiveness. Black exceptionalism points to the specific history and culture of African Americans and validates the distinct sensibilities and perspectives that have developed from that history.[13] At the end of "Conservation," Du Bois outlines the objectives of black particularity: "We believe it the duty of the Americans of Negro descent, as a body, to maintain their race identity until this mission of the Negro people is accomplished, and the ideal of human brotherhood has become a practical possibility" (DB 46). At the end of *Souls,* he makes a similar point. Although he claims that white and black have become "inextricably interfused" (James's phrase) in the making of a national culture, the two races have not blended beyond recognition. The "slave song" is "still distinctively Negro" (DB 234). The development has been "side by side," where the "elements are both Negro and Caucasian" (DB 234).

In contrast to Kallen, who uses a logic of non-blending to preserve the particularity of Jewishness at a time of increased contact with non-Jews, Du Bois invokes "Black blood" at a time of enforced racial segregation, when contact was policed and intermarriage outlawed. "Black blood" has produced American culture, which in turn is a sign of black humanity. Although both men oppose assimilation, Kallen's essentialism cannot be conflated with Du Bois's. Kallen's use of ethnic descent was a way to affirm Jewishness at a time of incorporation, whereas Du Bois invokes racial descent as a way to legitimate the humanity of African Americans at a time of racial persecution. As John Higham has pointed out, Kallen was trying to save a tradition, while Du Bois was attempting to consolidate and create an emergent one (*Send* 213).

Nationalizing Subcultures

So far I have outlined two points of intersection between Kallen and Du Bois: their common use of subcultural particularity to oppose Anglo-Saxon assimilation and commercial standardization; and their use of essentialism to secure subcultural distinctiveness. The third point of connection is universalism, understood as a logic of asymmetry in which a certain subculture becomes dominant. Kallen and Du Bois appropriate the Jamesian "each-form" as well as his "scale of values" to make a case for minority exceptionalism. It is important to point out that subcultural uniqueness is not an end in itself, but the means for refashioning modern Americanism, in which a sense of specialness is transferred from the subculture to the nation. Their nationalist perspectives foreground an exceptionalist perspective that privileges the partisan in modern configurations of the nation and the world. This move from identity culture to cosmopolitanism captures an important quality of Jamesian pluralism, its sense of contingency and dynamism in which "each-forms" are not anchored to a particular setting. In *A Pluralistic Universe,* James describes this quality: "The centre [of consciousness] works in one way while the margins work in another, and presently overpower the centre and are central themselves" (*PU* 761).

Subcultural autonomy does not lead simply to balkanization, a permanent state of marginalization, but within the dynamic world of James's pluralistic universe, the margins can become central. This imperative characterizes the twofold mission of Kallen and Du Bois: first, to modernize a national identity and thus allow the nation's democratic spirit to be fully realized; and second, to become the international standard of cosmopolitanism. The conservation of ethno-racial difference is not just a provincial gesture, but is linked to a larger strategy of transnationalizing the nation.

Kallen underscores the centrality of the margins in defining modern Americanism through the trope of the hyphen. He defends the proliferation of hyphenated identities at a time when Woodrow Wilson, among others, argued that "any man who carries a hyphen about him carries a dagger that he is ready to plunge into the vitals of this Republic" (qtd. Brown "Identity Culture" 168). Although Kallen acknowledges that the hyphen may lead to "radically antagonistic allegiances," it is more likely to result in greater cohesion, since "the hyphen unites very much more than it separates" (*C&D* 63). The two terms that Kallen's hyphen unites are Jewishness and Americanism. The hyphen is Kallen's preferred metaphor because it does not entirely fuse the two terms into a hybrid union, but retains a degree of relative autonomy, so that Jewishness can have an identity of its own apart from Americanism. He is able to sustain the Jamesian dialectic between independence and "inextricable interfusion."

Although he imagines a hyphen-nation, as an ideal Euro-American democracy consisting of a "great cooperative commonwealth of nationalities, British, French, German, Slavic, Jewish," Kallen ultimately uses this connective trope to foreground Jewish exceptionalism. His model of a liberal democracy takes sides, linking Jewish uniqueness with modern Americanism: "Hebraism and English nationality—these are the spiritual background of the American commonwealth" ("Nationality" 82). Kallen's explicit use of a typographical hyphen fuses Jewishness with Englishness, setting Jews apart from other, mainly Catholic European immigrant groups. At the end of "Nationality and the Hyphenated American," Kallen again uses the hyphen to reinforce his central thesis of Jewish exceptionalism: "Our duty to America, inspired by the Hebraic tradition,—our service to the world, in whatever occupation,—both these are conditions, in so far as we are Jews, upon the conservation of Jewish nationality" ("Nationality" 86).

The task of the Jewish intellectual is to promote the particular in the name of the cosmopolitan. The mission of the Jewish "college-bred" is the focus of Kallen's Zionist writings, which were published during the same period as his work on cultural pluralism. Although his early-twentieth-century writings on Zionism are far too extensive to address here, I do want to gloss the intersection of Zionism and cultural pluralism to claim that Zionism is the necessary complement to his theory of American nationalism, because both were attempts to remain "distinct" in the midst of the assimilating forces of modernity. Zionism, according to John Higham, provided a way to save American Jewry from disappearance (*Send* 205). "Without a country," Kallen quotes the Italian nationalist Mazzini, "you have neither name, token, voice, nor rights, no admission as brothers into the fellowship of Peoples. You are the bastards of Humanity" (*Zionism* 47).

This same argument, that group autonomy results in national and international recognition, is at the core of his 1913 speech delivered at the convention of the Boston Order of the Knights of Zion: "As the individual Jew makes the best of himself as a citizen of the United States . . . only by developing and expressing what is best in his nature as a Jew freely and autonomously, so the Jewish people can give their best to civilization . . . only by expressing the nature of the race freely and autonomously" (qtd. Schmidt, diss. 80).[14] Kallen's theory of modern Americanism (cultural pluralism) is itself a tale about the Zionization of America: the subculture lays claim to the national in order to become internationally recognized. His Zionism converges with his pluralism through the Jamesian trope of the "federal republic," as the nation-state becomes the central unit of his understanding of culture, ethnicity, and community.

Like Kallen, Du Bois also insists on the power of the minority intellectual to consolidate and perpetuate what Cornel West has called "subcultures of criticism." For West, subcultures enable "intellectual freedom fighters" to position themselves within the dominant culture, "while clearly being aligned with groups who vow to keep alive potent traditions of critique and resistance" ("New Cultural Politics" 22). West's conception of subcultures is neither simply integrationist nor segregationist, but represents a space of relative autonomy where a marginalized people can "cultivate critical sensibilities and personal accountability." Similarly, Alan Sinfield has defined subcultures within the context of sexuality as "any space at all that is not entirely incorporated, in which we may pursue our own conversations" (43). Sinfield's definition of gay subcultures is also a defense of relative autonomy, understood as a space from which to constitute "partially alternative subjectivities," which are at times connected to the dominant culture and other times not. This is precisely why intellectuals from outside the Anglo-patrician community of New England would be attracted to James's theory of margins: its indeterminacy and mobility create the conditions of possibility for "minority" intellectuals to lay claim to the national while at the same time maintaining a critical space of separation.

Du Bois incorporates the instability of James's marginal/center paradigm in order to show the centrality of an African-American subculture in the formation of a national culture. "Conservation" concludes with a defense of African-American exceptionalism as the basis of national uniqueness: "We are that people whose subtle sense of song has given America its *only* American music, its *only* American fairy tales, its *only* touch of pathos and humor amid its mad money-getting plutocracy"

(DB 44; emphasis added). At the end of *Souls,* Du Bois reiterates this point: "Actively we have woven ourselves with the very warp and woof of this nation . . . Our song, our toil, our cheer, and warning have been given to this nation in blood-brotherhood. Are not these gifts worth giving? Is not this work and striving? Would America have been America without her Negro people?" (DB 238). Du Bois uses black exceptionalism to humanize an ostracized population as well as to transform the dominant culture through its subculture. Du Bois's initial philosophical premise, as Hazel Carby has argued, is that "black people and black cultural forms do not exist in opposition to the ideals of the American republic, but, on the contrary, embody them" (*Race Men* 28).

In configuring the subculture and the nation as complementary rather than antagonistic terms, Du Bois locates "the symbolic power of nationalism, of Americanness, squarely within the black cultural field" (*Race Men* 28). Du Bois performs what James theorizes: that the margins have the potential to "overpower" the center and redefine it as their own. Just as Kallen Hebraizes the "federal republic," so Du Bois Africanizes it. This illustrates that identity culture in the modern period did not shun power as an inherently oppressive force but actively pursued it as potentially liberating.

Du Bois's theory of power centers around the black intellectuals, the "exceptional men" of his generation whom he refers to as the "Talented Tenth" and the "Negro college-bred." In 1903, the same year in which *Souls* was published, there appeared two of his early manifestos on the black intelligentsia, "The Talented Tenth" and "The Training of Negroes for Social Power." In "The Talented Tenth," Du Bois prophesies that the "Negro race, like all races, is going to be saved by its exceptional men" (Paschal 31). He proposes a scheme of subcultural "development" as an instance of "human progress," in which the "submerged tenth" will be raised through the efforts of the "aristocracy of talent and character." "Was there ever a nation on God's fair earth civilized from the bottom upward? Never; it is, ever was and ever will be from the top downward that culture filters" (Paschal 36).

Just as the expansion of "civilization" in James's anti-imperialism depends on what I call "trickle-down culture," so the uplift of the race depends on a similar process: "The Talented Tenth of the Negro race must be made leaders of thought and missionaries of culture among their people" (Paschal 50–51). The "missionary" relationship between the "college-bred" and the Filipino subject in James is reproduced within the African-American community as the distinction between the "college-bred" and the folk. Consistent with James's outlook of genteel reform, in which social change is understood as a pedagogical mission, character-building is part of a larger process of nation-building. Du Bois shares with James an Arnoldian faith that culture can overcome crisis; it will provide the social glue that will link individuals with groups and subcultures with the dominant society. This faith in the therapeutics of "good" culture is inextricably tied to a trust in intellectual leadership, in the "talented tenth" as the reparative force that will save the modern nation from disintegration. This ideology of racial uplift, as Kevin Gaines has argued, has as much to do with race as with class, in that it is rooted in a condescending attitude toward the masses as a way to produce a positive black middle-class identity, as "bourgeois agents of civilization" (Gaines 2–3).[15]

In contrast to Booker T. Washington's theory of development that focuses on the artisan, Du Bois's theory centers around the formally trained intellectual. The first step toward solving the "Negro problem," according to Du Bois, is "the spread of intelligence" (DB 356). It is the "higher, healthier tune" that will transform the racial margins into a social force. While culture in the colonial context and even in Arnold's sense of the term conventionally functions as an anodyne, placating conflicts rather than inciting them, culture as a form of character-building operates within the black community as a source of empowerment. In "The Training of Negroes for Social Power" (1903), Du Bois offers a theory of "social power," defined as "the growth of initiative among Negroes, the spread of independent thought, the expanding consciousness of manhood; and these things to-day are looked upon by many with apprehension and distrust" (DB 355). Du Bois adapts the Jamesian spirit of "inner spiritual Harvard" to life "behind the Veil" to offer a radical pedagogy, in which education motivates rather than subjugates: "Men openly declare their design to train these millions as a subject caste, as men to be thought for, but not to think; to be led, but not to lead themselves" (DB 355). Despite the fact that Du Bois's "college-bred" is gendered masculine in ways that contradict James's far more gender-inclusive language (after all, James delivered his speech on the "college-bred" at Radcliffe), both highlight the point that intellectuals still matter in the modern age. "The history of civilization seems to prove that no group or nation which seeks advancement and true development can despise or neglect the power of well-trained minds" (DB 356).

Du Bois's insistence on the centrality of black intellectuals in any plan of racial uplift is a critique of the anti-intellectualism of Booker T. Washington, who spoke dismissively of "mere book education" and perpetuated the stereotype of the "educated Negro" as a mockery of the genteel class donning "a high hat, imitation gold eye-glasses, a showy walking-stick" (*Up From Slavery* 57). Du Bois counters this effete image of the black intellectual-as-dandy with one of emphatic masculinity. Du Bois's conceptual framework of the black intellectual and race leader, as Hazel Carby has argued in *Race Men,* is "gender-specific; not only does it apply exclusively to men, but it encompasses only those men who enact narrowly and rigidly determined codes of masculinity" (*Race Men* 10). Besides acknowledging the deeply problematic gender politics of Du Bois's intellectualism, it is also important to examine how his masculinism operates in his discourse. Not only does his masculinism have to be seen in relation to Washington's effeminization of the black intellectual, but it also provides the rhetorical framework that places "social power" at the center of the agenda. It provides a means of encoding the black male intellectual as an active agent. For James and Du Bois, intellectual responsibility is inextricably tied to social power and authority, since as Du Bois opines, "responsibility without power is a mockery and a farce" (DB 354).

Furthermore, Du Bois's strategy of basing his internationalism on racial particularity intersects with Kallen's in that Du Bois finds in Zionism the conceptual foundations for his Pan-Africanism. In 1919 Du Bois outlined what would become the basic tenets of twentieth-century Pan-Africanism: "The African movement means to us what the Zionist movement must mean to the Jews, the centralization of race effort and the recognition of a racial front. To help bear the burden of Africa does not mean any lessening of effort in our own problem at home. Rather it means increased interest. For any ebullition of action and feeling that results in an amelioration of the lot of Africa tends to ameliorate the condition of colored peoples throughout the world."[16] Du Bois's internationalism explicitly borrows from a Jewish diasporic tradition in conveying an experience of discrimination, dispersal, and suffering in the modern age of the "racial state." As Paul Gilroy has suggested, the concept of diaspora can provide the means for exploring the complicated relations between blacks and Jews and the difficult political questions that arise, such as the status of identity and the power of nationalism (207).

Furthermore, Du Bois's Pan-Africanism explicitly connects internationalist concerns to national ones, leading him to conclude that an interest in Africa actually increases an awareness of "home." Pan-Africanism, moreover, is not a means of transcending the local or the national but of highlighting them, of cultivating a degree of African-American consciousness through awareness of international concerns. This trajectory is dramatized a year later in *Darkwater*, a book that represents Du Bois's internationalist critique and cosmopolitan vision, which aptly returns to Harlem.

Up to this point, Kallen and Du Bois seem to have more similarities than differences. They adopt primarily two elements from their mentor: first, a "scale of values" that privileges certain beliefs (or cultures) over others; second, the centrality of intellectuals as a social force in manifesting these beliefs. Without a sense of individual and collective agency, a scale of values can never be realized. Kallen and Du Bois ultimately acknowledge a pluralistic model of democracy structured in dominance, in which "social power" privileges certain values and cultures over others. This is seen in their respective formulations of modern Americanism, in which a distinct subculture lays claim to the dominant culture in the name of democracy. This is a quintessentially Jamesian maneuver in which the margins "overpower" the center, so that the ethnic or racial subculture redefines the national. Even though Kallen and Du Bois have essentialized the each-form through various biological and familial tropes, the each-form can still move; it can still usurp the center.

What his two students develop is James's understanding of partisan liberalism, a form of liberalism dependent on the ethical expression of taking sides. Yet the actual ethical content of James's liberalism is contingent on context. An exploration of the content of Kallen's and Du Bois's versions of modern Americanism will reveal the fundamental differences between James's two students.

From Jewish Puritans to the Black Adam

Before entering Harvard, Kallen understood Jewishness and Americanism as antithetical identities, the former representing the "ancient" and the latter the "modern." The "modern," for Kallen, required a break with the past, which he experienced personally in terms of a family schism between him and his father. Kallen arrived with his family in Boston in 1887 when he was five years old. The son of an orthodox Jewish rabbi, expelled from Germany as a foreigner, Kallen rebelled against the strict Hebraic rituals and traditions of his father. As an adolescent he sporadically ran away from home.

Raised in Boston's Jewish ghetto, Kallen entered Harvard at the age of eighteen as a secular subject and a prodigal son, having rejected Judaism and intentionally separating himself from a Jewish identity. But during his undergraduate studies Kallen revised his understanding of Jewishness. Just as Jamesian pragmatism defines the "marriage-function" of truth as marrying "old opinion to new fact" (P 61), so Kallen's cultural pluralism syncretically blends the "ancient" and the "modern." Modernity is now defined according to a principle of continuity rather than rupture; but in the process of grafting the past to the present, the past is radically changed. Kallen does not ultimately reject the tradition of his father; he just dramatically revises it.

At Harvard Kallen encountered another intellectual influence besides James, to whom he also dedicated a book: the patrician Barrett Wendell, a professor of English and among the first in the country to teach courses in U.S. literature. *Culture and Democracy,* which includes a reprinted version of Kallen's seminal essay on cultural pluralism, is dedicated to the memory of Barrett Wendell: "Poet, Teacher, Man of Letters, Deep-seeing Interpreter of America and the American Mind, In Whose Teaching I Received My First Vision of Their Trends and Meanings." In his sophomore year, at James's suggestion, Kallen took Wendell's course on American literary history. In this course, Wendell approached American literature through a Hebraic lens, underscoring the role of the Old Testament in the formation of a U.S. literary tradition. Pilgrims such as William Brewster and Puritans like John Cotton were Christian Hebraists, whose interest in the Old Testament led Cotton, among others, to the serious study of Hebrew.

Wendell's pedagogical emphasis on the Puritan veneration of the Hebrew tradition had a transformative effect on Kallen. Years later, reflecting on the impact of Wendell's teaching, Kallen recalled that his professor "showed how the Old Testament has affected the Puritan mind [and] traced the role of the Hebraic tradition in the development of the American character" (qtd. Konvitz 76). It was through the study of U.S. literature that Kallen developed an interest in the Hebraic, which he defined as "the secular, the non-Judaistic component of the entire heritage" (qtd. Konvitz 77). Prior to Wendell's class, Kallen had understood Hebraism and Americanism as incommensurable identities. Through various private conferences with his New England Protestant professor, which often resulted in arguments, Kallen was eventually reconverted to Judaism. In an interview shortly before his death, Kallen said that at Harvard, "a Yankee, named Barrett Wendell, re-Judaized me" (Sollors "Pure Pluralism" 182).

But Kallen's reconversion to Judaism was intellectual rather than theological; it did not lead him back figuratively or literally to his father. Kallen maintained this distinction between the intellectual and theological years later when comparing himself to George Santayana: "He was an atheist who rejected Catholicism without alienating the Catholic ways of thought, just as I reject Judaism without alienating the Hebrew Jewish ways of thought" (*What I Believe* 181). While at Harvard he founded the Menorah Society, which sought to preserve a selective tradition of Hebraic culture, namely its intellectual confluence with what Kallen (and Barrett Wendell) called the "American Idea." This was the belief that the Old Testament provided the catalyst for the Declaration of Independence and the Bill of Rights. The Old Testament encouraged, according to Sarah Schmidt, "the formation of a free society with notions of equal liberty to all individuals and to all groups, no matter how different" (Schmidt, diss. 77). What Kallen found of value in the work of both James and Wendell was that they captured the Hebraic intellectual tradition as a living practice rather than an ancient tradition. They modernized the Jewish past to make it a paragon of contemporary Americanness.

In "Democracy versus the Melting-Pot," Kallen applies Wendell's teachings to an understanding of modern Americanism, in which Jewish immigrants represent the new Puritans, reviving the nation's foundational values for the twentieth century. "The Jews come far more with the attitude of the vaunted earliest settlers," argues Kallen, "than any of the other peoples; for they more than any other present-day immigrant group are in flight from persecution and disaster" (*C&D* 76–77). Within this narrative, the United States represents a promised land for the Puritans and Jews alike. Jewish migration to the United States, therefore, does not break with the past but revitalizes and expands it. Anglo-Americans can relive the plight of their Puritan ancestors through modern-day Jewish immigrants. In a later essay in the same volume, "'Americanization' and the Cultural Prospect," Kallen revises the national narrative of Puritan settlement through a Spencerian trajectory, which depicts national development as a shift from the homogeneous to the heterogeneous. By the mid-nineteenth century, Kallen writes, the nation no longer contained "the homogeneous population of the Puritan age" (*C&D* 220). Through the advent of the "industrial machine," "cities grew and multiplied" (*C&D* 220).

As a result of the heterogeneous population of modern America, a national narrative has to be expanded to include its "non-British communities." But by including such communities, Kallen reminds the reader that the nation does not forsake its founding principles; its spirit remains the same. This argument allows Kallen to bypass the issue of assimilation by implying that Jewish immigrants do not need to change; their story is already told in the dominant narrative of the Puritan exodus from Europe and their resettlement in the New World.

Du Bois offers a dramatically different version of modern Americanism. He does not universalize African Americans in order to graft them onto the dominant national narrative of Anglo-American settlement. Rather than identify with John Cotton, Du Bois authenticates the African-American presence on the continent through the position of the "native": "Your country? How came it yours? Before the Pilgrims landed we were here" (DB 639). In emphasizing that African Americans are "warp and woof" of the nation, he again rewrites the story of national origins in stating that "there is nothing so indigenous, so completely 'made in America' as we" (DB 639). This same rhetorical strategy of *indigenismo* is also seen in Du Bois's contemporary Anna Julia Cooper, who uses the trope of the "native" to naturalize the "educated Negro," that figure whom Booker T. Washington ridicules for his emulatory excess: "Alien neither in language, religion nor customs, the educated colored American is today the most characteristic growth of the American soil, its only genuinely indigenous development. He is the most American of Americans for he alone has no other civilization than what America has to offer" (Cooper 213).[17] Similar to Cooper's, Du Bois's main strategy is to de-naturalize Anglo-American claims to authenticity in order to Africanize the "American Adam" as the originary citizen.

What differentiates Kallen and Du Bois is the ends to which their common strategies are directed. Whereas Du Bois challenges whiteness and the Anglo-American narrative of national settlement, Kallen consolidates whiteness by expanding the dominant national narrative to include Jewishness within an ideology of manifest destiny. Whereas Du Bois identifies with the indigenous, Kallen aligns himself with the Pilgrims. Whereas Du Bois uses the politics of difference to decenter the status quo, Kallen uses it to strengthen it. James's partisan pluralism develops according to two different trajectories, demonstrating the contingency and indeterminacy of James's politics of plurality. As a result, Jamesian pluralism in the next generation represents mutually exclusive understandings of modern Americanism, which take the partisan liberalism of James in antithetical directions. Du Bois, I argue, pushes the radical limits of James's genteel liberalism, showing how marginalizing the center dramatically transforms the center, whereas Kallen uses such a strategy to reinforce the same historical relations. To Africanize America at the turn of the century was a far more radical gesture than to re-Judaize it, especially considering how Du Bois rewrote the story of national genesis, replacing the Pilgrims with the Black Adam as the indigenous presence of the nation.

The Black Residuum

Although Du Bois uses Jamesian pluralism to reclaim the center, Kallen's cultural pluralism actually keeps African Americans marginal and even invisible. They occupy the "residuum" of Kallen's pluralistic universe, a term that James introduces in the 1880s to refer to the unassimilated excess of pluralistic systems. The "residuum," which literally means "the more," is the return of the repressed, a reminder that no system, including monism, can incorporate all elements. After all, "nothing includes everything, or dominates over everything . . . Something always escapes" (*PU* 776). Within the context of science, the "unclassified residuum," for James, represents that which exceeds explanatory categories, the "irregular phenomena" and "outstanding exceptions" that trouble authoritative claims. As Ross Posnock has pointed out, "the unclassified residuum spoke directly to black intellectuals" (*Color* 66). It created a subcultural space of critique and reflection, where black intellectual autonomy could be cultivated and consolidated. But the residuum designates not only a space of "second-sight." It is also a point of exclusion, a repository for those subjects who cannot be integrated within the pluralistic universe as "neighbors" or "intimates" (to use variations of James's tropes). Within Kallen's rendition of Jamesian pluralism, African Americans occupy this space of exclusion, the suppressed term of Kallen's cultural pluralism.

Kallen's most famous metaphor—the orchestra—excludes as much as it includes. These exclusions are most salient in "Democracy versus the Melting Pot" (1915), where Kallen introduces this metaphor to describe his "federation of nationalities" model of Americanism:

> Thus "American civilization" may come to mean the perfection of the cooperative harmonies of "European civilization"—the waste, the squalor and the distress of Europe being eliminated—a multiplicity in a unity, an orchestration of mankind. As in an orchestra every type of instrument has its specific *timbre* and *tonality*, founded in its substance and form; as every type has its appropriate theme and melody in the whole symphony, so in society, each ethnic group may be the natural instrument, its temper and culture may be its theme and melody and the harmony and dissonances and discords of them all may make the symphony of civilization. With this difference: a musical symphony is written before it is played; in the symphony of civilization the playing is the writing. (124–125)

Kallen's pluralism is a sanitized revision of James's murky and turbid "federal republic." As the highbrow trope of the orchestra suggests, cultural pluralism is an exclusive arrangement of distinct and discrete cultures, which excludes not only communities of color but also impoverished European immigrants who embody the "waste, the squalor and the distress of Europe."[18] Those who are included must keep to their place, because each ethnic group, like each instrument, has its "specific *timbre* and *tonality*." In contrast to his mentor's messy heterogeneity, Kallen's version is whitened, cleansed, and purged of undesirable elements. He Hellenizes the gothic turmoil of James's pluralistic universe to produce a harmonious world that more closely resembles the classical beauty of monism, which is precisely what James opposed.

Years later in another essay also included in *Culture and Democracy*, Kallen aptly refers to the exclusion of African Americans in a footnote, which is itself the textual equivalent of the "residuum." In this footnote he explains his neglect of the African-American influence in regional literature, saying that it is "at once too considerable and too recondite in its processes for casual mention. It requires a separate analysis" (*C&D* 226). Kallen avoids a discussion of the African-American impact on U.S. culture because of its "recondite" subject matter. But the primary reason Kallen excludes any mention of African Americans is the impact this would have on the foundations of the Euro-American narrative that he is re-creating. Whether in Kallen's orchestra or his national narrative of Jewish exceptionalism, there is no conflict in his pluralistic world. The residuum, for Kallen, is not a category of subversion but a mechanism of racial exclusion.

The suppression of African Americans from Kallen's cultural pluralism goes back to the concept's origins. The black residuum actually gave rise to cultural pluralism when Kallen first conceived of it while a graduate student at Harvard. He recollects its genesis: "It was in 1905 that I began to formulate the notion of cultural pluralism and I had to do that in connection with my teaching. I was assisting both Mr. James and Mr. Santayana at the time and I had a negro student named Alain Locke, a very remarkable young man—very sensitive, very easily hurt—who insisted that he was a human being and that his color ought not to make any difference. And, of course, it was a mistaken insistence. It *had* to make a difference and it *had* to be accepted and respected and enjoyed for what it was" (qtd. Sollors "Pure Pluralism" 269). Alain Locke, who was an undergraduate when Kallen was a doctoral candidate, was to become a philosophy professor at Howard University and the "father of the New Negro" during the Harlem Renaissance.[19] A friend of both Kallen and Du Bois, the latter of whom he met in the 1920s while Du Bois was editing *The Crisis,* Locke played an instrumental role in the early formation of Kallen's cultural pluralism. Their friendship underwent a difficult time while they were both in Oxford in 1907–1908, which coincided with James's visit to deliver the Hibbert Lectures.

Kallen's cultural pluralism originally emerged as a response to racism, as a failed attempt to resolve the problem of community among American Rhodes scholars abroad. Locke, who was the first African-American Rhodes scholar, was not invited to join the other Rhodes scholars for Thanksgiving dinner, because the white Southerners refused to dine with him. Recounting this experience, Kallen says that one or two others, who were "authentically" American, refused to attend as a gesture of solidarity with Locke, though he does not specify whether he was one of them.[20] The crisis erupted into a lively exchange about the value of racial difference. "We had to argue out the question of how the differences made differences," Kallen recalls, "and in arguing out those questions the formula, then phrases, developed—'cultural pluralism,' 'the right to be different' and 'pluralistic society'" (*What I Believe* 173). These conversations resulted in an awakening for Kallen, an awareness of the differences between being a white ethnic and being a racially marked other. Remembering this incident years later, he acknowledged that "Alain Locke's Negro difference" presented him "with a challenge of identity far more poignant and critical than mine" (173). In recognizing the deep division between being perceived as a "white ethnic" and being perceived as black, he admitted that "the impact of that kind of experience left scars" (132).

In his epistolary exchanges with Barrett Wendell, however, Kallen seemed less disturbed about the white racist attitudes toward Locke and more conflicted about his own mixed feelings about African Americans. Telling Wendell about the incident in 1907, Kallen writes: "As you know, I have neither respect nor liking for his race—but individually they have to be taken, each on his own merits and value, and if ever a negro was worthy, this boy is" (Sollors "Pure" 270). In his response, Wendell conveys his personal "repugnance" toward blacks: "My own sentiments concerning negroes are such that I have always declined to meet the best of them—Booker Washington, a man whom I thoroughly respect,—at table" (Sollors "Pure" 270). In the next letter, Kallen shares such "sentiments of repugnance": "you have phrased my own feeling toward the race, so well that I don't see that there is anything more to say . . . So he is to come to tea again tho' it is personally repugnant to me to eat with him." Kallen then ends with a reference to "Shylock's disclaimer," which is the point in *Merchant of Venice* (I.iii.35ff), where Shylock declines Bassanio's dinner invitation and says: "I will buy with you, sell with you, talk with you / walk with you, and so following; but I will not eat / with you, drink with you, nor pray with you." Kallen invokes Shylock's disclaimer not as a way to distance himself as a Jew from the dominant culture but just the opposite: to bond with the dominant Anglo-American culture through a shared racial repugnance toward blacks. Kallen and Locke share an intellectual friendship and an institutional connection as "Harvard men," but it is a friendship ultimately circumscribed by racial boundaries. Socializing together is off limits or if not clearly off limits, as Kallen's invitation to Locke for tea indicates, then at least fraught with tensions and reservations.

If Kallen's use of Shylock's disclaimer illustrates the personal distance between him and Locke, it also suggests the familiarity between himself and his former professor. That Kallen cites this passage in a letter to the Boston Brahmin implies that the letter-writer and the reader can share that which neither of them can share with Locke: their common experience of identifying as white. To what extent is the Yankee-Jewish bond, the very bond that allowed Kallen to rediscover his Jewishness under Wendell's guidance, based on the recognition of mutual whiteness? Besides a shared identification with the Old Testament, the Yankee and the Jew can also bond through their shared repugnance toward African Americans.

But Kallen's letters to Wendell also betray a certain insecurity about this bond, in the sense that intellectual philo-semitism did not necessarily translate into a liking for Jewish people. Philo-semitism was not so much a love of Jews in the flesh (as "moderns") as it was a veneration of an ideal type (as "ancients"), which was constructed from reading the Hebrew Scriptures. In Wendell's book *Liberty, Union and Democracy,* which was published a year before the Locke Affair and which Kallen approvingly mentions in his 1915 essay on cultural pluralism, Wendell expresses his antipathy toward the "foreign influences" in New England, which include "Irish, German, Italian, Jewish, whatever else" (11). He describes student class lists at Harvard as becoming more and more alienating each year, with surnames that are "absolutely foreign in all the implications, to the traditions by which we of New England have been nurtured" (7–8). Wendell could have just as easily invoked his own disclaimer in relation to both Locke and Kallen. Aware of the anti-semitic undercurrent of much New England philo-semitism, Kallen uses Locke to strengthen the Yankee-Jewish bond. Locke's blackness reinforces Kallen's Americanism by making Jewishness less alienating to the New England patrician.

In Kallen's pluralistic orchestra, exclusion of African Americans ensures an "associative harmony" between Anglo and Jewish Americans. But what happens when the African American steps outside the "residuum" and occupies the orchestra? Far more than Kallen, Du Bois is the one who actually sustains the "unharmonizable variety" of his mentor's work. "The Nation," Du Bois writes in the first chapter of *Souls,* "has not yet found peace from its sins; the freedman has not yet found in freedom his promised land" (DB 104). This line informs Du Bois's appropriation of the highbrow trope of the orchestra, which he uses to portray the nation not as a Hellenic utopia but as plagued by racial conflict. In chapter 12 of *Souls*, "The Coming of John," Du Bois interprets the orchestra as a sign of racial and class privilege. More specifically, it is a site of racial exclusion, where the "white John" and the "black John," boyhood friends in their Georgia town, unknowingly sit next to each other at a posh New York City concert hall. Although the "black John" loses himself in the music of "Lohengrin's swan," listening to it with all his "heart" (which attests to the profound aesthetic sensibility of the African American, a point that Du Bois makes throughout), he is nonetheless asked to leave. As he turns to exit from his seat, he recognizes the "white John," the Judge's son, and realizes that it was he who pressured the management to remove him. Former friends, they now look each other in the eye: "The white John started, lifted his hand, and then rose into his chair; the black John smiled lightly, then grimly, and followed the usher down the aisle" (DB 224).

Written a decade before Kallen's "Democracy versus the Melting-Pot," Du Bois's short story underscores the disjuncture between the melodious music performed and the racialized space of the performance. In contrast to the bars of "Negro folk-songs" that appear at the start of each chapter in *Souls* and reappear at the end, the orchestra represents the institution of high culture, whose privilege is predicated in part on the exclusion of African Americans, including the Talented Tenth. For Du Bois, the most "American" music resounds not from the metropolitan portals of high culture but from the rural communities of the black poor.

What is significant is that Du Bois's critique of the orchestra as a site of racial exclusion occurs after a scene in "The Coming of John" in which John Jones (the "black John") enjoys the various sights of New York City. As an urban *flâneur*, John likens the streets of New York to a "changelessly changing" sea, characterized by contrasts, "so bright and dark, so grave and gay" (DB 222). "He scanned their rich and faultless clothes, the way they carried their hands, the shape of their hats." Taken up with the moment, he sighs: "This is the World." John ends up at the orchestra precisely because he loses himself in the excitement and exhilaration of the metropolis. Modernity is depicted as a liberatory and thrilling experience, in which the city's anonymity provides a sense of detachment through connection. He is literally transported through the streets, "past stores and gay shops, across a broad square, until with a hundred others they entered the high portal of a great building" (DB 223). That this exterior scene of perambulatory pleasure precedes the interior one of racial exclusion underscores the African-American ambivalence toward modernity. The metropolis marks a liminal space of emergent freedom and residual prejudice; it designates a liberating zone of anonymity as well as a highly racialized sphere of segregation.

This narrative juxtaposition in "The Coming of John" illustrates Du Bois's own divided sentiments toward cosmopolitanism. These two scenes from "The Coming of John" suggest that persons of color can never transcend their racial particularity. There may be a momentary respite of anonymity, as when John is carried off by the moving crowd, but for the most part race is a living and determining force. The racial subject is constantly reinterpreted as "racial" through daily encounters. Any theory of humanism, which Du Bois calls a "a theory of human culture," must respond to this reality; it must be rooted in a recognition of identity culture rather than its transcendence. Universalism and humanism are not modes of escape from the challenges of identity culture but their fullest expression. Particularism and universalism are not antithetical elements, but like "Negro" and "American," they are complementary. Both Du Bois and Kallen use identity culture to theorize modern humanism, and their common strategy of universalizing the particular leads to conflicting versions of Americanism as well as to antithetical understandings of modernity and machine culture.

Modernity, Machine Culture, and the New Humanism

Modernity, for Kallen, is an actual reality; whereas for Du Bois it is also an ideal. Pluralism is Kallen's way to make modernity anodyne, to lessen its tensions and conflicts through various strategies of crisis management. It is a means of sustaining the status quo. Kallen uses the language of abundance, most notably the discourse of variety, as a way to diffuse the class and racial tensions associated with the modern age of industry. Just as Kallen does not rewrite the narrative of national genesis but only modifies it to include Jewish Americans as the modern-day Puritans, so he does not challenge the workings of a machine age, but instead applies the harmony of the orchestra to the workplace. Du Bois, in contrast, distinguishes between an industrial economy and an "industrial democracy." Modernity, for him, is both a present-day phenomenon of crisis and pleasure and a future ideal of equality, in which the abundance from the machine will be distributed evenly. Du Bois uses the language of difference to highlight rather than harmonize the division of global labor. For both men, the language of variety plays a central role in delineating the parameters and the possibilities of community in the modern age.

Culture and Democracy, which begins by bemoaning the suppression of cultural diversity at a time of "Kukluxitis," concludes on a radically different note: it celebrates the machine age as a time of new affinities and marks the arrival of a "new Humanism," which Kallen defines as the "Humanism of the industrial age." This new humanism conceives of the modern age as one of tolerance, catholicity, and fellowship. Kallen criticizes the anti-urbanism of the nineteenth century, epitomized in such figures as Carlyle and Tolstoy who saw in "the new economy of industry" impersonality, automatism, and compulsions. The modern inheritors of this cynical perspective include Randolph Bourne, the bohemian intellectual and rebel of Greenwich Village. Despite the fact that Bourne spoke highly of Kallen's cultural pluralism and used the metaphor of the orchestra as a springboard for imagining a "trans-national America," Kallen is rather critical of Bourne's rendition of modernity. According to Kallen, Bourne interprets the "institutions of modern life" as inextricably evil: "they inflict suffering, they suffocate independence and originality; they spread the pall of age and death on all things" (*C&D* 312). Although Kallen articulates a similar view in the early essays of *Culture and Democracy*, his perspective by the end of this collection has abruptly changed. The machine age is now recuperable, because it promotes diversity.

The industrial city, in attracting cheap labor from all over the globe, has consolidated the human population into diverse unities. The machine acts as a source of division by atomizing the production process but, more important, it establishes new modes of cohesion: "It simultaneously divides and unites men" (339). Industry has produced the industrial city where old world antagonisms dissipate into friendly fellowship: "Contact generates tolerance. Men learn to respect difference . . . Peoples of diverse origin, habits and standards are more at home with one another" (341). Kallen anticipates Iris Marion Young's ideal of the "unoppressive city," an ideal that has already been realized in the metropolis, which is the site of "organic" communion and "humane" alliances.

What is especially striking is how Kallen juxtaposes variety and diversity against class antagonism and labor unrest. At the end of *Culture and Democracy,* Kallen describes the benefits of trade unionism: "the story of workers' associations, and the trade-unions and the cooperative societies, and of the theories and philosophies which envision them, is direct witness of the pressure toward diversity, equality and cooperation in the domain of the industrial machine" (340). In contrast to Du Bois, who directly addresses racism within trade unions during this period in *The Crisis,*[21] Kallen celebrates worker organizations uncritically, as the place where old misunderstandings "wear down" and are replaced by new alliances. Kallen has fully incorporated pluralism within Progressive liberalism, as a way to placate middle-class fears that violence may erupt from industrial repression.

In the vein of Walter Lippmann, Herbert Croly, and Walter Weyl, Kallen was part of a new generation of theorists who imagined a modern philosophy of middle-class liberalism based on the *via media.* The crux of this "new Humanism" was a belief that an industrial economy of abundance would appease workers. As Weyl states in *The New Democracy:* "Where wealth is growing at a rapid rate, the multitude may be fed without breaking into the rich man's granary" (qtd. Forcey 63). The language of variety provides an important rhetorical salve for the worsening maldistribution of wealth. It democratizes plenitude at a time of disparity.

Kallen's cultural pluralism begins as a way to celebrate Euro-American immigrant cultures and specifically Jewish immigrants as exemplary Americans. It eventually becomes a defense of industrial capitalism, in which "diversity" is used to describe the image of the worker as a happy trade unionist, content with the goals of the machine age. Consistent with the trajectory of Progressive liberalism, Kallen's pluralism soon shifts from the happy factory hand to the consumer, from the mode of production to an economy of consumption, while the antebellum image of a nation of farmers changes into a nation of shoppers. The producerist ethos is now antiquated and potentially divisive, and its consumerist counterpart is perceived as a far safer alternative. The nation that shops together stays together. The real power emerging today in democratic life, opines Walter Lippmann in 1912, is consumer protest, which is "destined to be stronger than the interests of either labor or capital" (qtd. Forcey 165). Kallen reiterates this point in declaring that "mankind are, first and last, consumers" (*Individualism* 198).

Developed a year after the publication of *Culture and Democracy*, Kallen's theory of "consumptionism" represents an "innocent" way out of class stratification. In *Education, the Machine and the Worker: An Essay in the Psychology of Education in Industrial Society* (1925), Kallen radically transforms the identity culture of workers from the workplace to leisure. He accentuates the multiple loyalties—the hyphenated allegiances—that a worker has beyond the factory as a way of diffusing labor conflicts. "When he enters the shop, he [the industrial worker] is already the member of a very complex system of associations or communities. He belongs to a family, a church, a social club, a political party, a fraternal order, a school alumni association, and so on . . . They are, in a word, modes of consumption, and the interests of which they are constituted are interests of consumption. They are the modes of association through which the worker gets his plays and pleasures" (168). Industrial peace can be attained, Kallen seems to be implying, only if workers find interests away from work, away from the site of production, and toward play. Variety, therefore, can be seen as moving from a defense of ethnic particularity within an orchestration of modern Americanism to the "variety" shows and entertainments associated with working-class leisure.[22]

Kallen's pluralism responds to concerns about ethnic conflict and labor strife by placating them. By the end of *Culture and Democracy*, cultural pluralism signals a form of crisis management that actually brackets off crisis, suppressing and silencing it in the hope that troubling times will go away. Furthermore, Kallen's embrace of ethnic particularity is part of a larger attempt to incorporate identity culture within an economy of consumerism, in which ethnic difference adds distinctiveness to a potentially bland product. In this case, the product is American exceptionalism, which is itself, according to Kallen, a revision of European nationalities into a "truly 'trans-national America,' a new and happy form of associative harmony" (*C&D* 232). While James's pragmatism, as critics have long noted, incorporates the language of business, as in the "cash-value" of truth, Kallen's rhetoric uses the nascent discourse of professional advertising. Words such as "new" and "newest" pervade the pages of *Culture and Democracy*. Kallen is not just presenting his readers with a new pluralistic model of modern Americanism, but selling them a new national mythology, in which diversity safeguards rather than threatens the nation.

The multicultural descendant of Kallen's cultural pluralism is what has become known as the "Benetton effect," a term used to describe hegemonic forms of corporate multiculturalism that have become profitable means of commodification.[23] Benetton advertisements have, for instance, completed the consumerist shift that Kallen inaugurated in representing the colorful varieties of their products without a trace of their production. Kallen's theory of liberal consumerism, in which his pluralism plays a vital role, sets the conceptual groundwork for a postmodern and post-Fordist economy of consumption, in which consumers are seen in relation to lifestyles and tastes rather than to social class. Kallen's pluralism, however, is a transitional national allegory, in which trade unionists and factory workers still figure, though as "happy" stereotypes.

If Kallen represents an early stage in the Benettonization of Jamesian pluralism, Du Bois signals a more radical variation, in which pluralism is a critique of power relations within the nation and in the world. Whereas *Souls* revises the meaning of modern Americanism, *Darkwater* offers a scathing critique of the inequalities characterizing the world system in the aftermath of World War I. In "Of Work and Wealth," Du Bois moves from the national to the international in criticizing racialized structures of inequality in which "industrial oppression" rests on "the oldest and nastiest form of human oppression,—race hatred" (DB 530). In contrast to Kallen, who celebrates the benefits of the industrial age with little emphasis on its disparities, Du Bois turns to East St. Louis in the aftermath of the race riots of 1917. He describes the "flame-swept walls," the "streets almost wet with blood," and "the bones of dead men new-bleached" as the manifestations of uneven development, linking this black ghetto with the major centers of commerce in the United States and abroad (DB 525). "East St. Louis is a paradise for high and frequent dividends and for the piling up of wealth to be spent in St. Louis and Chicago and New York and when the world is sane again, across the seas" (DB 526). East St. Louis is a "microcosm," to borrow Du Bois's term, of industrial relations occurring on a global scale: the relations between East St. Louis and St. Louis depict the colonial connections between Europe, Africa, and Asia.

Contrary to Kallen, who employs the language of diversity to diffuse the animosities of class, Du Bois uses the language of racial diversity to accentuate the division of labor at an international level: "the world today consists, not of races, but of the imperial commercial group of master capitalists, international and predominantly white; the national middle classes of the several nations, white, yellow, and brown, with strong blood bonds, common languages, and common history; the international laboring class of all colors; the backward, oppressed groups of nature-folk, predominantly yellow, brown, and black" (DB 532). In contrast to "Conservation" and even *Souls, Darkwater* speaks of race not as a category in its own right but as a category that is sustained through industrial oppression. "American Negroes," writes Du Bois, "have exemplified the last and worst refuge of industrial caste" (DB 541).

In typical pragmatic fashion, most of *Darkwater* is dedicated to the task of problem-solving, in grappling with the fundamental concerns of the day: "Our great ethical question today is, therefore, how may we justly distribute the world's goods to satisfy the necessary wants of the mass of men" (DB 533). In answering this question, Du Bois adopts a strategy similar to the one he employs in defining Americanism. Just as he will not permit Stoddard to monopolize definitions of Americanism, so he will not let the Carnegies and the Vanderbilts control the meaning of industrialism. In *Darkwater,* he is not willing simply to dismiss the technological advances brought on by industrial development in favor of an antimodern agrarian utopia. Du Bois is a cosmopolitan modern through and through. He possesses elements of the Progressive intellectual in the vein of Charlotte Perkins Gilman. Machines can liberate women from housekeeping, just as they can free African Americans from menial service and domestic labor. "Cannot machinery, in the hands of self-respecting and well-paid artisans, do our cleaning, sewing, moving, and decorating?" (DB 543).

Du Bois's goal is to democratize industrialism to include a wider spectrum of the world's populations. The "history of the world," he writes, "is the history of the discovery of the common humanity of human beings among steadily increasing circles of men" (DB 557). A notion of an industrial commonwealth requires a "theory of human culture," in which the term "humanity" would be defined according to the world's demographics. "With Negro and Negroid, East Indian, Chinese, and Japanese they form two-thirds of the population of the world. A belief in humanity is a belief in colored men. If the uplift of mankind must be done by men, then the destinies of this world will rest ultimately in the hands of darker nations" (DB 507). Humanity, therefore, does not represent a de-racialized space of transcendence, but a term constituted by the brown, yellow, and black identity cultures of the world.

Du Bois's "theory of human culture" takes the term "human" and borrows its universalist connotations to elevate and empower the lowest castes of the world to the level of representative subjects. His radical humanism is based on the world's residuum, its colonized and disenfranchised people, who when taken as a whole make up the majority of the world's population. Du Bois's humanism is not a theory of symmetry, in which each of the world's races shares equal representation within an "orchestration of mankind," but an asymmetrical arrangement based on "proportionate representation" (DB 560).

Du Bois continues James's anti-imperialism but without the genteel ambivalence about self-determination. The colonized Third World, for Du Bois, does not consist as it did for James of individual subjects possessing psychological "inwardness." Instead, he anticipates Frantz Fanon in speaking of the potential power of the colonized through the formation of national movements. *Darkwater* is not just a portrayal of the tragedy of European colonialism, with special attention to its Third World victims; it is also a warning to the First World that the victims of colonialism will soon rise: *"The Dark World is going to submit to its present treatment just as long as it must and not one moment longer"* (DB 507). In redefining "humanity" as brown, Du Bois is also giving the "Dark World" agency, in that the destiny of the world is in "the hands of darker nations" (DB 507). Du Bois develops the trope of "hands" to emphasize further the potential agency of colonized peoples to throw off the yoke of imperial power: "The hands which Ethiopia shall soon stretch out unto God are not mere hands of helplessness and supplication, but rather are they hands of pain and promise" (DB 520).

The anti-imperialism of both James and Du Bois is an attempt to make "civilization" more humane; but whereas James operates within the racial and genteel conventions of this term, Du Bois democratizes "civilization" to include "the Negro, the Indian, the Mongolian, and the South Sea Islander" (DB 535). This move from "industrial imperialism" to "industrial democracy" is not antithetical to Jamesian pluralism but its most progressive realization. It takes the qualities that characterize "inner spiritual Harvard," specifically self-determination, autonomy, and individuality, and applies them to national sovereignty, national determination, and independence among the "darker nations."

Du Bois's ideal, however, is not only a decolonized world, where distinct nation-states are now autonomous and independent, but a more elaborate post-colonial ideal that he calls the "inter-nation." In *Darkwater* he refers to this ideal as a democratic "industrial commonwealth" that cannot "exclude the black and brown and yellow races from its counsels" (DB 556). In 1920, the year in which *Darkwater* was published, Du Bois also published an article in *The Crisis* called "Race Pride," in which he develops this cosmopolitan vision according to a radical disjuncture between people and place. "Let it be possible for whites to rise to the highest positions in China and Uganda and blacks to the highest honors in England and Texas" (Paschal 133). After World War I, Du Bois radically challenged the spatial politics of pluralism, its model of diversity-as-discreteness, by unsettling the tidy compartments that characterize Kallen's orchestra and his own ideal expressed in "Conservation" of a "side by side" union between white and black. This multicultural revision, however, does not elide identity culture.[24] Du Bois's cosmopolitan model of democracy, appearing in an article aptly entitled "Race Pride," is ethically, culturally, and politically based on the particularity of the Jamesian "each-form." Du Bois's "inter-nation" loosens the moorings of identity culture, and in doing so it maintains the importance of being black *and* English, or black *and* Texan. This is how cosmopolitanism sustains its rootedness, its ability to oppose discrimination without also obliterating racial particularity.

The inter-nation is realized, though not fully, in the metropolis. Manhattan is the site, according to Du Bois, where plurality and modernity intersect most positively, though still circumscribed within patterns of social and economic segregation. In *Darkwater* and specifically in "Of Beauty and Death," Du Bois reproduces the tensions from "The Coming of John," in which John Jones experiences both the pleasure and the racism of cosmopolitanism. The same excitement that characterizes John Jones's experience of the streets of New York unexpectedly reappears in one of the most pessimistic of Du Bois's early-twentieth-century works: "New York and morning: the sun is kissing the timid dew in Central Park, and from the Fountain of Plenty one looks along that world street, Fifth Avenue, and walks toward town . . . Humanity stands and flies and walks and rolls about—the poor, the priceless, the world-known and the forgotten; child and grandfather, king and leman—the pageant of the world goes by . . . these are the Ways of the World today" (DB 606). Even the metaphor of the "sea" from "The Coming of John" resurfaces in descriptions of the streets: "The glow of burning millions melts outward into dim and fairy outlines until afar the liquid music born of rushing crowds drips like a benediction on the sea" (DB 606).

From Fifth Avenue, the narrator-as-*flâneur* soon perambulates through the neighborhoods of Harlem: "The street is crowd and leisure and laughter . . . Orators declaim on the corners, lovers lark in the streets, gamblers glide by the saloon, workers lounge wearily home" (DB 607). Du Bois's Manhattan is a cosmopolitan ideal, not in the sense that exploitation and disparities are absent, but rather in the more mundane sense that the metropolis represents the greatest cross-section of the "human." By celebrating Manhattan as the apex of cosmopolitanism, Du Bois participates in a discourse of national exceptionalism that praises the metropolis for its transnationalism. New York is exceptional precisely because it already contains the world.

The city also represents spatial distinctions—the "black eyes" and "frizzled hair curled and sleek" of Harlem—a subcultural space of a world within a world that maintains its particularity, autonomy, and integrity. "Gone is the white world, the pale lips, the lank hair; gone is the West and North—the East and South is here triumphant" (DB 606). The black residuum is a source of pleasure, affirmation, and independence. It is also a sign of marginalization, the "ugly and evil" effects of racism. The American metropolis is not an "unoppressive city," in Kallen's sense of being a place of "general tolerance" and "widespread cooperative fellowship of individuals in which a society of free and equal men consists" (*Individualism* 97). Du Bois's American metropolis is exceptional because it displays the "beauty" and "ugliness" of modernity, as a place of difference and discrimination, of contact and segregation.

Cosmopolitan Humanism Revisited

Kallen's cultural pluralism reproduces the strategy of accommodation seen in his letters to Barrett Wendell. He exploits what G. Stanley Hall referred to as the "friendly feeling" and Edward Ross called the "cousinly feeling" between Yankees and Jews in order to create a spiritual and social "home" for Jewish intellectuals among the genteel "college-bred." Kallen's pluralism is a defense of Jewish distinctiveness—retaining the "Jew as Jew"—as well as a universalizing of Jewishness as quintessentially American. This allows Kallen to avoid the question of assimilation by suggesting that American exceptionalism is the logical extension of Jewish exceptionalism.

By contrast, Du Bois develops the radical possibilities of James's pluralism not by affirming the dominant narrative of Puritan settlement but by radically displacing it. He maintains the dialectical tensions between "each-forms" and "all-forms," and among the local ("inner spiritual Harvard"), the national ("federal republic"), and the international ("the cosmopolitan liberal party"). Du Bois translates "inner spiritual Harvard" into identity culture or an African-American subculture of criticism and affirmation. He transforms the "federal republic" into modern Americanism, which is unique and exceptional because of its African-American cultural and historical presence. He adapts "the cosmopolitan liberal party" into a "world federation" and an "inter-nation," which are manifested in the American metropolis. In the last instance, Du Bois's radical humanism returns to modern America. His cosmopolitanism does not transcend the nation-state but transforms it by presenting the American metropolis as a transnational chronotope. James's "pluralistic universe" is now situated in Manhattan, which is a place of autonomy as well as of overlap and hybridity; it is the site of "independence" as well as of "inextricable interfusion."

Du Bois offers an important point of contrast with recent theories of cosmopolitanism. Contrary to Du Bois's humanism, in which identitarian and nationalist claims still play a formative role in his transnationalist vision, contemporary cosmopolitanism often tends to view identity culture and, in some instances, the nation-state as irredeemably antiquated and provincial. The *bête noire* of contemporary cosmopolitanism seems to be identity politics, because it imposes limits, primarily limits on who can speak with authority. In a postethnic and postnational world, identity cramps our style; it designates a border in a borderless world. Cosmopolitanism enters the critical scene as the white horse to the rescue. It saves us from the restrictions of identity (a new euphemism for race); it promises to liberate us from the limitations of identity politics through the detachment of voluntary "cultural affiliations." It replaces essentialism with ethics so we can talk about that which really matters. It refers to the "atomizing politics of identity," as if identity politics created divisions that otherwise would not exist.[25] Essentialism and identity politics are dismissed as part of the problem, rather than seen as symptoms of and defenses against racism and discrimination. In denouncing identity politics as essentialist, some contemporary cosmopolitans have essentialized identity. They have condemned identity culture as restrictive, and therefore intrinsically conservative.

Although cosmopolitanism casts itself as a liberatory alternative to identity politics, it is not clear what the politics of cosmopolitanism actually are. What struggles will characterize cosmopolitanism? What will it oppose? What will it support? James's "cosmopolitan liberal party" arose in the specific context of opposition to the U.S. military invasion of the Philippines. Du Bois's "inter-nation" emerged out of a critique of national and global disparities in the aftermath of World War I; it specifically addressed, for instance, the East St. Louis race riots. It was a cosmopolitanism that was rooted, engaged, and partisan. For moderns like Du Bois, Kallen, and James, restrictions and limitations were not essentially oppressive; they could be, but they were not inherently so. Limits did not preclude an ethics but enabled an ethics to emerge. Politics and ethics required boundaries: they gave modern cosmopolitanism a content. Identity culture, whether it was "inner spiritual Harvard" or ethno-racial subcultures, provided the conceptual springboard for theorizing national and global communities. Modern cosmopolitanism did not transcend partisanism, but resoundingly and unequivocally reclaimed it.

In the next chapter, I explore how intellectuals from the regional margins of the United States used a similar strategy of resilient particularity to lay claim to the national. Pluralism, grafted onto land, legitimates the geographically "vanquished" (to borrow James's word) as central to the production of a national culture. In providing a counter-discourse of modernization, regionalism claimed to be a critique of uneven development not from the position of nostalgia but from the vantage point of the modern. Just as the ethnicization and racialization of James's "pluralistic universe" was a multidimensional and uneven process, so the regionalization of identity culture also produced a variety of intersecting and conflicting perspectives.

II

The Aesthetics of Diversity

3

The Uneven Development of American Regionalism

In the late nineteenth century, as pluralism appeared within the field of philosophy as a way to theorize the limits of an all-inclusive union by privileging the individuality of its component parts, analogous theories about local color emerged on the literary landscape as a way to imagine a national literature based on distinct localities. As early as 1868, John De Forest predicted that the "Great American Novel" would appear in "sections," since the United States consisted of a "nation of provinces." As the century progressed and the different regions of the nation became increasingly economically interdependent, De Forest's prediction gained in popularity. By the 1890s, when economic and cultural incorporation had intensified, so had the call for sectional uniqueness.

In his 1892 preface to his best-selling collection *The Hoosier Schoolmaster* (1871), Edward Eggleston reiterated De Forest's prophecy by claiming that the "great American novel" was indeed "appearing in sections." By the late nineteenth century, the "Federal nation," according to Eggleston, had finally "manifested a consciousness of the continental diversity of its forms of life" (7). This attempt to conceive of a national literary tradition in terms of "diversity" was also embraced by a new generation of writers such as Hamlin Garland and Frank Norris. In 1894 Garland proclaimed that a truly national literature would be based on the "local novel," since "it is the differences which interest us; the similarities do not please" (*Crumbling Idols* 49). Later in the same decade, Norris also imagined the "Great American Novel" as "sectional" and multiple, since one region of the nation was "very, very different from the life in another" (*Responsibilities* 229).

This move to theorize a national literature based on the particular, a move that conceived of localism and Americanism as interdependent, parallels on aesthetic terrain the pluralist configuration of a democratic commonwealth. Both pluralism and regionalism addressed the same dilemma: how to conserve the integrity and the individuality of a subculture, or what William James more abstractly calls the "each-form," in the midst of the standardizing forces of modernity. Whether it was Americanization for the pluralists or modernization for the regionalists, both wanted to show that incorporation did not necessarily mean assimilation. Pluralists and regionalists believed that the contemporary monisms of Americanization and modernization were not complete and all-encompassing; there was still "residual resistance," to borrow James's phrase, that could transform the whole. This did not mean that pluralists or regionalists rejected the notion of national unity and opted instead for a multiplicity without end. Rather, they wanted to imagine a unity that did not compromise the distinctiveness of its constitutive elements. Whereas Kallen and Du Bois argued for the conservation of ethnic and racial differences in the formation of modern America, local colorists claimed that the preservation of regional distinctions would contribute to a more dynamic national literary tradition.[1] Pluralists and local colorists alike invoked subcultural uniqueness as a way to refashion the Union, because they believed that the only way to save unity from becoming uniformity was to define it through differentiation.

Both the pluralists and the regionalists implemented this strategy—unity without uniformity—by invoking variables that were rather troubling to their contemporaries. Whether it was African Americans and Jewish immigrants, on the one hand, or the old bogey of sectionalism on the other, pluralists and regionalists took that which was considered divisive and made it the necessary ingredient for the twentieth-century nation. This revised attitude toward division and difference was presented as a sign of national stability, demonstrating that even sectionalism was no longer deemed a threat to the republic's security. But such configurations of unity-in-distinctiveness were also attempts to conceive of particularity in non-separatist terms. According to pluralists and regionalists, subcultural autonomy and national loyalty should coexist for a modern notion of national coherence that would be sufficiently adaptable to incorporate new populations and regions.

By reconciling particularity with national unity, regionalism was seen as a way of tempering the incorporative excesses of the period through a plan of moderation. Just as cultural pluralism was a response to anxieties about both too much homogeneity and excessive heterogeneity, so regionalism responded to a similar set of concerns. Like Randolph Bourne and other liberal cosmopolitans who feared that assimilated immigrants had lost their "foreign savor," many also worried that urbanization would lead to a sameness among regions. "No difference is countenanced between city and village," declared one anonymous observer. "Uniformity is the curse which our modern life willfully feeds upon" (qtd. H. M. Jones 261). In *The American Commonwealth*, Viscount Bryce, who was the British ambassador to the United States, noted that the one drawback of American life was "its uniformity" (618). Besides the "uniformity of landscape," according to Bryce, the towns and cities shared a "monotony [that] haunts one like a nightmare" (622). Henry James was similarly disappointed to discover during his 1905 trip to the United States that despite all the talk about "individuality and variety," there was actually a dull "fusion" that characterized the different people of the nation, a "dimness of the distinctions" (*American Scene* 333). He writes in *The American Scene:* "It was the scant diversity of type that left me short, as a story-seeker or picture-maker" (335).

Concomitant with these anxieties about spatial standardization, there were also contrary concerns that America was becoming too regionally varied. Like E. A. Ross, who feared that the new immigration would end any hope for a national common culture, many were also distressed that the Civil War specter of sectionalism would threaten a new generation of Americans. Despite President William McKinley's 1897 Inaugural Address, which assured Americans that the "North and the South no longer divide on the old lines" and that this was a "cause for true felicitation," there was still tremendous concern that the more the nation moved beyond its war-torn past, the more it was haunted by it. "The Union has not been reunited," warned Murat Halstead in 1885, "but sectionalism in its worst form has been revived" (245). In 1897 Woodrow Wilson, then a professor of political economy and jurisprudence at Princeton, believed that the "sectionalization of national life" prevented a true "economic and spiritual union" ("Making of the Nation" 3). Although he reassured his audience, as did McKinley, that there was no longer "any danger of a civil war," he expressed concern that the regions of the nation had developed at different rates with some far more prosperous than others. In contrast to Bryce and others who felt that uniformity had collapsed the distinction between the country and the city, Wilson insisted that modernization had exacerbated the distinction. The country and the city were growing further apart as they were becoming more intertwined.

Had modernization made sectionalism obsolete, replacing it with a national economy of uniformity? Or had modernization resulted in a revival of sectionalism in which regions competed for access to development? Like pluralism, regionalism responded to the conflicting trends of homogenization and differentiation, by which regional consolidation produced spatial hierarchies. According to the geographer Edward Soja, "nineteenth-century regionalisms developed mainly out of attempts to preserve distinct regional cultures in the face of increasing homogenization or to resist the particular spatial divisions of labour being imposed by expansive market integration and the equally expansive national state" (165).

Similar to cultural pluralism's response to concerns that America was becoming either too homogeneous or too heterogeneous, regionalism took a middle path between the two, insisting on a model of unity-in-distinctiveness. The nation was a federation of partial narratives, a collection of scattered texts. As one critic noted in the *Atlantic*: "we shall rely more and more on realistic fiction for a federation of the scattered states of this decentralized and diverse land of ours" (Nicholson 199). This tactic of moderation recognized regional differences but insisted that they did not threaten the Union, only strengthened it. Like William James's metaphor of pragmatic truth as the "half-way station" between extremes, regionalism signified the middle ground between the obliteration of regional distinctions and divisive sectionalism.

From Pluralism to Local Color

Horace Kallen, one of the first theorists of cultural pluralism, saw a direct connection between his theory of ethnic accommodation and local color. For Kallen, regionalism and pluralism demonstrated how the periphery could transform the dominant culture, not through a radical break but more gradually through a process of grafting. Middle Western literature, according to Kallen, was "not a transplantation from Europe; it was a graft from New England" (*C&D* 222). Though Garland, as I will later demonstrate, would oppose the notion of "grafting" to describe a regional literature, he shared with Kallen a project of decentralization.

Pluralists attempted to challenge Anglo-Saxonism as the only standard of Americanism, just as regionalists sought to de-center New England, and more generally, the Northeast, as the cultural arbiter of literary taste. Kallen saw in the work of Theodore Dreiser, Hamlin Garland, and Booth Tarkington a way to construct a truly national literature no longer exclusively based on the "New England School." For Kallen, such writers of "mixed or non-British blood and familial background" not only added an "ethnic plaiting" to American literature; they were also the leaders of an American "literary imagination," who contributed a "spontaneous" and "raw" language to the belletristic tradition of the Northeast. As the aesthetic counterpart to cultural pluralism, regionalism was able to fuse "geographic localism and cultural nationality" (226). Regionalism did for geography what the hyphen did for ethnicity: it linked a subculture with a national identity.

But ethnic and geographic variety were not as analogous as Kallen suggested. The parallel between cultural pluralism and local color had its limits. The racialization of variety certainly converged with the spatialization of difference, as we will see, but they were not identical processes. The fact that William Dean Howells came from Ohio did not prevent him from mingling with the genteel society of the Boston Brahmins; whereas for Du Bois, a New England birthright did not warrant him immediate entry into Harvard. It was assumed by the local elders of Great Barrington, Massachusetts, that Du Bois would be more at "home" in a black college in the South. His New England boyhood was thought to be at odds with his "natural" setting in the Black Belt. Region and race, therefore, were not always allied: they might in fact be perceived as antithetical in the determination of one's subject position. Although pluralists and regionalists grappled with similar dilemmas and recommended a common strategy of unity-in-distinctiveness, they targeted different subcultures. Whereas Kallen and Du Bois interpreted culture primarily in ethnic or racial terms, local colorists defined culture in geographic terms. Whereas one Judaized or Africanized the "each-form," the other spatialized it.

To attribute a culture to a distinct place seems for the late-twentieth-century critic to run the risk of obsolescence. "In an era of historical inquiry in which the categories of race, ethnicity, class, and gender have taken center stage," writes the historian Patricia Nelson Limerick, "both region and section register as relics and antiques" (84). But for the turn-of-the-century reader, the *lingua rustica* of local color was far more familiar than the affirmation of ethnic or racial difference. Josiah Royce, for example, found the emergent discourse of "race distinctions" disconcerting and instead identified himself as part of the "human race." But Royce had few qualms about identifying as a Californian. "Local pride," or what he also termed "wholesome provincialism," signified a devotional reverence for the place of one's origins. For Royce, racial identification should be universal or "human," but spatial affinities must be particularized. Yet to particularize one's regional identity was not to challenge a national identity but to complement it. Royce acknowledged that "the tendency toward national unity and that toward local independence of spirit must henceforth grow together" (66). To be a nationalist and to be a regionalist were not oppositional, but vital in order for both to prosper.

At the turn of the century, it was far easier to apply hyphenated identities to regional affiliations than to ethnic or racial ones. In contrast to Du Bois and even Kallen, Royce conveyed relatively little, if any, angst about negotiating his "twoness" between being a Californian and an American. One reason for this was that there was already a well-established language of regional affinity, which, according to Frederick Jackson Turner, even predated nationalism.[2] This explains, at one level, the popularity of local color literature. Compared to the relative obscurity of pluralism, which even Kallen admitted had few followers, local color was considered as "natural as whooping-cough." "Everybody writes 'local' stories nowadays," Edward Hale Jr. ruefully declared in his review of Garland's *Crumbling Idols* (Nagel 56). Part of the reason for the genre's popularity was that it relied on a residual discourse of localism, harking back to a Jeffersonian tradition of wholesome agrarianism that embodied the republican virtues of self-sufficiency and independence. "Those who labor in the earth," wrote Jefferson, "are the chosen people of God" (qtd. Johnstone 158).

At a time when the country and the city were now physically linked through a sophisticated network of railroads, telegraph poles, and electric wires, it is perhaps not surprising that modernization was seen as the end of independence. Although Josiah Strong, among others, envisioned dependency as a virtue, as a sign of modernity and the rise of a world-civilization, most Americans still viewed dependency with suspicion, in the Jeffersonian sense that it would "beget subservience and venality" (qtd. Johnstone 158). The popularity of local color was due in part to its reliance on a long-standing discourse of anti-urbanism, which championed the individual against the encroaching monopolies and trusts and celebrated the virtues of independence over dependency. Whereas Kallen and Du Bois established an emergent nationalist discourse of ethnic or racial pride, the regionalists combined a residual discourse of agrarian virtue with an emergent one that embraced the contemporaneous and the modern.

Regional Distinctions as Signs of Subordination

Critics have underscored that regionalism's connection to a rural past is symptomatic of its modern genesis. June Howard, for example, argues that the regionalist genre is "distinctively modern," emerging between 1870 and World War I as part of a larger "movement to invent traditions" (368). Richard Brodhead has claimed, along with Eric Sundquist, that regionalism surfaced during these same years of "rapid corporate-capitalist industrial development in America, with its reinsertion of agrarian and artisanal orders into a new web of national market relations" (370). This critical trend has both applied and extended Raymond Williams's distinction between the country and the city to the American context in explaining how the rise of local color as a popular genre in the periodical literature of the turn of the century coincided with the peripheralization of rural America. Regional distinctiveness was historically constructed according to a metropolitan narrative of progress and development. The distinctiveness of the local, moreover, appeared at the moment when it was rendered subordinate within the spatial hierarchies of urbanization.

Raymond Williams, in his landmark study *The Country and the City*, traces the development of the opposition between industry and agriculture, claiming that it signifies the culmination of a specialized and spatialized division of labor that did not originate with capitalism but developed under it to a dramatic extent (304). In "Region and Class in the Novel," Williams locates the emergence of the regional genre in the late nineteenth century, when there was growing consciousness about the centralization of culture, finance, and government. Regional literature was therefore largely a function of "centralized cultural dominance" (60), and represents a modern form of the city-country division, a point that Garland made during the height of his involvement in the populist movement: "The contrast of city and country, everywhere growing sharper, will find its reflection in this local novel of the immediate future" (61). Regional literature dialectically interrogated and reinforced the disparity between the city and the country, while also reconfiguring this disparity as a legitimate source of artistic creation. Rather than dismissing the disparate areas of the nation, regional literature instead validated the geographic "margins" as a rich and fecund space for cultural production. "Regionalism" described the attempt to level a national literature spatially and culturally and challenged the inferior and subordinate connotations of the local.[3]

One way in which regionalists challenged the negative meanings associated with the regional was through the rhetoric of authenticity. According to this rhetoric, to be from the geographic margins of the country was not a disadvantage but a privilege: it authorized one to speak for a distinct place and thus provided a way of gaining access to national letters. Authors were most national when they were most local. But who was to provide the authentic voice for a distinct locality? For Garland, "the tourist cannot write the local novel," since the local novel rejects the "picturesque" as a superficial mode of apprehending surfaces rather than depths (*Crumbling* 54). Although, as I will argue in the next chapter, the urban picturesque provided the middle-class *flâneur* with a way to comprehend the ethnic ghettos of the city as a "natural" part of the metropolitan experience, for Garland, only a native of the slums could write about that experience: "The novel of the slums must be written by one who has played there as a child, and taken part in all its amusements . . . It cannot be done from above nor from the outside" (*Crumbling* 61). The only person who could capture the interiority of a place was one "born out of its intimate heart." "To such a one," declared Garland, "nothing will be 'strange' or 'picturesque'; all will be familiar, and full of significance or beauty" (*Crumbling* 61).

In 1895 Mark Twain similarly noted that only the "native novelist" could write about a distinct region: "There is only one expert who is qualified to examine the souls and the life of a people and make a valuable report" ("Paul Bourget" 50). Just as Garland rejected the tourist, so Twain rebuked the foreigner, since the latter could only "photograph the exteriors of a nation" but not "its soul, its life, its speech, its thought" (50). Local colorists, then, practiced an identity politics of place. At a time when the boundaries separating the country from the city were made increasingly complex, the local novelist insisted on clear demarcations separating insiders from outsiders, natives from strangers. Authentic and indigenous depictions were defined against touristic or counterfeit ones. During this period of urban migration, uprootedness, and economic upheaval, the essentialist position of an authentic utterance promised to fix people to a distinct place. Similar to Du Bois and Kallen, local colorists used essentialism as part of a strategy to promote the conservation of differences. Both pluralists and regionalists legitimated their claims through genealogical appeals, but while Du Bois and Kallen traced descent through blood, Garland and other regionalists did so through land.

This regionalist appeal to the land, however, has been problematized in the work of Richard Brodhead and Amy Kaplan, among others, who have de-naturalized the relationship between the local colorist and the rural periphery. By understanding regionalism as a modern genre located within the metropolis, Brodhead and Kaplan have de-authenticated local color by rendering it a form of literary absenteeism. The regional writer did not actually inhabit the regions that she depicted, but more often than not, lived in the city fully immersed in the centralized institutions of the nascent mass media. An indigenous connection to the region was itself a product of the metropolis, in the literal sense that local color was a commodity within the periodical industry that dominated the literary mass marketplace by the late nineteenth century.

Kaplan has described regionalism as an instance of "literary tourism," which possesses the "perspective of the modern urban outsider who projects onto the native a pristine authentic space immune to historical changes shaping their own lives" ("Nation" 252). Brodhead has argued that nineteenth-century regionalism was bound together with "class privilege, and high-cultural hierarchy" (141). Rather than representing the authentic voice of the regional subaltern, it instead ventriloquized rural misfortune from the comforts of the metropolis. Although regionalism expanded literary access to groups historically excluded from highbrow culture, such as Hamlin Garland, whom Brodhead describes as "the first farmer to have entered American literature," it did so on certain terms. They were expected to construct the region as a refuge from the contemporary anxieties of immigration and modernization. The generic formula required that the region be rendered nostalgically, according to Brodhead, as a form of "cultural elegy" that memorialized a rural past, which was quickly disappearing under the engines of progress.

Such critics, who view regionalism as a product of the metropolis, provide an important antidote to the romantic claims of the local colorists, who see themselves as organically connected to the regions that they represent. By transforming Garland's and Twain's "native novelist" into a tourist, Brodhead and Kaplan have unsettled the genre's essentialist claims to authenticity. Regionalism can no longer be read, as Nancy Glazener has pointed out, as simply an advocate for rural people (228). Garland's focus on regional insiderism has to be seen, for instance, within a context in which geographic marginality was itself a source of an author's cultural capital. This critical move to disrupt the organicism of the genre has had the beneficial effect of challenging a potentially ultra-conservative political agenda, which came to fruition among the Southern Agrarians of the 1920s and 1930s.[4] A predominant trend of recent criticism is not to hail regionalism as a subversive and counter-hegemonic genre but rather to warn against its racial and ideological conservatism. As Roberto Maria Dainotto has argued, regionalism at first seems consistent with the liberal-left concerns of postcolonialism and multiculturalism, but it is ultimately a reactionary genre that configures the region as a pure space pitted against the fear of a hybrid society. Rather than embracing the heterogeneity of the United States, local literature actually provides idealized images of a homogeneous past.

Although this critical emphasis on the modern has allowed critics to complicate the relation between authorship and representation, this interpretive framework has not sufficiently problematized local color's relation to the present and the past. The past is seen as a symptom of modern angst, as a temporal retreat from the effects of modernization. This critical trend ultimately takes the form of a familiar narrative: that regionalism operates as a heuristic of nostalgia and elegy, mourning a lost community that has already been incorporated within a standardized national economy. Sundquist identifies the genre as a "literature of memory" (508), and Brodhead describes it as a form of "cultural elegy," as "memorializing a cultural order passing from life" and creating a prosaic souvenir "of a loved thing lost in reality" (120). Kaplan adds a different inflection to the regional response to modernization as a "retreat from modern urban society." Rather than claim that the regional genre uses the past to escape from the present, she argues that it actually wants to escape from history altogether in search of a timeless rural community ("Nation" 256).

Although these funereal or escapist responses to modernization certainly describe a common trait in a predominant strain of local color, evident in the work of Sarah Orne Jewett (who is the shared point of reference for these critics), they do not describe the entire genre. Not only are the claims of these critics too wide-sweeping, but as Judith Fetterley has pointed out, they are also reminiscent of what Lora Romero has called the "cult of the Vanishing American." This cult, according to Romero, uses an "elegiac mode" to perform "the historical sleight-of-hand crucial to the topos of the doomed aboriginal: it represents the disappearances of the native as not just natural but as having already happened" (87). To cast the region as the spatial equivalent of the Vanishing American is to silence and suppress those forms of local color which did launch a critique of uneven development. Not all examples of local color ran from the effects of modernization; some confronted this process and attacked it.

Regional Fiction as a Modern Genre

There is a tradition of local color that did engage with the modern, offering a critique of the impact of economic development on the geographical periphery. By foregrounding these emergent aspects of local color as a modern critique of social and spatial marginalization, I argue that the genre includes regional configurations that do not rely primarily on a residual discourse of cultural elegy. Although the relation between region and representation is largely determined by corporate institutions of reading, by which I mean the national publishing infrastructure of distribution and consumption, it cannot ultimately be reduced to these institutions. Local color is neither the authentic voice of the subaltern nor the mouthpiece of the metropolitan elite, but a locus for a variety of ideological positions that articulate the relation between city and country for a local and/or a national audience.

Nancy Glazener in *Reading for Realism* has warned that if we read regionalism exclusively in terms of its role in national consolidation and its problematic racial politics, "we risk losing sight of regionalism's share in other political projects" (194). At the height of populism in the late nineteenth century, the rural was not exclusively a site of nostalgia, but also one of "modern political challenges" (194). I want to extend Glazener's point to show how certain regionalists conceived of themselves as "modern," as active agents in their contemporary world who offered both a critique of the status quo and a remedy for the future. Local colorists in attributing agency to the periphery called for a new aesthetics of localism, which would capture the heterogeneity—rather than the uniformity—of a "composite" national literary tradition. They perceived regional writing as the embodiment of youth and modernity, as they urged their generation to break away from the past—to create and not to imitate—in order to imagine a future national art.

In *Crumbling Idols,* which Alfred Kazin describes as the first manifesto of naturalism, Garland explained the relation between the "youthful artist" of the present and the "masters" of the past in defining the potential of "American art": "Youth should be free from the dominion of the dead; therefore I defend the individual right of the modern creative mind to create in the image of life, and not in the image of any literary master, living or dead" (3). Local color, for Garland, was strictly a "modern" genre, one that he called "veritism," which translated the "infinite variety" of life to literature (21).[5] For Garland, the local, the national, and the modern were interdependent, linked together through a heterogeneous and flexible configuration of aesthetic unity. In an essay entitled "The Modern Novel in Germany and America," Garland applied a Spencerian trajectory to national literatures to argue that literature began as "homogenous, simple, direct" but that its growth was in "complexity and interdependence" (qtd. Pizer 11).

Local color was not a form of literary primitivism but the apex of aesthetic development, because it captured the heterogeneous web of spatial dependencies characteristic of the modern moment. According to Donald Pizer in his study of the early Garland, "local color had to become dominant because it was the sole literary mode capable of depicting the increasing heterogeneity which was the product of the 'law of development'" (20). Progress, development, and modernity, for Garland, were not homogenizing and standardizing processes but the culmination of heterogeneous forces that could now be unified. To criticize the consequences of modernization for rural communities was not to reject the "modern."

Garland distinguished between modernization and modernity. While modernization signified standardization, modernity, as Garland understood it, marked the unleashing of multiple impulses, a liberation of individual creative expression. Local colorists saw themselves as cosmopolitan figures who believed that modernity would flourish if only the fruits of modernization were justly distributed. There was still an optimistic belief in the late nineteenth century that development could be directed toward humane ends if only the privileged were sensitive to the ways in which the other half lived. Garland combined this optimism with a deterministic pessimism, which manifested itself in the conflict between his faith in human agency to correct inequality (as in his support of populism as a form of agrarian agency) and his belief that the greater forces of evolutionary development constituted the primary determinant of human destiny (as seen in the persistent poverty of many of his characters). In either case, the local was cast as inextricably modern, as both the site of future possibility and a symptom of contemporary malaise.

The writers I will discuss, María Amparo Ruiz de Burton, Hamlin Garland, and W. E. B. Du Bois, configured the region as a contemporary place of struggle rather than a nostalgic projection of a past community. These regionalists challenged the homogenization of incorporation by articulating the limits of standardization within the confines of the regional genre. Just as Frederick Jackson Turner saw the section as a bastion of individuality in the midst of national uniformity, so local color was a way to preserve and crystallize the "geographic peculiarities," to borrow Turner's phrase, of "minority sections." This emphasis on the conservation of differences illustrates a pluralistic maneuver, in the Jamesian sense that "residual resistance" prevents complete assimilation. Unlike monists, pluralists acknowledged that nothing could contain everything, since something always escaped.

These three local colorists clearly operated within a consolidated nation. Their respective regions—California, Wisconsin, and Georgia—had already been incorporated within a national and international economy of exchange. Despite their different political views, with Ruiz de Burton far more conservative than either Garland or Du Bois, they did not claim a pristine position outside of modernization, but instead positioned themselves from within the periphery to criticize the impact of urbanization on their particular underdeveloped regions. Their work demonstrates that although a term like "region" has been used to disavow conflict and to celebrate local peculiarities as an end in themselves, this does not mean these concepts are forever lost and forfeited. Terms like "region" can be reappropriated to unleash that which has been suppressed.

Privileging the Partial

Both Jamesian pluralism and local color attempted to disarticulate unity from its conventional association with all-inclusivity and direct it instead toward a pluralist notion of partiality. Whether at the level of philosophical inquiry or aesthetic practice, democratic expression defined itself against what William James called "bigness." A limited purview was considered far more judicious than an all-encompassing one; this was a secular refashioning of the Protestants' belief that they could reach God more effectively through their own discrete sect than through the bolder universalist claims of Catholicism.

This emphasis on non-mastery—that nothing can include or persuade everyone—is evident in James's theory of narrative that is based on a notion of partial stories. "The point of view of many is the more natural one to take. The world is full of partial stories that run parallel to one another, beginning and ending at odd times. They mutually interlace and interfere at points, but we cannot unify them completely in our minds" (P 143). It was precisely this embrace of the partial that made local color such a popular genre for representing the modern nation. As early as 1881, an anonymous author in the *Atlantic* noted that "our society is too scattered and heterogeneous ever to be reflected as a whole" (qtd. Glazener 191). The author suggested that only the short story with its "bright little sketches of local life and character" could capture the vastness of the nation. Though these sketches might be "partial," they were nonetheless "clear images." This sense that the "partial" could still be "clear" was an important premise of local fiction, because it associated representational clarity and truth with a limited purview. One could claim to understand the whole not from the position of a single all-encompassing gaze but through a modest glimpse. As the critic Meredith Nicholson claimed in 1902: "We [the United States] cannot be condensed into one or a dozen finished panoramas; he who would know us hereafter must read us in the flashes of the kinetoscope" (804).

A decade earlier, in his tirade against the French novelist and travel writer Paul Bourget, Mark Twain imagined a national literature comprising thousands of novels as a way, in part, to challenge the European traveler's assumption that America could be mastered in a single tour: "Does the native novelist try to generalize the nation? No, he lays plainly before you the ways and speech and life of a few people grouped in a certain place—his own place—and that is one book. In time, he and his brethren will report to you in life and the people of the whole nation . . . And when a thousand able novels have been written, there you have the soul of the people, the life of the people; and not anywhere else can these be had" (52). The "partial story," then, was not invoked to counter the "whole" or the "nation," but rather to present a national literary tradition as a collection of limited vantage points.

Ruiz de Burton, Garland, and Du Bois further developed the partial by inflecting it with its secondary meaning, namely partisanism. Partiality was both incomplete and biased; it was at once limited and interested. Although a narrative was situated in a specific locality, it could still comment on the larger picture. The partial story might not claim to speak for the metropolitan center, but it certainly had something to say about it. John Dewey would contend in 1920 that "the locality is the only universal"—a version of Howells's and Garland's aesthetic belief that universal art was the most specific to a time and place (Dewey 15). What made Shakespeare timeless, according to Garland, was that he didn't care about the eighteenth century (*Crumbling* 40).

This move to universalize the particular was not only a pluralist maneuver, as I argued in the previous chapter, but also a regionalist one. In both cases, the universal was the particular which became dominant. It was a notion of the universal that still preserved the integrity of the "each-form" and elevated that position to signify the whole: the universal privileges the particular, and as it does so, a specific subculture becomes dominant without losing its individuality. This particularist conception of universality applied to the modernist strain of local color in that agrarian localities designated the center—rather than the periphery—of urban prosperity. As the populist Henry Demarest Lloyd declared in *Wealth against Commonwealth*: "New York would begin to die tomorrow if it were not for Illinois and Dakota" (519).[6] The local was universal in the sense that its labor—providing food—was considered the life-blood for all.

The regional narratives that I will examine, Ruiz de Burton's *The*

Squatter and the Don, Garland's "Up the Coulee," and Du Bois's "Of the Black Belt," cast the periphery not as a fetishized and isolated region but as central to a national and international economy of uneven development. My position challenges, in part, Raymond Williams's configuration of the regional novel as a genre that "has initially so isolated its region, and thus projected it as internally whole—'organic'—that it is unable to recognize the complex internal processes, including internal divisions and conflicts, which factually connect with those wider pressures" ("Region and Class" 61).[7]

These three regional narratives attempt to characterize the divisions and conflicts that link a specific region to a larger economy. In thematizing the often fraught relations between the city and the country, these works configure the local in terms similar to Rob Wilson and Wimal Dissanayake's definition: "So situated, the local need not embody a regressive politics of global delinkage, bounded particularity, and claims of ontological pastness, where locality becomes some backward-gazing fetish of purity to disguise how global, hybrid, compromised, and unprotected everyday identity already is" (5). These three narratives depict the isolation of the farmer as a symptom of uneven development rather than a sign of autonomous self-sufficiency. Through the vantage point of the local, they demonstrate that a specific region is inextricably tied to national and global pressures. Though San Diego, La Crosse valley, and Dougherty County may appear distant and removed from the metropolis, their everyday realities are entwined with more powerful centers of commerce.

Pan-Patrician Regionalism

María Amparo Ruiz de Burton's *The Squatter and the Don* (1885), a "regional" novel set primarily in California during the 1870s, represents a transitional stage between residual and emergent formations of local color. The novel is residual in the sense that it invokes an elegiac mode of cultural mourning, because the Californios, the declining patrician class of the region, are systematically losing their land to Anglo squatters and the railroad monopoly.[8] Don Mariano, the patriarch of the Alamar family and the novel's primary spokesman for the Californios, pessimistically predicts the future of his class: "I am afraid there is no help for us native Californians. We must sadly fade and pass away. The weak and the helpless are always trampled in the throng. We must sink, go under, never to rise" (177). In contrast to the halcyon days before the Mexican American War of 1848, the future for the Californios looks grim.

But Ruiz de Burton's narrative does not take refuge in a golden ageism of Californio supremacy, and in this sense *The Squatter and the Don* is qualitatively different from the vast majority of Californio testimonials during this same period, which were primarily concerned with depicting life "the way it used to be" before the invasion.[9] Ruiz de Burton's narrative invokes the past in order to justify the Californios' attempt to reposition themselves within a modernized California. *Squatter* is residual only in terms of explaining to the Anglophone reader why the Californios should maintain their cultural, political, and economic authority in the future. This illustrates a project that I call "strategic residualism," in which a regional narrative expediently uses an elegiac mode primarily to advocate an emergent politics of adaptation. In the context of *Squatter,* the Californios are not an anachronism, residual and picturesque remains of a feudal past, but are cosmopolitan subjects, able and willing to adapt their ways to a commercial economy of speculation and investment.

Furthermore, *Squatter* is a regional novel by default. It had aspired to be a national novel, much like Ruiz de Burton's first novel, *Who Would Have Thought It?* (1872), which was published by the Philadelphia-based company J. B. Lippincott. But Ruiz de Burton's second novel had a different fate. Its hopes of a national readership were thwarted when the author had to borrow money from a friend to have the book published by a local company in San Francisco called Samuel Carson & Co. She describes the experience of holding the final product in a letter to a friend: "My book has seen the light of day. My poor little ugly child!" This comment suggests a rough-cast quality to the book, one that would certainly differentiate it at a material level from Garland's *Main-Travelled Roads* and Du Bois's *The Souls of Black Folk,* both of which were originally published by metropolitan firms.[10] It is therefore important to understand her conservatism partly within the context of a failed national novel. Its regionalism is a result of material conditions rather than choice.

The novel begins with Don Mariano's attempts to negotiate a compromise with the Anglo squatters who are killing his cattle in order to settle on his property and establish farms. As Rosaura Sánchez and Beatrice

Pita have pointed out, Don Mariano is depicted as an entrepreneurial individual, "accommodating and pragmatic," and able to adapt to his new environment. He offers to sell the squatters some of his cattle on credit to set them up as ranchers; then he offers to sell them land on the condition that they fence off their property. He also gives advice about growing crops in the arid climate of Southern California. While most of the squatters ignore Don Mariano's suggestions, Clarence Darrell, the novel's hero, who is the son of a Yankee squatter-farmer and a southern mother, insists on paying for his father's claim on the Alamar ranch. While negotiating the deal, Clarence has a glimpse of Don Mariano's daughter Mercedes, and the novel's romantic subplot begins. In addition to this love interest, there is a political plot in which Don Mariano and his wealthy son-in-law George Michlin, together with Clarence, go to Washington, D.C., to persuade congressional leaders to support a second transcontinental railroad to the Pacific, which would end in San Diego.

The novel shifts between the romantic subplot and the political main plot, as alternative strategies for Californio salvation. By the end, the government support for the Texas Pacific Railroad is thwarted because of a bribery scheme, and the Alamars are ultimately saved from penury by the twelve million dollars that Clarence Darrell has accumulated through mining speculations. The marriage of Clarence and Mercedes restores the Alamar family to their prior class position, but since they are now supported by capital investment and not by land, they must move from the country to the city, to the financial hub of the West, San Francisco.

Written at a time when the majority of Mexican ranchers had been reduced to farming rented property, the novel is primarily concerned with finding solutions to the modern crisis of Californio pauperization. Ruiz de Burton's task is as follows: how to save a declining patrician class through alliances with the northeastern metropolitan elite and with Anglo speculators, while at the same time conserving the particularity of Californio culture and identity. In order for the Californios to save their class position they must establish coalitions with other cultures and localities, including a pan-patrician alliance that would link the Californio elite of the West with their genteel counterparts in the Northeast. Transregional alliances, in other words, are both the source of the problem and its remedy.

The incorporation of California within a national and international economy has both positive and negative effects. On the one hand, "bad" interconnectedness has resulted in the monopoly of the Central Pacific Railroad, led by the "Big Four" (Leland Stanford, Mark Hopkins, Collis P. Huntington, and Charles Crocker). This form of mono-development, which favors San Francisco over San Diego, fosters uneven development both within the state of California and nationally. By privileging the northern half of the nation, this sole transcontinental railroad, completed in 1869, urbanized one half of the union, making it a magnet for industrial development, while peripheralizing the southeastern and southwestern United States.

On the other hand, Ruiz de Burton advocates three forms of "good" interconnectedness, which can counter the effects of underdevelopment through the establishment of alternative trans-regional alliances: (1) a southern transcontinental railroad; (2) pan-patrician alliances with the northeastern elite; (3) Anglo-Californio intermarriage. Ruiz de Burton does not attempt to protect the region of California or the Californio people from encountering other cultures and regions of the United States. Instead, it is through the reformulation of national contact that Ruiz de Burton finds various panaceas for her particular class-culture. While monopoly-government collusion homogenizes its component parts, crushing all opposition, other forms of trans-regional alliance can actually protect cultural and regional distinctiveness.

The first form of trans-regional alliance that Ruiz de Burton advocates is based on the historical example of Tom Scott's plan for a Texas Pacific Railroad. In the 1870s Tom Scott, a Texan railroad mogul, appealed to the federal government for public land and funds to build a competing national railroad that would favor the southern portion of the nation.[11] The anticipation of such a scheme resulted in a craze of speculation, in which the author and her husband Henry Burton participated and suffered losses once the railroad project initially failed. Written in the aftermath of the Big Four's successful annihilation of all competition, *Squatter* can be read as an attempt to replace mono-development with plural development, which is another way of saying that the narrative advocates competitive capitalism over monopoly capitalism. As Sánchez and Pita have pointed out, this novel attacks "the government-monopoly collusion, not the capitalist system *per se*" (29).

San Diegans, according to this novel, do not resist the "metropolitan corridor," but welcome it; in fact urbanization is described organically as a natural mode of development in the maturation of a place: "San Diego at that time—in July, 1873—be it remembered, was fresh and rosy with bright hopes, like a healthy child just trying to stand up, with no sickness or ill-usage to sap its vitality and weaken its limbs" (171). But government and monopolies work together to suppress plural or natural progress. San Diego is now a "crippled and dwarfed little city." Its suppressed growth has resulted in its disfiguration; its poverty is a result of unnatural development. Like Garland, Ruiz de Burton calls for decentralization, the diffusion of authority away from a single metropolis and toward a plurality of centers dispersed throughout the nation. But where Garland's call in *Crumbling Idols* is made in a spirit of optimism, Ruiz de Burton's is made in a tone of desperation.

A more promising form of trans-regional alliance is pan-patricianism, which assembles the genteel of both coasts within the metropolitan spaces of the Northeast. Patricianism does for Ruiz de Burton what populism does for Garland: both are ways of attributing agency to the periphery by imagining trans-local coalitions that link people who share a common class position but are geographically separated. Demonstrating their adaptability, the Alamar sisters, Mercedes and Elvira, temporarily leave their local setting and travel to the cosmopolitan centers of the East. The apparent reason for their cross-country trip is to lobby legislators to allocate funding for the Texas Pacific, but the ideological purpose is to convince the genteel northern reader that the elite of the West can mix and mingle in the most exclusive circles of the East.[12]

In blurring the distinction between the country and the city, Ruiz de Burton shows through a series of travel sketches from Newport to New York City and Washington that Mercedes and Elvira constitute a translocal "leisure class." In Veblenian fashion, they partake in the conspicuous display of wasted time through various activities, including croquet and sailing. Yet despite their successful ability to assimilate, they still maintain their cultural distinctiveness through the consumption of traditional Spanish dishes such as *tortita de aceituna* and *empanaditas de pollo* (142–143). Californios are both native and cosmopolitan; they can sing Spanish ballads by day and attend the opera by night. They designate the "half-way station" between exoticism and familiarity, between excessive particularity and homogeneity. They have sufficient "local color" to make them interesting to the northeastern reader, but not so much as to break the bond of genteel identification that Ruiz de Burton hopes will rally support for her displaced people.

Ruiz de Burton further establishes a trans-local alliance between the elite of two coasts through a strategy of a shared racial experience of whiteness and a common language. Upon seeing the Alamar men for the first time, Clarence notes: "They are gentlemen, no doubt." Once their class position is verified, Clarence then observes their race: "They look like Englishmen" (89). Californio whiteness is not just any kind of whiteness, but the most genteel kind. To allay any suspicion that the impending marriage of Clarence and Mercedes is an interracial one, Ruiz de Burton underscores Mercedes's whiteness throughout the novel through figurative and explicit references. When Clarence and Mercedes first meet, their common sexual and racial affinity is told through the hermeneutic language of blushing. When he first gazes into her eyes, her "face was suffused with burning blushes," to be matched by his "crimson blush" (98). The face not only provides a mirror into the characters' interior as the surface expression of internal desire, but also demonstrates their whiteness.

The translucence of the skin is a sign of a character's moral and racial purity. To be readable rather than indecipherable is evidence of *sangre azul*—blue blood—which was itself a traditional sign of whiteness and privilege in Spain through readability: if the blue vein could be seen in the neck, then the person was white. For the less alert reader, Ruiz de Burton supplies an excess of explicit markers of her character's whiteness, describing, for example, the "white throat" of the sleeping Mercedes (151). Californios and their Anglo sympathizers reconfigure whiteness, so as to include the Californios in order to secure their vulnerable elite status. To do this, the narrative establishes a racialized hierarchy, as David Luis-Brown has argued, with respectable Anglos and Californios at the top of the social order, and with Anglo "riff-raff," *mestizos*, Indians, and blacks grouped at the bottom (820).

After this first sighting of the Alamar family, the next scene resolves any possible doubt about the whiteness of the Californios. Again, Clarence is the legitimating agent of their whiteness and their gentility, but this time through his ears rather than his gaze. Like the narrative voice, the Californio characters seem to speak without an accent, in the same standard English as the respectable Anglo characters. Even when Don Mariano apologizes about his English at his first meeting with the squatters, his speech does not betray an accent: "If you don't understand me I will repeat my words until I make my meaning clear" (90). Clarence insists that an interpreter is not necessary: "We understand you perfectly"

(90). The accentless English is a sign of the commonality between Anglo and Spanish elites, a sign that they can understand each other perfectly not just in the literal sense of comprehension but in the sympathetic sense of compassion.

Whereas accentless speech suggests commonality, accented speech underscores class and racial differences. The white characters who do have accents are some of the squatters, who reassure the Don at their first meeting that they "ain't in a hurry" (90). The sole character who does have a consistent accent throughout the novel is Tisha, the black servant of the Darrell family, who refers to the protagonist as "Massa Clary." Black southern dialect, which Du Bois refuses to use in his account of the Black Belt in *Souls,* has the purpose in this novel of reinforcing the whiteness of the Californios. Because the Spano-Americans sound white, they therefore must be white.

What further differentiates the Californios from the white squatters around them is that they signify a cosmopolitan elite. It is important to note that trans-regional alliances in *Squatter* are not made in the name of internationalism, but rather in that of a cosmopolitan Americanism. The Californios are patriotic subjects, loyal citizens of an Anglo-American past, who are seen at their most American when Mercedes and Elvira visit Mount Vernon.[13] At Washington's grave, Mercedes and Elvira demonstrate their reverence for the nation, their loyalty to the United States rather than to Mexico. Their hyphenated identity as Spano-Americans does not lead to dualistic angst, but rather to an unequivocal allegiance to the founding fathers. The trip to Washington's tomb is described not as a touristic leisure outlet but as a sort of pilgrimage, on which their "patriotism" can be "fulfilled with due reverence" (214).

Their sojourn is also confirmation of a certain tradition within an Anglo-American past, namely federalism. One would think that visitors from the geographic margins of the nation would visit Monticello, the home of the localist Jefferson, whose brand of democracy embraced the individualism associated with a decentralized government. But their visit to Mount Vernon suggests allegiance to a specific tradition of liberal republicanism, one that privileges federalism as a way to integrate the various parts within the union.[14] At this point in the narrative, the characters are still hopeful that the federal government will save San Diego by authorizing funds for the Texas Pacific. The remedy for regional ills can still be found at the national level.

This faith in the federal government to redress the wrongs perpetrated by monopolies fades toward the end of the novel when two alternative remedies for the regionally vanquished come to the fore: speculation and populism. Though these two panaceas were seen as mutually exclusive, as evident in Garland's populist reproach of speculation as a form of parasitism, the narrative is desperately trying to resolve the crisis of both the Californios and the Californians.[15] Once the narrative returns to the West, more time is spent in trying to figure out ways to save both the Alamar family from penury and "the people" of California from monopolies than in trying to convince genteel readers on the other coast that the characters are deserving of their respect and sympathy. Speculation resolves the fictional plot of the Alamar crisis, and populism attempts to solve the contemporary crisis of monopolies. The "Redeemer" of Ruiz de Burton's fictional plot is Clarence, who is worth over twelve million dollars through investments in Colorado and Arizona mines.

Ruiz de Burton admires the "lucky investor" for the same reason Garland loathes such a figure: speculators profit without having to produce. To get rich without having to work is the ideal way to rescue the declining patricians. The problem is that the Alamar family does not have the necessary capital to invest, despite the fact that they are open to new enterprising ways of acquiring wealth. They must therefore depend on Clarence, who is embarrassed about his choice of occupation, confessing to his investment broker that his father would consider him a "thief" (107). The novel acknowledges this residual attitude toward speculation, embodied in the yeoman values of the anachronistic father, only to replace these values with a modern outlook that views speculation as a new form of entrepreneurialism. Clarence personifies a spirit of competitive capitalism, modernized for a new era, when the individual can realize the American Dream through good luck rather than hard work.

The novel also speculates at another level in recommending that the best way for the Californios to secure their future is to intermarry with wealthy Anglos, to establish what the historian Douglas Monroy has called a "united elite" (222). This third form of trans-regional alliance, in which a transplanted Anglo and a "native Spano-American" marry, was the most familiar scenario for Californio financial salvation in the nineteenth century, and was evident in the author's own marriage to U.S. Army Captain Henry Burton. According to the historian Albert Camarillo, "only a small number of the once wealthy Spanish-speaking elite escaped the subsequent social and geographic segregation and were effectively assimilated into American society, largely through intermarriage" (25).

What is significant about *Squatter* is the dwindling role that this marriage plays. The novel has been classified as a historical romance, and it certainly begins as one with the romantic display of mutual blushes when Mercedes and Clarence first meet. But the nature of their relationship becomes far less romantic and far more expedient toward the end of the novel. The marriage scene, which one would assume to be the apex of the plot, is perfunctorily told in a few vague sentences: "As everything was ready, the marriage ceremony took place as the priest arrived" (359). There is no description of either the bride or the groom, only of the mother, Doña Josefa, weeping with her daughters. By this late point in the novel, Mercedes has almost entirely receded into the background, and the focus is now on the details of Clarence's speculation schemes. In fact, Clarence spends far more time with his investment broker Hubert Haverly than he does with his wife, which only seems appropriate given his self-identification as "a money-making Yankee" (360). The cursory role of the marital union suggests that Ruiz de Burton is ultimately concerned with restoring financial security to the Californios rather than with exploring the cultural negotiation of Anglo Protestantism and Mexican Catholicism or the psychological dimension of a cross-cultural union. We learn nothing about the interiority of the relationship. Their union serves the purely pragmatic function of rescuing the Alamar family from financial ruin.

The final panacea that Ruiz de Burton offers is a populist one, which occurs in the last chapter, "Out with the Invader," when the tenor of the book abruptly changes from the fictional to the oratorical and the narrative vantage point also alters from the Californio to the Californian. The characters disappear, and Ruiz de Burton speaks directly to the reader in a call to action: *"the people of California take the law in their own hands* and seize the property of those men [the Big Four], and confiscate it, to re-imburse the money due *the people*" (366). That the book, which up to this point focuses on various forms of pan-patrician alliance, should end with a populist summons to "the people" is hardly convincing, especially when considering that the populist character in the novel, Peter Roper, is portrayed as a calculating demagogue.

What this sudden shift from speculation to populism suggests is that the novel is desperately trying to find a remedy for the Californio/an crisis. From elite alliances with New York Society to populist coalitions with Anglo "riff-raff," the novel is important precisely because it uses a variety of strategies—an excess of solutions—to save Ruiz de Burton's own particular class-culture. That the novel employs widely divergent ideological strategies, which frequently contradict one another, is symptomatic of the urgency and anxiety surrounding this specific historical moment as well as of the regional genre more generally. Ruiz de Burton understands that alliances are necessary to counter the power of government-monopoly collusion, but she is uncertain about whether such alliances should be inter-regionally elitist or intra-regionally populist. Should Californios align themselves with the patricians or the people? At a time of crisis, Ruiz de Burton grasps at both straws, regardless of the ideological incompatibility between investment banking and populism. This suggests that perhaps the novel's contradictory conclusion is ultimately a gesture of futility and political pessimism rather than a bona fide call for insurrection on the part of the "white slaves" of California. Perhaps Don Mariano's prophetic words inform this final appeal: "We must sink, go under, never to rise" (177).

From Patricians to Populists

Whereas populism for Ruiz de Burton is a last-ditch attempt to save a former patrician class, it signifies a far more serious strategy in the work of Garland and Du Bois. Garland's short story "Up the Coulee" and Du Bois's sketches of the Black Belt employ an emergent aesthetics of populist dissent to grapple with the modern political challenges facing farm workers. Both Garland and Du Bois render modern locality in ways that stress interconnectedness at two levels: first, in terms of the antagonistic relation between the rural region and more powerful metropolitan spheres of influence; and second, in terms of the collusion of aesthetic practice with political intervention.

Similar to Ruiz de Burton, Garland and Du Bois configure the local as an interconnected region, in which a common class experience links people who are geographically distant. But Garland and Du Bois view trans-regional alliances in different class terms than Ruiz de Burton, from the perspective of tenants and sharecroppers, a class that even populist leaders frequently marginalized in favor of land-owning farmers.[16]

Both Garland and Du Bois use the genre of local color to launch a populist critique of a world-system, a critique based on the ethos of producerism in its strictly organic sense of agriculture. Land is both the source of the problem and the remedy, since it is at the fundamental level of the maldistribution of land that the "great world-industry" goes awry.

In contrast to *Squatter*, which represents a transitional phase of local color, combining the residualism of Californio mourning with a contemporary critique of monopoly development, Garland and Du Bois are more firmly situated in the modern moment. When they do refer to the past, it is primarily as a point of contrast, as an irrecoverable period whose memory haunts rather than comforts those living in the present. This is ultimately what differentiates the transitional localism of Ruiz de Burton from the modern localism of Garland and Du Bois. Her conservative politics and their progressive critique of uneven development stem in part from their contrasting views of both history and metropolitan authority. Whereas history authenticates the Californios as the legitimate owners of California property and the metropolis may offer the promise to actualize this historical "fact," the past for Garland and Du Bois informs but does not necessarily determine the present.

They are far more focused on criticizing the contemporary forces of agrarian poverty, which are located primarily within the metropolis, than on making prior claims to land ownership (and in the case of most African-American tenant farmers in the 1890s, who were little more than a generation removed from slavery, prior ownership was not a pertinent issue). The metropolis, for Garland and Du Bois, is the source of regional underdevelopment rather than an agent of salvation. By focusing on the tensions between the city and the country, rather than their alliances, they make an ethical and political argument for land ownership instead of a historical one based on reclamation.

In the late nineteenth century, Garland was a reformer and a radical, who was active in Henry George's Single-Tax League in the late 1880s and became a frequent speaker in support of the Farmers' Alliance and the Peoples' Party at the height of the movement in the early 1890s.[17] In addition to empowering farmers to assert themselves politically, a point he explores in *A Spoil of Office* (1892), populism provided Garland with the conceptual means to link the Midwest with the Black Belt, whites with blacks. "There are ten millions of poor whites and negroes in the South," he wrote in 1894, "who must also be counted out of the question; and, last, there are ten millions of artisans in the Northern states essentially cut off" ("Land" 166–167).[18] Populism allowed Garland to take a holistic approach toward the nation's problems, one that rendered the nation an interconnected body, in which a disease in one part affected the whole: "We begin to perceive that the nation is a solidarity, and that whatever produces disease in one part of the social body produces distress on the whole body; that the poor sewing girl, the farmer, the artisan, *cannot be crushed without a certain reaction upon art*" (167).

This organic perspective of an interdependent nation also characterizes Garland's aesthetic theory. The "land question" is as much an artistic issue as it is an economic one, since the liberation of labor will also liberate art. For there to be change in art, society must also experience a transformation: "The whole social order must undergo change before American art will become the jubilant and perfectly wholesome art it should be" (174). Regionalism, therefore, is not exclusively a residual genre preoccupied with an irrecoverable past, but also an emergent discourse, which conceives of aesthetic practice as a form of political and social intervention.

Whereas Garland's affiliation with the populist movement has been well documented, Du Bois's populist sympathies have received less critical attention. Better known for his elitist concept of the "talented tenth," Du Bois became increasingly interested in what he called the "submerged tenth." By the late 1890s he began to rethink the laissez-faire economics that he had been taught in Frank William Taussig's seminars at Harvard, as he became increasingly doubtful that the market could reestablish equilibrium without some sort of outside intervention. "'Populism,' he now started to believe, 'was a third party movement of deep significance'" (qtd. Lewis 186). Populism offered the possibility of redistributing property on more equal terms, a policy that would have dramatic consequences for the black population of the turn of the century, which was primarily rural.[19]

Like Garland, Du Bois acknowledged the symbiotic relationship between art and politics. Rejecting the Victorian notion of aesthetic disinterestedness, Du Bois argued that artistic representations are inevitably partial. "All Art is propaganda," he proclaimed. "I do not care a damn for any art that is not used for propaganda" (Paschal 94). Black art has to work as propaganda, according to Du Bois, because that is the only way whites will recognize blacks as human: "until the art of the black folk compels recognition they will not be rated as human" (Paschal 96). Local color was for Garland and Du Bois an explicit form of agitprop, a way to unsettle familiar perceptions of the agrarian "other" by foregrounding the structural forces that resulted in the disparity between the country and the city. Such a focus could highlight the humanity of those living in the "minority sections."

"Up the Coulee" as Fraternal Allegory

Garland's short story "Up the Coulee" portrays the costs of uneven development between the country and the city through a fraternal allegory of irreconcilable union. Considered by critics to be the most autobiographical of Garland's short stories, "Up the Coulee" depicts Howard McLane, a "wonderfully successful" author and actor of the New York stage, upon his return to his native Wisconsin after many years of little or no contact with his mother and brother.[20] The story begins with Howard's arrival at the small railroad depot, a sign that this peripheral region is within metropolitan access, a connection point along what the historian John Stilgoe has called the "metropolitan corridor."[21] While walking up the coulee to his brother Grant's farm, Howard drinks in the beauty of "the majestic amphitheater of green wooded hills" and absorbs the "coolness and the fragrance and the color of the hour" (*Main-Travelled Roads* 55, 59).

At this point, Garland satisfies the expectations of his urban readers by offering them picturesque descriptions of the landscape. As yet untouched by the machines of modernity, La Crosse valley retains a pristine innocence and beauty. This pastoral scene, however, abruptly ends when Howard arrives at the farm and the two brothers gaze in silence at each other. Howard feels the bitterness and anger of his brother, who stands before him "ragged, ankle-deep in muck, his sleeves rolled up, a shapeless old straw hat on his head" (61). Here the country-city distinction is portrayed through class distinctions between the two brothers, the older a successful and well-traveled actor living in New York, and the younger an impoverished farmer forced to sell the family home and live on a rented farm with his wife, his mother, and two children. Garland intensifies the class differences between the brothers by juxtaposing brief descriptions of clothing. While Howard dresses in the latest cosmopolitan fashions, which include a négligé shirt, a windsor scarf, russet shoes, and a tennis hat, Grant wears a worn-out "checked shirt without vest" and suspenders, whose once bright colors now stain the shoulders of the shirt.[22]

The fraternal class differences are intensified further through the racialization of their respective bodies. Upon their first meeting, the brothers are unable to shake hands, because Grant's hands are covered with mud, while he notices "the gleam of Howard's white hands [which] angered him" (61). Throughout the narrative, the whiteness of Howard's body is contrasted with the bronzed skin of Grant, whose daily exposure to the sun has made him as "brown as leather" (64). Prefiguring Mary Austin's definition of race, in which the environment rather than heredity produces racial differences, Grant describes his arduous and exploited labor in racialized terms: "This cattle-raisin' and butter-makin' makes a nigger of a man . . . I'd like to know what a man's life is worth who lives as we do? How much higher is it than the lives the niggers used to live?" (85–86).[23] Grant's relation to the land as a laborer on a rented farm, rather than as an owner of the farm, produces his blackness. His racialization is a product of labor, both in the sense that his racialization is produced from his relation to the land, and in a metaphoric sense of describing the arduousness of his labor.

The rhetoric of economic oppression takes its strength from the language of racial oppression, but it is not only the regional subaltern who is racialized. Howard's stay in Wisconsin—"the place of his birth"—constructs his whiteness, as he becomes more aware of what his body signifies in the antagonistic space of his brother's home: "He looked down at the sleeve of his soft and fleecy nightshirt, at his white, rounded arm, muscular yet fine as a woman's" (67). Howard's whiteness is gendered in ways that effeminize his intellectual labor and portray him as an urban aesthete or dandy. Garland, however, carefully avoids overemphasizing Howard's effeminacy by quickly resolving the open-endedness of his bachelorhood. Garland reassures the reader that despite his associations with poets and artists, Howard is nonetheless "sought after by brilliant women" (72). Yet even here the ambiguity of the bachelor is not fully resolved, evident in the passive voice structure that effaces the question of whom Howard has sought after.[24]

Notwithstanding Howard's effeminate and decadent appearance, he also represents culture, theater, and art. As he tells his family about various concerts and performances, Howard senses "a sudden change . . .

they grew sober, and he felt deep down in the hearts of these people a melancholy . . . They were hungry for the world, for art—these young people" (85). Hungriest for the cultural life of the city is Grant's wife, Laura, who would "like to go to a city once . . . I've never seen a play, but I've read of 'em in the magazines. It must be wonderful . . . I hate farm life" (89). In contrast, the country is defined in terms of the absence of "culture," as the negation of the city: "There were no books, no music, and only few newspapers in sight—a bare, blank, cold, drab-colored shelter from the rain, not a home" (92).

Garland characterizes culture as distinctly urban and primarily manifested in "high" cultural institutions such as theaters and concert halls. Access to this cosmopolitan "culture" is available through the magazines of the late nineteenth century, in which plays are read but not seen. Magazines produce for Laura the desire to visit the city and consume theater, music, and art; she aspires to be both a tourist and a consumer of the urban experience. As vehicles of "culture," magazines reinforce the distance between the urban and the regional—making Laura aware of what she lacks—while also making the city strangely familiar, a place of projected desires and dreams that link the margins with urban centers in highly connected and disparate ways. With no reference to folk or rural forms of community, Garland's short story suggests that the countryside is entirely bereft of culture, that culture comes to it second-hand through glossy periodicals.

Garland addresses the unequal relations between the country and the city in the form of a question: "Why was he [Howard] living in the crush and thunder and mental unrest of a great city, while his companions, seemingly his equal, in powers, were milking cows, making butter, and growing corn and wheat in the silence and dreary monotony of the farm?" (73). Before returning to New York City, Howard attempts to rectify the "infinite tragedy of their lives" by offering to purchase the family farm from its present owners, a family of German immigrants. Not only is there little hostility expressed toward the German immigrants, (in fact, Howard insists on making the offer of purchase in his broken German), but Garland refuses to resolve this fraternal disparity through philanthropy.

Despite Howard's desire to see his family return to the boyhood farm, where a people and a place can be united once again, "Up the Coulee" resists the impulse to re-anchor a people onto a place as a form of narrative and spatial resolution. In refusing his brother's offer, Grant confides: "I'm a dead failure. I've come to the conclusion that life's a failure for ninety-nine per cent of us. You can't help me now. It's too late" (97). The narrative abruptly ends with a handshake: "the one fair-skinned, full-lipped, handsome in his neat suit; the other tragic, somber in his softened mood, his large, long, rugged Scotch face bronzed with sun and scarred with wrinkles that had histories, like saber cuts on a veteran, the record of his battles" (97). By resisting a "happy ever after" ending in which the wealthy New York actor rescues his Wisconsin family from poverty, Garland illustrates the limits of filial union. He demonstrates that a charitable gesture cannot rectify the seriousness of regional and economic disparity by simply putting the family back where they belong.[25]

Unlike Edward Eggleston's midcentury tales of Hoosier life, which consist of light-hearted dialect stories and humorous adventures, Garland's stories possess a bitterness, as Howells points out in his review of *Main-Travelled Roads,* which translates the "Peasant's War into modern and republican terms" ("Editor's Study" 639). Speaking specifically about "Up the Coulee," Howells describes it as an "allegory of the whole world's civilization: the upper dog and the under dog are everywhere, and the under dog nowhere likes it" (639). Within this sketch of a particular locality, the reader discovers an indictment against a "whole world's civilization." Garland refuses to depict La Crosse valley in a vacuum, as an isolated and pristine community untouched by modernization; instead the story rejects nostalgia in order to provide an allegory of uneven development, by showing how the relations that influence a world and a nation also affect a family. The narrative is partial in both senses of the word. It is specifically situated in the local, not claiming to provide a panorama of both the city and the country; and it is highly partisan, eliciting guilt from the metropolitan reader.

Though La Crosse valley may be geographically distant, the reasons for its poverty can be traced, figuratively speaking, to the urban reader's own backyard. This goes against the metropolitan interpretation of the agrarian crisis of the early nineties. David Starr Jordan, who was president of Stanford University, epitomizes this dominant position in an article published the same year as *Main-Travelled Roads,* in which he blames the "agricultural depression" on the "habitual idleness" of the farmers (243). In challenging this blame-the-victim approach to agrarian poverty, Garland's "Up the Coulee" unequivocally opposes the disparity that urban contact produces within peripheral regions.

Touring the Black Belt

Whereas Howells was Garland's ideal reader, seeing in the narrative a modern allegory of social critique, William James was a far less insightful reader of Du Bois's sketches of the deep South. James tended to rely on residual readerly expectations of landscape description, which bordered more on ethnographic and touristic notions of geographical otherness, rather than viewing the work as a critical intervention about regional underdevelopment. This tension between readerly expectations and writerly practices, in which readers expect elegiac or curious representations of a valorized rural community while writers enact a social critique, is seen in William James's letter to his brother Henry about Du Bois's *Souls of Black Folk*. "I am sending you a decidedly moving book by a mulatto ex-student of mine, Du Bois, professor of history at Atlanta (Georgia) negro College. Read Chapters VII to XI for local color, etc." (qtd. Aptheker 70). This description of such chapters as "Of the Black Belt" and "Of the Quest of the Golden Fleece" as "local color" is certainly not a generic classification we would associate with the book today. But for William James, this particularist mode of categorizing authorship and text seemed to be the convention, evident in Henry's response that further differentiated Du Bois's book in terms of race and region. In *The American Scene,* Henry James praised *Souls* as "the only 'Southern' book of any distinction published for many a year" and noted that its author was one of the "most accomplished members of the Negro Race" (307).

Both Henry and William James underscored the book's distinctiveness, as "Southern," "local color," and "negro," distinctions that the Jameses did not themselves experience in that their racial and regional identification as "white" and "Northern" rarely, if ever, framed their own work. Horace Kallen's explanation of how marginal writers can use localism to gain access to "national letters" can be useful for understanding how the James brothers interpreted Du Bois's book. For writers to "enter into the national letters," according to Kallen, they need to attain the "perfect utterance of their race and place" (226). They must strive to portray "racialized localities" as a way to flaunt their authorial authenticity in order to gain a national readership. The more writers stick to the local the more they will succeed nationally. It is precisely this equation between locality and authenticity that seems to inform both Henry and William James's reading of *Souls.*

What is significant is that William James did not consider the entire book an example of "local color," but only particular chapters, namely those which dealt specifically with the rural South. Du Bois seemed to be aware of this potential reading in his earlier version of these chapters, which appeared in an 1899 U.S. Department of Labor bulletin. In these sketches, Du Bois explicitly promises the reader a "glimpse" of the Black Belt for the chief purpose of its "local color" (401). Notice how this earlier version differs from its later incarnation in *Souls.* Whereas these earlier "social sketches" focus exclusively on the "property holding people," the Black Belt sketches in *Souls* emphasize the plight of the "black tenant." Du Bois only uses "local color" in the 1899 version to refer to the middle-class African Americans of southern towns, the part of the population which has "succeeded best in the struggle of town life" (417). The explicit use of the term "local color" disappears in *Souls* when he focuses on the "submerged tenth." This later work wants to resist a localized reading, which would reduce a national "social" problem to a specifically southern one.[26]

Furthermore, Du Bois's government sketches of the Black Belt offer "no attempt at a complete study," whereas his later work tries to link Dougherty County, Georgia, with a larger economy of cotton production: "the Negro forms to-day one of the chief figures in a great world-industry; and this, for its own sake, and in the light of historic interest, makes the field-hands of the cotton country worth studying" (171). In contrast to his earlier sketches, which celebrate the successful landowning sector of the Black Belt as "local color," the later sketches are far less comfortable operating under this rubric. They are less interested in providing the reader with "glimpses" than in examining the conditions of the black farm worker.

Du Bois's 1903 sketches of Dougherty County, Georgia, the erstwhile capital of the antebellum Cotton Kingdom, operate within the genre of local color in the sense of providing a tour of the post-Reconstruction rural South as a "racialized locality," but they do not work exclusively within this mode. Du Bois seems to be challenging the generic limits of "local sketches" by undermining the basic requisites of local color: (1)

picturesque landscape descriptions, (2) quaint dialect, (3) isolated communities. More than Garland's "Up the Coulee," Du Bois's Dougherty County sketches go through the conventional motions of local color as an ethnographic tract in which the specific characteristics of a distant place are disclosed to the metropolitan reader. Like Garland's tale, Du Bois's sketches go beyond the aesthetic conventions of local color to ask larger questions about the postbellum underdevelopment of the rural periphery: "Such an economic organization is radically wrong. Whose is the blame?" (178). From the position of the local, these sketches reproach an entire system, a cotton economy that ties people from different parts of the nation and the world together in unjust ways.

"Of the Black Belt," which according to William James begins the section of "local color," opens with a scene similar to the opening of "Up the Coulee." The narrator rides in a train from the metropolitan center on his way to the periphery; but unlike Garland's story, which begins at the end of the train journey, Du Bois's narrative starts with the actual trip from the "North." Early on, Du Bois challenges the assumption that the South is peripheral, stating that the southwest region of Georgia, where he is headed, is the "centre of the Negro Problem" (158). The emphasis on the journey allows Du Bois to begin the tour while still on the train, with descriptions of the landscape outside his window.

Du Bois, however, is not a conventional tour guide. He refers to Atlanta, not as the modern capital of the New South, but as the "ancient land of the Cherokees." Like Garland, he portrays the picturesque terrain, the "red clay and pines of Northern Georgia," but then he combines aesthetic description with historical horrors, describing how the bloody history of Native American expulsion and chattel slavery are still inscribed within the "crimson soil." At another stop along the "metropolitan corridor," he indicates the site of the "Delegal riots," and later he mentions the place where "Sam Hose was crucified" (158).[27] From the vantage point of the "Jim Crow Car," Du Bois attempts to monumentalize an alternative history of the South as a "scarred land."[28] Unlike Thomas Nelson Page and other southern regionalists who romanticize the plantation myth, Du Bois demonstrates that the past continues to haunt the post-Reconstruction South.

Du Bois not only challenges how the past has been rewritten in plantation novels but also implicitly criticizes how the "modern" South has been ignored by both fiction writers and sociologists. In addition to being a nostalgic projection, the South is a complex living reality, which in turn is divided by internal schisms between the country and the city: "Once upon a time we knew country life so well and city life so little. Now the world has well-nigh forgotten what the country is" (160). Du Bois criticizes the privileging of the urban, which he actually contributed to in *The Philadelphia Negro* (1899) and later in *Darkwater* (1920), because it has led to the silencing of the countryside. His sketches of Dougherty County signify a modern intervention on behalf of African-American farmers, but they also intervene on behalf of a region.

To speak about a specific race and class required that one take into account the politics of space. Region is central for Du Bois's understanding of the relations between economics and racism. He takes a holistic approach to economic peripheralization by approaching the underdevelopment of a class of black workers as concomitant with the exploitation of land. The regionalization of his work on race radicalizes his political critique, from one preoccupied with racial distinctiveness as in "The Conservation of Races" to a more volatile discussion about a world economy of cotton production that implicates race, region, and class.

To show how race and class intersect in specific localities of agricultural production, Du Bois invokes certain readerly expectations while also undermining them. Just as he uses the language of the picturesque travel tour to foreground incidents of racial brutality, so he uses the same travel discourse of landscape description to point out the desolation (rather than the revival) of plantation lore. "The whole land seems forlorn and forsaken. Here are the remnants of the vast plantations of the Sheldons, the Pellots, and the Rensons; but the souls of them are passed. The houses lie in half ruin, or have wholly disappeared; the fences have flown, and the families are wandering in the world" (DB 161). This region, which was once celebrated as the "Egypt of the Confederacy," has experienced its own exodus of capital, leaving it underdeveloped, as a peripheral point in the New South economy of mechanized farming. But there is a residual slave economy still in existence, the remains of the feudal relations of the antebellum era in which a new generation of landowners maintain the same relations between people and place through peonage labor or what Du Bois aptly calls "debt-slavery." Although the tour begins with a historical overview, it is now fully immersed in the modern, in the contemporary relations of tenant farmer and land baron that replicate for another generation the relations of the plantation.

Du Bois further maneuvers within the local genre by depicting individual tenant farmers as "distinct characters quite out of the ordinary" (DB 167). The deep South is still a bastion of individuality and eccentricity, a familiar requisite for regional and especially southern uniqueness. He recounts various individuals he meets, figures such as Sam Scott and Luke Black. Some are prosperous, such as a man named Jackson who owns one hundred acres, while others are destitute. Within a single county there is a hierarchy of conditions, with the northwest corner of the county far more "modern" than its southwestern part.

What is missing in his depictions of these individual figures, regardless of whether they are freeholders or tenants, is dialect. Without the slightest indication of a regional accent, an elderly man sitting along the roadside recounts the abuses under slavery: "This land was a little Hell. I've seen niggers drop dead in the furrow, but they were kicked aside, and the plough never stopped" (DB 164). Another "distinct character" summarizes his philosophy of life with little sign of a distinctly southern accent: "Look up! If you don't look up you can't get up" (DB 166). That Du Bois depicts these voices without dialect, a dramatic break from the conventional local color portrayals of rural blacks, renders these subaltern voices similar to the middle-class speech of the sketches' readers. This vocal similarity creates an uncomfortable degree of proximity between the black southern farmer and the cosmopolitan reader within a genre that is expected to provide a distanced look at how the other half lives.

In depicting the lives of these individual tenant farmers, Du Bois rejects the aestheticizing language of picturesque variety and local color. Similar to Garland's descriptions of rural life in the Midwest, Du Bois underscores the monotony of life in the Black Belt: "With the grown men of the county there is little variety in work" (DB 175). The absence of "variety," Du Bois implies, is due in part to the absence of a "leisure class." "The dull monotony of daily toil is broken only by the gayety of the thoughtless and the Saturday trip to town. The toil, like all farm toil, is monotonous" (DB 175). Variety is associated not only with leisure but also with town life, which represents an "atmosphere of excess."

What informs much of Du Bois's work of the late 1890s is the concern that young people will abandon the farms and move to the city, a migration that would unsettle the foundation of black southern culture. This move to the city is itself predicated in part on the desire for variety, on the need for "amusement": "Its parks and play grounds, its theatre and galleries, its music and dancing" ("Amusement" 33). In an 1897 piece entitled "The Problem of Amusement," Du Bois does not censure the desire of young people to seek variety but understands why people move to cities. In a tone similar to Garland's on the appeal of urban life, Du Bois writes: "You who were born and reared amid the kaleidoscopic life of a great city scarcely realize what an irresistible attraction city life has for one who has long experienced the dull, lifeless monotony of the country" (32). The language of variety structures Du Bois's distinction between the country and the city, in which the city is associated with variety, abundance, and leisure, while the country is analogous to monotony, scarcity, and work.

Like Garland's, Du Bois's response to the city-country division is complicated. On the one hand, both writers are critical of metropolitan centrality and regional peripheralization and use the local sketch to underline their resentment at such economic and cultural disparity. Yet on the other hand, they recognize the pleasures of the city with its variety of amusements and cultural institutions. Du Bois portrays the black South in these sketches as culturally deprived, a point at odds with the conclusion of *Souls,* which celebrates the "Sorrow Songs" and folk music in general as emblematic of the "Negro Spirit." In his early Black Belt sketches, the rural South is as bereft of culture as Garland's La Crosse valley. For both Du Bois and Garland, culture may be romantically celebrated as part of the rural "folk," but as an everyday practice it is ultimately located in the city.

Torn between celebration and pathos, Du Bois's ambivalence toward the black rural South is somewhat resolved by the end of his Black Belt sketches, where he portrays the rural South not as an isolated "backwater" but as the "warp and woof" of an international economy. He redeems this region by showing how Dougherty County is interconnected with the metropolitan centers of the world, not through variety and leisure, but through the monotonous toil of cotton production. The historian Paul Buck has pointed out that during this period "the economic interests of the South could not be separated from those of the country at large" (300). The 1890 Census explicitly describes the interdependence between the southern cotton crop and the northern industrial system: the "sheetings and print cloths of the South are consumed in Northern homes and Southern yarns are woven on Pennsylvania looms and made into hosiery on New York and Pennsylvania frames" (Buck 301). According to Du Bois, the racial composition of the southern labor force supporting the Cotton Kingdom has changed since the Civil War, "from the Black to the White Belt" and the "Negro of to-day raises not more than half of the cotton crop" (DB 171). Despite the migration of cotton production from black to black-white labor, Du Bois argues in "The Quest of the Golden Fleece" that African Americans still constitute "one of the chief figures in a great world-industry" (DB 171).

Rather than the "talented-tenth," he speaks of the "submerged tenth," the peonage labor in the Black Belt whose toil is a crucial part of cotton production. His sketches are local in the same way as Garland's: both launch a critique of an international system from the vantage point of the particular.[29] Du Bois's sketches are at once situated and partisan. Not tracing cotton to the northern mills or its export abroad, Du Bois focuses exclusively on its production, on the "modern Quest of the Golden Fleece in the Black Sea" (DB 170). This focus allows him to underscore the role of cotton workers, rather than the consumer products associated with cotton, so that figures who once peopled the backdrop of rural landscapes are now its main protagonists. Whether it is a sharecropper like Luke Black or a tenant farmer like Grant McLane, Du Bois's and Garland's local sketches portray these figures as speaking subjects who articulate the inequalities of uneven development without sentiment and without accent.

A Plea for Asymmetrical Regionalism

The combination of Garland's and Du Bois's populist sketches with Ruiz de Burton's patrician regionalism demonstrates that the privileging of locality as a site of "residual resistance" does not guarantee a specific political orientation. There is no ideological position intrinsic to locality. Partiality—in both senses of a localized and partisan critique—can refer to the "residual resistance" of a sharecropper as well as to the plight of a displaced aristocrat. There are a variety of ways to be local. To return to the topic of the uses of variety in reconceiving a national literature, it is important to remember that Garland did not support a relativist notion of regional diversity. At the turn of the century, the embrace of variety also meant the recognition of limits. Partiality operated not only as a mode of collecting—with each region having its distinct arrangement of stories—but also as a way of ordering local narratives according to a principle of national cohesion.

In *Crumbling Idols*, only particular uses of local color will count toward a national aesthetic, only those sketches which challenge the aesthetic standards of the East and promote a "new composite" will be considered "American" (122). For Garland, western literature has, unfortunately, become "an annex of the East," which has "imitated imitations" since the East is itself an imitation of Europe (121). The purpose of western literature is not to convince the easterners that its regional writers can write like them. Western writers must reject this "desire to write for the applause of its masters in the East" (121), and instead create an alternative mode of aesthetic practice, which he refers to as a "difference of treatment" (120). In contrast to Kallen's gradualist language of "grafting," Garland's theory of localism is reminiscent of Whitman as a declaration of aesthetic independence, not exclusively in the name of a distinct region but in terms of a national literary tradition: "The centre of this literature of national scope, therefore cannot be in the East" (122). It will be "something new; it will be, and ought to be, American,—that is to say, a new composite" (122).

Although Garland is rather vague about the details of this new aesthetic, what is significant is his dual strategy of preserving the character of the "minority section," as well as nationalizing it as indicative of the nation. This asymmetrical configuration of union, in which Garland nationalizes the local, is similar to Du Bois's design in "The Conservation of Races." Both break with the strategy of integration through mimesis: accept us because we are similar to you. Instead, they lay claim to the national, not by pleasing its dominant sectional/racial group, but by differentiating themselves from it. Just as Du Bois in "The Conservation of Races" claims that blacks are at their most American when they resist Anglo-American assimilation, so Garland argues that local literature, and particularly that of the West, best exemplifies a national literature when it rejects eastern aesthetic standards. As a result, they reconcile a modern notion of individuality with national citizenship. Contrast this to Ruiz de Burton's strategy of ingratiating the Californio elite with the genteel reformers of the East. Whereas Garland and Du Bois configure national incorporation through a strategy of resilient individuality, Ruiz de Burton imagines it through identification.

Garland's own partiality about local color, that only specific uses of locality can represent Americanness, is certainly open to criticism: he clearly privileges realism over romance, the West over any other region of the United States, and populism over any other political agenda.[30] His anti-assimilationist claim, like Du Bois's, is also problematic: both Garland and Du Bois are already inscribed within the very eastern metropolitan values that they want to challenge. I am, however, less interested in debating the degree to which these two writers are already implicated in the dominant culture than in examining how they invoke a strategy of persistent particularism to offer an alternative plan of national incorporation. How did they negotiate subcultural distinctiveness with national representativeness? How did they configure national unity through differentiation?

The lesson that Garland's theory of local color provides for us today is that a critical practice concerning the local must itself be partial. Rather than take conceptual refuge in symmetrical thinking and configure regional variety in exclusively relativist terms, as a complicated and contradictory set of social discourses that interact and combine in numerous ways, critics of regionalism need to acknowledge rather than suppress a principle of determination: to privilege certain uses of local color over others. A fundamental danger of symmetrical thinking, according to Raymond Williams, is that it evades the point "that in the production of human society some activities are more fundamentally determining than others" (Eagleton "Williams" 169). Symmetrical thinking also avoids the uncomfortable task of exclusion: that any project of collection requires a principle of rejection.[31]

In *The Country and the City,* Raymond Williams addresses the importance of asymmetrical thinking in the context of regionalism:

> Very few titles to property could bear humane investigation, in the long process of conquest, theft, political intrigue, courtiership, extortion and the power of money. It is a deep and persistent illusion to suppose that time confers on these familiar processes of acquisition an innocence which can be contrasted with the ruthlessness of subsequent stages of the same essential drives . . . The "ancient stocks," to which we are sentimentally referred, are ordinarily only those families who had been pressing and exploiting their neighbours rather longer . . . If we have humanity to spare, it is better directed to the unregarded men who were making and working the land, in any event, under the old owners and the new. (50)

Not all victims of the land are created equal. Ruiz de Burton's defense of the "ancient stocks" of California as "natives" to the land is not equivalent to the struggle of the sharecroppers and tenant farmers in Garland's and Du Bois's sketches. Garland and Du Bois use the local to foreground labor: to accentuate the irony that those who work closest to the earth reap the fewest rewards. Whereas Ruiz de Burton invokes the local to maintain a privileged distance from the land, Garland and Du Bois use the local to underscore the tragedy surrounding those who are most proximate to it.

Garland's theory of local color provides a heterogeneous conception of a unified national literature that is structured by a specific emphasis. This emphasis, which privileges certain regions and particular aesthetic practices over others, characterizes more generally turn-of-the-century conceptualizations of variety. Whether it is early configurations of pluralism, analogous theories of regionalism, or as we will see in the next chapter, the formation of the urban picturesque, all three examples inscribe the language of variety within limits, so as to retain a principle of determination that produces a hierarchy of values. Rather than take refuge in symmetrical thinking, which disavows conflict through a relativist principle of equivalence, they instead foreground partiality, which unabashedly favors certain formulations of local individuality over others. They demonstrate that one can theorize variety without relinquishing a notion of boundaries.

But boundaries also vary. In the next chapter, I show how the metropolis rather than the countryside is perceived as the authentic site of variety. Practitioners of what I call the "urban picturesque" claim that the city is the apex of modernity, that ethnic variety is a sign of development (in contradistinction to the underdeveloped and homogenous countryside). The equation of variety and modernity can be applied to disparate contexts, invoked to justify either the city or the country as the primary spatial and cultural determinant of the nation. The question then is not whether variety is a progressive or a conservative concept, but rather how is it used and who is using it. The elasticity of its invocations highlights the need to locate agency, to specify and explicate the contexts in which the various meanings of variety are produced.

4

The Urban Picturesque and Americanization

By the late nineteenth century, regionalists such as Hamlin Garland as well as literary critics more generally considered the picturesque "superficial," an overused and commercial mode of representation (*Crumbling Idols* 60–61). This opinion was commonplace as early as the 1850s, when Hawthorne's *The Blithedale Romance* was criticized for its "picturesque detail" and its consequent lack of "moral depth and earnestness."[1] More concerned with surfaces than depths, this aesthetic continued to fall into disfavor with the literary establishment when the term saturated the marketplace of guidebooks and travel narratives with such titles as *Picturesque America, Picturesque Italy, Picturesque California,* and *Picturesque New York,* to name but a few. Nearly every nation in Europe, not to mention almost every state in the Union, seemed to have its own illustrated book attesting to its regional uniqueness.

Despite this context of critical disrepute and commercial excess, the term played a formative role in the popular representation of American modernization. In the flourishing magazine culture of the 1890s, the picturesque sought to make modernity less terrifying by making it familiar through a gradualist approach that linked old concepts with new phenomena. Its hackneyed language promised to turn the urban realities of class disparity and ethnic heterogeneity into customary sights and even potentially pleasant aspects of the modern experience.

Of all American cities at the turn of the century, New York best satisfied the material requirements for the picturesque, namely a dramatic chasm between rich and poor combined with ethnic heterogeneity. In 1890 it became the first American city to reach a population of one million, and by 1910 over three-fourths of its inhabitants were either foreign-born or the children of immigrants. In Robert Hunter's classic 1904 study of the urban poor, he estimated that no less than 25 percent of the people of New York City lived in poverty (27). Among immigrant workers, he claimed that over 40 percent were unemployed for some part of the year (34).[2] In 1892 Lyman Abbott noted that New York represented a "microcosm" of "all the contrasts of our modern life,—its worst and its best aspects" (39).

Anxieties about modernity focused on New York; it became the site where the fears of unruly and polyglot hordes and the "dangerous classes" were projected and elaborated. For Josiah Strong, New York signified a "City of Destruction," a bastion of Romanism, socialism, and decadence that threatened the yeoman ideals of an earlier age. For Joaquin Miller in *The Destruction of Gotham,* it represented a "new Babel" on the brink of collapse: "All Europe, all Asia, all Africa, the whole wide earth has sent up her best, worst, weakest, strongest, most wicked, wild, and reckless people, to the building of this new Babel" (12). Gendering New York as a woman and presenting catastrophe as female hysteria, Miller concluded that the city's excessive heterogeneity had "made her mad." A generation before the 1920s, heterogeneity and New York City were already fused in the American imagination as "Mongrel Manhattan," to borrow Ann Douglas's phrase. For some this fusion inspired disturbing images of bedlam, while for others it created the positive basis for redefining and modernizing American nationhood.

In contrast to the sensational fiction of sublime terror or the nativist anxieties of looming catastrophe, what I call the "urban picturesque" provided another way of representing the metropolis, one that transformed the everyday marvels of modernity into a "whole wondrous spectacle" (Fullerton 664). The urban picturesque was the aesthetic expression of Herbert Spencer's notion of "progress" as the evolution from "homogeneity to heterogeneity," which played into a triumphalist narrative of national development: New York City displayed to the nation and to the world that its "heterogeneous foreignness" was a "real triumph" (Dwight 544). At its most fundamental level, the urban picturesque offered a new way of apprehending urban space by making inequality and immigrant diversity expected elements of modernity. It signaled a constellation of aesthetic practices and meanings that rendered the heterogeneity of the city as "charming" and "quaint" rather than exclusively deleterious.[3] It also offered a much needed aesthetic vocabulary for middle-class inhabitants of the city who did not resist otherness but actively pursued it.

The journalist Viola Roseboro, for example, enjoyed strolling through Mulberry Bend because she found the Italians "delightfully picturesque." When observing the arrival of immigrants at Castle Garden, she admitted that the immigrant "adds to the picturesqueness . . . throughout all the lower part of Manhattan island." For the journalist John Corbin, the immigrant subcultures of New York supplied the city with "richness and variety" by bringing a "greater variety of food cooked with a finer art than is to be had in any other city the world over" (270). In contrast to Josiah Strong and Joaquin Miller, who found the diverse immigrant populations a source of dread, journalists for *The Cosmopolitan* and *Harper's*, among other New York–based periodicals, configured these same subcultures as repositories of picturesque pleasure. New Yorkers depended on the immigrant subcultures to provide their city with its "highly distinctive savor" (Dwight 544).

In Chapter 3 I explored how regionalism sought to modernize America by preserving its local peculiarities, so that a national literature would not appear in a single "Great American Novel," but as distinct and discrete regional stories that would decenter the metropolis as the literary hub of the nation. The urban picturesque also operated as a form of local color, which captured the Old World customs and peculiarities that existed in the heart of modernity. But where regional variety consisted of "native" voices, picturesque variety relied on foreign accents. It was part of a more general attempt to nationalize the transnational as distinctively American. The urban picturesque was an important vehicle for transforming immigrants from social threats to cultural resources, as signs of an urban identity as well as a national one. It was part of a larger process of urbanizing a national identity by linking New York cosmopolitanism with modern Americanism.

Although this shift was not officially recognized until the 1920 Census, when for the first time the urban inhabitants outnumbered rural ones, the ideological practice of modernizing American identity through its metropolitan center was already under way by the end of the nineteenth century.[4] As early as 1882 the journalist James McCabe considered New York "thoroughly American": the "people of New York represent every nationality upon the globe, and thus give to the city the cosmopolitan character which is one of its prominent features. But no city on the continent is so thoroughly American as this" (54).[5] Both regionalism and the urban picturesque tried to preserve cultural peculiarities as distinctively American, but they did so through antithetical attitudes toward the city. Whereas Garland decried New York City as a "literary dictator" that needed to be overthrown, the urban picturesque privileged the metropolis as definitive of the nation, and even of the world.

My objective is to explore how the aesthetic discourse of the urban picturesque helped to equate ethnic variety and urbanism with modern Americanism. More specifically, I am interested in how this discourse operated within a larger narrative of Americanization, defined not in terms of assimilation but rather along the lines of Jamesian pluralism, which sought to reconcile the "each-form" within a "loose" and "concatenated" union. In 1916 Randolph Bourne would translate James's "pluralistic universe" in explicitly nationalist terms as "Trans-National America." In contrast to the melting pot, the predominant trope of American acculturation by which cultures were to blend in order to form a new synthesis, Bourne's model of national incorporation was based on unity-in-discreteness. According to this model, immigrants must retain their "foreign savor," which would distinguish modern America from the supposedly homogeneous nationalities of Europe. In *The American Scene,* Henry James similarly deplored the "great assimilative organism" with its "huge white-washing brush" of Anglo-Saxonism; he preferred that immigrants retain signs of quaint and distinctive alienness (97). The "picturesque," for James, resided in the "unconverted residuum," a variation of his brother's pluralistic term to refer to those who had not yet surrendered to the "assimilative force" (95).

The main task of the urban picturesque was to capture immigrant peculiarities as a way to demonstrate to middle-class readers that "richness and variety" were part of the metropolitan experience. To do this, periodicals used a genre that I call the "intra-urban walking tour." As the modern descendent of the eighteenth-century genre of urban spectatorial literature, which provided panoramic tours of London in installments, the intra-urban walking tour produced glimpses or brief sketches of New York rather than comprehensive descriptions.[6] The intra-urban walking tour was a genre ideally suited for the emerging figure of the urban commuter. While sitting on the avenue "L" or on the crosstown trolley, reading about downtown perambulations afforded a sense of contact with the "other half," cross-cultural encounters that the new technologies of mobility were making more difficult to experience directly and meaningfully. Both the intra-urban walking tour and its generic counterpart, the regional short story (also popular in magazines during this period), supplied increasingly busy readers with a sense of "rough and rugged pleasure" at a time when urban space was becoming highly differentiated according to race, ethnicity, and class.

The intra-urban walking tours exemplified the Bournean model of cultural incorporation by casting cultural difference in terms of unity-in-discreteness. The urban picturesque ensured that particularity would be maintained by mapping cultural difference onto distinct neighborhoods. The picturesque represented the aesthetic counterpart to economic segregation by transforming the class, racial, and ethnic divisions that characterized urban space into a spectacle. This tendency to use the picturesque to highlight the internal diversity of the city also characterizes Theodore Dreiser's early sketches of New York from the 1890s. Though Dreiser did not explicitly use the term "picturesque" to refer to New York (he primarily employed the term when describing conventional rural scenes), his sketches nevertheless exhibit the picturesque mode of apprehending urban space, one that interprets the economic chasm and ethnic variety of the city as a fecund space for aesthetic representation. His sketches, which originally appeared in *Harper's Weekly* and the *New York World,* among other mainstream periodicals, demonstrate how the discourse of the urban picturesque was employed more generally to cast New York as a spectacle, in which the daily dramas of triumph and tragedy were staged.

Whether it was the mainstream walking tours of *The Cosmopolitan* or Dreiser's sketches of the 1890s, the urban picturesque did more than simply naturalize economic and ethnic variety as part of the urbanscape. It also established a hierarchy of racial preferences in which certain types of poor urban populations were included at the expense of others. On the one hand, the urban picturesque was representationally generous, expanding the bounds of sympathetic depiction to include the visages of impoverished European immigrants who were more frequently portrayed as either a threatening mass or a marginal presence. On the other hand, the urban picturesque rarely strayed from these immigrants, and when it did, as I will later elaborate, it turned typically to the Chinese.

Omitted entirely from its field of vision were African Americans, who were also arriving in New York City in record numbers at the turn of the century. In 1903 Du Bois noted that "the most significant economic change among Negroes in the last ten or twenty years has been their influx into northern cities" (qtd. Meier 274).[7] But picturesque perambulators rarely ventured into the black neighborhoods of the Tenderloin to comment on the "quaint" atmosphere or the "charming" visages.[8] Blackness signaled the representational limit of the picturesque. Concerned with the "smiling aspects" of modern life, the picturesque could not address "uncomfortable" topics such as racism and racial segregation. The picturesque disavowed the social and cultural consequences of the nascent black migration northward by placing them beyond its field of vision.[9]

In stark contrast to the urban picturesque's refusal to "see" blackness, the same aesthetic went to great lengths to present Southern and Eastern European immigrants as "charming." One way in which this was done was to make swarthiness beautiful. Viola Roseboro, for example, found the Italians "delightfully picturesque," largely because "the street is full of swarthy, unkempt men" (398). In William Dean Howells's novel *A Hazard of New Fortunes*, Basil March took pleasure in the "picturesque raggedness" of the Italian immigrants, and he especially "liked the swarthy, strange visages," because "he found nothing menacing for the future in them" (259).[10] The urban picturesque emerged at the intersection of ethnicity and class, where swarthiness was inextricable from poverty and both were potentially "delightful."

Making swarthiness picturesque was part of a larger process of expanding the racial category of whiteness to include its swarthier hues. Although the Harvard scientist Nathaniel Shaler in 1897 lumped blacks together with the new immigrants as permanently inassimilable, many social scientists as well as magazine journalists sought to distinguish between blacks and what are today known as "white ethnics."[11] Scholars such as William Z. Ripley, an economist at MIT, spoke of the "varieties of whites" as a way to include Alpines and Mediterraneans with Anglo-Saxons in a discussion about the "races of Europe." Henry Pratt Fairchild similarly referred to the "European varieties within the white race." Edward Ross, a liberal populist-progressive sociologist and eugenicist who coined the phrase "race suicide," referred to Slavic immigrants as a "race," as a "nationality," and as "white." In his 1914 article "The Slavs in America," Ross commented: "No doubt between five and six per cent. of the whites in this country are of Slavic blood" (590). Although Ross referred to them as a "race," he found no disturbing inconsistency between being white and being Slavic. His use of "race" when referring to Slavic immigrants is more akin to the late-twentieth-century notion of ethnicity.[12]

This understanding of "race" as a sign of white ethnicity is also seen in Alfred Holt Stone's 1906 article on racial tensions in the United States: "We speak loosely of the race problems which are the result of European immigration. These are really not race problems at all. They are purely temporary problems, based upon temporary antipathies between different groups of the same race, which invariably disappear in one or two generations, and which form only a temporary barrier to physical assimilation by intermarrying with native stock" (679).

There was a growing sense that the category of "race" was limited, that it could not take into account differences that were perceived as cultural rather than biological. Writing before the emergence of the contemporary use of ethnicity, these scholars were searching for a language with which to expand and differentiate whiteness. Although Shaler, among others, saw immigrants as racially other (more akin to African Americans than to Anglo-Saxons), there were numerous sociologists, comprising conservatives and progressives, who were trying to broaden the category of whiteness to include "temporary antipathies." In *Whiteness of a Different Color: European Immigrants and the Alchemy of Race*, Matthew Frye Jacobson has demonstrated that "becoming American" and "becoming Caucasian" were intertwined. He argues that the incorporation of European immigrants as a normative model of assimilation was the result of their racial status as "free white persons." Their inclusion was dependent on "the racial exclusion of others" (12). "The European immigrants' experience," writes Jacobson, "was decisively shaped by their entering an arena where Europeanness—that is to say, whiteness—was among the most important possessions one could lay claim to. It was their *whiteness*, not any kind of New World magnanimity, that opened the Golden Door" (8).[13] As an aesthetic corollary to the historical process of Americanization, the urban picturesque deemed European immigrants "charming" precisely because they were a different shade of white.

This is not to say, however, that the expansion of whiteness was entirely a democratizing gesture, as race theorists such as Ripley still maintained an internal hierarchy with Nordics at the top. Racialism still occurred within shifting perceptions of whiteness. The Senate Commission on Immigration reported in 1911 that Poles were "darker than the Lithuanians" and "lighter than the average Russian," which suggests that European immigrants were not perceived as monolithic, but differentiated according to racial nuances and phenotypical gradations (qtd. Jacobson 69).

As whiteness became more inclusive it also became more segmented, a tension that was at times strategically suppressed through the egalitarian rhetoric of variety. When Henry Pratt Fairchild, for example, referred to the "European varieties within the white race," he did so to consolidate the new immigrants with the already established native white population as a way to cohere the racial formation of the nation. The expansion of whiteness relied on the rhetoric of variety to create a sense of racial coalition, while at the same time utilizing internal hierarchies among the different varieties to maintain Anglo-Saxon supremacy. The revision of whiteness in the urban picturesque was a response to as well as a reformulation of nativist sentiments.

Analogous to this sociological trend, the aesthetic discourse of the picturesque produced racial distinctions that ultimately legitimated the new immigrants as potential citizens at the expense of African Americans. While one became part of the color and variety of the city, the other by implication was rendered invisible. By embracing the good immigrants while banishing dangerous citizens, the urban picturesque raised questions about what kinds of variety were considered acceptable within the American commonwealth. How various could variety be? The answer to this question was partly the result of a growing economic rivalry in the early twentieth century between black and European immigrant labor, a rivalry that the *New Republic* described as a "silent conflict on a gigantic scale" (qtd. Steinberg 201).

The racial limits of the picturesque were also determined by the concept's residual meanings. From its temporal migration from eighteenth-century Britain to late-nineteenth-century America and its spatial migration from the country to the city, the picturesque brought with it ideological baggage that contained, among other things, racial prescriptions. The picturesque, moreover, was highly racialized long before it arrived in the United States. In order to understand the residual racial traces of the turn of the century urban picturesque, it is important to highlight formative moments of its eighteenth-century incarnation.

The Picturesque as a Traveling Theory

That a concept which migrated from Britain to America should be the aesthetic for Americanizing the European migration to New York City exemplifies Edward Said's notion of a "traveling theory." Accounts of theoretical transplantation and circulation, according to Said, necessarily involve the acknowledgment that movement into "a new environment is never unimpeded" (226). There are new modes of representation and institutionalization that differ from the original usage. With regard to the picturesque, this would include the differences between rural landscapes and ethnic urbanscapes, between the pictorial composition of "high" art and the periodical sketches associated with "low" art. But there are also similarities. A "traveling theory" still possesses a "discernible and recurrent pattern to the movement itself" (226). There are two recurrent patterns that link the eighteenth-century aesthetic practice of the picturesque with its modern counterpart.

First, the picturesque, whether in the context of the countryside or the urbanscape, operates as an aesthetic middle ground. Originally theorized in the late eighteenth century by the Reverend William Gilpin, then further conceptualized at the turn of the nineteenth century by Uvedale Price and Richard Payne Knight, the picturesque emerged as a third category of aesthetic pleasure beside the sublime and the beautiful. It includes within its domain those objects, such as trees, rocks, and groves, which give delight to the eye but cannot be classified within those two Burkean categories. Not requiring the classically trained eye necessary to detect beauty and not possessing the infinite awe of the sublime, the picturesque is somewhere in the middle, a domesticated sublime that transforms shock into mild surprise. Lacking the vastness of the sublime and the smoothness of the beautiful, the picturesque represents "roughness," "sudden variation," and "untouched varieties." This eighteenth-century aesthetic, with its emphasis on vision and on landscape as an ornamental surface, finds in the contrasts between streams, hills, and foliage, together with the decayed cottage and disheveled gypsy, endless occasions for entertainment.[14]

In contrast to the beautiful, which signifies a harmonious and symmetrical blend of equivalent parts, the picturesque refers to asymmetrical distinctions and hierarchies of preference. Contrary to the sublime, which suggests "infinity" and a "boundless ocean," the picturesque, according to Uvedale Price, depends on the "shape and disposition of its boundaries" (*Essays* 84). What ultimately distinguishes the picturesque from its parent categories is that it represents an asymmetrical composition defined within distinct boundaries. Like William James's psychological concepts of "attention" and "emphasis," the picturesque "eye" "learns how to separate, to select and combine" (Price, *Essays* 5). It does not claim to include everything within an all-encompassing panorama, but rather it provides modest glimpses and sketches of particular scenes.

The second recurrent pattern in eighteenth- and nineteenth-century uses of the picturesque is the concept's racial politics, in which blackness is the banished term that defines "picturesque variety." In *A Dialogue on the Distinct Characters of the Picturesque and the Beautiful* (1801), Price associates "variety" with whiteness and "absolute monotony" with blackness. While whiteness signifies a chromatic "union of all other colors," blackness represents the "extinction of all colors." Price endows these colors with moral significance in which whiteness is synonymous with inclusivity and "purity," while blackness is pejoratively defined as pure "absence."

The allegorical language of white superiority and black inferiority, which takes the form of variety versus monotony, is ultimately abandoned and replaced with an unabashedly racist discussion of the politics of hair:

> One very principal beauty in hair, is its loose texture and flexibility; by means of which it takes . . . a number of graceful and becoming forms, without any assistance from art; and, like them too, is capable of taking any arrangement that art can invent. Add to this, the great diversity of colours, from the darkest to the lightest in all their gradations; the glossy surface; the play of light and shadow, which always attends variety of form: and then contrast all this with the monotony of the black wooly hair of the negro! Its colour, nearly the same in all of them, and the form, without any natural play or variety, and incapable of receiving any from art! (58).

Price associates the picturesque with the "loose texture and flexibility" of white people's hair, and conversely links the anti-picturesque with the "monotony of the black wooly hair of the negro." The picturesque in its very origins uses the language of variety to promote white supremacy. Its aesthetic proclivities highlight a moral allegory: variety becomes synonymous not only with "beauty in hair" but also with virtue and probity, while blackness refers to the "absence" of moral rectitude. The racial aesthetics of hair also suggest two opposing forms of civil society. Whereas white people's hair describes a varied, "loose," and flexible union, a democratic union, black people's hair implies a union of sameness, uniformity, and "monotony," a union that excludes flexibility and variety, bordering on totalitarianism. Uniformity, which Price describes as "so great an enemy to the picturesque," is given a racial inflection that explicitly casts democratic values and black people as incompatible.

Price's contemporary Richard Payne Knight does not define the picturesque and its opposite in such blatantly racist terms, but he does describe the ideal figure of picturesque beauty, a figure who encapsulates both the "roughness" and the "otherness" of the English countryside. For Knight, this figure consists of "gypsies and beggar girls," whose "dirty and tattered garments, the dishevelled hair, and general wild appearance . . . are often picturesque" (Copley and Garside 146). From its beginning, the picturesque traveler has embraced a "variety of tints," which translate into a racial spectrum whose limit is swarthiness. Just as the picturesque was interposed between the sublime and the beautiful, so swarthiness represents that liminal stage between whiteness and blackness. The aesthetics of landscape description explicitly and implicitly provide a racial allegory of civil society, using the language of abundance and variety to demarcate the point of racial exclusion.

From Gypsies to Rag Pickers

If the picturesque was a traveling theory, then gypsies and beggar girls were its traveling figures. They were the eighteenth-century antecedents of the late-nineteenth-century immigrant, and both were emblematic of the migratory movements of the dispossessed, the mobility of those who did not own property but went in search of it. The immigrant traversed the city rather than the pastoral landscape, gleaning the remains of overproduction in the shadows of opulence. Gypsies and immigrants represented the racial limits of the picturesque, with their swarthiness, but they also represented its class limit. Just as the eighteenth-century picturesque travelers were not interested in the small farmer working hard to maintain a modest crop but in the peripatetic figures of the countryside, so the late-nineteenth-century urban picturesque travelers were not intrigued by the economically mobile immigrant family, moving from their downtown tenement to their Brooklyn home. Nor were they generally curious about the working classes.

The urban picturesque tended to represent the *Lumpenproletariat,* which only seems appropriate given that *Lumpen* means "rags and tatters."[15] Rag pickers roamed the city streets searching through refuse for fragments of clothes and morsels of food that they could either consume or sell. Through their scrutinous gaze, waste acquired value. Refuse was recycled into second-hand commodities. Alfred Stieglitz's 1893 photograph "The Rag Picker" (Figure 1) highlights a solitary woman under a street lamp in the Bowery sifting through the detritus of the city.[16] As the modern counterpart of gypsies and beggar girls, the immigrant as rag picker became an archetype in the periodical sketches. For Viola Roseboro, "much of the picturesqueness" of the Neapolitan immigrants on Crosby Street was that they were "rag-pickers," and represented "the poorest and dirtiest of their race" (396). In 1892 Mariana Van Rensselaer explored "Shantytown," that liminal space of New York where the rag pickers congregated, because she found "perpetual picturesqueness in their tottering, pitiful, vanishing" ways, reminiscent of those "often greenly environed, relics of bucolic days" (320). Located on the metropolitan periphery, Shantytown designated a transitional space between the country and the city, between the residual agrarian setting of the picturesque and its emergent urban one.

The rag picker was also a figurative analogue to the picturesque traveler. The rag pickers' search for valuables amid refuse mimicked the traveler's own quest for unusual sights amid ruins. The urban picturesque captured the consumerism of the poor, an impaired consumerism that both disturbed and fascinated the picturesque travelers as a grotesque counterpart to their own pecuniary desires. "Modern consumption," according to Rachel Bowlby, "is a matter not of basic items bought for definite needs, but of visual fascination and remarkable sights of things not found at home" (1). Similarly, Gilpin acknowledged that the "love of novelty is the foundation of this pleasure" (41). By drawing a parallel between the rag picker's pursuit of material goods and the picturesque traveler and reader's quest for visual curiosities, the picturesque sketches mediated the economic and ethnic chasm between the abject immigrant—"the poorest and the dirtiest"—and the middle-class consumer. By inscribing immigrant rag picking within the consumerist

1. "The Rag Picker," by Alfred Stieglitz

rhetoric of pecuniary desire, the picturesque traveler naturalized immigrants' poverty alongside their swarthiness.

Penury and ethnicity became linked as familiar sights of modernity; so when late Victorian perambulators witnessed rag picking firsthand, they were reminded of the "pictures" from their parlor-room reading. The picturesque tours of New York are examples of what Stephen Rachman in a slightly different context has called "devotional seeing," which is a form of "cultural recognition" that translates actual sights into a form of literary insight, by which "cities are imagined before they are experienced" (663). But while Rachman refers to "formal literature," the urban picturesque relied on representations from the nascent mass media. The late Victorian *flâneur* recognized poverty and swarthy immigrants as familiar sights of modernity partly on the basis of textual cues of such genres as the intra-urban walking tours. By making the alienation of the rag picker less alienating for the viewer, these tours transformed the shock of modernity into a mild surprise.

The Rise of Professional Spectatorship

Modernity's scribe was the journalist whom Walter Benjamin called the descendent of the midcentury *flâneur.* But unlike that earlier figure, who wandered the Paris arcades satisfying his appetite for urban observation as an end in itself, the late-nineteenth-century journalists were far more concerned with pleasing their readers with extraordinary spectacles amid the "picturesque decay" of the urban ghetto.[17] Pressured by deadlines as well as by sales, late Victorian journalists were far from the leisurely perambulators of an earlier generation. In their search for novelty, these journalists, eschewing the sensationalism of George Lippard and other lurid chroniclers of the midcentury city, unveiled the nooks and crannies of the metropolis in the daylight rather than in the more mysterious gaslight as a way of presenting modernity as a curious and picturesque spectacle of wholesome amusement.

Portraying downtown in daylight also created a space for the female *flâneuse* (and for her female readers), expanding the opportunities for journalists such as Viola Roseboro, Mariana Van Rensselaer, and Alice Harrison to stroll through Little Italy, Shantytown, and Chinatown. The late-nineteenth-century journalist also possessed elements of the bohemian, the predecessor of the *flâneur,* who would walk around the less popular thoroughfares of the city rather than among the crowds on Broadway. Most important, this late-nineteenth-century urban observer transformed the amateurism of the *flâneur* and the bohemian into the professionalism of the journalist, who, like her eighteenth-century predecessor, had a sharp "eye" to find obscure visual delights in the midst of urban decay.

Gilpin described his perambulations in terms of "hunts" and "searches," and his late-nineteenth-century urban counterpart actively pursued "pictures." The teleological gaze of the picturesque traveler parallels that of the rag picker, since neither could return home empty handed. To be successful, the picturesque traveler needed an experienced eye. This prerequisite is consistently stated in the eighteenth-century formulation of the picturesque, with Gilpin insisting that the traveler should possess "an eye *learned in the art*" (62). Uvedale Price likewise claims that the traveler must know "how to separate, to select, and combine" (*Essays* 5). Where the picturesque eye "discovers a thousand interesting objects," Price continues, "a common eye sees nothing but ruts and rubbish" (qtd. Hussey 112). In *Picturesque America* (1874), William Jennings Bryan provides the American reader with similar advice: "People in search of the picturesque should understand the importance of selecting suitable points of view" (qtd. Halloran 240).

Who better to select the appropriate perspective than an experienced observer of the city, one who walks its streets with a degree of ease and familiarity that only a cosmopolitan *savant* can have? Contrary to Hamlin Garland's claim that the picturesque is exclusively the domain of the tourist, the periodical sketches suggest that the ultimate guide to the "other half" is a metropolitan insider, someone comfortable with cross-cultural encounters and knowledgeable about the city's less traversed regions.

For example, a turn-of-the-century review of Jacob Riis's *How the Other Half Lives* commended the book for its worldly perspective: "It is from beginning to end as picturesque in treatment as it is in material. The author's acquaintance with the latter is extremely intimate. The reader feels that he is being guided through the dirt and crime, the tatters and rags, the byways and alleys of nether New York by an experienced cicerone" (qtd. Gandal 61). A confident guide was the key to the picturesque's success. After all, how was one to overcome one's own anxieties about immigration and modernization with someone equally as nervous? For the picturesque to work, that is, for the reader to find pleasure in the seemingly frightening areas of the city, the dauntless manner of the picturesque traveler must put the reader at ease. At a time when advertisements in periodicals were encouraging readers to trust in a company's products, the intra-urban walking tour persuaded its readers to explore the city's immigrant ghettos with a trustworthy guide, a connoisseur rather than a weekend amateur or worse yet, a European visitor.

H. G. Wells and Paul Bourget, for instance, were rather overwhelmed by New York City, with Wells complaining about its "noise and human hurry" and Bourget describing the streets as simply a "rushing sense of the foreign." Where Wells heard noises, the cosmopolitan *savant* would hear a comprehensible variety of tongues; where Bourget saw only impressionistic blurs, the cosmopolitan found picturesque details. This preference for the insider was part of the professionalization of spectatorship, when readers were encouraged to leave the looking to the urban connoisseur. But it could be said that the picturesque was never intended for dilettantes. Richard Payne Knight defined the picturesque as a "manner of seeing" with an "eye" trained in compositional principles of landscape painting. The intra-urban walking tours provided a sort of pedagogy of spectatorship, instructing the reader how to transform the congested and impoverished districts of the metropolis into a sense of "rough and rugged pleasure."

The intra-urban walking tours, unlike conventional travel narratives about New York City, frequently strayed from the popular commercial thoroughfares of Fifth Avenue and Broadway and wandered into the more obscure side streets of lower Manhattan. Exhibiting traces of the romantic bohemian, the narrators promised to take their readers "off the beaten track" and to the areas that Dreiser called the city's "strange and unAmerican regions." From *flâneurs* like Hutchins Hapgood to *flâneuses* like Viola Roseboro and Alice Harrison, the narrator-as-guide intrepidly ventured into the out-of-the-way restaurants and shops in the immigrant quarters. Roseboro, for example, promised her readers that she would go beyond the familiar stereotype of Italians behind the "hand-organ or a fruit stall" and instead portray them in their communities along the "Crosby Street sidewalks." In *The Cosmopolitan,* Wong Chin Foo invited his readers to the least-known immigrant community, the *terra incognita* of "Little Hong Kong."

To reinforce the authenticity of this genre, in terms of both the cosmopolitanism of the guide and the local color of the immigrant quarters, the intra-urban tours typically shunned the material comforts of elevated trains, cars, and carriages; instead, the quest for the authentic required the abandonment of technology and the adoption of walking. Walking was perceived as a democratized form of travel, a form of social leveling in which the streets became a contact zone for cross-class intermingling. In a 1904 treatise on walking tours in *Harper's Weekly*, the anonymous author views walking as a way to purge "our overfed, overclothed, overeducated, glutted lives" and to see the world from the tramps' perspective ("Walking" 1382). Making the streets a site of encounter between Americans and immigrants was the aim of M. E. Ravage, a Jewish immigrant writing for *The Century*, when he addressed his readers in the second person, inviting them to leave their "cushioned vehicles": "if you would only come out of your cushioned vehicles and let me take you about a bit and give you a glimpse of the splendid things that lie beneath this crude exterior, I promise you would come away with a very much changed impression of us" (26).

Intra-urban walking tours were part of what Michael Cowan calls "a tradition of self-conscious street walking" in which walking in the American city was not taken for granted but was seen as part of a teleological narrative of national development. Direct experience of the ghetto (or at least reading about another's experience) consisted of consuming the foods of various ethnic restaurants or visiting the marketplace filled with exotic commodities, which affirmed the global centrality of the nascent world power. Walking, in other words, created the conditions for controllable cross-cultural and cross-class encounters that legitimated the new immigrants as an energizing and desirable presence within the nation.

These narratives of locodescription were highly appealing to late Victorian readers because they could indulge their desires for vitalist encounters without having to get dirty. Readers could pursue what Jackson Lears has called the "cult of experience" by reading about the walks of others. Late-nineteenth-century journalism, according to Alan Trachtenberg, provided a "surrogate experience" and actually "deepened the separations it seemed to overcome—deepened them by giving them a precise form: the form of reading and looking" (*Incorporation* 125). The tours, therefore, translated walking into a visual spectacle that domesticated the modern by reducing it to appearances. "The whole spectacle of poverty," observed William Dean Howells, "is incredible. As soon as you cease to have it before your eyes,—even when you have it before your eyes,—you can hardly believe it, and that is perhaps why so many people deny that it exists" (*Impressions* 120–121).[18] Walking suggests a comparatively intimate form of travel, in which the perambulator experiences the city along the sidewalks, face to face with alien "others." But representations of walking actually create a distance, in the double sense that the experience occurred for someone else and that reading about this experience produces a gap of signification between the signs on the page and the referential world outside.

A fundamental premise of the picturesque is that such a distance can also be comforting, and is in fact necessary in order to find "delight in ruins." Pain and danger can be terrible, according to Richard Payne Knight, when viewed too closely, but from a safe distance the same scene can be "delightful" (qtd. Hussey 81). Howells reiterates this point by noting that the "shabby avenues" of New York yield a "repulsive picturesqueness" except "at a distance" (*Impressions* 205). This distance is also produced through the synchronicity of the tours, as a series of brief and fleeting snapshots or glimpses that affirm a specular world of appearances. The picturesque relies on this sense of perambulatory distance: that getting up close and personal with the immigrant poor would paradoxically result in their remoteness. Keith Gandal's observations about Riis's *How the Other Half Lives* also pertain to the intra-urban walking tours: both oscillate "between intimacy and estrangement" (71).

The picturesque signifies an anti-commercial form of tourism, an alternative mode of commodified vision that explores the unknown, the unfamiliar, or the conventionally unseen. Much like contemporary postmodern travel packages that promise "tourist free" areas where you can pursue the authentic without running into someone else wearing Bermuda shorts and carrying a camera, the picturesque sketch represents a nineteenth-century version of anti-touristic travel.[19] But as Jonathan Culler has pointed out, the "distinction between the authentic and the inauthentic, the natural and the touristy, is a powerful semiotic operator within tourism" (131). The picturesque traveler's position as consummate insider depends on her ability to distinguish between "natives" and tourists.

In the effort to find someone more touristy than oneself, the confident manner of the cosmopolitan *savant* begins to disclose its insecure underside. In a walking tour published in *Scribner's*, the popular writer Jesse Lynch Williams condescendingly refers to the ogling of a busload of rural tourists: "real people from the real country, and their mouths are open and they don't care" (57). He then contrasts the tourist with the "typically New York" or "as New Yorkish as New York can be"—phrases he uses with authority and aplomb. Picturesque travelers legitimate their own subject position as authentic cosmopolitans through a litany of comparative signifiers. The identity politics of place are not the sole preserve of the rural native novelist. They also belong to the professional journalist, who combines the romantic bohemian's love of slumming, the midcentury *flâneur's* ease among crowds, and the picturesque traveler's discriminating eye.

Because of its emphasis on professionalism, the intra-urban walking tour is the most appropriate genre to examine when considering how the concept of the picturesque was disseminated in turn-of-the-century America. Not only was it the genre in which the actual term "picturesque" was used most frequently, but it also accrued the most authority in defining what the picturesque elements of city life were. Confined to the parameters of a distinct neighborhood or ethnic group, the walking tours did not overwhelm the reader with panoramas, but merely titillated them with brief sketches. Offering only a partial view of the city, the picturesque was an unabashedly subjective discourse, characterized by such terms as "interesting" and "charming." The power of the intra-urban walking tour came from its partiality, in terms of both its limited gaze and its predilections. What gave this partiality credibility was that it supposedly came from an urban professional. Not just anyone's opinions mattered but only the opinions of those who possessed the skill, knowledge, and confidence of the cosmopolitan expert.

This, as I will later elaborate, is precisely the tradition that Dreiser challenges not by undermining the notion of the professional guide but by expanding it to include the ultimate insider, namely the expert who lives among the poor. Before elaborating on this variation of the picturesque, it is important to explain how the commercial walking tours, which exemplify the dominant tradition of the picturesque, incorporated European immigrants as citizens by keeping them culturally and visually "different."

Spectacles of Americanization

Just as the picturesque as an aesthetic category represents a domesticated sublime in which boundlessness is converted into finitude, so the urban picturesque Americanizes foreignness through a notion of narrative incorporation. Whether it is Roseboro's study of the Italians of New York or Hapgood's account of the Lower East Side, these intra-urban walking tours invoke the picturesque as a way to tame the wildness of the "other" by inscribing foreignness within the aesthetic parameters of cultural peculiarities. By converting the exotic into a mild curiosity, the intra-urban walking tours are narratives of Americanization, in which descriptions of the foreignness of immigrants turn into discussions of their potential contributions as citizens. These narratives of incorporation, however, do not define Americanization as homogenization or, as Randolph Bourne calls it, "Anglo-Saxonising" ("Trans-National" 112). Instead, they configure Americanization in the vein of William James's "pluralistic universe," where the individuality of the each-form would be preserved within the "federal republic."

In addition to being the complement of Jamesian pluralism, the urban picturesque is the literary analogue to Bourne's "transnationalism," which imagines American national identity in terms similar to Kallen's orchestra, as a federation of distinct European cultures. "America is transplanted Europe," writes Bourne. "Its colonies live here inextricably mingled, yet not homogeneous. They merge but they do not fuse" ("Trans-National" 114). Reminiscent of Price's description of the picturesque as "blended but distinct" and Knight's notion of civil society as divided parts connected to a whole ("Divide the parts, and yet connect the whole"), Bourne's configuration of a heterogeneous union follows a similar cultural cartography, namely unity-in-distinctiveness or what Bourne calls a "side by side" union in which the parts are arranged as distinct and discreet within a national whole, an ideal that he describes as "a world-federation in miniature" ("Trans-National" 117).[20]

In order for the United States to be unified but not uniform, the immigrants would have to retain cultural markers of authenticity. The "dangerous" Jew, according to Bourne, is one who has "lost the Jewish fire," whereas the "good" Jew "sticks proudly to the faith of his fathers" ("Trans-National" 113–114). Bourne loathes immigrants who do not remain "distinct" and refers to them as "cultural half-breeds," because they compromise their authenticity by adopting the tastes of mainstream American culture. "Our cities are filled with these half-breeds who retain their foreign names but have lost the foreign savor" (113). They now attend American movies, sing popular songs, and read cheap newspapers. No longer containing the traces of the Old World, the assimilated immigrant puts the picturesque, and its larger project of a revamped American exceptionalism, into crisis. With the "half-breed" now consuming the same commercial culture that the picturesque traveler is trying to avoid (and that ironically the journalist relies on to sell sketches to national periodicals), the question arises: How can authentic otherness be conserved?

The best way to conserve the "foreign savor" of immigrants, while at the same time incorporating them within a national union, is to adopt a notion that Bourne calls "dual citizenship." This means that immigrants have to be politically and spiritually "welded" as citizens but remain culturally distinct. In the intra-urban walking tours, the urban picturesque operates as a textual sign of ethnic distinctiveness and authenticity; it reassures the reader that otherness still exists among the "poorest and dirtiest," and that it is a necessary element of modern Americanism. Within this genre, the objective of the picturesque is to perform this ideal of "dual citizenship" by converting urban denizens into national citizens without sacrificing the cultural particularity of the immigrant group. Viola Roseboro's "Italians in New York" (1888) illustrates the possibility of "dual citizenship" by representing the Italians as both "picturesque foreigners" and good potential "citizens."

Roseboro's tour begins on Crosby Street, the heart of the downtown "colony," which is described as an "uncommonly foreign-looking" street because of "its narrowness, together with the height of its big gloomy tenements" (396). But Roseboro soon admits that the street is "rather attractive," largely owing to the fact that the "inhabitants return to their native habits" in the hot summer months of New York and "camp out in domestic platoons on the sidewalk." The tour finds much "picturesqueness" in the costumes and customs of the ghetto: the "big gold rings in their ears regardless of sex," the women's "flatly braided hair," and the peasant "head-dress" of a linen bonnet that is "so charmingly becoming to their dark faces" (396). This catalog of cultural peculiarities represents an index of their authenticity: they are "good" immigrants rather than assimilated "half-breeds."

The picturesque descriptions of Italian peculiarities are presented as a series of "pictures" that attempt to preserve these cultural distinctions by freezing them in time. Just as the *flâneur,* according to Walter Benjamin, establishes *tableaux vivants* from the fleeting moments around him, so the urban picturesque traveler stalls the gradual loss of "foreign savor" by arranging the immigrants into various still postures. During one of her tours to Crosby Street, Roseboro "saw one not-to-be-forgotten little picture," which she describes to the reader: "It was a woman, a beautiful young woman, with a beautiful child upon her arm, and her dark, coarse shawl drawn over her own head and the child's, and around him, achieving one of those mysteriously simple and artistic effects that semi-barbarians, and they only, seem able to master. 'Picturesque' and 'charming' and 'artistic' are words apt to be badly overworked in writing about the Italians" (390).

Roseboro, in apologizing for using such a hackneyed word, demonstrates a familiar anxiety surrounding the picturesque: that it is both a sign of particularity and a representational cliché. It signifies the liminal space between distinctiveness and stereotype, between specificity and generality. But the overuse of the term has the advantage of naturalizing the Italians' presence: their association with the city becomes as expected as the word "picturesque" is to describe them. Yet in an attempt not to make their presence too ordinary, Roseboro has to depict them as moderately exotic. Exemplifying the residual meaning of the picturesque as the "half-way station" between the sublime and the beautiful, Roseboro refers to the Italians, and particularly the image of mother and child, as "mysteriously simple" rather than "mysteriously" enigmatic or complex, and in terms of "semi-barbarians" rather than complete primitives.

Furthermore, Roseboro inscribes the mother and child within a familiar image of Catholic iconography. At the turn of the century there was a growing enthusiasm for the premodern, and specifically Catholic *objet d'art*—as emblematic of ritual and sacrament in the midst of an increasingly secular culture. Walking tours such as this one, which attempted to incorporate the Italians within a modern and revised notion of Americanism, also contained elements of antimodernism, which Jackson Lears has described as a "taste for the exotic, a desire to preserve the old," which could coexist with "a zeal for industrial growth" (*No Place* 187). But there is also a more generous reading of this "picture," which underscores the positive attributes of being cast as premodern. By inscribing the impoverished Italian mother and child within the topos of classical Renaissance painting, Roseboro converts the profane into the sacred. As an example of "devotional seeing," with painting rather than literature as the referential medium, the urban picturesque sanctifies the poorest of Mulberry Bend, by enshrining Catholic mothers as signs of inviolability in the midst of slum life.

Another way in which Roseboro presents the Italians as picturesque immigrants and safe potential citizens is by emphasizing their indifference toward labor unions: a defensive move in a post-Haymarket climate that associated immigrants with radicalism.[21] "The Italians are generally, and so far remarkably, little influenced by our labor agitations" (399). The subtext of this picturesque tour is an attack on "organized labor," and against the dangerous immigrant who is actively involved in the "labor question" (403). Just as the religious imagery elevates the Italians above the everyday struggles for survival, so this second use of the picturesque further removes them from the larger tensions and conflicts of the city. The Italians, for Roseboro, are "delightfully picturesque" not only because the women wear "bonnets" but also because the men and women are "indifferent to politics." As citizens, their contribution to the nation will be in terms of culture, in sharing with the nation their "artistic instinct" (404). By marking the Italians as picturesque, this tour incorporates their presence within a national public culture on specific terms: that they add a degree of local color without challenging the structures of class differentiation. They can be included within the national orchestra, to use Kallen's metaphor, as long as they stay in their place.

Whereas the picturesque operates in Roseboro's tour as a way to make the Italians less threatening through their political indifference, it works in Hutchins Hapgood's "A Picturesque Ghetto" as a way to make the socialism of the Jewish immigrants benign. In both instances, the picturesque is a way to depoliticize immigrant communities and to reduce the inhabitants to specular oddities rather than active agents. This sketch, which was published in the *Century Magazine* in 1917 though based on material written at the turn of the century, employs the familiar language of comparison to define the Jewish ghetto as "richer than any other" (471). The picturesque is synonymous with the rhetoric of subcultural exceptionalism, in which the traveler is on an endless quest to find the "most interesting" immigrant quarters. Like Bourne's transnationalism, in which subcultural uniqueness reinforces cosmopolitan supremacy, the ghetto, we are told, is a metaphor of New York, since both embody "infinite variety," "vitality," and "picturesqueness" (471). The "picturesqueness" of the ghetto emerges from Hapgood's unequivocal admiration and fondness of this world within a world, qualities that contrast with Henry James's far more hesitant (and therefore less picturesque) response to the Jewish ghetto in *The American Scene* as a "phantasmagoric" place, "swarming" with an "ant-like population" (101, 102).[22]

For Hapgood, the "picturesque" attribute of the Jewish immigrant can be found in the conflict between the "old culture" and "new ideas." What emerge from this clash between residual habits and new ideas are "Socialistic difficulties," which seem out of place in "American conditions" (472). Hapgood expounds upon this point about residual socialism in his urban sketches, which were later collected and published as *The Spirit of the Ghetto*. He refers to the "Intellectuals of the Ghetto" as its "most picturesque and interesting" element (39). The entire book is a study of this intellectual community, which consists of anarchists, socialists, editors, and writers. In assessing the significance of socialism among Jewish immigrant intellectuals, Hapgood notes that "socialism is not a permanently nutritive element in the life of the Ghetto, for as yet the Ghetto has not learned to know the conditions necessary to American life, and can not, therefore, effectively react against them" (39).

What is considered most dangerous—immigrant radical politics—is a source of "picturesque" pleasure. For Hapgood, Jewish "socialism" is a residual mode of thought that only serves to make coffeehouse discussions more engaging. Jacob Epstein's accompanying illustrations reinforce this point by depicting the intellectual socialists in passionate debate in cafés rather than on picket lines (Figure 2). Though the tours include various scenes of immigrants, few portray them working. They may be walking home from work but they are rarely at work. Rather they are portrayed as consumers: drinking a cup of coffee, buying a newspaper, or shopping at the market. The picturesque is used to take the sting out of subcultural dissent by reducing opposition to a sign of cultural uniqueness. Hapgood's and Roseboro's intra-urban tours incorporate Southern and Eastern European immigrants into the American scene by framing them as mainly producers and consumers of a distinct European subculture. Socialism is to Jewish immigrants what "bonnets" are to Italian women: a quaint and charming indicator of cultural authenticity, which poses no real threat to the cosmopolitan nation.

Depoliticizing immigrants was the price of the ticket for their admis-

2. "A Political Discussion at the 'Independent Café' on Grand Street," by Jacob Epstein

sion into a transnational America. On the one hand, the urban picturesque signified an altruistic aesthetic: it expanded the bounds of representation to include "the lowest races of Europe" within a modernized notion of American nationalism. On the other hand, the urban picturesque included these newcomers only on certain terms. First, immigrant cultures had to be depicted as premodern, as the cultural relics of an earlier time that existed within the belly of the beast of modernity. Second, the new immigrants were portrayed primarily as icons of culture rather than of work. Culture was bracketed off from politics and reduced to an assortment of images ranging from lighting the Sabbath candles to rag picking in Little Italy. Like the gypsies and beggar girls of eighteenth-century landscape painting, the immigrants of the late nineteenth century were used to provide an ornamented surface for the urbanscape. They decorated the street scenes of Mulberry Bend and Hester Street with a hint of local color that reassured readers that modernization did not necessarily mean either cultural insipidity or political revolution.

This embrace of European immigrants as the distinctive feature of U.S. modernity was indicative of emergent attitudes toward urbanization. Rather than posing a threat to a national identity, ethnic difference now constituted a necessary element in the modern revision of Americanism. A national mythology shifted from the country to the city, from the yeoman ideal to a cosmopolitan one, and the immigrant became an icon of modernity, expressive of the mobility and transience of the new age. New York was seen as the modern city, with its diverse culture of dislocation considered to be the most indicative of a national spirit rather than its aberration. "This city has always been an open door to foreign immigrants," wrote the New York *Sun* reporter Julian Ralph in 1891, "and lately it has been their principal gateway. A few always linger here at the threshold of the New World, and, being thrown together again, establish so-called colonies or foreign quarters. Therefore we have the Bowery as it is. It does not offer any new problem or confront us with an unfamiliar condition." David Graham Phillips, a journalist and later a novelist, similarly wrote of the Bowery that it was "the true cosmopolitan thoroughfare of New York": "a bit of gay color from South Italy here, the wooden shoes and yarn stockings of a German peasant girl there, a fez from Turkey or Arabia, a coat from China."[23]

The emergent discourse of the urban picturesque was neither the exclusive nor the dominant mode of representing the metropolis. It existed alongside competing aesthetic discourses, such as Joaquin Miller's sensationalist exposés, in laying claim to the national. The urban picturesque was also part of a much larger trend at the turn of the century to naturalize and nationalize the city as quintessentially American, as the fullest expression of its internal diversity. Alongside an older tradition of anti-urbanism, which underscored in gothic fashion the sublime terror of the city, the urban picturesque turned yesterday's fears into modern pleasures. The extent to which the United States is now primarily identified by its metropolitan centers reveals the success as well as the predominance of this once emergent perspective.

Dreiser and the Spectacle of Extremes

The urban picturesque, as I have been underlining, was a way to naturalize both swarthy immigrants and poverty as expected elements of modernity. The discourse of the picturesque also went beyond the explicit use of the term in mainstream intra-urban walking tours. I include Theodore Dreiser because his urban sketches of New York expand the conventional uses of the picturesque by showing that it represents a general mode of perception not confined to explicit terminology or to a specific genre. In the late 1890s Dreiser explicitly uses the term "picturesque" to refer to conventional rural settings, such as Brandywine, Pennsylvania, the historic site of a Revolutionary War battle. But in his urban sketches of New York, written in the 1890s and later collected and published as *The Color of a Great City* (1923), he uses a picturesque mode of apprehending urban experience in capturing the positive energies and associations of metropolitan life through the more general language of "variety" and "color." His field of vision elaborates this process of naturalizing ethnicity and poverty as intrinsic elements of modernity. Dreiser's urban sketches, therefore, demonstrate the prevalence of the picturesque, its expansiveness as an aesthetic mode that exceeds its explicit uses. Furthermore, his sketches disclose the material conditions required for this metropolitan spectacle. More than either Roseboro or Hapgood, Dreiser unabashedly celebrates the economic and ethnic extremes of city life as necessary qualities of visual pleasure.

Dreiser's interest in creating "brief pictures" of city life initially attracted him to a career in journalism and eventually to fiction writing. For Dreiser, Stephen Crane, and a host of others, the urban sketch, in particular, was influential in the development of late-nineteenth-century realism. Dreiser begins his autobiography, *Newspaper Days,* by acknowledging the central role that the sketch had in his early experiences as a writer. Inspired by Eugene Field, the dean of American journalism, Dreiser appreciated Field's sketches of Chicago life at a time when the genre mainly depicted European scenes and people. Dreiser credited Field with Americanizing the genre by focusing on the everyday spectacles and ordinary figures that populate the American urban scene. When Dreiser arrived in New York in 1894, he was determined to bring Field's flair to his own sketches of the metropolis. He thought the plethora of sketches that filled the pages of New York newspapers and magazines were far too dull and predictable, representing just "practical accounts" with no suggestion of "the color, the emotion, the sorrow, the rage" (*Color* 274). Dreiser introduced an aesthetics of affect to the urban sketch, with his "brief pictures" combining literary and journalistic writing, observation and emotion, and rich and poor people into a dramatic spectacle that depicted the contrasts and variations of city life.

Despite his attempt to transform the genre, Dreiser's descriptions of New York often use the same celebratory rhetoric of the picturesque found in the intra-urban walking tours. In a tone of exhilaration, Dreiser exclaims: "The glory of the city is its variety. The drama of it lies in its extremes" (*Color* 156). Economic disparity is the precondition for the city's variety, a necessary evil that produces a glorious "drama." At this point, the emphasis is on variety rather than class divisions; economic extremes are a means to an aesthetic end and not the subject of reflection. The rhetoric of variety is at its most unequivocal when describing the ethnic diversity of Manhattan, with its "varied and foreign groups": "Bucharest and Lemberg and Odessa come to the Bowery, and add rich, dark, colorful threads to the rug or tapestry which is New York" (*Color* 6).[24] He then spatializes this "colorful" tapestry according to distinct neighborhoods, reminiscent of Jacob Riis's color-coded map of New York that he likened to the stripes of a zebra: "the Irish in the lower East and West Sides; the Syrians in Washington Street, a great mass of them; the Greeks around 26th, 27th and 28th Streets on the West Side; the Italians around Mulberry Bend; the Bohemians in East 67th Street, and the Sicilians in East 116 St. and thereabouts. The Jews are chiefly on the East Side" (*Color* vii-viii). Absent from Dreiser's map are African Americans, a population that Riis describes in more substantial detail. Similar to the picturesque tradition of the intra-urban walking tours, Dreiser includes a spectrum of hues that stops at blackness. African Americans represent the suppressed term of his urban sketches, the "dark" thread not visible in the otherwise "colorful" tapestry.

Dreiser does, however, break with the genre of the intra-urban walking tour in two respects. First, he outdoes the professional journalist since he not only knows the hidden nooks and corners of the other half but actually lives there. Far more than the professional intra-urban tours, Dreiser's sketches, which frequently appeared in the same periodicals such as *Harper's* and *McClure's,* possess the flavor of the romantic bohemian, who lives among the very people about whom he writes. In the highly competitive world of journalism in the 1890s, new reporters had to distinguish themselves to catch the editor's attention. This led to stylistic innovations, such as Dreiser's strategy of self-authentication: that he was "tramping with the tramps" (to borrow the title of Josiah Flynt's 1899 book) to provide his readers with an inside glimpse of the everyday occurrences in lower Manhattan.

Dreiser turned his own economic misfortune when he first arrived in New York in the mid-1890s into a productive source of literary creativity by the end of the decade.[25] He was the city's native informant, not as a stylish New Yorker but as the urban bohemian, the perambulator who could blend in with the working people and even with the tramps of the Bowery. F. O. Matthiessen, one of Dreiser's earliest biographers, considered him an "insider" of urban poverty (in contrast to Crane, whose *Maggie* he deemed the work of an "outsider"; 91–92).[26] Dreiser shared in this sense of his own insiderism when he accused William Dean Howells in a 1900 interview entitled "The Real Howells" of being too detached from the poor by being overly committed to "literary" rather than to "direct experience."

It was precisely Dreiser's claim to "direct experience" that gave him a degree of literary clout as an author. In writing about Hell's Kitchen and the Bowery, he explained that his ability to mingle with the poor was the result of his own experiences of living in the slums, in "the shabbiest, most forlorn neighborhoods which the great metropolis affords." At one point during the winter of 1894–1895, he wandered the streets of New York sleeping in flophouses (Lingeman 162). To distinguish himself from the uptown slumming parties (which were in their heyday during the 1890s), Dreiser flaunted his contact with the poor as a sign of his own authenticity, as a badge of courage that legitimated him to write about these districts. He epitomized Garland's native novelist: only one who lives in the slums can write about them.

In 1899 Dreiser wrote a sketch about Hell's Kitchen, not as a sensationalist voyeur, a stance that typified most journalistic accounts of this area, but as an insider who once lived there. His decision to move to this "region" was supposedly made out of choice rather than necessity: "Interested in the stark pictures of slum life so often painted, I finally went to reside there for a period" (*Color* 184). This illustrates a form of "devotional seeing" extended to the level of action: Dreiser has already imagined the slums before actually living in them. His reference point is not literature but a visual aesthetic, which demonstrates the growing alliance between newspaper journalists and illustrators. Some of Dreiser's closest friends in the 1890s were in fact illustrators, figures like William Glackens, George Luks, and John Sloan, who eventually founded the Ashcan School.

The second way in which Dreiser's sketches depart from the conventional use of the picturesque in the intra-urban walking tour is that they represent labor strife or individual moments of exploitation. Though Dreiser abides by the same racial parameters of the urban picturesque—finding its limit with swarthiness—he does depict that which the urban picturesque conventionally disavowed. In "The Sandwich Man," Dreiser integrates affect into the depiction of the human billboards who walk the streets of New York advertising the consumer goods that they themselves cannot afford. In contrast to the walking tours, whose subjectivist discourse merely extends to what is "interesting," Dreiser speaks explicitly about feelings and pathos. The sketch begins: "I would not feel myself justified mentally if at some time or other I had not paused in thought over the picture of the sandwich man. These shabby figures of decayed or broken manhood, how they have always appealed to me" (*Color* 260).

Dreiser employs the conventional markers of the picturesque, framing a fleeting moment of city life in terms of a "picture" that includes a degree of "decay." But unlike Roseboro's "picture" of the Italian immigrant mother and child, which is removed from the everyday streets of Mulberry Bend and sanctified as "classical" art, Dreiser's "picture" of penury focuses on the material conditions of the individual sandwich man, starting with a description of his actual body which is "cold, red, and often wet" (*Color* 261). Dreiser's materialist approach implicates a system of "overproduction," which he describes through the irony of the "perambulating packhorse of an advertisement" inviting others to buy when he has "but life enough to walk" (*Color* 260). The sandwich man ironically advertises a pair of shoes when he has none to wear; he publicizes a sale on winter coats when his body is exposed to snow. These are the "extreme" contrasts that characterize the spectacle of modern variety.

In his sentimental and maudlin prose, Dreiser describes the disparities and misery of the city, but he never actually relinquishes the picturesque mode of seeing. The extremes of urban life are ultimately part of a Darwinian struggle for existence performed daily on the metropolitan sidewalks. In 1896 he recommends that people should not simply read about "this world of struggle and discontent" but should go "into the places where misery gathers and "do something for them" ("Reflections" 81). Writing about the bathos and misery of this struggle is for Dreiser a source of activism. This is his way of doing "something for them." But it is also a way for Dreiser to naturalize class conflict as part of the modern experience by elevating it to the level of a Manichean struggle: "Weakness confronts strength, poverty wealth, health sickness, courage cowardice, fortune the very depths of misfortune, and they know each other not—or defy each other" (*Color* 169). In 1900 Dreiser self-righteously accuses Howells of providing no "theory of improvement." Howells merely "watches the changeful scene, rejoices or laments over the various and separate instances, but goes no further" ("Real Howells" 102). But one must ask whether Dreiser accuses Howells of the very specular approach that he himself adopts, namely presenting his reader with a series of "pictures" and then going no further.

This absence of a "theory of improvement" becomes most apparent in Dreiser's 1923 introduction to *The Color of a Great City*, in which he bemoans the appearance of social services to alleviate poverty in the ghettos. Now the East Side is (regretfully) "beschooled and beserviced." As a result of the progressivist reforms that began at the turn of the century, the dramatic extremes so necessary for a vitalist encounter with modern life have to some extent been mitigated. The postwar city has become "duller because [it is] less differentiated" (*Color* vi). New York "was more varied and arresting and, after its fashion, poetic and even idealistic then than it is now" (v). The New York of the 1920s is "commonplace and almost [a] bread and butter world" (v). The urban picturesque in *The Color of a Great City* figures as an elegy for the prewar New York of 1900–1914. Dreiser never rejects the picturesque mode of representing New York in terms of extremes, perhaps because the opposite of extremism, namely moderation, bores him: "a strictly median condition [is] never wholly or easily attained in life, and never, apparently, seriously desired by it, as an end in itself, and never quite satisfactory" (*Hey* 210). Disparities are disturbing, yet inevitable (and aesthetically necessary). After all, "Nature adores extremes" (*Hey* 211).

Chinatown and the Racial Limits of Variety

Despite Dreiser's fondness for extremes, his sketches ultimately reinforce the racial limit of swarthiness by rendering blackness invisible. There is, however, one type of intra-urban walking tour that does attempt to expand the racial boundaries to include not just European ethnicities but also the Chinese. The urban picturesque, in other words, provides a cultural index of how larger questions about the boundaries between ethnicity and race were negotiated. In the late nineteenth century, the most contested site for negotiating this boundary was Chinatown. Attitudes toward Chinese exclusion, for example, are revealed through the aesthetic terminology used to describe these subcultural communities. The flexibility and variousness of the picturesque, the very qualities that Uvedale Price embraced (and associated with white people's hair), find their racial and ideological limit in determining whether the Chinese qualify as a picturesque immigrant group. This is the point, moreover, at which intra-urban travelers display their true colors. As an aesthetic analogue to the Chinese exclusion acts that began in 1882, the picturesque, for some urban travelers, stops at Mott Street. For Jacob Riis, the Chinese epitomize the anti-picturesque because "Mott Street is clean to distraction" (77). Contrasting the Chinese to the nearby Italians, Riis concludes: "Chinatown as a spectacle is disappointing. Next-door neighbor to the Bend, it has little of its outdoor stir and life, none of its gaily-colored rags or picturesque filth and poverty" (77).

The picturesque was a highly comparative discourse, in which hierarchies were established among immigrant groups according to individual preferences. The prevalence or absence of such conventional picturesque markers as "filth," colorful rags, and crowded streets determined whether the Chinese were considered a legitimate presence in the late Victorian urbanscape. While writers such as Sui Sin Far, a Eurasian immigrant from Britain, describe the streets of Chinatown as lively and crowded, full of a motley assortment of pedestrians, Riis's Chinatown is bereft of street life, a point visually reinforced by the accompanying photograph of a lone Chinese man walking toward the camera along an empty street. As an urban semiotician, Riis interprets this solitary scene as itself a sign of the "stealth and secretiveness" of Chinese culture (78).

Compare Riis's depiction of Chinatown with that of Wong Chin Foo, a U.S.-educated Chinese immigrant who was among the first to use the term "Chinese American." Wong, a journalist, social worker, and civil rights leader, organized a political association in the aftermath of the Geary Law called the Chinese Equal Rights League, which initiated the drive to demand citizenship for the Chinese.[27] A political exile from China, Wong was an important interlocutor who wrote for the New York Chinese immigrant press as well as for mainstream periodicals. As Qingsong Zhang has argued in "The Origins of the Chinese Americanization Movement," Wong launched an internal critique in the *Chinese American (Hua Mei Xin Bao)*, trying to eliminate opium smoking, prostitution, and gambling, while in the mainstream media he attempted to counter negative racial stereotypes with more positive depictions.[28]

In his intra-urban tour "The Chinese in New York," which appeared in *The Cosmopolitan* in 1888, Wong represents the ideal subcultural *savant*, the "native informant" who is prepared to guide the late Victorian reader through this unfamiliar district. Working within the picturesque convention, he begins the tour by accentuating the uniqueness of his particular subculture. "Every one knows the French, German, and Irish districts," but the "most interesting of all to Americans" is New York's "Little Hong Kong" because it represents the "exact antipodes of this continent" (25). At first, Chinatown suggests an urban frontier, an antitouristic tourist zone where only the adventurous go. But as the narrative develops, its initial sensationalism is replaced with a tone of ordinariness. The narrative does not visit forbidden places, as slumming narratives frequently do. It portrays the everyday sites of Chinatown, ranging from restaurants to markets, in an attempt to demystify the Chinese presence in the city.

While less sympathetic and sensational depictions focus primarily on the opium dens, this tour depicts the occasional man smoking opium, but it is far more interested in the preparation and consumption of food (Figure 3). The sketch even provides a glossary acquainting the reader with translations of common menu items. The glossary is an apt metaphor for understanding the role of Wong: he is a cultural mediator who translates "foreignness" into familiarity, and in doing so, incorporates Chinese culture within the day-to-day rhythms of the American metropolis. Although the term "picturesque" is not explicitly used, the sketch nonetheless follows the picturesque formula in combining foreignness

3. "A Chinese Kitchen," by J. Durkin

with citizenship, portraying the immigrant as sufficiently peculiar to be interesting but also familiar enough to be nonthreatening. As a narrative of Americanization, Wong's sketch refers to what the Chinese can contribute to a national culture: they are hard-working, "well-educated people" who write poetry and maxims and are "very clean in their cooking." In addition, Chinese men make ideal husbands for white ethnic women, often marrying "Irish, German or Italian wives." Most important, the Chinese husband "never beats his wife, [and] gives her plenty to eat and wear" (308). Wong also notes that there are over a hundred Eurasian children in New York (308). Whereas miscegenation was usually a source of concern (resulting in a ban in California), Wong reassures the New York reader that Chinese "children speak the English language, adopt the American ways and dress" (308).[29]

Although Wong's intra-urban tour Americanizes the Chinese through the common ground of food and family, it also seeks to retain a degree of local color, a picturesque element of distinctiveness: "they can not be expected to give up . . . peculiar peculiarities" (311). His notion of Americanization anticipates Kallen's: citizenship marks the ground of commonality, whereas culture is the point of differentiation. Chinese immigrants should not become mimetic reproductions of Euro-Americans, but should retain their distinctiveness, primarily in the realm of religious belief. In a gesture reminiscent of Bourne's contempt for the Americanized foreigner, Wong abruptly interrupts the tour with the following caveat: "So long as a Chinaman continues a heathen he is generally honest; but look out for him when he once becomes 'converted'" (299). This admonishing tone seems more characteristic of the picturesque traveler. But Wong's narrative demonstrates that the desire for distinctiveness was shared by the cosmopolitan Euro-American and immigrant alike. A "sense of specialness," to borrow Trinh T. Minh-ha's phrase, was also cultivated within the subculture (Trinh 86). Specialness and authenticity, however, signify differently for Wong than they do for Bourne, the latter finding authenticity a sign of modernist resistance against uniformity. For Wong, the retention of certain "peculiarities" is a political move against assimilation, directed specifically at Christian missionaries.

In contrast to most Americanized Chinese at the turn of the century, Wong refused to convert to Christianity. As a child growing up in China, he had been highly influenced by Christian missionaries (and as Zhang points out, his education in the United States was sponsored by Christian missionaries), but as an adult, exposed to the sinophobia of the United States, he was struck by the breach between "brotherly love" and racial violence. In "Why Am I a Heathen?" published in the *North American Review* in 1887, he portrayed the variety of Christian sects as bewildering, with "each one claiming a monopoly of the only and narrow road to heaven" (169–170). He also said that the primary teachings of Christianity had already been stated by Chinese philosophers such as Confucius.

Wong embodies the very ideal of Americanization that he promotes: that national citizenship and subcultural membership are not conflicting alliances. Equal rights (sameness regardless of race) and subcultural difference are ultimately commensurable. Food and family link the public and private spheres in two ways: first, they demystify the "otherness" of the Chinese in order to claim that political rights must be multicultural; second, they demonstrate that the private sphere of domesticity (whether in the home or in the Chinatown restaurants) is already multicultural. In his intra-urban tour in *The Cosmopolitan,* Wong illustrates this through his discussion of intermarriage and Eurasian children, in which the home is already a site of racial and cultural blending. He also underscores this point of cultural intermingling through descriptions of the interiors of Chinese restaurants. We are told, for example, that "at least five hundred Americans take their meals regularly in Chinese restaurants in orthodox Chinese fashion, with chopsticks" (305). Chinese restaurants are already heterogeneous spaces where the American consumer is not a unique presence but a regular one. Wong uses the picturesque convention in his intra-urban tour to translate the racial sublime into a charming curiosity. Chinatown is not a homogeneous space of hermetic otherness, but a lively and heterogeneous site of culinary (read: innocent) encounters.

The urban picturesque also extended beyond the parameters of New York City to refer to the Chinatowns of other American cities.[30] Alice Harrison, a *flâneuse*-journalist, published a walking tour of San Francisco's Chinatown for the *Overland Monthly,* a journal formerly edited by Bret Harte and the original forum for his poem "The Heathen Chinee." Whereas Harte's poem helped crystallize sinophobia in the 1870s, Harrison, writing a generation later, explicitly invokes the language of the picturesque to cultivate sympathy for this maligned community. Chinese culture is synonymous with gastronomical excess, variety, and abundance. In contrast to Riis's emphasis on scarcity, secrecy, and solitude, Harrison underscores the "astonishing variety" of fruits in the markets as well as the "bilious pyramid of yellow-green cakes of bean cheese" and "every variety of fish known to the coast waters." Contrary to Frank Norris's "The Third Circle," which portrays the horrors of reversed assimilation when an East Coast middle-class woman visits San Francisco's Chinatown only to be kidnapped and made into an opium addict, Harrison reassures the "fair lady" that the "stoic silence" of the Chinese is not from the concealment of vile thoughts but a sign that the "epicure [is] serenely full."

As a way to "humanize" the Chinese, which can be interpreted as a mode of "residual resistance" against the Geary Law, Harrison and Wong use the intra-urban tour to focus on those public places conventionally associated with the domestic: restaurants, markets, and kitchens. Whereas Riis perceives Chinese culture as impenetrable and indecipherable, Harrison's and Wong's tours disclose its busy exteriors and interiors. Food and the picturesque sites of its distribution, preparation, and consumption provide the basis for the Chinese immigrant's inclusion within a transnational America.

Food and the (Anti)-Picturesque

That the picturesque and immigrant foods should so frequently intersect in the intra-urban walking tours is not surprising. Both provide a way of talking about cultural variety in ways that are pleasurable and non-threatening. Chop suey, which was a culinary fad among the cosmopolitan youth in the 1890s, was far more palatable to the middle-class reader than a discussion about sinophobia, labor union harassment, and the massacre at Rock Springs.[31] The urban picturesque and food worked in tandem to define the limits of American cosmopolitanism. This is no better seen than in a series of articles that John Gilmer Speed wrote in 1900 for *Harper's Weekly*. A regular contributor to the magazine, Speed is a pivotal figure in turn-of-the-century configurations of food, the picturesque, and cosmopolitanism, because he employs the "food question" to celebrate the diversity of New York as well as to explore the limits of that diversity. In "Food and Foreigners in New York," which was published in the magazine's "Imperialism" issue, Speed finds New York to be a microcosm of the world: "we cross two whole continents within three minutes, from Italy to China, Rome to Canton" (847). In contrast to the "sameness" of the European diet, the "varied and abundant food-supply" of New York makes the metropolis "immensely cosmopolitan." To eat in New York is to take a "pilgrimage of the world." Food also protects the cultural distinctiveness of New York's "diversity of types": "the food products of every other country [are] available to a variety of palates, these racial dissimilarities are maintained and encouraged rather than diminished" (846). Anticipating at one level Bourne's transnationalism, Speed assures his readers that the "diversity exists and will exist for generations."

Speed's celebration of metropolitan exceptionalism changes into a somber discussion in an article published three months later, entitled "The Negro in New York." In response to the New York race riots of August 1900, Speed speaks of African Americans and food, not in terms of consumption but rather in terms of labor.[32] The language of diversity disappears entirely as he launches a critique of racist labor practices within the food service industry. Much like Dr. Olney in Howells's *An Imperative Duty,* who returns to Boston to find that the African-American waiters have been replaced by Irish immigrants, Speed observes that the "trade of waiting, as far as the negroes are concerned, has practically died out in New York." Pointing out that black waiters have been replaced by the "new immigrants," he nostalgically recalls the famous black caterers and restaurateurs of a previous generation, who "ranked as Sherry's and Delmonico's do now." While the "food question" was originally a positive trope to describe the multiculturalism of New York, it is now a divisive and loaded term that is more closely associated with racial discrimination. His two articles in this series demonstrate that the flexibility of the picturesque can embrace immigrant unity, but cannot provide an adequate language for discussing the marginalization of black labor.

Seven years later the African-American activist and writer Mary Church Terrell also examined the juncture of food, race, and cosmopolitanism in her autobiographical sketch "What It Means to Be Colored in the Capital of the United States." Originally published in the progressive magazine *The Independent* in 1907 and later included in her autobiography *A Colored Woman in a White World* (1940), this narrative uses the genre of the intra-urban walking tour to create a counter-tour that underscores the racial limits of the picturesque. In contrast to Speed, who speaks of blacks as erstwhile waiters, as laborers rather than consumers, Terrell is a well-to-do consumer who walks not out of choice, a prerequisite for the *flâneur*, but out of necessity as she searches for admission into a Washington, D.C., restaurant and hotel for the evening. The daughter of a wealthy Memphis real estate dealer and educated at Oberlin, Terrell became the first president of the National Association of Colored Women and a member of the Washington Board of Education. Married to Robert Terrell, the first African-American graduate of Harvard College and eventually a magistrate in the District of Columbia, Mary Terrell was one of the few black women to win recognition in both the white and black worlds during her lifetime. Generally considered to be "middle-of-the-roaders," both she and her husband epitomized talented-tenth leadership in the early twentieth century (Meier 183).

Terrell's narrative describes walking in terms of "wandering about" like "a stranger in a strange land." But unlike Georg Simmel's notion of the stranger as a "potential wanderer" who willfully perambulates, Terrell must wander the public spaces involuntarily, since she is unable to find private interiors that will accommodate her: "As a colored woman I might enter Washington any night . . . and walk miles without finding a place to lay my head . . . [or] without finding a single restaurant in which I would be permitted to take a morsel of food" (379).[33] In contrast to the picturesque traveler, Terrell narrates not where she goes but where she cannot go, naming places and restaurants that exclude blacks. Whereas Hapgood and Roseboro, among others, walk in and out of various eateries and coffeehouses, Terrell experiences the public space of the street far differently, as an internal exile rather than a curious traveler. For her, the limits of perambulation implicitly circumscribe the picturesque, so that she describes urban spaces not as "colorful" but as "colored."

Terrell's counter-walking tour illustrates how the whiteness of middle-class Washington establishments produces her blackness, making her a stranger in a place, a denizen rather than a citizen within, ironically, the nation's capital. It narrates, moreover, her de-Americanization. Yet Terrell's walking tour demonstrates not only the racialization of urban space and the subsequent production of difference but also the racialization of consumption. Like walking, consuming is a racialized activity, especially for the emergent black middle class, who have the money but cannot spend it. Although Terrell is "abundantly supplied with money," she is still barred from purchasing a meal. The democratization of money, heralded by Simmel among others as the "great leveller," finds its point of exclusion with the black consumer. "Indians, Chinamen, Filipinos, Japanese and representatives of any other dark race," writes Terrell, "can find hotel accommodations, if they can pay for them. The colored man alone is thrust out of the hotels of the national capital like a leper" (379).

For the African American walking in the city, "unassimilated otherness" was not a position of curiosity and pleasure but rather a mode of social and cultural exclusion. Urban spaces contain silences, which become articulate only when, for example, Terrell runs across a "chance acquaintance" who recommends a black boardinghouse in the black part of town. She can only eat when she "knows her place," when there is a one-to-one correlation between black people and black spaces. Mapping distinct people onto discrete spaces is the basis of segregation, which reveals the disturbing underside of Kallen's orchestra and Bourne's transnationalism. Whereas Bourne considered a "side by side" union to be potentially "peaceful," Mary Church Terrell devoted much of her life to challenging the exclusive racial and spatial politics of such unions.[34] Her counter-tour discloses the borders of the urban picturesque, namely the juncture of class and race. Just as she is unable to be a consumer in the material sense, a prerequisite for the traveler, so she is also unable to consume at a visual level. Her blackness further precludes her from being either the object of the picturesque gaze or the actual figure of the traveler. As a result, her narrative delineates the ideological limits of the rhetoric of variety, since scarcity rather than abundance characterizes her relation to the city.

The "Transnational Imaginary" and U.S. Exceptionalism

In contrast to the model of scarcity that shapes black relations to the city, even for wealthy African Americans such as Terrell, an attitude of abundance characterizes the relation between the urban picturesque and Eastern and Southern European immigrants. In 1897 Joseph Senner, an official at Ellis Island, claimed that "immigration is welcomed with open arms" as long as there is "an abundance to divide" among newcomers and the "older settler" (1–2). The representational generosity of the urban picturesque toward these newcomers is premised on the assumption that there is plenty to go around. As both a source and a sign of American abundance, the urban picturesque incorporated Europe's swarthier hues into a national narrative of American exceptionalism.

The cosmopolitan practitioners of the urban picturesque participated in this process of Americanization by translating the process of transnational migration into a distinctively American metropolitan phenomenon. The urban picturesque represents what Rob Wilson and Wimal Dissanayake have called in a different context the "transnational imaginary," the process by which the practices of everyday life are shaped and reshaped through a "spatial dialectic" of local and transnational forces. Whereas Wilson and Dissanayake use this term to refer to the de-nationalization of local spaces within a world that is becoming increasingly "borderless" (2), the early-twentieth-century practitioners of the urban picturesque viewed a transnational imaginary as a distinctively national project, as a way of inscribing a global process within the borders of the American metropolis.[35]

As an aesthetic practice located within a much wider project of material and ideological modernization, the urban picturesque nationalized the transnational as a sign of American uniqueness. George Yúdice has called this tendency to universalize American diversity the "we are the world complex." Such a mindset, Yúdice argues, disavows class antagonism, social problems, and economic disparity in order to celebrate American diversity. Yet this "we are the world" attitude is not unique to the contemporary moment. It also characterizes the modern period, as a way to reconfigure American nationalism at a time of internal and international migration, labor strife, and spatial consolidation within the metropolis. In this context, the urban picturesque naturalized ethnic heterogeneity and class inequality as expected signs of modernity. As the journalist James McCabe noted in 1882, the "population of New York is more cosmopolitan than that of any city in the Union, and the majority of the people are poor" (507).

Cosmopolitanism came at a cost, and the best way to mediate that cost was to switch the focus from concerns about the growing economic chasm to a celebration of ethnic variety. The aesthetics of diversity provided an important palliative that did not deny poverty but made it more colorful. The reason New York was exceptional was that it could contain the world within its borders, and that it could also nationalize the newcomers as a vital part of the modern scene. While some were concerned that the new generation of immigrants signified excessive heterogeneity, the intra-urban walking tour reassured its readers that they were not, to quote one observer in 1906, "inherently more difficult to Americanize than were the immigrants of the past" (Huebner 675).

Although Hapgood claimed that the picturesque possessed a "disinterested point of view," it actually signaled a highly selective and partial mode of seeing. It reconfigured the national motto of *e pluribus unum* according to a "transnational imaginary" that followed a path of moderation.[36] By trying to find the "half-way station" between excessive heterogeneity and oppressive uniformity, practitioners of the urban picturesque established a formula that was similar to the sociologist Franklin Giddings's recommendation: "Somewhere between excessive heterogeneity and complete homogeneity will be found that precise composition of a people which ensures progress and is yet compatible with personal freedom and a liberal social organization" ("Sociological Questions" 253). Excessively heterogeneous societies do not have a common ground, according to Giddings, and "really homogeneous people" do not encourage progress (253). Giddings's prescription for heterogeneity—*via media*—demonstrates the common patterns structuring aesthetic and sociological practices at the turn of the century.

The picturesque as the halfway point between the sublime and the beautiful provided an aesthetics of moderation in reconceiving a national identity for the modern period. In an attempt to reconcile "progress" with national unity, it expanded the parameters of whiteness to include the "lower races of Europe," while occasionally admitting the Chinese and barring African Americans and other people of color. The residual racial politics of the picturesque also informed its modern incarnation. Just as blackness for Uvedale Price signified "absence," and specifically an absence from democratic unions, so the urban picturesque rearticulated this allegory of civil society by excluding blacks from the urban scene as well as from the national public culture.

The black fiction of the same period, however, tells a different story. In the next chapter, I show how black women intellectuals, such as Frances Harper and Ruth Todd, employ the same cultural cartography of the urban picturesque, cultural pluralism, and Bourne's transnationalism—unity-in-distinctiveness or a side-by-side union—to create a public space for African Americans as citizens. In the work of these writers, the rhetoric of variety, combined with the politics of racial distinctiveness, makes up a subcultural strategy for national intervention. Black women writers appropriated the equation of variety and Americanism to privilege African Americans, in Du Boisean fashion, as the source of a subculture's and the nation's salvation. Like the practitioners of the urban picturesque, these writers naturalized the relation between heterogeneity and democracy in claiming that a true commonwealth requires a variety of representatives. But in contrast to the urban picturesque, African Americans naturalized this relation for a racial rather than an ethnic subculture. While the urban picturesque made the impoverished European immigrant visible, the fictional work of Frances Harper made the middle-class black woman the exemplary citizen. These two chapters taken together demonstrate that the benevolence of variety was essentialized, while its parameters remained highly contested.

III

Heterogeneous Unions

5

Biracial Fictions and the Mendelist Allegory

Although blackness was rendered invisible in the perambulatory aesthetics of the urban picturesque, it played a pivotal role in scientific debates about human variation. Scientists debated whether Africans (including African Americans) were a racial variety, along with Asiatics and Caucasians, or constituted a distinct species beyond the parameters of the human. In scientific writing throughout the nineteenth century, "variety" and "species" were highly racialized terms that were most commonly understood in relation to sexual selection. "Variety" represented minor and temporary differences within a single species, and "species" referred to permanent and unbridgeable differences, where sexual unions would produce (if anything) "hybrids," biological anomalies that would probably be sterile.

Darwin's theory of evolution countered such nineteenth-century naturalist assumptions by showing that the human species designated a highly dynamic and heterogeneous category, with Africans constituting a human variety rather than a separate species: "[that races] graduate into each other, and that it is hardly possible to discover clear distinctive characters between them" (*Descent* 536).[1] For Darwin, variety was necessary for the struggle of life and vital for natural selection since it provided the generative force for "new and distinct species." He spoke of "species and variety" as unstable categories whose boundaries were constantly undermined by the vicissitudes of nature, which made the term "variety" "difficult to define" (*Origin* 38).[2]

This explicit recognition of the instability and vagueness of variety was lost in the work of Darwin's American contemporaries. On the eve of the Civil War, an Alabama physician, Josiah Nott, became a leading exponent of polygenesis, a pre-Darwinian theory that sought to explain the origins and persistence of human diversity. Polygenesis, a term invented in America though the idea was not, claimed that man originated in multiple places by several separate acts of creation, and that since then the "diversity of the races" had maintained their distinctiveness.[3] In *Types of Mankind* (1854), which was published five years before *The Origin of Species* and went into eight editions before the start of the Civil War, Nott and George Gliddon argued that even if one were to contest creationism, what was certainly indisputable was "the *permanence* of existing physical types" (50). In contrast to Darwin's configuration of variety as always changing, Nott spoke of "congenital varieties" and "permanent varieties," in which differences were essentialized as constant and fixed. Polygenesists invoked the language of diversity and variety to argue for the biological basis of racial difference as a way to justify Negro inferiority and the institution of slavery. "Nations and races, like individuals," wrote Nott and Gliddon, "have each an especial destiny: some are born to rule, and others to be ruled" (79).

After the Civil War, there was still a residual polygenesis that influenced scientific and social thought, namely Nott's theory of biraciality, which considered the mulatto to be short-lived and in many instances infertile.[4] In 1866 Nott accepted Darwin's thesis as to the basic unity of humankind, but Nott saw nothing inconsistent between admitting this point and arguing that the races of man constituted, if not distinct species, then at least "permanent varieties" (Haller 80). This position allowed Nott to uphold his polygenesist thesis that intermarriage would lead to the extermination of both blacks and whites. He argued that the mulatto was a hybrid of two separate species, a human equivalent of the mule, which would result in the degeneration of the United States both culturally and physically.

This racist theory of biraciality influenced evolutionary theorists such as Herbert Spencer, who believed that interracial unions among widely divergent "varieties" were "physically injurious" to the offspring, producing a "worthless type of mind—a mind fitted neither for the kind of life led by the higher of the two races, nor for that led by the lower—a mind out of adjustment to all conditions of life" (qtd. Haller 130). This parallel between Nott and Spencer suggests a certain ideological connection linking polygenesis to Social Darwinism, a connection stemming from the shared belief that different races represented "permanent varieties" and their crossing would lead to an inferior hybrid. Although Social Darwinists like Spencer claimed to apply Darwinian evolution to social contexts through the Spencerian thesis of the "instability of the homogeneous," they actually relied on certain pre-Darwinian assumptions, specifically a rigid understanding of racial "variety" in relation to sexual selection.[5]

At the end of the nineteenth century, when Reconstruction codes were repealed in Southern legislatures and white-black relations regressed to antebellum patterns, it is not surprising that the scientific thinking of that earlier period was given new legitimacy to justify the post-Reconstruction move to Jim Crow. In 1890, when over one-third of the United States from Alabama to Colorado had passed or was about to pass anti-miscegenation laws, the Harvard naturalist Nathaniel Shaler wrote: "We can see how English, Irish, French, Germans, and Italians may, after a time of trouble, mingle their blood and their motives in a common race, which may be as strong, or even stronger, for the blending of these diversities. We cannot hope for such a result with the negro, for an overwhelming body of experience shows that the third something which comes from the union of the European with the African is not as good material as either of the original stocks" ("Science" 37). For racist accommodationists such as Shaler, white and black could work together but not sleep together, since the product of such unions would be a "third something," a biological deviant that would defy the Manichean dualism of the American racial order.[6] For Shaler, along with the social scientist Henry Pratt Fairchild, the ideal interracial union was a "side by side" one, with white and black working together in what Shaler called a "perfect civil union" but "without the bond of kinship in blood." It was the "duty" of each race to "remain apart."

At the same time as the discourse of "variety" surfaces in the aesthetic discourse of the urban picturesque to reconstitute and expand the category of whiteness, it also appears in hereditarian debates about racial hybridity as a way to solidify as well as to expand the parameters of blackness. While variety in the context of the picturesque was used to bracket off African Americans from a multicultural vision of modern Americanism, in scientific debates it was used to account for the persistent presence of African Americans within a racially hybrid culture. Variety, in other words, was not solely a means of Americanizing European white ethnicities, but also a racial term for discriminating between whites and blacks at the height of segregation. In the post-Reconstruction era, the language of variety provided multiple ways to discipline as well as to restructure the meaning of race fusion within definitions of "modern Americanism."

Residual Polygenesis and the "Third Something"

American scientists such as Nathaniel Shaler would embrace Darwin's theory of evolution but not its indeterminate principle of biological variation. The result was a theoretical hybrid, a "third something," which integrated Darwinian evolution with a residual polygenesis. Absent from American formulations was the Darwinian sense of contingency and change, or what Darwin referred to as "accidental variations," the accumulated influences that constitute the inherited "baggage" of the animal at birth. Although the Americanization of biological variety ossified Darwin's notion of variety, this does not mean that applications of static diversity were equally as rigid. The polygenesist notion of "permanent varieties" was actually quite flexible. Its determinate rhetoric could not control its indeterminate uses. Though the polygenesist/Social Darwinist notion of biological variety was primarily invoked as a racist attack against miscegenation, it also had other meanings. Biological variety was employed by racists and anti-racists alike to underline hereditarian influences on black and biracial subjectivity. In contrast to Darwin, whose notion of variety did not engage in a sustained way with questions of genetic transmission, variety in the age of eugenics became a highly contested discursive field that reached far beyond a small coterie of scientists to influence cultural and literary representations of racial inheritance.

African-American writers such as Charles Chesnutt, Ruth Todd, and Frances Harper responded to racist theories of biracial degeneration by appropriating the scientific language of hereditarian character and adapting it for anti-racist ends. In doing so, they made the "third something" untragic, and even an exemplary figure in its ability to transform a position of racial marginality into one of personal strength and political conviction. African-American writers, however, were not uniform in their appropriation of hereditarian debates; in fact, their use of different theories demonstrates the multiple ways in which black writers vindicated biracial subjects.

I focus on two competing theories of heredity from the turn into the twentieth century: blending inheritance ("soft" heredity) and particulate heredity ("hard" heredity). The first theory, blending inheritance, was the predominant paradigm of hereditarianism in the nineteenth century, surfacing in Chesnutt's model of race fusion, which he defined in nationalist terms as the "future American." Racial extremes, according to this theory, combine into a neutral third term, an average of the two parents. The second theory was particulate or "hard" heredity, which came to fruition with the revival of Mendelian genetics at the turn of the century. This theory claimed that certain traits do not blend but retain their dominant or recessive character. This notion of hierarchical or asymmetrical inheritance represents a fundamental premise of racial identification for Frances Harper and Ruth Todd, whose work illustrates how the "white Negro" identifies unequivocally as black.

I call such anti-passing narratives "Mendelist allegories," which is a variation of Fredric Jameson's notion of a "nationalist allegory," in which "private individual destiny" in minority literature has a political and public dimension.[7] Jameson's "nationalist allegory" is in large part a defense of nationalism for subordinated peoples, a nationalism that advocates self-determination and independence, while at the same time transforming the dominant "first-world culture." Like the "nationalist allegory," the Mendelist allegory examines the importance of nationalism among subordinated populations. But unlike Jameson's trope, the Mendelist allegory, in privileging matrilineal lines of descent, illustrates the convergence of black nationalism with feminism in the formulation of a strategy of counter-essentialism. The Mendelist allegory takes "biological" definitions of race, which dominated the hereditarian discourse of the late nineteenth century, and turns them against themselves in order to argue for a black identity that was "permanent," persistent, and female. I use Mendelism allegorically rather than literally, since neither Harper nor Todd explicitly referred to Mendel as Madison Grant would do a generation later. Harper wrote on the eve of the revival of Mendel's work, and Todd wrote during the revival's early stages in the 1900s.

The coupling of Mendelism with black women's writing may at first seem incongruous. After all, what does a eugenicist revival have to do with black women's uplift fiction? Despite the fact that this revival initially occurred among a small group of eugenicists, there is a common logic that informs both the theory of Mendelian inheritance and black women's anti-passing fiction. However unlikely this pairing may seem to us today, reform-minded race writers a century ago found in fixed notions of biological inheritance the possibility of representing the black community as a unified family. Mendelian scientists and black feminist nationalists claimed that inheritance was disproportionate, that certain traits would predominate over others without necessarily losing their discreteness.

The logic of particulate inheritance supported the aims of black women's writing of the period: that racial fusion did not preclude cultural unity but actually guaranteed it. Both represent theories of persistent particularity.[8] I see the relation between Mendelism and black women's anti-passing fiction as fundamentally allegorical in the way Jameson uses the term as a rhetorical mode, which is "profoundly discontinuous, a matter of breaks and heterogeneities, of the multiple polysemia of the dream rather than the homogeneous representation of the symbol" (73). In contrast to the traditional notion of allegory, which is based on a "one-to-one table of equivalences" between archetypes and personifications, Jameson's model of allegory highlights the very dynamic of Mendelism, namely an understanding of change and transformation as highly uneven and unequal processes.

My purpose in examining black nationalist feminists' use of the language of racial variety is twofold. First, I want to show how a highly racist theory of biraciality, which was employed at the time to support a range of policies from anti-miscegenation legislation to the "one-drop" rule of negritude, could be appropriated to defend black humanity and black citizenship as well as to Africanize modern Americanism. This supports my larger claim that the language of variety in its philosophical, cultural, and scientific manifestations could not be stabilized to support a single political or social agenda. As Darwin said of biological variety, it is "difficult to define." Although variety was employed to defend essentialist positions, there was nothing essentialist about its significations; it represented a highly indeterminate and flexible discourse, whose meaning was constantly being re-produced in a range of different contexts. A Mendelian logic of asymmetrical inheritance, I argue, defended minority identities (especially borderline cases such as the "white Negro") in order to save them from absorption within the majority culture as well as to establish race leaders to consolidate a racial subculture and eventually the nation.[9]

The effects of biological essentialism were at times anti-racist and feminist and at other times deeply reactionary: biology cast black women as reparative agents of a subculture and a nation, ideal citizens who were paragons of virtue. The parameters of citizenship were curtailed in political ways, narrowing the spectrum of legitimate social action. The Mendelist allegory incorporates Du Bois's emphasis on Africanizing Americanism with Kallen's wariness toward socialism. The result is a conceptual hybrid, in which the "Talented Tenth" are primarily black women defined against certain forms of political radicalism. The Mendelist allegory represents a "third something," a cross between Du Bois's "genuine democracy" and Kallen's cultural pluralism.

My second purpose in linking black women's literature with hereditarian science is to intervene in critical debates about race and culture in the modern period. Critics have tended to tiptoe around the uncomfortable issue of racial essentialism, especially in instances when African-American writers use the rhetoric of "blood" to defend biological definitions of racial distinctiveness. Susan Gillman, in her study of Pauline Hopkins and the scientific rhetoric of "blood," refers to Judith Butler's notion of semiotic "excess" to dislodge a biologized term into a multivalent sign located in "multiple cultural contexts," which include biology alongside culture and "pan-racial harmony." Gillman uses the critical terminology of variety—"multiple contexts" and "excess"—to evade rather than to engage with the question of racial essentialism. "Culture" functions as a form of evasion, saving the critic from having to grapple with the consequences of racial essentialism. Questions that do not surface include: Why are the biological meanings of "blood" intrinsically unappealing? Why does a "seamless" and "unitary" representation of black selfhood have to be dislodged through semiotic excess?

The critical move from the biological to the cultural is also seen in George Hutchinson's *The Harlem Renaissance in Black and White*. In a parenthetical remark, Hutchinson lauds Franz Boas in part for advancing discussions of group identity through the term "culture": "By the end of the 1920s, partly because of Boas' influence, 'culture' would replace blood and spirit as the effective category of group identity for Kallen and Du Bois" (78). This shift from biology to culture is cast as a sign of conceptual progress, reaching its zenith with Alain Locke's notion of "cultural racialism," which leaves behind Du Bois's and Kallen's early romantic racialism. Again, essentialism is avoided through recourse to culture. Biology represents the conceptual building block that one plays with but eventually outgrows.

What is most refreshing about Walter Benn Michaels's argument in

Our America is that he challenges the move from biology to culture by showing that "culture" is a "modern" mode of reconceptualizing and preserving the essential contours of racial identity. "Culture," according to Michaels, is a "way of preserving the primacy of identity while avoiding the embarrassments of blood" (13). Pluralizing culture was not a means of de-biologizing race but just the opposite: it reinscribed it within nativist and essentialist terms. Culture is not innocent for Michaels; it is not safely contained within a dyadic structure that is antithetical to biology. The strength of Michaels's argument is the way he collapses the binary of culture versus biology, showing that culture is in fact a racialized and biologized term, especially when it appears to be most plural. The weakness of Michaels's critique, however, is that he never analyzes and interrogates essentialism. Identity politics, for Michaels, is *ipso facto* nativist, localist, and racist. There is no dialectic. Despite their different conclusions, Michaels, Gillman, and Hutchinson share the assumption that biological essentialism is politically and ideologically retrograde. Either it has to be culturalized (Gillman and Hutchinson) or it has to be done away with altogether (Michaels). In either case, there has been strong resistance to any recourse to biology.

I work from a different premise: that the biological was a powerful means for black women to reclaim the bodies of mothers and daughters, specifically the reproductive bond that frequently (in the days of slavery and afterward) had to be silenced. Whereas passing ruptures the biological bond between brown mother and fair daughter, anti-passing re-naturalizes this familial connection as persistent and inviolable, able to be reconstituted even after years of separation. My discussion of how black women writers used biology and racial essentialism is informed by two feminist interventions: Elizabeth Grosz's reflections on nature and biology and Diana Fuss's interrogation of the discourse of essentialism. Grosz has suggested that feminists need to rethink their relationship to the question of nature, no longer seeing it as a conceptual impasse toward cultural, historical, and social processes, but as the *object* of such processes. As a way of opening up the study of feminism and biology, she poses the following questions: "How does biology provide the conditions for culture and history, those terms with which it is traditionally opposed? What are the virtualities, the potentialities, within biological existence that enable cultural, social and historical forces to work with and actively transform that existence? How does biology—the structure and organisation of living systems—facilitate and make possible cultural existence and social change?" (31–32).

To put such questions at the forefront of an analysis of black feminist invocations of biology would shift the critical focus from either criticizing or evading the implications of "blood" toward a more complicated account centered around the use-value of essentialism. We would move from "Is she an essentialist?" to far more productive and nuanced angles of inquiry: How does the text use racial and sexual essentialism? What are the larger political and social objectives that the biological enables? Such questions would also develop within literary and historical contexts Diana Fuss's project of deconstructing the binary of essentialism versus constructionism in order to focus on the construction of essences. This *modus operandi* would allow critics to think beyond essentialism as the nemesis of difference and to analyze how essentialism produces differences.

By examining the *production* of the biological and the essential, I hope to analyze the uses of what could be termed late Victorian identity politics. This will make it possible to analyze the means through which certain African-American writers represented black bodies (even those that signified as white) as natural and nationalizing forces. At a time when theories of biraciality sought to de-naturalize the mulatto body, in particular, as biologically anomalous and deviant, a "third something" that defied proper classification, black writers re-naturalized the biracial body as "genuine" and "authentic." Before elaborating on such narratives, I turn to the hegemonic uses of biraciality and biological essentialism, since it was this tradition that the Mendelist allegory addressed and challenged.

Biraciality, White Supremacy, and the Tragic Mulatta

The Mendelist allegory's effacement of an intermediary position of biraciality was consistent with the predominant white attitude toward mixed-race people. As Carl Degler has written, "there are only two qualities in the United States racial pattern: white and black. A person is one or the other: there is no intermediate position" (qtd. Sollors *Neither Black* 112). One way in which white America attempted to disavow this "intermediate position" was through anti-miscegenation laws, which would reduce the mulatto to the Vanishing American of the postbellum period. In 1890 Atticus Haygood, a white Southern Methodist bishop and a conservative defender of black rights, commented on the success of anti-miscegenation laws in reducing the size of the mulatto population: "it is absolutely settled that the tendencies against miscegenation increase in both races. Fewer mulattoes are born each year. The moral tone of the Negroes does improve. The white man recoils from amalgamation more than in former days; and law teaches all" (Mencke 106). The populist Tom Watson, who was considered a friend of African Americans, sanguinely wrote in 1892 that the "'black belts' of the South are getting blacker. The race is mixing less than it ever did. Mulattoes are less common (in proportion) than during the times of slavery. Neither the blacks nor the whites have any relish for it" (Mencke 107).

One physician, however, challenged the effectiveness of anti-miscegenation laws in confessing that the white male's "desire for variety" could not be suppressed. A major in the Army Medical Corps, Dr. Robert Shufelt, ruefully admitted in *The Negro: A Menace to American Civilization* (1907) that it was the "desire for variety" that led white men to have interracial sex. "The pressure or demand to satisfy the sexual appetite in the [white] male—even if he be an individual endowed with refinement—often completely blinds him, rendering him practically irresponsible in many cases, and, the desire for variety coming into play, carries him over almost anything" (Mencke 111). Similar to Josiah Royce's definition of "true variety" as "inbred" and "unchangeable," Major Shufelt claimed that the "desire for variety" was a biological urge that could not be curtailed through cultural "refinement" or legal prescriptions.[10]

The legal and the biological did converge, however, in turn-of-the-century definitions of racial identity. "Descent" was a hereditarian term to suggest that racial affinity was primordial and essential. The law of hypodescent was epitomized in the "one-drop rule," the commonly held belief that biracial subjects were unequivocally black if they had any black ancestors, regardless of how white they appeared. "The ultimate absurdity in America's attempt to draw a race line with the one-drop rule," according to Joel Williamson, "was the fact that many mulattoes themselves simply did not know whether they were white or black" (98). As Pauline Hopkins asked in *Of One Blood* (1903), "The slogan of the hour is 'Keep the Negro down!' but who is clear enough in vision to decide who hath black blood and who hath it not? Can any one tell?"

(607). The courtroom frequently became the site of racial deciphering, evident in a District of Columbia appeals case, *Wall v. Oyster* (1910), in which Isabel Wall, who appeared white, was restricted from attending a white school on the grounds that her great-grandmother was a "very light mulatto woman." As there was no "ocular evidence" of her blackness, the defense's case rested on Wall's genealogy, concluding in the scientific language of fractions that the "child's proportion of negro blood is one eighth or one sixteenth" (53). In contrast to Homer Plessy in *Plessy v. Ferguson* (1896), who challenged the principle of racial segregation on the grounds of the Fourteenth Amendment, Isabel Wall contested the parameters of whiteness. Her case demonstrates the close relationship between genealogy and science to provide legal certainties (or approximations thereof) when biracial mixtures are no longer detectable to the eye.

The language of fractions suggests that blood does not blend but retains its distinctiveness as a discrete unit that can be measured. When blackness cannot be seen, it can still be quantified. In the late nineteenth and early twentieth centuries it was commonly believed that blood carried the hereditary qualities of an individual. Hereditarian character explained moral character. The paradox of the "science of blood" is that it represents a theory in which supposedly permanent traits are stabilized through the perpetual movement of bodily fluids. Circulation creates stasis.

This common assumption that traits of temperament and intelligence are inborn in races shaped the familiar literary stereotype of the tragic mulatta, whose sense of inner turmoil, of being a product of both worlds but a member of neither, was seen as a result of incompatible blood. This stereotype was founded in the anti-slavery fiction of the antebellum period but gained new force at the turn of the century, largely because of the "new" scientific interest in genetic transmission that incorporated the residual polygenesis of an earlier era. Throughout the nineteenth century the tragic mulatto, according to Sterling Brown, was considered "a victim of divided inheritance; from his white blood came his intellectual strivings, his unwillingness to be a slave; from his negro blood came his baser emotional urges, his indolence, his savagery" (160). It was believed that the character of the mixed-blood subject could be determined according to a "mathematical computation of the amount of white blood in a mulatto's veins" (162).

The Irish-American playwright Dana Boucicault gave literary expression to this stereotype in his play "The Octoroon" (1859). This early fictive depiction of the biracial subject crystallized the relations between aesthetic representation, scientific "fact," and social opinion. It acquired a degree of cultural currency that influenced the ways in which African-American writers would portray this figure. In this play, Zoe, who ultimately poisons herself when it is realized that she cannot marry her beloved white suitor George Peyton, declares: "Of the blood that feeds my heart, one drop in eight is black—bright red as the rest may be, that one drop poisons all the blood; those seven bright drops give me love like yours—hope like yours—ambition like yours—life hung with passions like dew-drops on the morning flowers; but the one black drop gives me despair, for I'm an unclean thing—forbidden by the laws—I'm an Octoroon" (383). This scene combines sentimentalism with what Werner Sollors has called "the calculus of color" to cultivate sympathy among a white audience. At one performance in Maine, an abolitionist leapt onto the stage and begged Zoe to escape rather than to drink the poison (Sollors *Beyond* 355).

Despite the play's sympathy toward its tragic protagonist, it still assumes that blood can be quantified. By repeating the simile "like yours," Zoe implies that the seven drops of blood make her more white than black. The play stays within the logic of mathematical calculations, that blood is discretely racialized and contains character traits like "love" and "ambition." In fact, the tragedy depends on the deterministic nature of blood: it presents an insurmountable barrier preventing George and Zoe's love from ever being fulfilled. Boucicault's play contests the asymmetry but not the principle of inherited racial distinctions. This combination of social and literary stereotype with "scientific" claims to quantification continued to play a powerful role in late-nineteenth-century configurations of biraciality. At a time of Jim Crow, when white and black were considered to be socially, biologically, and legally distinct, black writers engaged with the paradox of biraciality, in which a mathematical model of racial discreteness was used to understand biological fusion.

Race, Science, and Transvaluation

Although the dominant whites invoked the laws of heredity to render the "third something" a tragic and conflicted character, the language of heredity was not the sole preserve of those in power.[11] African Americans also benefited from a hereditarian logic but in significantly different ways. They did not use hereditarianism to defend race purity, as whites commonly did, but rather to argue that biraciality was a normative attribute of black identity. From this point of view, Shaler's "third something" was the representative black subject. As Harryette Mullen has written, "African-Americans tend to preserve, at the level of family oral history, an acknowledgment that their genetic heritage is the product of different races and that their traditions are syncretisms of interactive cultures. Our elders often preserve oral memory of ancestors with 'white blood' or 'Indian blood'" (72).[12] At the turn of the century, black thinkers invoked hereditarian language to claim a position of racial distinctiveness through an acknowledgment of racial heterogeneity. Genetic variety produced black unity.

In her 1895 speech on the value of "Race Literature," Victoria Earle Matthews described Negroes as a "people of varied nationality," a claim she supported by quoting a passage from a scholarly article entitled "Mixed Races": "The American Negro is a new race, and is not the direct descent of any people that has ever flourished" (173). Hereditarian rhetoric was used to support a black nationalist notion of a unified community that was fundamentally heterogeneous. This goes against our contemporary mindset that assumes racial essentialism and black nationalism promote a homogeneous racial identity. Michael Dyson, for instance, has argued that racial essentialism has suppressed the "intriguing variety" and "vibrant diversity" of African-American culture (218). By contrast, race reformers a century ago claimed that the "laws of heredity" would reveal the varieties of blackness. They appropriated the essentializing language of genetics for anti-homogenizing arguments of African-American diversity.

This appropriation of biological essentialism to defend racial heterogeneity was part of a more general strategy that Nancy Stepan and Sander Gilman have called "transvaluation."[13] "Reactive and defensive though transvaluations may have been," Stepan and Gilman argue, "the result was often empowerment" (92). African Americans took the idioms of science to challenge the charges of racial inferiority and to make the case for an emergent black nationalism. In contrast to Kevin Gaines's argument that the nationalist ideology of racial uplift clashes with the determinism of heredity, I argue that through a strategy of transvaluation black reformers transformed the racism of biological determinism and turned it into a sign of black exceptionalism and resilience.[14] The hereditarian discourse of blood transforms what Etienne Balibar has called "fictive ethnicity" into a "natural" and lived experience. This has the advantage of making nationhood appear less of an arbitrary abstraction and more of an "expression of a pre-existing unity" (Balibar 96).

The process of establishing black unity in the post-Reconstruction era relied on genealogical appeals to "common blood." Since genealogy, and specifically matrilineal descent, had been used to enslave blacks, and after manumission it was used to keep them racially other, then the same logic of descent could be employed for the positive promotion of "race development." Genealogy, moreover, played a crucial role in assuming black unity in the process of trying to construct it. If it could be claimed that blackness was already in the blood, or as Du Bois put it, that the "Negro spirit" was present in the "Negro blood," then Negro consciousness merely required the release of latent, biologically entrenched proclivities.

Heredity, therefore, is an invention of pastness that constructs a notion of peoplehood for the present and future. This sense of peoplehood, according to Wilson Moses, was distinctly bourgeois in Gilded Age black nationalism, which Moses does not dismiss as simply a fantasy or a mode of escape, but calls "a rational attempt to manipulate the hostile environment in which it was conceived" (29). The middle-class black family was considered a biological unit, which epitomized a pluralistic union in that characters possessed a diverse range of skin colors and yet were connected through what Du Bois called "common ancestry." This fusion of the biological and the national illustrates Balibar's point that "the idea of eugenics is always latent in the reciprocal relation between the 'bourgeois' family and a society which takes the nation form" (102). Blood, nation, and family constituted the triadic terms of a "scientific" construct that both excluded African Americans and was used by them to create a national public space of political intervention.

In his 1905 review of Du Bois's *The Souls of Black Folk,* the black sociologist Kelly Miller praised the book for its application of "scientific accuracy and method to the study of the race question" (617). Du Bois also used scientific methodologies for framing race issues in his earlier work "The Conservation of Races" (1897). Stepan and Gilman view this text as an exemplary model of transvaluation, because it countered "the charge of biologically based racial inferiority of the black population by asserting a distinctive and positive psychic-biological identity for African-Americans" (182). Biological distinctiveness, which had been the basis of black inferiority from polygenesis to the one-drop rule, is now seen as a source of collective strength and vitality, as the basis of what Du Bois called "race pride" (DB 43). Anthony Appiah has persuasively argued that Du Bois's concept of race as a sociohistorical concept is premised upon the biological assumption of common ancestry and "common blood." For Appiah, "The Conservation of Races" illustrates the "classic dialectic," in that Du Bois did not transcend the nineteenth-century definition of race but depended on it in order to revalue blackness in the face of scientific explanations of racial hierarchy ("Uncompleted" 25).

Although Du Bois acknowledged the limits of scientific definitions of race, pointing out that the scientific "criteria of race are most exasperatingly intermingled," he still held on to the language of "blood." Whereas the science of race accentuated differences in speaking about the distinct varieties of blood, a viewpoint that was taken to its extreme in Nott's belief in the "diversity of origin," Du Bois invoked Darwin to make a contrary point, namely that we are all of one blood: "as Darwin himself said, that great as is the physical unlikeness of the various races of men, their likenesses are greater, and upon this rests the whole scientific doctrine of human brotherhood" (DB 40). Du Bois translated the science of race from a defense of racial particularities to a humanistic belief in a common humanity. By doing this, he showed that science could be invoked to promote a vision of connection rather than of segregation.

Du Bois's appropriation of science was not unique. Pauline Hopkins, Victoria Earle Matthews, and Anna Julia Cooper, among others, referred to the "laws of heredity" to counter scientific claims of black inferiority with an alternative notion of affirmative consciousness. Like Du Bois, Pauline Hopkins in a short story about interracial marriage, "Talma Gordon" (1900), claimed that the "law of heredity" "makes us all one common family," a point that she would explore further in her novel *Of One Blood*. In 1895 Victoria Earle Matthews used "the law of heredity" in a Lamarckian sense of acquired characteristics, by which each generation's achievements would be passed on to the next: "we must begin to form habits of observation and commence to build a plan for posterity by synthesis, analysis, ourselves aiming and striving after the highest" (182).[15]

Anna Julia Cooper in *A Voice from the South* also used a Lamarckian notion of acquired characteristics to describe how contemporary examples of criminality could be traced back to an individual's progenitors: "Now whatever notions we may indulge on the theory of evolution and the laws of atavism or heredity, all concede that no individual character receives its raw material newly created and independent of the rock from whence it was hewn. New life is bound up within the period of its conscious existence. No personality dates its origin from its birthday" (234–235). Cooper concluded that a person's "character" was the accumulation of forces over the course of many generations, so that "in order to reform a man, you must begin with his great grandmother." That Cooper traced the black "character" to the great grandmother rather than through patriarchal lines of descent was a distinctive feature of black appropriations of hereditarian logic. Just as the slave status of the biracial offspring was determined by the mother's position in the antebellum period, so a child's maternal genealogy determined his or her character in the aftermath of slavery. Furthermore, Cooper linked moral character with hereditarian character, a strategy that challenged an individualist or "blame-the-victim" approach to black "deviance."

Richard Hofstadter has pointed out that the early interest in eugenics was largely motivated by reformist concerns in that it "spoke in terms of the collective destiny of the group rather than of individual success" (*Social Darwinism* 167). For Lamarckians such as Matthews and Cooper, the environment was still a vital component of heredity, since one had to take into consideration a history of slavery and the failure of Reconstruction when judging the black race. For Matthews heredity signified future possibilities, whereas for Cooper heredity was a way to show how the past still haunts the present. In both cases, heredity was at the center of turn-of-the-century notions of individual integrity. As Howard Horwitz has noted, it was "fundamental to the period's idea of what constitutes persons and culture and of how one detects and represents character" (323).

In appropriating the scientific discourse of heredity to rewrite the stereotype of the tragic mulatta, African-American writers demonstrated that "modern science" was "already multicultural," a point that Sandra Harding has recently reiterated (348). I am specifically interested in how the debate about genetic transmission, which centered around Galtonian blending versus Mendelian particulate heredity, figured allegorically in these writers' various depictions of biraciality.[16] One way to resolve biracial angst was through fusion or blending inheritance, which Charles Chesnutt elaborates in "The Future American" (1900). If whites and blacks were to have interracial sex over the course of many generations, then whiteness would no longer exist as a "pure" category and racial discrimination would gradually disappear. Biological fusion was an idealistic recipe for social reform: if whites had black blood in their veins, then they would cease to be racist.

The second way that black writers resolved the tragic mulatta stereotype was also through hereditarian principles applied to social ends. Particulate heredity or neo-Mendelism claimed that certain traits were inherited unblended and untainted; it was a way to preserve at the level of science the integrity and distinctiveness of the Jamesian "each-form." Applied to literature, and specifically to the black feminist work of Ruth Todd and Frances Harper, this hereditarian logic represents a Mendelist allegory, in which blackness is the dominant trait that resolves the duality of the "white Negro." Through asymmetrical descent, in which one genealogical line predominates over another, the mixed-race protagonist can focus on reconstituting the black family, and more generally, healing the black community through racial uplift.

I argue that the "one-drop rule" of negritude, used to marginalize the "white Negro," was actually appropriated by black thinkers to argue for the dominance of African blood. Hereditarian character, in other words, was transferred to black character, as a sign of survivability and persistence. "If survival or ability to reproduce was going to be a eugenical criterion for race potential," according to Marouf Hasian, "then African-Americans were going to make the most of biological discussions. As one black would triumphantly observe, 'Unlike the Indian, the Negro is destined to remain a big factor in our civilization. He is here to stay'" (Hasian 60). If the hereditarian trope of "blood" was used to essentialize blackness, even among those who could pass, then African Americans were to use the same rhetoric of biological essentialism to demonstrate race loyalty. The blond, blue-eyed Iola Leroy, for instance, does not want to be white and even rejects her most desirable white suitor, and instead embraces her one drop of black blood to work for "race organization."

Galtonian Blending

Scientific debates on heredity provided a language in which to imagine the biracial subject, and particularly the "white Negro," as a unified figure, no longer divided by conflicting racial heritages. To resolve mulatto angst in his ideal of the "future American," Chesnutt relied on the predominant nineteenth-century model of genetic transmission, namely blending inheritance. It was, according to the historian Peter Bowler, a "confused theory" according to which the traits of the child were always the average of its parents.[17] As a form of "soft heredity," blending inheritance assumed that the transmission of characters to the offspring could be altered by changes in the parents' bodies or in the general environment. Parental bodies, moreover, played an active role in transmitting traits directly to the offspring, which was an intermediate version of its parents. Darwin believed in this notion of blending heredity, that parental differences were fused in the child so that variation was constantly being diminished (Olby 55). Darwin's cousin, Francis Galton, who coined the phrase "eugenics" in 1883, similarly supported blending inheritance, by which the parents were the primary contributors to the child's genetic makeup.

Galton also developed a Law of Ancestry, which claimed that a child's progenitors, primarily the grandparents, also played a role. This Law employed a formula of democratic contribution, whereby each generation influenced the offspring in proportion to its generational proximity: "The share that a man retains in the constitution of his remote descendants is inconceivably small. The father transmits, on an average, one-half of his nature, the grandfather one-fourth, the great-grandfather one-eighth; the share decreasing step by step, in a geometrical ratio, with great rapidity" ("Hereditary Talent" 70). Galton acknowledged instances of "particulate inheritance," when a trait from a grandparent would not blend, which was typically found in eye color. Galton observed that the children of a light-eyed and a dark-eyed parent usually took the eye color of one parent over the other, rather than a blended hue (*Natural Inheritance* 12). Although he conceded that some traits remained distinct, either latent or patent, he was more interested in the process of amalgamation. One such example was skin color, since the "children of the white and the negro are of a blended tint; they are neither wholly white nor wholly black" (*Natural Inheritance* 12). The biracial child, in other words, was understood as an intermediate hybrid, a symmetrical fusion of whiteness and blackness. Stable inheritance through proportionate blending was ultimately a genetic recipe for moderation.

For sociologists such as Lester Ward, it was precisely Galton's belief in blending inheritance which made him so important for theorizing the transmission of culture. In 1891 Ward defended Galtonian fusion: "in the union of opposites nothing is lost of the qualities of either, but only the tendency to extremes is checked" (318). Applying Galtonian blending to sociological concerns, Ward admitted his own willingness to neutralize a "few of even the noblest attributes" for a "leavening of the whole mass of society" as a moderate and unthreatening force. He also saw in Galton the idea that parents still matter, which created a flexible model of transmission that would accommodate a latent Lamarckianism, so that education and culture could be seen as acquired characteristics that influence future generations. Although Galton vehemently opposed Lamarckianism, his theories were nonetheless considered adequately vague and open-ended to include environmental influences. Even Ward had to acknowledge that Galton did "strongly" oppose the Lamarckian doctrine of the transmission of acquired qualities, but he also noted that Galton's *Hereditary Genius* claimed that intelligence ran in certain families. Ward found in Galton a residual Lamarckianism, in which environment was still potentially significant. This highlights the general flexibility of Galton's theory of blending inheritance, in that it could incorporate a variety of views into an inoffensive synthesis. Galtonianism was about establishing a common ground, an intermediary space where genetic (and ideological) extremes were neutralized. It was founded on a premise of democratic equivalence, with generations contributing in proportionate gradations and each parent contributing equally.

Galtonian Fusion and Chesnutt's "Future American"

Like Lester Ward, who saw in Galton a way to mediate social extremes, so Chesnutt favored the logic of Galtonian blending because it established the mulatto as the normative racial subject. Blending inheritance provided Chesnutt with a way to challenge the quantification of "African" and "Caucasian" blood. He wanted to go beyond the mathematical language of fractions to dismantle the boundaries that separated the races. To do this, Chesnutt promoted a model of fusion, an implicit incorporation of Galtonianism or blending inheritance, in which the offspring is the intermediate of its parents. This strategy of vindicating biraciality provides an important alternative to the Mendelist allegory, demonstrating the variety of ways in which biraciality was negotiated among African-American writers.

In using Chesnutt to complicate African-American appropriations of hereditarian logic, it is important to point out the complexities and contradictions within his own use of the "laws of heredity." On the one hand, Chesnutt invokes hereditarian science as an authoritative discourse that can undermine racial categories. On the other hand, he mocks the explanatory authority of science, and particularly Lamarckianism, to explain black behavior.

To illustrate this mockery, Chesnutt's short story "A Victim of Heredity," published in 1900, the same year as "The Future American," is a satirical critique of hereditarian logic to explain individual agency. The story centers around the dilemma faced by a northern property owner in North Carolina named John after he captures Sam Jones, a black chicken thief. John is torn between his sympathy for Jones, who he learns has a sick wife and no job, and the need to use him as an example of the evils of stealing. He then runs into "old Julius," the local historian and storyteller, and Julius explains that the African-American proclivity for chicken stealing is "in the blood," the result of a goopher (a spell) from the antebellum days. Years earlier, the slaveowner McDonald wanted to cut his food costs, so he went to a local conjurer to decrease the appetite of his slaves. But when the slaves were becoming malnourished, McDonald returned to the conjurer to have her create a counter-spell that would make the slaves desire chicken meat.

Heredity, in the form of conjuring, is a way to get Sam Jones off the hook: his desire to steal chickens is not a matter of choice but the legacy of an antebellum goopher. Like so many of Chesnutt's sympathetic white characters, John's wife earnestly believes Julius's story that Sam Jones is innocent because he is the victim of a goopher. As in Anna Julia Cooper's example, hereditarianism is a way of comprehending how the past still haunts the present, even in the form of conjuring. It is finally John's (unnamed) wife who decides that Julius should release Sam Jones from the smokehouse, since he was under "the influence of heredity" and not fully responsible for his actions (131). Sam Jones was not the only "victim" of a goopher; the narrator's wife was also fooled. She is the one under the spell of Julius's conjuring tale and cannot be entirely responsible for her decision to release Jones. Chesnutt points to the irony of the "laws of heredity," in that Julius's conjure story is able to do what knowledge of Jones's ill wife and unemployed status cannot do: cultivate white sentiment. Whites are more willing to believe a story that casts blacks as hereditarian victims than one that casts them as agents responding to the conditions of poverty.

This ironic critique of hereditarianism, however, disappears in Chesnutt's fictional depictions of biraciality, especially of Rena Walden (Rowena Warwick) in *The House behind the Cedars*. In this novel, also published in 1900, Chesnutt adopts a far more sympathetic view toward the "laws of heredity," which actually tends toward a Mendelian interpretation of the "white Negro" rather than one based on harmonious blending. *The House behind the Cedars* compares the experiences of passing between a brother, John Warwick, and his sister, Rena Walden. While the brother is able to pass and marry into one of the elite families of South Carolina, his younger sister is plagued by guilt about leaving their ailing mother and fear that her "heritage" will be disclosed, particularly to her white suitor George Tryon. SallyAnn Ferguson has described Rena Walden as a "failed 'Future American,'" because she is never able to fuse entirely with the white world and decides to return to North Carolina to be with her mother. As Rena says when she returns to her mother's black world: "I'll not leave mother again. God is against it. I'll stay with my own people" (121).

Despite the fact that Rena Walden displays far more angst about biraciality than, as I will elaborate, the "flat" characters of the Mendelist allegory, the Mendelian element of this narrative surfaces in the depiction of daughterly loyalty to the black mother as a parable of anti-passing. Rena's death at the end of the novel from "brain fever," however, reinscribes her within the stereotype of the tragic mulatta. In contrast to the characters of the Mendelist allegory, Rena's identification with her black mother leads to her downfall rather than to her liberation.

Although *The House behind the Cedars* can be read as a Mendelist allegory, albeit to a limited extent, Chesnutt's most coherent and detailed engagement with hereditarian discourse is clearly toward Galtonian blending. This appears most unequivocally in the nonfiction essays he published as a series of articles in the *Boston Evening Transcript* in 1900. Entitled "The Future American," his articles outline the relation between racial hybridity and national identity.[18] Similar to Du Bois's incorporation of scientific "proof," a strategy that Kelly Miller applauded, Chesnutt explicitly refers to "recent scientific research" in order to argue that racial fusion leads not to national degeneracy, as residual polygenesists were wont to claim, but rather to national strength. He engages with "modern research" to dismantle certain racist assumptions ranging from mulatto infertility to racial purity. Chesnutt's theory of the "future American" illustrates a larger point: that African-American intellectuals during this period did not shy away from racial science but actively appropriated it, using scientific research for antithetical ends. Chesnutt, like Du Bois, invoked science to argue for a common humanity.

Like Du Bois's "The Conservation of Races," Chesnutt's "The Future American" hinges on a biological-cultural definition of race: "I use the word 'race' here in its popular sense—that of a people who look substantially alike, and are moulded by the same culture and dominated by the same ideals" (19). Cultural and ideological coherence depends on physiological similarity: the people who look alike also think alike. This premise forms an important component of Chesnutt's ideal of the "future American," who is a complete fusion of "white, black and Indian" and now represents a new composite race. Science and history work in tandem to demonstrate the inevitability of racial fusion. "Proceeding then upon the firm basis laid down by science and the historic parallel," writes Chesnutt, "it ought to be quite clear that the future American race—the future American ethnic type—will be formed of a mingling, in a yet to be ascertained proportion, of the various racial varieties which make up the present population of the United States" (18–19). Science confirms what history has been showing all along, namely that slavery was "a rich soil for the production of a mixed race" (22).

Chesnutt's use of science is also specific, centering on the work of William Z. Ripley's *The Races of Europe* (1899). Ripley, a young economist at MIT whose research was an interdisciplinary blend of anthropology, statistics, and geography, argues that the European races are composed of three types: Teutonic, Alpine, and Mediterranean. There is "no single European white race of men," since the types are "all more or less blended together by the unifying influence of civilization" (194). In a gesture reminiscent of the Spencerian notion of progress as an "advance from the homogeneous to the heterogeneous," Ripley attributes the development of European culture to its biological variety: "No continental group of human beings with greater diversities or extremes of physical type exists. That fact accounts in itself for much of our advance in culture" (104). The significance of Ripley's work is that he was among the first generation of Anglo-American scholars to claim that Europeans represented a neutral and intermediate type, descended in part from the

African race. Although Madison Grant among other nativists would use Ripley to argue for white supremacy in underscoring the superiority of Europeans, particularly those of Nordic blood, Chesnutt employs the strategy of transvaluation to demonstrate the varieties within whiteness.

The single passage that Chesnutt quotes from Ripley's study is precisely the one that nativists ignored: that the "European races, as a whole, show signs of a secondary or derived origin; certain characteristics, especially the texture of the hair, lead us to class them as intermediate between the extreme primary types of the Asiatic and Negro races respectively" (18). The European is the Galtonian intermediate, already a blend of African and Asian traits, which makes the notion of white purity—the foundational premise of the one-drop rule—a fiction. In summarizing the importance of Ripley's work for his own ideal of the "future American," Chesnutt cites "scientific circles" to claim that "the progress of Europe has been found in racial heterogeneity, rather than in racial purity" (18). Ripley's Europe is already a hybrid space. Chesnutt finds in Ripley's thesis a fractured and heterogeneous whiteness, which is sufficiently destabilized for him to interject his theory of racial fusion.

Chesnutt adopts an evolutionary approach to the gradual mingling of the races, arguing that a scientific and historical process will eradicate racism by effacing blackness. How will this happen? In language reminiscent of Galton's proportionate blending, Chesnutt elaborates a genealogy of race fusion.

> Taking the population as one-eighth Negro, this eighth, married to an equal number of whites, would give in the next generation a population of which one-fourth would be mulattoes. Mating these in turn with white persons, the next generation would be composed one-half of quadroons, or persons one-fourth Negro. In the third generation, applying the same rule, the entire population would be composed of octoroons, or persons only one-eighth Negro, who would probably call themselves white, if by this time there remained any particular advantage in being so considered. Thus in three generations the pure whites would be entirely eliminated, and there would be no perceptible trace of the blacks left. (21)

Critics have disagreed about how to interpret Chesnutt's formula of racial descent. Is he privileging whiteness or deconstructing it? SallyAnn Ferguson has argued that the "future American" is assimilationist for claiming that racial uplift can only occur through self-extinction: only when blacks biologically disappear will white racism end. Yet Stephen Knadler has offered a more generous interpretation of Chesnutt's theory of fusion: that rather than trying to efface blackness, Chesnutt is destabilizing "nostalgic identities" (438). Chesnutt's emphasis is not on black absorption into the white race, according to Knadler, but rather on overturning the faith in white racial purity, a radical notion in Jim Crow America.

Like Knadler, I believe that Chesnutt's model of fusion tends toward blackening whiteness rather than toward preserving it as a pure category. As Chesnutt sarcastically says, "it would probably be put, the white race would have absorbed the black" (21). He rejects the term "white race" and instead speaks of the mulattoization of America as a way to invert the figure of the mulatto from tragic to exemplary. All future Americans will be "mulattoes," but untragically so: "Any dream of a pure white race, of the Anglo-Saxon type, for the United States may as well be abandoned as impossible, even if desirable" (19). In regard to genetic regression or atavism, Chesnutt simply responds, "If now and then, for a few generations, an occasional trace of the black ancestor should crop out, no one would care, for all would be tarred with the same stick" (21).

Chesnutt favors Galtonian blending for the same reason that the sociologist Lester Ward prefers it to "hard" heredity: it aims toward neutralizing the extremes by creating an average or what Chesnutt calls a "uniform type" (22). Progress depends on "a composite and homogeneous people," so that the "civil life" is no longer plagued by "racial discord." Chesnutt reiterates the dominant assumption of his day, epitomized in Senator Wade Hampton's claim in 1890 that "the prosperity and the perpetuity of government depend most on the homogeneity of its people" (132). Chesnutt similarly imagines a more peaceful "civil life" based on homogeneity, but whereas Wade assumes that "homogeneity" is Anglo-Saxon, Chesnutt sees it as biracial. Through Galtonian blending, whiteness will be made mulatto, so that the marginal "tragic" subject will become the representative citizen. As a way to diffuse race conflict, Chesnutt's model presents a notion of variety-in-moderation, in which extremes are neutralized toward a general average that ultimately moves toward homogeneity.

Defining the Mendelist Allegory

Compare this symmetrical model with the second theory of genetic transmission, particulate heredity. In 1885 a German geneticist, August Weismann, published *Germ Plasm,* in which he made a case for "hard" heredity, a theory that reduced the biological significance of parents to the role of receptacles of genetic matter. This marked the death knell of Lamarckianism, in that environment was rendered superfluous to the transmission of character. Not surprisingly, Lester Ward considered Weismann's theory, in contrast to Galton's, "absolutist" and inflexible. Despite such criticism, Weismann's "hard" heredity set the conceptual groundwork for the Mendelian revival at the turn of the century. The midcentury pea studies of Gregor Mendel, which had quickly fallen into obscurity with the enthusiasm over evolutionary theories, were rediscovered in 1900 and became a predominant paradigm of scientific thought by 1910. In the first decade of the twentieth century, Mendelism won over the vast majority of biologists in the United States (Cravens 40). In 1867 Mendel demonstrated that hereditary characters are transmitted intact from parent to offspring. These factors do not blend with others; they maintain their integrity and distinctiveness.

Mendelism is a theory of genetic autonomy and of persistent individuality. It shows that characters are stable, independent, and particular. To quote Mendel: "The course of development consists simply in this: that in each generation the two parental characteristics appear, separated and unchanged, and there is nothing to indicate that one of them has either inherited or taken over anything from the other" (Ames and Siegelman 322). This observation of nonblending traits was precisely the point that was underlined in early-twentieth-century descriptions of neo-Mendelism. In a 1912 article acquainting general readers with the contributions of Mendelian genetics, Percy Stickney Grant summarizes Mendel's notion of heredity: "The essential part of Mendel's discoveries is the principle of the segregation of characters in the fusion of the reproductive cells or gametes . . . Mendel did not believe in blends, but in the unit character of heredity" (Grant 516). In contrast to Galton's notion of democratic equivalence, in which white and black contribute in equal portion to the formation of the biracial child, Mendelism rests on a premise of nonreciprocity, in which one trait predominates over others in unequal measure. While Galtonianism supports symmetrical blending, Mendelism is asymmetrical, with dominant traits more often than not prevailing over recessive ones.

This asymmetrical understanding of biraciality, according to which certain traits dominate over others, implicitly informs African-American representations of the fair mulatta. I will focus on two such narratives, Ruth Todd's short story "The Octoroon's Revenge" (1902) and Frances Harper's *Iola Leroy* (1892). Published ten years apart, and framing the decade that witnessed the emergence of neo-Mendelism or "hard" heredity, these two narratives illustrate a Mendelist allegory, in which matrilineal lines of descent undeniably prevail. The picturesque adage "blended but distinct" aptly describes the female protagonist of the Mendelist allegory, who is racially blended but whose sensibilities and loyalties are distinctively black. The Mendelist allegory is a way to retrieve an anti-assimilationist position for the "white Negro" by making the protagonist's private destiny the source of a subculture's and a nation's salvation.

At a time when one-drop definitions of negritude prevailed, the Mendelist allegory demonstrates that on the battlefield of social relations (as on the battlefield of heredity) blackness wins: it is the dominant mode of identification even for those who appear white. Whereas a Galtonian logic blurs particularity within a synthetic blend, Mendelism protects the genetic "each-form" through generations of interracial unions. The Mendelist allegory uses the discourse of variety to link racial particularity with national representativeness, with the black-identified "white Negro," especially the activist, being heralded as a paragon of Americanness. The Mendelist allegory is the fictional complement to Du Bois's "The Conservation of Races," since both claim that those who are most distinctively African American are the nation's exemplary citizens.

The Mendelist allegory dramatizes in the context of race, heredity, and nationalism a cultural pattern that characterizes the rhetoric of diversity at the turn into the twentieth century. The recognition of ethno-racial variety, together with regional peculiarities and individual eccentricities, was not valued as an end in itself, but as part of a larger strategy to incorporate the subculture as definitive of the nation. The Mendelist allegory possesses the boldness of Du Boisean conceptions of black agency in claiming that African Americans are the "very warp and woof of this nation" (DB 238). It also intersects with Jamesian pluralism in incorporating a "scale of values" to redefine modern Americanism according to a narrative of black exceptionalism. The discourse of variety is structured according to a principle of subordination, with certain identity cultures privileged over others. Like Jamesian pluralism, the Mendelist allegory asserts boundaries as part of an ethical vision that replaces ambivalence with positionality and inbetweenness with taking sides. The premise of the Mendelist allegory is that African Americans are heterogeneous: they designate a racial subculture that is regionally, economically, and phenotypically diverse. By appropriating a Mendelian logic of dominant and recessive traits, feminist writers such as Harper can forge a subcultural common ground—a variety in unity—that can elevate a race as well as the nation.

A strategy of appropriation or "transvaluation" was actually a common practice. It characterized literary representations as well as more general discussions about racial parameters. Booker T. Washington, for instance, took the "one-drop rule," which sought to keep whiteness pure, and inverted it to show the hereditarian dominance of blackness. In *The Future of the American Negro* (1899), Washington writes: "It is a fact that, if a person is known to have one percent of African blood in his veins, he ceases to be a white man. The ninety-nine percent of Caucasian blood does not weigh by the side of one percent African blood. The white blood counts for nothing. The person is a Negro every time" (158). Washington's disinterested tone in rehashing the one-drop rule of negritude betrays a certain irony. In presenting it as a "fact" he also highlights its absurdity. Through the statistical language of percentages, Washington demonstrates the irrationality behind the rule, by which "one percent" prevails over "ninety-nine percent."

What is interesting, however, is that in Washington's implicit critique of this statistical imbalance there is an acceptance of its basic premise: he maintains the distinction between "African blood" and "Caucasian blood," so that the two can be quantified. There is also a way in which Washington, in refraining from explicitly criticizing this rule, demonstrates that it renders whiteness genetically weak. Through a process of transvaluation, he reverses the one-drop rule to show that "white blood counts for nothing." In the game of heredity, blackness wins every time: it is the ultimate racial determinant. Similarly, Mendelian genetics ensures heterogeneity by demonstrating that a particular trait can come into contact with other traits and yet retain its distinctiveness.

Both one-drop definitions of negritude and Mendelian genetics are formulas for preserving a model of variety-in-discreteness. They incorporate heterogeneity through a principle of dominance, by which certain traits prevail over others rather than pluralistically combine. Hybrid unions are not relativistic, a democratic synthesis of various "each-forms," but structured according to what William James called "a right scale of subordination." According to the historian Everett Johnstone, "the vast majority of 'white Negroes' made no effort to desert the mulatto group." They instead remained loyal to families and friends (qtd. Kinney 25). John Mencke has made a similar point in claiming that blacks as well as whites accepted the "fact" that there were intrinsic racial qualities: "Afro-Americans seem to have been as firmly convinced as whites were that the two races were fundamentally different because of basic inner qualities. Hence mulattos, because they had some degree of black blood in them (and therefore black traits as well), could not ever be truly white, regardless of their appearance or socioeconomic background. They would always be closer to blacks in an inner, psychic sense, and their identification should therefore be with the black race" (159).

This same logic of hierarchical distinctions—that even the "white Negro" was intrinsically black—was also used to support racist arguments. In 1909 Alfred Schultz cited various ethnographic studies, including anthropological work on the populations of South America and the Caribbean, in order to deny that the mulatto is an exact mean of his two parents: "In the immense majority of cases his characteristics are borrowed from both races, but one of them is always predominant, and that is nearly always the negro race" (8–9). In the following decade, Madison Grant in *The Passing of the Great Race* explicitly refers to Mendelian laws to argue that the races cannot blend. The results of intermixture are "not blends or intermediate types, but rather mosaics of contrasted characters" (14). Applying this Mendelian logic to distinct racial groups, Grant concludes that "the cross between a white man and a Negro is a Negro" (18). The white supremacist appropriation of Mendelian laws was part of a two-pronged attack against interracial sex: first, Mendelism or hard heredity was invoked to argue against the possibility of fusion, since white and black blood could not blend; second, it was used to demonstrate that blackness always predominates. Therefore, according to Schultz, the "intermarriage of people of one colour with people of another colour always leads to deterioration" (1). The "new" science of

Mendelism was put to old uses: to give new legitimacy to a residual polygenisism that associated hybridity with degeneration.

In black appropriations of the same hereditarian laws, the "one-drop rule" creates a state of resolution within the black psyche. The Mendelist allegory empowers blackness by using the very logic of white supremacy, replete with its biological assumptions of unblended inheritance. It rewrites the tragic mulatta stereotype into an untragic figure, who is not beleaguered by the Du Boisean language of "double consciousness," "warring selves," and "irreconcilable strivings." Instead the untragic protagonist of the Mendelist allegory unequivocally identifies with her black mother, an identification that also determines her choice of suitor. Marriage, and more specifically marrying into the black race, resolves the racial ambiguity of the "white Negro." Unification comes not through fusion but through persistent particularity, in privileging one discrete component over another to resolve the angst of twoness. Marital union provides psychological quietude for the protagonist and narrative closure for the reader.

This contrasts with what Susan Gillman has called the "race melodrama," a genre that exhibits an "ambiguous fascination" with the tragic mulatto. A variation of Peter Brooks's "the melodramatic imagination," the American race melodrama creates a Manichean world view, a world polarized by binary conflicts between good and evil that lead to unresolved conclusions. Both the race melodrama and the Mendelist allegory include the restoration of the black family as a microcosm of the nation within a female-centered narrative. However, the race melodrama, epitomized in Pauline Hopkins's *Of One Blood*, offers "no possibility of restoring the American social and moral order" (232). Moral polarities result in unresolved racial conflicts that lead to strained and tragic endings. Lois Lamphere Brown has shown that Hopkins's "traumatized mixed-race women" are often on the brink of rescue, but their circumstances change for the worse: "they are exiled, silenced, or driven to death" (58).

What differentiates the female protagonists of the Mendelist allegory from those of the "race melodrama" is the absence of trauma and interiority. Whether it is Lillian Westland in "The Octoroon's Revenge" or Iola Leroy, these "white Negroes" convey little or no sense of angst about the knowledge of being black. Although Iola undergoes tragic experiences similar to those of the typical Hopkins character, such as rape, slavery, and familial separation, she is surprisingly unscathed. Though this seems implausible, and for some readers has been a source of criticism, my purpose is not to criticize the female characters of the Mendelist allegory for their "flatness" or superficiality but rather to examine how the absence of psychological crisis operates as a sign of black affirmation.

The Mendelist allegory resolves the inner conflict of the tragic mulatta by having her choose sides: by allying with black people, the fair mulatta finds a sense of moral purpose and personal happiness. These narratives are essentialist, programmatic, and reductive, but they are also necessary to resolve the "double consciousness" of the tragic mulatta through an alternative figure who finds a sense of wholeness by identifying with the biologically "dominant" part of her "blood." One will find completeness, moreover, by identifying with the "part" rather than the "whole." Partiality—both in terms of blood and sentiment—produces a unified subject. Rather than negotiate one's "warring selves" into a symmetrical union, the Mendelist allegory recommends choosing an asymmetrical mode of identification.

Some critics have used the psychological work of William James to interpret the fictional characters of Pauline Hopkins's novels;[19] James's work is also pertinent for understanding the "flat" characters in the Mendelist narratives of Ruth Todd and Frances Harper. Of particular relevance is James's concept of "heterogeneous personality," which first appears in *The Varieties of Religious Experience*. According to James, such a personality is the "result of inheritance" and occurs when an individual possesses "the traits of character of incompatible and antagonistic ancestors" that are "supposed to be preserved alongside of each other" (154). Although James does not explicitly racialize this concept, critics have used a notion of the "divided self" to interpret the conflicts of the tragic mulatta figure, whose inheritance made it difficult, if not impossible, for her to reconcile her twoness. As Judith Berzon has pointed out, mulatto angst was commonly reduced to "racial disharmony," "the clash of blood," and "unstable genetic constitution" (100).

What is significant in terms of the "flat" characters of the Mendelist allegory is that James's "heterogeneous personality" is curable through a "period of order-making." This involves a "scale of values" or the creation of "a stable system of functions in right subordination" (159). The "process of remedying inner incompleteness," according to James, requires an asymmetrical principle of domination and subordination, or to put it in colloquial terms, a strong sense of priorities. The protagonists of the Mendelist allegory do not represent the symptom of the "heterogeneous personality," but illustrate its cure. By choosing sides, the biracial subject finds happiness through a principle of subordination that produces what James calls "healthy-mindedness."

The Mendelist allegory reconstitutes the autonomous self at the very time when it was coming under scrutiny. According to Jackson Lears, the "autonomous self, long a linchpin of liberal culture, was being rendered unreal—not only by the growth of an interdependent market but also by a growing awareness of the constraints that unconscious or inherited drives placed on individual choice" ("Salvation" 9). While the dominant Victorian culture was becoming increasingly fascinated with multiple selves and the psychological mysteries of "hidden selves," black women writers such as Frances Harper used a Mendelian logic to reaffirm Victorian moral boundaries that were becoming blurred. Black women reclaimed those moral codes and conceptions of selfhood that had been historically withheld from them at the same time as the dominant culture rendered such concepts oversimplified and obsolete.

The Mendelist allegory takes this obsolete notion of unified selfhood in order to refashion Americanness to include what T. Thomas Fortune called its "voteless citizens." It incorporates a hereditarian logic of matrilineal descent in order to naturalize a notion of community that appeared or "felt" essential. The strategy of essentialism, the British anthropologist Pnina Werbner has remarked, requires an acknowledgment of contexts and agency, which should not be dismissed unconditionally as "essentially" conservative. Self-essentializing, according to Werbner, is a "rhetorical performance in which an imagined community is invoked. In this regard, the politics of ethnicity are a positive politics; they serve to construct moral and aesthetic communities imaginatively" (230). Self-essentializing provides such writers as Frances Harper with a mechanism for rewriting the tragic mulatta stereotype, in transforming the "heterogeneous personality" into "healthy-mindedness." As Terry Eagleton has pointed out: "Nobody can live in perpetual deferment of their sense of selfhood, or free themselves from bondage without a strongly affirmative consciousness of who they are" ("Nationalism" 37).

The hereditarian and nationalist logic that underlies the Mendelist allegory provides this sense of "affirmative consciousness" that casts black identity as desirable and even destined. The "white Negro," who could so easily slip into white society and reap its economic and social privileges, could not resist the appeal of blackness. This sense of persistent ethnicity, that even after contact with white culture African Americans retain their distinctiveness, is a powerful form of subcultural unification, whereby "voteless citizens" imagine intervening nationally not through passing, but through affirmative blackness.

The Mendelist allegory dramatizes the conversion of mulatto angst into black activism. As a therapeutics of loyalty, it bridges public and private realms and creates a unified sense of subcultural identity and national citizenship. It illustrates a rhetoric of essentialism that is not strategic, since this implies a degree of distance and disinterestedness from which essentialism can be invoked or not invoked at will. Instead, the Mendelist allegory illustrates a form of counter-essentialism that represents what Raymond Williams has called "structures of feeling," as deeply embedded assumptions about community, family, and identity that were part of the lived experience of being black in Jim Crow America. Not geared toward depicting blacks as exclusively the victims of history, the Mendelist allegory employs a deterministic logic of hereditarianism to argue for black agency: it articulates an oppositional African-American cultural criticism that acknowledges the differentiation of black life within an essentialist framework of race loyalty.

The Mendelist Allegory and the Law of Maternal Descent

In Chesnutt's adaptation of Galtonian blending, there is no dominant or subordinate trait, but only a neutral plane of mediation. "There would be no inferior race to domineer over," according to Chesnutt, and "there would be no superior race to oppress those who differed from them in racial externals" ("Future American" 21). The fusion ideal resolves the social marginality and internal angst of the biracial subject by making her normative; she signifies the middle ground of race blending. The Mendelist allegory is another strategy of resolving the social and racial liminality, one that represents an asymmetrical mode of identification where blackness predominates over whiteness at the level of sensibility. As a specifically feminist and black nationalist approach to biraciality, the tragic mulatta is made untragic not by fusing with whites, but through an antithetical strategy based on reclaiming her blackness, which was a more general gesture of reclaiming matrilineal lines of descent. In contrast to Chesnutt's notion of the "future American," which understands social change only in evolutionary and reproductive terms (sex + time = change), the Mendelist allegory foregrounds agency, and especially the willfulness of female characters. Social change will happen only if private (maternal) devotion turns into public commitment.

Whereas Chesnutt's fusion is inevitably a fantasy, the Mendelist allegory is focused on pragmatic solutions to mulatto angst and black uplift. At a time when miscegenation was outlawed in much of the country, how would racial fusion happen at the scale that Chesnutt imagines? He does not actually delineate a policy that would result in a hybrid America.[20] The Mendelist allegory, by contrast, offers ways for black activists to cope psychologically and to maneuver politically in Jim Crow America through strategies of racial reform and organization.

Houston Baker has accused black women writers of this period, especially those who focused on the "white Negro," of creating a "mulatta utopia" that ruptures any connection with a "foremothered past" and instead represents a nonplace where motherless daughters dream. "Summoning to view black southern mothers," argues Baker, "was for the daughters at the turn of the century taboo. For such a summons could only evoke a place of inescapable erring and difficulty whose representation might well bring *contempt* and not the fiercely sought sympathetic white public opinion" (30). I use the Mendelist allegory to demonstrate the opposite, that the white daughter commits race treason by identifying with her mother's people. To use Noel Ignatiev's term, the black-identified white daughter is a "dissident so-called white."[21] Loyalty to one's mother is loyalty to the black race. Narratives such as Todd's "The Octoroon's Revenge" and Harper's *Iola Leroy* enthusiastically and unhesitatingly reclaim the maternal bond, a bond that also provides ample opportunities for daughters, in particular, to come out of the white closet.

Ruth Todd's "The Octoroon's Revenge," which appeared in *The Colored American Magazine* in 1902, contains the familiar plot line of the Mendelist allegory: the fair protagonist, the darling of southern society, is in fact black. Lillian Westland, the only daughter of Jack Westland, "one of Virginia's royal blue bloods," falls in love with her mulatto coachman Harry Stanly, who cannot pass as white. She decides to elope with Stanly, then move to Europe, to be free from the racism and the anti-miscegenation laws of the United States. When Lillian's aristocratic father reads her letter confessing all, he commits suicide and leaves everything to her. We are told by Mammie Nellie, an octoroon servant, that she is in fact the mother of Lillian. Having been Jack Westland's mistress for nearly two years, Nellie became a scorned woman once Westland married a distant cousin. To get revenge, she switched babies when Westland's legitimate heiress died as an infant. Nellie does not disclose her secret to Westland (or to Lillian) until after the elopement. It is the news of the switched babies, we are told, that leads to his suicide. The final scene takes place in New York City, where both Harry and Lillian greet Mammie Nellie and exclaim in unison: "My poor abused mother!" They plan to spend several years traveling in Europe, since "even here in New York race feeling sometimes runs very high" (144).

What is significant about this story is the absence of trauma surrounding Lillian's blackness. There is no "crisis experience," as in Mark Twain's *Pudd'nhead Wilson* when Tom Driscoll finds out from Roxy that he is in fact black. In contrast to Tom, whose blinding rage leads him to raise a club to his mother, Lillian is emotionally and psychologically unscathed.[22] The switch from calling Nellie "mammie" to "mother" is depicted as inconsequential. Lillian is also completely unaffected by the suicide of her father; she simply sees it as her mother's just revenge. For it is Nellie, and not her father, with whom Lillian ultimately identifies. One could dismiss Todd's untragic mulatta as a "flat" character, lacking adequate interiority and psychological depth. One could also interpret Lillian's lack of interior turmoil as an affirmation of black consciousness, which is explained, in part, through a biological essence manifested at the level of a "natural" bond.

The narrative suggests that Lillian's attraction to her Negro coachman is a product of an inexplicable "feeling." While sitting on a mossy bank, Lillian explains to Harry her affinity to his race. "I only wish, dear, that I also was possessed of Negro lineage, so that you would not think me so far above you. As it is dear—perhaps it is but the teaching of Mammie Nell—but I feel something as though I belonged to your race, at any rate I shall very soon, for whither you go, there too I shall be" (137). Todd implies that Lillian's attraction to Harry could be a matter of environment, and more specifically the result of Mammie Nell's teachings. (This point is underlined later when Nell, speaking directly to the reader, attributes Lillian's defiance of white privilege entirely to "the teachings of her old mammie Nellie"; 143.) But Lillian, in using the word "perhaps," is not persuaded that Nellie's teachings account for the entire appeal of blackness. She adds, in a more confident and unequivocal tone, "I feel something as though I belonged to your race." It is as if black blood communicates a certain sensibility, which Lillian cannot precisely convey other than through the sentimental language of feeling.

Besides the lack of internal angst, the Mendelist allegory also foregrounds mothers. If mothers disappear at one point in the narrative, then they reappear later. In "The Octoroon's Revenge," Nellie is the primary force behind the romantic relationship, and she even joins her daughter and son-in-law in Europe, where all three live happily ever after.[23] The story reverses Chesnutt's fusion: the white negro does not disappear further into whiteness, but with the help of the black mother she returns to the fold, and in this case marries a man who cannot cross the color line. The maternal character prevents rather than encourages future race blending not on the grounds of race purity, which was the position of white nativists such as Madison Grant and Thomas Dixon, but in terms of reconstituting the black family. Biological essentialism or hereditarian character is put to social and cultural ends.

Toward the end of Todd's short story, we are told that Nellie had been cultivating Harry Stanly as a possible suitor for her daughter when he was still a boy. When Jack Westland expressed his gratitude for the care which Nellie was giving his heiress Lillian, he asked Nellie if there was anything he could do in exchange. "There was one thing I desired above all others, and that was the education of a mulatto lad of ten years of age, who worked about the stables. I asked him if he would send the lad to some industrial institution, which request he readily granted" (143). The black mother plays an instrumental role in orchestrating the romance between the southern belle and her mulatto coachman. Through romance rather than violence, the black mother gets her revenge against what Mark Twain calls the "First Families of Virginia."

Some critics have interpreted the mulatta figure as a conciliatory gesture to appease white readers. The untragic mulatta of the Mendelist allegory, however, unhesitatingly rejects the white world, including its most "aristocratic" suitors. Far from flattering white readers, the Mendelist allegory actually unsettles dominant assumptions about the desirability of whiteness. Lillian shows no desire to pass, to become part of the aristocratic world to which she could so easily belong. Lillian's unequivocal identification with blackness, and of Nellie as "mother" rather than as "mammie," illustrates affirmative black consciousness, an early-twentieth-century version of "black is beautiful." In her discussion of the "fair" mulatto, Kimberly Wilson has defined this figure as "symbolic of racial fusion," who can be seen as "deconstructing essentialist notions of race" (104). In the Mendelist allegory, however, the mulatta is untragic precisely because the narrative constructs rather than deconstructs essentialist notions of race. Although the mulatta in this context represents historical fusion, a residual reminder of slavery, she also signifies a future commitment to blackness. Psychologically, she does not sit on the proverbial fence in a constant state of liminality, but chooses sides as a way to heal the rifts within the black psyche as well as within the black community.

Marital union is maternal reunion, which leads to the reestablishment of the black family. Unlike the traditional tale of the tragic mulatta, which typically ends in her exile or death, Todd's short story concludes on the hopeful note of resolution. Todd incorporates a constructivist notion of black identity (through Nellie's teachings) with a biologically inherited one ("I feel something") to argue against passing for the "white Negro." Happiness can be found through the (surprisingly) unpainful process of self-outing.

The Mulatto as a Mediation of Black Variety

Hazel Carby has argued that the mulatto is a "narrative device of mediation," operating as a "vehicle" for both the "exploration" and the "expression" of black-white relations. The mulatta figure, according to Carby, "allowed for movement between two worlds, white and black, and acted as a literary displacement of the actual increasing separation of the races" (*Reconstructing* 90). Carby configures mediation in terms of a black-white axis, highlighting the separation and differences between the two races. The mulatto figure, as I see it, is also a form of mediation within the African-American community, who unites the variety of hues within a consolidated notion of black consciousness. Even Nathaniel Shaler, who argued against miscegenation, celebrated the variety of hues among African Americans, which was (ironically) the manifestation of racial fusion: "In a large body of American negroes, we find a wide range of hue, some being relatively quite light colored, though the other African marks are very strong" ("Science" 41). Shaler developed this observation to claim that the variety of hues among African Americans was in fact a sign of American exceptionalism: "If we can trust the reports of travelers, no such wide variation is found among the blacks of the Guinea coast, or indeed among any of the distinct races of Africa" ("Science" 39).

African Americans also celebrated the internal variety of the black community, as in the ball scene in Du Bois's *The Quest of the Silver Fleece* (1911), which takes place, appropriately enough, in the nation's capital: "The color of the scene was wonderful. The hard human white seemed to glow and live and run a mad gamut of the spectrum, from morn till night, from white to black; through red and sombre browns, pale and brilliant yellows" (305). Fannie Barrier Williams also addressed internal variety, but in the context of the black family: "Parents and children, sisters and brothers of different complexions are often found openly living apart yet cherishing a secret and abiding love for each other, which may be exhibited only under cover and when free from the interfering forces of prejudice" (422). Since the light-skinned members of the black family frequently passed, a decision that Williams fully supports, familial love must go underground as a "secret" but no less "abiding love." The Mendelist allegory celebrates the black family as a model of *e pluribus unum*. Because its fairest members refuse to pass, the black family can be reconstituted above ground rather than underground, as a public union of white and black, united under the rubric of "race pride." The fair mulatto represents an important vehicle of mediation within the black community, as the unifying figure that brings the various branches and hues of the family together.

Within the logic of the Mendelist allegory, the mulatta figure, as a trope of mediation, becomes the ideal national citizen precisely by establishing a common ground within the subculture. By identifying with the particular, she epitomizes the national. The mulatta figure is not a vehicle of mediation in the sense of a symbiosis between Self and Other, or what Homi Bhabha has called "inbetweenness." She brings black and white together through her loyalty to the black subculture. The black woman, and more specifically the "fair" mulatta, becomes the exemplary citizen by retaining what William Dean Howells has called the "quality of Afro-Americanness." Despite race blending to the point of whiteness, the white Negro represents resilient particularity. Loyalty to one's race is loyalty not only to one's mother but also to one's nation. Claiming racial distinctiveness is not synonymous with a politics of separatism, but rather with a process of national incorporation in which the subculture serves as a model of national development. Hereditarian character is connected to national character, whereby the "mulatta's genealogy," to quote Lauren Berlant," is "a genealogy of national experience" (470).

At one level, the Mendelist allegory is the African-American counterpart to Bourne's "Trans-National America," in that it defends African-American distinctiveness as a sign of representative Americanness. Just as Bourne argues that the "good" Jew is one who practices the faith of his fathers, so the "good" black citizen is one who remains loyal to his "mother-race." In 1909 the social scientist Francis Hoggan considered such loyalty, especially for the fair mulatto, heroic: "A black skin is a very serious handicap in the United States, and those who, from race love and devotion, elect to remain with the dark race, though fair enough to escape into the white one, are cast in heroic mold, and deserve in fullest measure the admiration and respect of both races" (355). Whereas Bourne's "transnationalism" opposes assimilation, wanting instead to preserve the "foreign savor" of the newly arrived immigrants, the Mendelist allegory opposes passing, arguing instead for the "white Negro" to align with black kin and friends and thus reject white privilege. While Bourne wants to preserve the "foreign savor" as a way to celebrate the variegated nationality of the United States, writers such as Harper want to claim black distinctiveness for different ends: to consolidate a black subculture in order to move from the national margins to the center. Whereas Bourne celebrates distinctiveness for aesthetic purposes, Harper uses it for political and social ends.

Loyal Daughters and National Citizens

Whereas Todd locates the reunited black family, replete with its racial variations, in Europe, Frances Harper in *Iola Leroy* situates the reunited black family, in all of its variety, in the South. This return to the rural South, the feminized site of organic origins, adds a point of emphasis to the Mendelist allegory that Todd's short story does not have, namely an investment in social reform through a commitment to racial uplift. Harper's protagonists are activists, expressing their loyalty at the level of the community as well as that of the family. They represent, in the words of William Dean Howells, "exemplary citizens." In a 1901 article entitled "An Exemplary Citizen," Howells remarks that in mixed-race writers, such as Paul Laurence Dunbar, there is a "loving loyalty to family and race." At the turn of the century, loyalty was considered a sign of private devotion as well as of public commitment, an ethical position that was synonymous with "good citizenship." In *The Philosophy of Loyalty,* Josiah Royce claims that loyalty "forbids cowardice; it forbids hesitancy [and] it forbids me to play Hamlet's part" (187–188).

Loyalty, moreover, promotes action rather than ambivalence, a commitment toward a definite set of goals rather than to continual doubt and reflection. Similar to María Amparo Ruiz de Burton, who originally published *The Squatter and the Don* under the pseudonym "Loyal Citizen," Harper's *Iola Leroy* represents the public manifestation of private values, in which individual belief combines with collective ideals. In *Iola Leroy,* Harper reinvents national citizenship through the black community, in which African-American nationalism provides, to quote Lauren Berlant, a "model of dignity and justice that white American citizens will be obliged to follow" (467). In Mendelist fashion, the part defines the whole: a distinct subculture becomes representative of the nation as a whole.

The plot of *Iola Leroy* follows the familiar trajectory of the Mendelist allegory: the beautiful and wealthy daughter of a southern slaveowner discovers after her father's death that she is black. Her mother, Marie, who epitomizes the tragic mulatta, had tried to pass as white to protect her two children, Iola and Eugene, but an error in the manumission contract signed by her now deceased husband has rendered the document invalid. Now Leroy's cousin, Alfred Lorraine, claims ownership of all the property, sending Marie and Iola "down the river" to the auction block. Iola suddenly falls from grace, from southern belle to exploited chattel, when race and class privilege disappear. Although at this point the narrative abruptly shifts forward to the Civil War, it is implied that Iola while a "white slave" in the deep South was a victim of sexual assaults by her owners. The narrative focuses on her work as a nurse in the Union army, healing the body politic by tending to the maimed bodies of its warring soldiers. By caring for the physical wounds of the nation, she heals the psychological wounds of slavery.

During this period, Dr. Gresham, a New England physician who comes from an abolitionist family, proposes to Iola. When Iola "outs" herself as a black woman, which she does proudly and frequently, Dr. Gresham insists that her genealogy does not matter. Yet when Iola raises the issue of family, that a child of theirs may in fact be too dark to pass as white, Dr. Gresham pauses. Iola interprets his hesitation as further validation of her plan: to dedicate her life to finding her mother. Her priority is in repairing the fractured black family, rather than in cultivating an interracial one. Years later in Philadelphia, where Iola is working as a store clerk, she runs into Dr. Gresham and he proposes once again. This second proposal affords Iola a chance to restate her commitment to her black family, which is already restored and living together in the city. It also gives Iola the opportunity to announce her grander plan: to work for racial uplift in the South. Through a *conversazione* among the "talented tenth," Iola meets her future husband, the fair mulatto Dr. Frank Latimer, who, like her, sacrifices the privileges of whiteness in order to work for the racial uplift of their "mother-race." In contrast to Todd's story, in which the newlyweds move to Europe, Iola and Dr. Latimer move with their family to North Carolina, where they work to establish a model of nationhood based on a "Christian commonwealth."

Although *Iola Leroy* was one of the best-selling novels by an African-American writer prior to 1900, its contemporary critical reception has been mixed. Paul Lauter reported that in the editing of *The Heath Anthology of American Literature* Frances Harper "emerged as one of the most consistent candidates for cutting, in whole or in part" (28). The main criticism of *Iola Leroy* focuses on its characterization, or lack thereof. "Characters do not act," writes Houston Baker in his appraisal of the novel, "they talk—endlessly" (32). Even for feminist critics who are sympathetic toward Harper's social and political project, Harper's protagonists lack a "distinct self." For Deborah McDowell, they represent a "status symbol" rather than a "dynamic character": "As Iola fulfills her role as exemplary black woman she comes to resemble a human being less and less and a saint more and more. We learn very little about her thoughts, her inner life. Nothing about her is individualized, nor does this seem to be Harper's chief concern, for she is creating an exemplary type who is always part of some larger framework. That larger framework is moral and social" (286). McDowell concludes that the lack of interiority of the characters is the result of Harper's "propaganda motive" (286): the characters are trapped "in an ideological schema that predetermines their identities." Too much emphasis on civil concerns results in a lack of development of individual concerns, or what McDowell has referred to as the absence of "unique voices."

Iola Leroy has been primarily valued as a historical and sociological artifact, applauded for its feminist aspirations but neglected for its aesthetic and narrative techniques. There is a sense in which the "imperative duty" of the mulatta protagonist also informs our critical understanding of the author. Just as the mulatta heroine must fulfill public needs rather than private desires, so Harper must sacrifice character development for the promotion of race development. Aesthetic concerns are commonly interpreted as secondary to political and civic activism. Rather than displace the issue of "undeveloped" characters with a focus on the moral and social aims of the novel, I want to discuss both aesthetic technique and the novel's public purpose. To what extent are "flat" characters necessary for the novel's depiction of the exigencies of black community formation? And at the level of "individual" character, isn't it precisely the absence of internal angst that makes coming out so appealing?

In his introduction to *The Autobiography of an Ex-Colored Man* (1912), William L. Andrews comments on the lack of "soul-searching" in the black fiction of the turn of the century: "In the African-American novel of the late nineteenth and early twentieth centuries, the leading characters almost always have a choice between self-interest and self-sacrifice in the name of uplifting the race. Generally, the choice is in favor of the latter; usually little soul-searching is required" (xviii). Maryemma Graham, in her entry on Harper for the *Dictionary of Literary Biography*, has similarly observed that "Iola experiences no inner conflict regarding her black racial identity" (171).

This lack of inner turmoil is a reworking of a familiar scene in nineteenth-century biracial fiction, namely the "crisis experience" when the white protagonist is told that she is in fact black. It is the point when the mulatto becomes "conscious" of his or her own blackness. According to Everett Stonequist, who coined the phrase in his 1937 study of the mulatto or "marginal man," the degree of trauma associated with this experience reflects the extent to which the individual has assimilated into the dominant culture. The more accepted the individual is in white society, the more shattering the experience. Similar to Du Boisean "double consciousness" in which the black subject is torn between "two irreconcilable selves" and "two warring ideals," Stonequist's "marginal man," in the words of Judith Berzon, is "torn between two courses of action and is unable calmly to take the one and leave the other" (Berzon 122).

Berzon, in her study of the mulatto in American fiction, was the first to apply Stonequist's concept to literature. From Mark Twain's Tom Driscoll to Sinclair Lewis's Neil Kingsblood, Berzon traces the various scenes of mulatto strife, which are emblematic of "human" struggles associated with Sartrean existentialism: "How can the human being define himself?" (131). As a metaphor for the human condition, the biracial figure expands from the particular to the universal, and in so doing changes from a fictive "character" to an exemplary "individual." For the writer, the crisis experience is the narrative technique necessary to establish psychological depth, because it provides a "dramatization of the mulatto's anguished search for self-definition" (137). In the biracial subject's painful struggle against "the objectification of his being" (130), we are all reminded, or so this argument goes, of our existentially cognizant quest for identity.

What is significant is the absence or brevity of the crisis experience in the Mendelist allegory. In Todd's "Octoroon's Revenge," this scene is never depicted. Lillian Westland goes from calling Nellie "mammie" to calling her "mother" without any sign of self-consciousness, never mind interior angst. In *Iola Leroy*, written ten years earlier, there is a "crisis experience," when Marie tells her daughter that in fact they are all black and will be sold into slavery: "I have negro blood in my veins. I was your father's slave before I married him. His relatives have set aside his will. The courts have declared our marriage null and void and my manumission illegal, and we are all to be remanded to slavery" (105). Harper depicts Iola's response, first, through a description of her face: "An expression of horror and anguish swept over Iola's face, and, turning deathly pale, she exclaimed, 'Oh, mother, it can't be so! you must be dreaming!'" (105). Then Harper describes Iola pacing the floor, "almost wild with agony," and with "crushing anguish upon her mind" (105). Finally, Iola bursts into "paroxysms of tears succeeded by peals of hysterical laughter" (106).

Iola's crisis experience is told through a series of bodily stages, beginning with a close-up of her facial expression and ending with her pacing on the floor, fluctuating between emotional extremes. "An individual character," according to Berzon, "may experience more than one reaction in the first period after the discovery of his Negro background" (123). Berzon rather clinically elaborates on the crisis in Harper's novel: the "world reels, consciousness is lost, or a dazed state ensues" (123). What is not mentioned in Berzon's analysis of the crisis experience in

Iola Leroy is its brevity. Within ten lines, Iola is "growing calmer," asking questions about who is behind this scheme of "downright robbery." The mother and daughter then discuss Christianity, and Marie encourages her daughter to "strive to be a Christian." By the end of the chapter, Iola has pledged her loyalty to her mother—"Mother, I will never desert you in your hour of trial"—and is sitting by the bedside of her dying sister Grace. Holding Grace's hands, Iola listens to her sister's final words: "Dear Iola, stand by mother" (108).

As is characteristic of the Mendelist allegory, in which identification with one parent predominates over the other, Iola's terse crisis experience portrays the intersection of black consciousness with fealty to the mother. As in "The Octoroon's Revenge," there is no daughterly mourning for the deceased father, just complete and unequivocal devotion to the black mother. Conventionally, characters' first reactions to the disclosure of their blackness are supposed to indicate the degree to which they have internalized white racist views of blackness. "Their immediate reactions," according to Berzon, "reveal their attitudes toward race, status, and self-esteem" (123).

The crisis experience, furthermore, gives white readers an opportunity to rehearse their own racist sentiments, with becoming black signifying "horror" and also inspiring sympathy. The brevity of this scene in *Iola Leroy* actually undermines the function of the crisis experience. In this particular scene, becoming black does not lead to exile, marginality, or perennial conflict, but to the affirmation of a female-centered extended family, which includes "Mammy Liza" and not a single male character (white or black). The "crisis experience" is less about individual turmoil and more about reimagining black genteel nationalism in feminist and Christian terms.

At the beginning of the chapter in which this scene appears, entitled "School-girl Notions," Iola defends slavery to her New England classmates. For her, it is an institution of benign paternalism, since she had never witnessed her father "strike any one of them [the slaves]." Adopting her father's stance on slavery as her own, Iola explains that "slavery is not wrong if you treat them well and don't sell them from their families" (98). By the end of the chapter, Iola is told that she herself will be sold into slavery. It is ultimately her mother's blood, and not her father's blue blood, that sends her down the river to the auction block. This chapter narrates Iola's shift in parental identification from daddy's little girl to her mother's loyal daughter. It depicts a twofold conversion, in which becoming black-identified is concomitant with becoming woman-identified. In *Iola Leroy* the "crisis experience" is actually an awakening, the point at which an emergent black nationalism and genteel feminism intersect with Christian ideals—"have faith in the darkest hour" (107).

Most of the authors of this period, as Berzon has pointed out, rely on the "heredity-race formula" to interpret mulatto character (34). *Iola Leroy* uses this formula to naturalize Iola's identification, and that of other fair mulattos in the novel, as black. In contrast to the tragic mulatta, whose blood is depicted as clashing, the untragic mulatta privileges her mother's blood over her father's in an attempt to reject a position of ambivalence and liminality. As Iola declares publicly: "The best blood in my veins is African blood, and I am not ashamed of it" (208). Iola does not represent James's "heterogeneous personality," but a united self that has incorporated a principle of "order-making" to resolve conflict. To demonstrate such "healthy-mindedness," the novel consists of numerous occasions when Iola and other fair mulattos "out" themselves as black. It is as if public declarations of blackness reaffirm and naturalize the characters' new subject position as unified.

Self-outing also provides an occasion for the fair mulatta to underscore the absence of trauma: public composure is evidence of internal serenity. As Iola says to her white suitor Dr. Gresham: "The intense horror and agony I felt when I was first told the story are over. I have passed through a fiery ordeal, but this ministry of suffering will not be in vain. I feel that my mind has matured beyond my years. I am a wonder to myself" (114). The primary hierarchical principle for Iola and the other characters is founded on maternal identification. Iola unequivocally rejects Gresham's proposal, stating that her priority after the Civil War is to find her mother: maternal love is greater than romantic love, and by extension, love for the black race is more important than an interracial love. "Oh, you do not know how hungry my heart is for my mother! Were I to marry you I would carry an aching heart into your home and dim its brightness. I have resolved never to marry until I have found my mother" (117–118).

In her reading of this novel, Elizabeth Young has argued that the Civil War operates as a "complex metaphor for struggle about identity," in which external conflict is internalized as a "model for the construction of subjectivity" (287, 274). The problem with this interpretation is that it cannot acknowledge the *absence* of internal conflict. In rejecting Dr. Gresham's proposal, for example, Iola is not wallowing in doubt and regret. Instead she admits that "she had never for a moment thought of giving or receiving love from one of that race who had been so lately associated in her mind with horror, aversion, and disgust" (111). Iola is the personification of Roycean loyalty: unequivocal dedication to a principle. Through her "flat" characters, Harper portrays racial identification as a form of loyalty to the mother. In doing so, she proposes a radically different model of mulatta subjectivity, one in which the mulatta is unified rather than discordant, directed rather than traumatized.

The flatness of these characters underlines the point that identifying as black is not a "bad thing": it is an identity of love rather than repulsion, loyalty rather than betrayal, sacrifice rather than expediency. In speaking again to Dr. Gresham after his second proposal, Iola is given another opportunity to link blackness with a late Victorian notion of "womanism": "Nor am I wholly unselfish in allying myself with the colored people. All the rest of my family have done so. My dear grandmother is one of the excellent of the earth, and we all love her too much to ignore our relationship with her" (235).[24] In the Mendelist allegory, biracial characters, upon discovering that they have a drop of negro blood, identify as black—with only a brief initial response of "wild agony." This Mendelist maneuver uses flat characters to establish a bounded and celebrated notion of black culture that is free from internal conflict, including class differences and colorism. Ambivalence is rejected for a black subjectivity that reconciles twoness through identification with one's maternal genealogy.

In Harper's novel, it is not only the fair mulatta who unhesitatingly identifies with her mother and grandmother, but also the male "white Negroes" who reclaim their mothers in the name of blackness. As Iola's brother Harry confides to his uncle: "I confess at first I felt a shrinking from taking the step, but love for my mother overcame all repugnance on my part" (203). Iola's future husband, Dr. Frank Latimer, "outs" himself publicly before a group of doctors in Philadelphia using the "scientific" discourse of blood: "'The blood of that race is coursing through my veins. I am one of them,' replied Dr. Latimer, proudly raising his head" (238). Later Iola asks him why he has not "slip[ped] out" of the race, and he replies: "My mother, faithful and true, belongs to that race.

Where else shall I be?" (263). In claiming their black mothers, both Harry and Frank marry black women. Frank weds Iola and they move to North Carolina, where Frank becomes the "Good Doctor" who is also a "leader in every reform movement for the benefit of the community" (279), while Iola teaches Sunday School. Harry marries Lucille Delany, an African-American woman of "unmixed blood." When he proposes to her, Lucille raises the issue of racism within the black community: "You know, Harry, complexional prejudices are not confined to white people" (278). Harry reassures his future bride that the women in his immediate family, Marie and Iola, are "too noble to indulge in such sentiments" (278).

Just as Lillian Westland marries a spouse who cannot pass as white, so Harry's choice of mate also represents an interracial union under the rubric of blackness. The mulatto is a trope of mediation, but primarily a mediator within the subculture, bridging racial differences in reconstituting the black family as a heterogeneous union. There is a sense in which Galtonian fusion or what Chesnutt calls the "future American" is indeed occurring, but exclusively among those who identify as African American.

The connection between allegiance to the subculture and the nation is made at the novel's end, which is precisely the point when the white characters disappear. As Lauren Berlant has pointed out, black nationalism serves as a model of national futurity, the standard to which white Americans should assimilate: "Harper's *Iola Leroy* seizes the scene of citizenship from white America and rebuilds it, in the classic sense, imagining a liberal public sphere located within the black community . . . Harper's civic and Christian black American nationality depends not only on eliding the horizon of white pseudo-democracy; she also imagines that African-American nationalism will provide a model of dignity and justice that white American citizens will be obliged to follow" (467). The Mendelist allegory operates at the level of individual allegiance and national development. Not only does the white Negro choose sides, but so does Harper in selecting the ideal standard of national citizenship. She reinvents, to quote Berlant, "a truly African American-centered *American* citizenship" (468).

In a speech entitled "Duty to Dependent Races," Harper explains why African Americans are the ideal citizens: "America needs the Negro for ballast if for nothing else [because] his instinct for law and order, his inborn respect for authority, his inaptitude for rioting and anarchy, his gentleness and cheerfulness as a laborer, and his deep-rooted faith in God will prove indispensable and invaluable elements in a nation menaced as America is by anarchy, socialism, communism, and skepticism poured in with all the jail birds from the continents of Europe and Asia" (qtd. Warren 63). In contrast to the urban picturesque, which privileges European immigrants and sometimes the Chinese over African Americans, Harper privileges the population that has been rendered invisible. To do this, she invokes hereditarian rhetoric to justify black moral character: the aptitude for "good citizenship" is an "instinct" and "inborn." African Americans now represent law and order in contrast to disruptive immigrant radicals. With the Haymarket Affair still fresh in the American memory and an important nativist rallying cry in the 1890s, Harper plays on such fears to vindicate black citizenship.

On the Uses and Abuses of Essentialism

The Mendelist allegory is in some ways politically radical and in other ways deeply conservative. The most praiseworthy aspect of the Mendelist allegory is that it transvalues the racist policies of segregation, anti-miscegenation laws, and one-drop definitions of negritude into sources of black affirmative consciousness. It transforms segregation into subcultural distinctiveness; it counters anti-miscegenation with a celebration of *intra*racial black-white unions; it corroborates one-drop definitions of negritude through the "white Negro's" rejection of white privilege. The Mendelist allegory is in part a narrative of white dissidents, of race traitors, who identify with the minority culture rather than pass as genteel Anglo Americans. Through a deterministic logic of hereditarianism, the protagonist of the Mendelist allegory, ironically, chooses sides and in doing so, discovers a sense of agency, imagines a program of social change, and finally becomes a paragon of citizenship. Biology offers black women, in particular, a sense of social responsibility through social belonging, an ideal of a woman's community centered around the black mother, and an unequivocal allegiance to a racial subculture. Biology, in other words, provides a conceptual means for fusing black nationalism, feminism, and national citizenship. It naturalizes the relationships between ostracized subcultures, voteless women, and national leadership.

The role of women in Chesnutt's passive model of gradual race fusion is as procreators, with social change reduced to interracial sex. The Mendelist allegory offers a far more interventionist notion of social change, in which women are off their backs and on their feet. Ironically, biology is used to liberate women from their biology as reproductive subjects. Furthermore, the Mendelian emphasis on the discreteness and segregation of gametes does not translate literally into a hermetic and atomistic notion of a black subculture. Instead, it provides the means for elevating black subcultural uniqueness—identity culture—into a model of modern Americanism. Black culture becomes the dominant rather than the recessive trait of national character. Black exceptionalism, as in Du Bois, will save the "federal republic." But unlike Du Bois, the saviors will not necessarily be the "college-bred" or even the "Negro college-bred," but black women who represent an "aristocracy of character" cultivated in the school of hard knocks.

The Mendelist allegory, however, affirms the "healthy-mindedness" of the black psyche and the national representativeness of the black community at a cost. In contrast to Du Bois's *Darkwater*, a book that was dismissed by some critics for promoting "Black Bolshevism," Harper's use of black exceptionalism in her 1893 speech at the World's Congress of Representative Women is predicated on the demonization of European and Asian immigrant workers, especially socialists and anarchists.[25] Identity culture is invoked for an anti-socialist agenda, whereas Du Bois in *Darkwater* uses it precisely to imagine a decolonized and democratic "industrial commonwealth." What unites the Mendelist allegory with the urban picturesque and even with Kallen's pluralism is the belief that the "good" citizen is ultimately one who remains distant from labor struggles. Just as the urban picturesque uses citizenship as a way to privilege certain European immigrant cultures (especially those not traditionally affiliated with labor unions) over African Americans, so the Mendelist allegory legitimates black citizenship by excluding immigrant radicals.[26]

In her 1893 speech, Harper's rendition of the "cheerful" African-American worker is reminiscent of Kallen's depiction of the "happy" trade unionist and the urban picturesque's evasion of work. Harper in this same speech naturalizes black citizenship and cheerful laborers through the biological language of "race" instincts: inherent in black character are the "instinct for law and order" and the "inaptitude for rioting and anarchy." This suggests that biology can be used to include as well as to exclude, to privilege as well as to silence. Essentialism is highly variable, in that a racial "essence" is cast as permanent and fixed in inconsistent ways.

I have focused on two competing notions of modern Americanism: Chesnutt's model of unity-in-fusion and Harper's counter-example of unity-in-discreteness. While one model dissolved racial boundaries between white and black, the other reconstituted them, reinforcing racial distinctions through a hereditarian logic of non-blending. Taken together, these two opposing theories of race contact dramatize the dialectical tensions of Jamesian pluralism, that is, the conflicting desire for "connection" and "autonomy," as well as for "inextricable interfusion" and "independence." In the next chapter I shift from racial encounters to religious ones (though the two are by no means mutually exclusive), from the national to the international, from the literary to the oratorical. At the 1893 World's Parliament of Religions, which was an auxiliary event at the Columbian Exposition along with the World's Congress of Representative Women, the competing models of unity-in-variety (fusion versus discreteness) surfaced in debates about the possibilities and limits of a "universal religion." A year after the publication of *Iola Leroy*, anxieties about blending and non-blending manifested themselves in the religious sphere, where some participants imagined a "Buddhized Christianity" while others insisted on Christian uniqueness.

6

East Meets West at the World's Parliament of Religions

On September 11, 1893, the chairman of the World's Parliament of Religions, John Henry Barrows, welcomed nearly four thousand people, including representatives from twelve different world religions, to the opening of the congress. "Welcome, most welcome, O wise men of the East and of the West!" (WPR I:73). Barrows's words of greeting soon turned into a series of oratorical rules, with the Presbyterian minister sounding like a referee briefing the players before a competition: "We are met in a great conference, men and women of different minds, where the speakers will not be ambitious for short-lived, verbal victories over others, where gentleness, courtesy, wisdom and moderation will prevail far more than heated argumentation" (WPR I:75). If anyone should offend a spirit of fellowship, he advised the audience, "let him not be rebuked publicly or personally" (WPR I:75). This caveat was reiterated by the president of the Auxiliary Congress, Charles Frank Bonney, who claimed that "each system of Religion stands by itself in its own perfect integrity, uncompromised, in any degree, by its relation to any other" (WPR I:72).

Compare this non-conflictual model of religious diversity with that offered by the third speaker, Archbishop Freehan of Chicago, who was later forbidden by the Vatican (as were all U.S. Catholic clergy) to attend any future interreligious gatherings. At this overwhelmingly Protestant event held during a time when there was a wave of anti-Catholic attacks in the United States, the archbishop imagined a far different model of religious diversity, one in which the participants would be "meeting together and *talking together* and seeing one another" (WPR I:80; emphasis added). A "diversity of opinion" would cultivate "a sincere respect and reverence and a cordial and fraternal feeling of friendship" (WPR I:80). Archbishop Freehan's model was far more dialogic and indeterminate than the one proffered by the Protestant organizers, and it was therefore seen by some as threateningly flexible.[1]

The opening moments of the parliament revealed the tensions underlying the event, tensions that would grow during the subsequent two weeks. These tensions centered around two contrasting conceptions of diversity: first, as discrete and atomized, with the autonomy of the "each-form" protected and preserved; and second, as dialogic and indeterminate, with boundaries blurred. This dynamic between discreteness and fusion is also seen in the general outline of the parliament, which Bonney formally described in his introduction to the published transcripts. On the one hand, the parliament aimed to "promote and deepen the spirit of human brotherhood among religious men of diverse faiths." Yet on the other hand, it sought to set forth "the important distinctive truths held and taught by each Religion" (WPR I:18). The same tensions that characterize William James's "pluralistic universe," tensions between autonomy and connection, separation and "inextricable interfusion," also inform this late Victorian religious chronotope. The Reverend John Keane, the Anglo-Catholic controversialist and the most prominent Catholic leader in the United States, framed these tensions between particularity and connection in the form of questions: "Shall the future tendency of religion be to greater unity, or to greater diversity? Is it to be a process of elimination, or by a process of synthesis?" (WPR II:1333).[2]

The World's Parliament of Religions was another occasion at the turn of the century when the relations between unity and diversity were theorized and debated. From James's "each-form" to Kallen's and Du Bois's defense of ethno-racial subcultures, I have traced the various attempts from the late nineteenth to the early twentieth century to determine the value of variety in relation to local, national, and transnational modalities of union. Questions that have appeared throughout this book surfaced at the parliament with a religious inflection: How could a "spiritual human brotherhood" include a variety of religious beliefs without sacrificing the particularity of each sect within an ecumenical melting pot? Was religious variety a sign of strength or weakness? Should the world's religions be condensed into one powerful union or loosely brought together into "friendly fellowship"?

The World's Parliament raised important questions about the value of variety, because the physical presence of Buddhist, Hindu, and Shinto representatives from Ceylon (now Sri Lanka), Japan, India, and China in the metropolitan space of Chicago rather than in the missionary fields of the East encouraged serious reflection about the consequences of cross-cultural contact. It sought to construct a common religious discourse in recognition of an increasingly global society, but the status of individual religious faiths remained contested. Some imagined a unity-in-fusion, whereby a "Buddhized Christianity" and a "Christianized Buddhism" would emerge; whereas for others, a model of unity-in-discreteness, or what was referred to as a "side by side" union, signified an ideal arrangement of religious comity.

These competing visions of religious diversity (fusion versus discreteness) also informed the parliament's understanding of religion and nationhood. Some imagined an ideal of conversion, which dislodged the one-to-one relation between people and place either by Hinduizing the American Protestant or by Christianizing the Easterner. Others wanted to reinforce the national parameters of religious belief with Americans as representative Christians, and Indians, for instance, as representing different variations of Hinduism. The prevalence and confusion of this nationalist framework appeared in the parliament's opening ceremony, when the representatives entered the Hall of Columbus "arm in arm," walking "beneath the waving flags of many nations" (WPR I:62). What is significant about this description of the opening ceremony is the role of national flags: they were displayed but not associated with distinct groups of delegates. The delegates entered "arm in arm" rather than according to national affiliation. Despite the often confusing ways in which a nationalist discourse was invoked, it nonetheless provided a familiar way to articulate the racial, cultural, and religious differences among the delegates. The display of various flags also contributed to the visual spectacle of the event, a sign of its cosmopolitanism.

Held in the Hall of Columbus on Michigan Avenue from September 11 to 27, as an auxiliary event at the 1893 Columbian Exposition in Chicago, the parliament attracted a total of almost 150,000 spectators to hear nearly 200 speakers. The most heavily attended of the twenty supplementary congresses, the parliament was the first of its kind to invite participants from all over the globe to take part in an interreligious forum that was open to the general public.[3] For the majority of audience members, who were overwhelmingly middle-class and Protestant, the parliament marked the first time that they encountered representatives of Eastern religions or what were then referred to as the "ethnic religions." The event included such speakers as Anagarika Dharmapala from Ceylon, Pung Kwang Yu from China, and Swami Vivekananda from India. Despite its cosmopolitanism, with more than forty papers delivered by Asian delegates, the event was predominantly Christian and Euro-American, with over 65 percent of the 400 delegates being Protestant (Figure 4).

There were no representatives of Native American religions other than Alice Fletcher, an anthropologist and a student of Franz Boas, who spoke briefly on the subject. Only three African Americans participated, including the Chicago Unitarian Fannie Barrier Williams.[4] The Jewish delegation was also small, consisting primarily of Dr. Kaufman Kohler, a leader of the Reform movement, and Henry Mendes from New York's Sephardic community. There were no representatives from African "tribal" religions. Although Barrows claimed that "equal freedom [was] gladly accorded to all races and both sexes," roughly 10 percent of the speakers were women, which amounted to approximately twenty women, including Elizabeth Cady Stanton.[5]

Historians have commented on the predominantly "Christian flavor" of the event, or in the words of James Ketelaar, on its "Eurocentric and

4. Delegates during a session at the World's Parliament of Religions

Christocentric understanding of the world" (259). This characteristic was not lost on observers of the parliament. The missionary Dr. George William Knox said that "the parliament was distinctively Christian in its conception, spirit, prayers, doxologies, benedictions; in its prevailing language, arguments, and faith" (Barrows, "Results" 138). Though Christians were a clear majority, there were deep divisions within this group that prevented a strong sense of solidarity. Paul Carus, a participant at the parliament and a founder of the Open Court Press (which soon became a major vehicle for bringing Eastern texts to Anglophone readers), distinguished between two types of Christians: "narrow" and "broad."

"Narrow" Christians were those who represented a residual model of religious sectarianism and orthodoxy, shunning contact with other faiths in the fear that boundaries would be dismantled. "Narrow" Christians preferred an isolationist stance, a form of religious protectionism in which old borders could remain unchallenged and hermetic. There was an anti-assimilationist subtext to "narrow" Christianity, a subtext that rejected contact because it feared conversion or reversed assimilation through the seductive rhetorical powers of the charismatic "heathen." By contrast, "broad" Christians, like Carus, considered themselves "theological progressives," and saw in an East-West encounter the means of revitalizing and modernizing Christianity. For Carus, the parliament represented the changing of the guard, the "extinction" of "narrow" Christianity as an obsolete mindset, and the beginning of a "new era of broader and higher religious life" (14).[6]

In this chapter I build on the earlier ones in presenting a historical instance in which the question of variety was consciously and explicitly discussed. The virtues of variety were not debated in a social vacuum, but in dialogue with other concerns such as national exceptionalism, minority resilience, and modern internationalism. For the organizers of the event, the parliament was intended, in part, to demonstrate the inextricable relation between Christian exceptionalism and modern Americanism. In his opening remarks, Barrows illustrated how the two were intertwined. "There is a true and noble sense in which America is a Christian nation, since Christianity is recognized by the supreme court, by the courts of the several states" (*WPR* I:74). The parliament, however, was not exclusively about the consolidation of dominant forms of national and religious identity. Although the organizers desired a monological event of discrete presentations, without debate or argumentation, the exigencies of the parliament produced quite a different affair.

Occurring at the height of imperialism, the event was an unmanageable encounter between dominant and subordinate religions and races in a hall filled with over four thousand people. Within this dynamic space, where the audience frequently interrupted speeches with boos and cheers, the minority presence of the Asian delegates became overwhelming, with their colorful robes overshadowing, literally and figuratively, the black raiment of the Christian clergy. During the two-week event, speakers such as Anagarika Dharmapala and Swami Vivekananda became instant celebrities, pursued by fans and soon lecturing across the country. One eyewitness, Matthew Trumbull, a labor organizer in Chicago, sardonically noted that the "heathen carried away the prizes of most value, while the agnostic and unbelievers cheered" (Seager, *World's Parliament* 146). Charles Little, a Methodist speaker, observed a similar dynamic but in more generous terms: "people expected pagans. And pagans, they thought, were ignorant and impotent of mind, with no reasons for their worship and no brains in their theology. To them the Parliament was a stunning revelation" (211). The "wise men of the East," according to another attendee, provided "a surprise to the whole Occidental world" (Neely 973).

This point was not lost on the Asian representatives. In an 1897 interview Swami Vivekananda said: "The Parliament of Religions, as it seems to me, was intended for a 'heathen show' before the world; but it turned out that the heathens had the upper hand, and made it a 'Christian show' all round" (qtd. Basu and Ghosh 700). Virchand Gandhi, a Jain delegate from India, wrote in the *Arena* that "at least a third and sometimes two-thirds of the great audience of Columbus Hall would make a rush for the exits when a fine orator from India had closed his speech" (qtd. Burke 68). By moving from the margins to the center, the Asian representatives altered the Christian logic of the event, transforming a potentially Orientalist spectacle into an anti-colonial critique. This shift from the margins to the center is also reflective of William James's pluralistic philosophy, a pluralism that was itself partly the result of his engagement with the teachings of Dharmapala and Swami Vivekananda, both of whom he met many years after the parliament: "The centre [of consciousness] works in one way while the margins work in another, and presently overpower the centre and are central themselves" (*PU* 761).[7]

This move of the Asian speakers from the margins to the center is reminiscent of Du Bois's and Kallen's strategic shift from the subculture to the nation. By becoming central, the Asian delegates de-Orientalized the parliamentary space by giving it a content firmly situated in the exigencies of the colonial world. This oratorical coup disrupted the conventional relations between West and East, the metropolis and the periphery, in creating a highly unstable forum that represents a useful counter-balance to the anthropological exhibits of the "main" event at the Columbian Exposition.

The center (Christianity) and the margins ("ethnic religions") worked in opposite ways, with the latter ultimately "overpowering" the event. I will first examine the consolidation of religious variety to substantiate modern Americanism and Christian exceptionalism, then explore the converse: how the Asian representatives used the pluralistic format of the event to usurp the central position. As Archbishop Freehan predicted in his opening remarks, a sense of a "common humanity" would be produced, not through atomized monologues, but through dialogue. This event was another instance when the rhetoric of pluralistic variety was destabilizing, able to be appropriated by different groups toward competing visions of modernity. In this context, it was used to promote syncretic (unity-in-fusion) and non-syncretic (unity-in-discreteness) models of diversity toward radically different understandings of religious cosmopolitanism.

From the Midway to Michigan Avenue

> I thought th' Fair was mixin' an' th' Midway made me crawl,
> But th' Parl'ment of Religions was th' mixin'est of all!
>
> I see th' Turks agoing round th' Midway in th' Fair,
> But our minister reproved me when he seen me peep in thair,
> "Defilin' place" he called it, an' th' Turk "a child of sin";
> But th' Parl'ment of Religions took all them heathen in.
>
> —Minnie Andrews Snell, "Aunt Hannah on the
> Parliament of Religions"

Many observers and participants, including the Columbian Exposition's chief of construction, Daniel Burnham, confidently predicted that in a hundred years the fair would be forgotten, while the parliament would long be remembered.[8] The event's chairman, John Henry Barrows, the head of the First Presbyterian Church in Chicago and a professor of religion at the University of Chicago, contrasted the parliament with the World's Fair: "while the fair was no novelty, the parliament was unique and unexampled" ("Results" 136). The chairman elaborated on the exceptionalism of the parliament by inscribing it within the familiar discourse of American exceptionalism: both the parliament and the United States were signs of religious tolerance and individual freedom. Quoting a letter from an invited guest from India who was unable to attend, Barrows announced at the opening ceremony "that only in this western republic would such a congress as this have been undertaken and achieved" (WPR I:74).

For Paul Carus, a liberal philosopher of religion, editor of *The Monist*, and a German immigrant, the parliament was "unique in its way" and a "landmark of the evolution of religion." It was also "typically American," an event which is "still looked upon as all but impossible in conservative Europe, where the idea still prevails that a man can mount a platform only in company with those whose opinions he would indorse [sic]" (8). Professor Estlin Carpenter of Oxford University similarly noted that "no country in the world possesses the needful boldness of conception and organizing energy save the United States of America" (WPR I:28). This popular perception about the exceptionalism of the parliament was rather short-lived. Burnham's prediction that the parliament would be remembered long after the fair was not fulfilled. Today, over a century later, the Exposition has become a favorite topic of historians and literary scholars, while the parliament, except for the work of a few historians of religion, has fallen into relative obscurity at a time of increased scholarly interest in multiculturalism.

One reason for the popularity of the fair and the neglect of the parliament is suggested in Aunt Hannah's use of "mixin'," a term that refers not only to people of doubtful character but also more generally to a muddled and confusing situation. Where the Midway was "mixin'," the parliament was "mixin'est," a distinction that implies that the fair offered a more coherent arrangement of diverse cultures, one that followed evolutionary lines portraying humanity in its most "civilized" stages down almost to its animalistic origins. The mile-long strip of land, which the *Chicago Tribune* labeled the "Royal Road of Gaiety," consisted of a populist display of discrete ethnographic exhibitions of nonwhite people who performed their "native" customs. Such an arrangement told a linear narrative that reinforced Victorian America's longstanding racial and cultural prejudices. This arrangement not only reiterated an evolutionary understanding of "progress" but also relied on imperial modes of seeing, which Edward Said has described as "the vision of Orient as spectacle" (*Orientalism* 153). The fair, and more specifically the Midway Plaisance, has become a popular chronotope of contemporary study precisely because it exhibits the conventional power dynamics of Orientalist performance. The Occidental gaze managed the Oriental "other" through a constellation of disciplinary practices that portrayed Asianness as an ethnographic prototype of backwardness.

The parliament, by contrast, was a far less stable affair, which could not easily be reduced to an Orientalist spectacle. Rather than silently performing "native" customs along the Midway, Asian representatives directly addressed the largely Christian audience, not in unfamiliar tongues that were then translated but in English. Many of the Asian orators spoke English fluently, a point that was frequently noted in private and public accounts of the parliament. Of Swami Vivekananda, a popular Hindu speaker from Calcutta, the *Chicago Advocate* stated: "His knowledge of English is as though it were his other tongue" (qtd. Chetanananda 59). Regarding an equally popular orator, Dharmapala, the Dubuque, Iowa, *Times* reported that his "peroration was as pretty a thing as a Chicago audience ever heard" (qtd. Burke 75).

Asian representatives were also highly conversant with Christian doctrine, able to draw conceptual parallels between Hindu and Buddhist philosophy and biblical parables. Dharmapala, who had been educated in Roman Catholic missionary schools, described his leather-bound Bible as "falling apart from constant use" (682). They were colonial mimics gone awry, using their knowledge of the imperial religion to describe its failings in mellifluous prose. Dharmapala highlighted the contradiction between Christian charity and the slaughter of animals by declaring the "great slaughter-houses in Chicago a disgrace to civilization and to the world." He explained that "the people of the East" could not understand a "religion which allows such practices." Swami Vivekananda similarly underscored Christian hypocrisy when he addressed his audience directly: "You Christians, who are so fond of sending out missionaries to save the soul of the heathen—why do you not try to save their bodies from starvation?"⁹ Their linguistic and cultural fluency was a source of oratorical power, which inspired religious doubt among many earnest attendees.

Because of the openness of the spoken word and the unpredictable nature of the relation between speaker and audience, the critical paradigms used to analyze the fair are not readily transferable to the parliament. If the fair illustrates the Victorian preoccupation with otherness as order, classification, and discipline, then the World's Parliament typifies the equally Victorian concept of otherness as unorganized collections, messy and contradictory attempts to assemble the heterogeneous. Although the Protestant organizers structured the parliament according to discrete and distinct presentations with the different religions, like the different Protestant denominations, arranged in a "side by side" manner, the actual event was far less orderly. The parliament had a distinctively carnivalesque atmosphere, with speakers running between the Hall of Columbus and the adjacent Hall of Washington to deliver and redeliver their papers to overflow crowds. At times, speakers did not even show up, especially for the afternoon sessions, which required the organizers to gather anyone they could for an impromptu speech. Some observers described it as "bedlam" and "babel."

I see the Parliament of Religions as a representative event of the late Victorian period, because it depicts modernity as a process of encounter between dominant and subordinate peoples in a world plagued by colonialism, missionaries, and a global economy of uneven development. Though the organizers wanted to exclude these extra-religious concerns, they crept back in with a vengeance. This highly unstable forum is an important corrective to "White City," the event that concludes Alan Trachtenberg's *The Age of Incorporation*. White City, located in the center of the World's Columbian Exposition in Chicago, was the showpiece of the event, depicting a future city of harmony and technological advancement. There were displays of electric kitchens, electric bulbs, dynamos, and railroads. The master plan of the city highlighted the coordination of space and structure with the Court of Honor, the hub of White City, designed in a uniform neoclassical style in uniform whiteness. The architecture accentuated symmetry in form, harmonious arrangement, and visual sameness, which, as Trachtenberg aptly notes, served as an allegory of the corporate age, an age that idealized a future without conflict.

Although White City is a response to an imperial, corporatized world, it legitimates this world, as Trachtenberg demonstrates, through an ideal society of symmetry, whiteness, and uniformity. Whereas Trachtenberg focuses on the "main" event of the Columbian Exposition, I choose an auxiliary one. Whereas White City represents a corporate ideal of organization—of unity through subordination—blanketed in the aesthetics of whiteness and harmony, the parliament was far less predictable, an event that aspired toward harmony and symmetry but failed. To end with the World's Parliament of Religions rather than White City is to bring a different emphasis to the familiar narrative of incorporation: an emphasis informed by Jamesian pluralism, whereby "nothing includes everything, or dominates over everything ... Something always escapes" (*PU* 776).

The Crisis of Christian Variety

> Then a Cath'lic man got up an' spoke, about Christ an' th' cross;
> But th' Christians of th' other creeds, they giv' thair heds a toss.
> When th' Babtist spoke, th' Presbyterians seemed to be fightin' mad,
> 'Tel th' Parl'ment of Religions made my pore old soul feel sad.
> —"Aunt Hannah on the Parliament of Religions"

The parliament signified not only a crisis of variety between Christianity and the world's other religions but also an internal crisis in which the very definition and future direction of Christianity were at stake. Had Christianity become too heterogeneous, so that it could no longer be unified? If Christians within one nation could not find a common ground, then how could they expect to found a "human brotherhood" with the religions of the world? The Presbyterian minister Charles Briggs believed that the only way to save Christendom was to dissolve the various denominations and form one organic church. The "process of dissolution has gone on long enough," Briggs wrote in 1899; "the barriers between the Protestant denominations should be removed and an organic union formed" (*Whither* xi). A similar sentiment was expressed by those on the missionary front. George Candlin, an English Methodist missionary in China who spoke at the parliament, insisted that "our denominational distinctions have for the most part become anachronisms. They rest on certain hopeless arguments which can never be settled one way or another. Our divisions are strangling us." He supported, instead, the "catholic development of Christian thought" (WPR II:1184–85).

A single church would make Christianity more appealing and simpler to sell to potential converts. As it was, the "unsophisticated pagan" was so bewildered by the confusion of sects as he was bombarded by Episcopalians, Presbyterians, Calvinists, Armenians, Unitarians, and Trinitarians, that he finally gave up in despair "the vain attempt to ascertain what Christianity is" (WPR II:1188). Both the domestic theologian and the Methodist missionary insisted that Protestantism must be consolidated in order to be saved. The only way to preserve the power and appeal of Protestantism at a time of waning interest was to opt for a unified Christian church rather than the diversity of "jarring sects."

This anxiety about the internal variety of Christianity was part of a larger spiritual crisis at the turn of the century, which was fundamentally a crisis of plausibility. Christian discourses were losing their explanatory power to make sense of a dramatically changing world. Religious doubt, rather than faith, characterized middle-class Protestant attitudes toward evolutionary theories of development, new scientific discoveries, and the secularization of progress. In 1886 a writer for *The Forum* observed that "Christianity appears to many of the wisest to be at the present day in deadlier peril than it has been at any time during the eighteen hundred years of its existence" (qtd. P. Carter 10). Also writing for *The Forum*, Charles Briggs noted soon after the event that Christianity was experiencing an "ebb-time," since it could not keep pace "with the progress of knowledge" ("Alienation" 366). These anxieties were compounded by the changing demographics of the nation.

Immigration from Southern and Eastern Europe during the last two decades of the century significantly increased the membership of Jewish organizations and of the Catholic Church at the same time as Methodism, traditionally the most popular of the Protestant denominations, showed a steady decline. Henry King Carroll, a Methodist leader and director of the Division of Churches for the Eleventh U.S. Census (1890), acknowledged this decline in his talk at the parliament, entitled "The Present Religious Condition of America." Carroll stated in a disinterested tone that the Roman Catholic church was "now the largest of the churches in number of communicants" and the wealthiest in terms of the "value of house property" (*WPR* II:1164). Methodism, he noted, was second. Seven years later, in an article in *The Independent,* Carroll adopted a far more concerned tone in acknowledging "the indubitable and uncomfortable fact" that the membership of the Methodist church was significantly decreasing (38).

These concerns about the waning authority of Protestantism surfaced at the World's Parliament of Religions in numerous ways. While some, such as George Candlin, considered Protestant variety a source of weakness, others believed that it was a sign of individual liberty and freedom. Whether one embraced religious variety or rejected it, the language of diversity played a central role at the parliament in reconfiguring Christianity for the next century. In his commentary on the parliament for the *Methodist Review,* Charles Little perceptively noted that Christian variety was a source of power but also contributed to Christianity's lack of coherence: "The display of Protestant Christianity . . . lacked unity and coherence. It was abundant in variety and abundant, too, in power. One thing, however was painfully and conspicuously absent, namely, a clear, definite, and powerful statement of the fundamental positions of Protestantism" (216). What had been considered the strength of Christianity, namely its internal variety, was now seen as a source of its vulnerability. How could one be loyal to a set of beliefs if those beliefs were "conspicuously absent"?

Protestantism was looking more like the vague lines of an impressionistic painting than like the definite metal marks of an etching. Its character was impressionable and susceptible rather than steadfast and loyal. In reacting to this perceived assault on Protestant character, Herrick Johnson objected to the parliament because "it confounds moral distinctions." Johnson claimed that declarations of "fellowship" and "universal fraternity" obliterated "important peculiarities" of each religion: "Nothing could be better calculated to shade away the eternal distinctions between right and wrong, between truth and falsehood, than such a conspicuous 'fellowship' and 'co-operation'" (401). Contact in the name of "fellowship" ultimately threatened Christianity, a threat that Johnson perceived in the parliament's tendency toward "blending and obliterating" religious distinctions.

Though Carus dismissed such speakers as "narrow" Christians, Johnson and others raised important questions about the necessity of boundaries in establishing religious identity and convictions. In contrast to the

Mendelist allegory, which sought to abet a crisis of multiple loyalties through a hereditarian logic of non-blending, the post-reformation trend of Christian diversification resulted in a full-blown crisis at the parliament. Many of the Christian participants called for a need to re-reform Christian variety in more cogent and homogeneous terms. One way to curtail Christian plurality was to shun contact with religious others. One Methodist representative, T. McKendree Stuart, explicitly expressed such a position in commenting that the "Christian system cannot admit any other system on the same plane of divine authority with itself" (42). The Archbishop of Canterbury went even further in refusing to attend the parliament altogether on the grounds that appearing on stage with representatives of other faiths would create a scene of parity that would call into question the authority of Christianity as "the one religion."[10]

Cross-cultural contact did prove helpful for some Christian participants in reassuring them that their own variety was still manageable in contrast to the perceived excessive diversity of Eastern religions. T. McKendree Stuart alleviated his own concerns about Christian superiority by noting that the Eastern religions were too "heterogeneous" to be spiritually satisfying. According to Stuart, only those who were "most vague and unreasonable" seemed to find "inspiration" in the "vast, complex, heterogeneous, and irrecoverable systems of Asiatic religions" (42). Reverend Gordon, a missionary and educator in Japan, similarly commented on Buddhism's "lack of unity and homogeneity" (*WPR* II:1294). Reverend Slater, a Christian missionary in Bangalore, India, also found Eastern religions, and specifically Hinduism, excessively diverse. He described Hinduism as a "vague eclecticism, the sum total of several shades of belief, of divergent systems, of various types and characters of the outward life" (*WPR* I:456). A Presbyterian missionary and president of the Imperial Tungwen College in Beijing, W. A. P. Martin, called the state religion of China a "heterogeneous cult" (*WPR* II:1140). Four years after the parliament, Barrows visited Poona, India, and observed "the lack of unity prevailing in India." "It is an aggregation of the peoples, governments, religions and classes where the divisions are woful [*sic*] indeed" (*Christianity* 168).

In contrast to the excessive heterogeneity of India, Christian variety seemed less daunting and threatening. The disorderly "other" reconstituted Christian unity by reconfiguring denominational variety as a source of strength and superiority. Cultural contact actually reinforced

Christian provincialism. As Reverend Burrell of New York commented, "God be praised for this congress on religions. Never before has Christianity—the one true religion—been brought into such open and decisive contrast with the other religions of the world" (qtd. Trumbull 339–340).

While Protestants turned to India to appease concerns about their own denominational excess, they looked toward Catholicism for assistance in imagining a broader Christian community. Distance from Indian variety meant proximity to Catholic unity. In fact, one of the most satisfying aspects of the parliament for Barrows was the dialogue that was established between American Catholics and Protestants. Despite attacks against Catholicism in the immediate aftermath of the parliament, there was now a "better understanding," according to Barrows, "between Catholics and Protestants in America than ever heretofore" ("Results" 143). The Eastern other played a crucial role in making Catholicism less alien within the United States. Eastern heterogeneity resulted in Christian consolidation. Charles Little juxtaposed Catholic unity against the petty squabbles among Protestant denominations. Influenced by his experiences at the parliament, Leonard Woosley Bacon wrote the definitive history of American Christianity in 1897, in which he supported the ideal of a Christian union that included the Roman Catholic Church.

In contrast to the concerns about denominational unity among Protestant speakers, Catholic participants at the parliament asserted a confident tone toward an ideal of heterogeneous unity. While "broad" Christians were reconceiving American Protestantism as a multicultural faith, Catholics claimed that they were already cosmopolitan. Bishop Keane announced that Catholicism "alone is world-wide and cosmopolitan embracing all races and nations and peoples and tongues" (WPR I:487). Isaac Hecker, an erstwhile Methodist and Catholic convert, noted that "Catholics were the only religious body in the United States not torn asunder by sectional strife during our civil war" (qtd. P. Carter 142). Protestant leaders found in Catholicism a confident and uncontested sense of unity, which appeared especially attractive when the common ground of denominationalism seemed vague and unstable.

With the help of the Eastern "other," the parliament represented a site where the crisis of Christian variety was both expressed and remedied.

The event witnessed the modernization of American Christianity, in which Protestantism fused with Catholicism, creating a cosmopolitan faith that was both various and unified. One could now mingle with the Eastern other without worrying about forsaking one's own Christian character. At the parliament, this modernized Christian union found its strongest expression in the speech by Philip Schaff, a retired professor of religion at the Union Theological Seminary in New York City. Too ill to deliver the paper (he died a few days later), he sat on the stage listening to his student declare: "Variety in unity and unity in variety is the law of god in nature, in history, and in his kingdom. Unity without variety is dead uniformity. There is beauty in variety. There is no harmony without many sounds, and a garden incloses all kinds of flowers . . . The world will never become wholly Greek, nor wholly Roman, nor wholly Protestant, but it will become wholly Christian, and will include every type and every aspect, every virtue and every grace of Christianity—an endless variety in harmonious unity, Christ being all in all" (WPR II:1194). As an "endless variety" kept in check by "harmonious unity," Schaff's pluralistic Christian union was not only a sign of aesthetic beauty—"There is beauty in variety"—but also the best illustration of the "new and improved" Christianity that the parliament sought to promote.[11] It signified the apex of religious development, a theological corollary to Spencerian progress. "We must remember that denominations are most numerous," Schaff remarked, "in the most advanced and active nations of the world" (WPR II:1193).

In his prefatory remarks to his two volumes of parliamentary proceedings, Barrows used the trope of white light as a visual corollary to Schaff's Christian pluralism: "Religion, like the white light of Heaven, has been broken into many-colored fragments by the prisms of men. One of the objects of the Parliament of Religions has been to change this many-colored radiance back into the white light of heavenly truth" (WPR I:3). The former president of Spain, Emilio Castelar, who covered the parliament in the Spanish press, similarly observed that "Christianity, like light, has many colors" (qtd. WPR I:642). As a metaphor for modern or "broad Christianity," white light contains all colors, a chromatic example of variety-in-unity, which ultimately disciplines the "endless variety" of its constituent elements through the "harmonious unity" of whiteness. "White light" is also a metaphoric defense of particularity, since through a prism the distinct colors are still identifiable—not completely blurred or blended with the other elements of light. This model of diversity within unity, which is then circumscribed by whiteness, served as the organizational principle for the arrangement of cultures at the parliament.

A Side-by-Side Union

Through its format of individual speeches and the actual arrangement of speakers on the stage, the parliament typified a Protestant mode of organization that underscored the "distinctive truths of each religion." Centered around individual presentations, the format suppressed the relational character of religious thought and instead promoted a reified view of each discrete creed. Like the Methodist metaphor of Christian union, wherein each denomination signified a separate string of the harp, the parliament organized the different faiths so that each speaker represented a distinct theology. Even when the speakers in the second half of the event were asked to lecture on the future of religion and evaluate their faith in relation to others, the information was still conveyed through individual presentations with little or no room for dialogue and debate. The organizing committee also arranged for "separate and independent" denominational congresses to concur with the parliament, with the aim of more fully describing "their doctrines and the service they have rendered to mankind" (WPR I:68).

At least one observer of the period criticized the parliament for structuring the conference around individual presentations rather than interfaith discussions: "This cosmopolitan assembly was not strictly a parliament, because extemporaneous debate was absent. It was rather a World's fair of theological exhibits with a sort of Midway Plaisance attachment for the *bric a brac* of creeds" (Trumbull 334). Considered by some as a "hierological museum" of exotic specimens, the parliament reinforced the disparity and distinctiveness of religions through its organizing principle of unity through discreteness. The leap from "distinctive truths" to "brotherhood," however, was not convincingly made. The parliament seemed to be caught between its structural emphasis on individuation and its rhetoric of universalism.

The Protestant notion of unity, or what I call "unity-in-discreteness," conceived as a loose collection of particularities, also structured the arrangement of delegates on the stage. In the proceedings, Barrows quotes an eyewitness report of the closing ceremonies:

> Never since the confusion of tongues at Babel have so many religions, so many creeds, stood side by side, hand in hand, and almost heart to heart, as in the great amphitheater last night. On the great platform of Columbus Hall sat the representatives of creeds and sects that in bygone days hated one another with a hatred that knew no moderation. The last and closing scene of the great Parliament of Religions is one that will live forever in the memory of those who were so fortunate as to be spectators . . . On the stage, beneath the folds of the flags of all nations, were the representatives of all religions. The dull, black and somber raiment of the West only intensified the radiantly contrasted garbs of the Oriental priests. (WPR I:158)

This orderly arrangement of diversity resembles William James's pluralistic universe, which is based on a notion of "nextness," in which proximity suggests unity but also autonomy.[12] Both models promote a "side by side" union, with each element seen as distinct yet also linked through its "nextness" to others. Such a union embraces variety, but a domesticated variety that does not blend its distinctive elements in order to form an eclectic synthesis. Reflecting on the parliament, Crawford Toy wrote in the *New World:* "It was not intended to be a scientific gathering, but rather a friendly meeting for the exhibition of different religious ideas side by side" (Toy 737). The arrangement of people "side by side" also describes the arrangement of ideas that were articulated from the same podium but were not to intermingle. One reason a "side by side" union was a necessary organizing principle for the Protestant architects of the event was that it preserved not only the uniqueness of American Protestantism but also the distinctiveness of the "Oriental Other." The Protestant clergy and the Asian priests must be arranged side by side, so that the distinctiveness of each defined and reinforced the uniqueness of the other. Proximity generated difference.

As Barrows's contrast between "black raiment" and "radiantly contrasted garbs" suggests, religious difference was frequently depicted in terms of distinctions in dress. The press regularly described this visual contrast as a "picturesque spectacle." The *Chicago Times* described the delegates' vestments as having an aesthetic content apart from the speaker's words:

> Yellow and blue, red and lavender, old gold and green, cardinal, crimson and scarlet . . . a bewildering kaleidoscope of tints, punctuated and emphasized by the still black and white of American and European . . . Strange costumes of rich silks, satins, and velvets were next neighbor to common flannel. One son of Asia dressed his limbs in blue and pink percale pantaloons, and another in some soft good of shrimp pink . . . At the eastern end of the stage sat . . . [the representatives] of Japan. Their rich silk vestments, delicate in texture, and gorgeous in their richly blended tints and shades, looked in the distance like a flower pot in a garden of black.[13]

This description underscores a point repeatedly made in comments about the parliament, namely that it was, to borrow Paul Carus's words, an "unprecedented spectacle," which was "often picturesque" (Carus 389). The arrangement on the stage dramatizes Thomas Wentworth Higginson's metaphor of a "symphony of religions" in Technicolor rather than in sound, a visual performance in which variety signified not the dissolution of discrete creeds but a cosmopolitan celebration of them all.[14] In this "kaleidoscope of tints," there was still a clear arrangement of orderly variety. The "black and white" colors associated with the West were contrasted with the carnivalesque blend of the Orient's "exotic" yellows, blues, and reds. Chromatic intermingling occurred exclusively in the East, which was appropriately displayed on the "eastern end of the stage," so that the "garden" of Western Protestantism—perhaps arranged along the western end of the stage—could remain purely black, in a visual and figurative sense, as the absence of color.

What the liberal Protestant gaze demonstrated in these descriptions of variety's theatricality was that heterogeneity was not a threat to coherence but ensured it. The result was a pleasurable, harmonious, and visually exciting union that enlivened the drabness of Christianity without the Eastern montage of colors actually fusing with it. This parallels historically what many non-Christian participants considered to be the purpose of the event: "to aid a beleaguered Christianity in meeting the demands of the modern age [in order] to teach Christianity both what it lacked and what it had lost" (Ketelaar 281). Just as the colorful garb rejuvenated the dull raiment of the West, so the spiritual wisdom of the East was expected to prepare Christianity for the coming century. Such a panacea, by which the East rescued the West from its own spiritual ennui, occurred at the level of aesthetics with the reconciliation of the pluralist dilemma: the distinctiveness of East and West could still be preserved in a heterogeneous union.

The Heathen's Jeremiad

> I listened to th' Buddhist, in his robes of shinin' white,
> As he told how like to Christ's thair lives, while ours was not—
>   a mite,
> 'Tel I felt, to lead a Christian life, a Buddhist I must be,
> An' th' Parl'ment of Religions brought religious doubt to me.
> —"Aunt Hannah on the Parliament of Religions"

Paul Carus observed that although "discussion had been excluded from the programme so as to avoid friction, it could not be entirely controlled" (388). There were still unpredictable moments when the Asian speakers stood behind the podium before a crowd of thousands. The "side by side" model that the Protestant organizers tried to maintain was easily put into disarray. One evening, for example, Dharmapala went far beyond his allotted time, and the next morning's schedule was adjusted so that he could finish his lengthy lecture on the Vedanta philosophy. Swami Vivekananda, whom the *New York Times* dubbed "the greatest figure in the Parliament of Religions," gave an impromptu talk the first afternoon, which soon resulted in a mandate for ten more appearances.[15] The audience's affection for certain figures, most if not all of them Asian, transformed the schedule, making the event far more accommodating than the organizers had originally intended.

Not only did the charismatic presence of the Asian speakers result in schedule changes, but they were perceived by some as possessing the power of a "propagandist" who could potentially convert the Christian maidens in the audience (Figure 5). Their very popularity stirred up fears of reversed assimilation. The *St. Louis Observer* noted that Dharmapala "looked the very image of a propagandist, and one trembled to know that such a figure stood at the head of the movement to consolidate all the disciples of Buddha and to spread 'the light of Asia' throughout the civilized world" (Seager *World's Parliament* 110). Vivekananda claimed to have converted nearly four thousand Americans to Hinduism during his stay. The *Indian Mirror* reported that the "tide of conversion seemed to have rolled back from the East to the West—the tables were completely turned" (French 69). Such figures as Vivekananda and Dharmapala unsettled the side-by-side union, not only in the literal sense of the meeting's format, but also at a deeper level. They represented a specter of conversion through oratorical seduction.[16]

What is especially intriguing is that the Asian delegates managed to seduce their Protestant audience by vociferously attacking Christianity. The harsher the Asian jeer, the greater was the Christian cheer. When Protap Chandra Majumdar, the author of *The Oriental Christ* (a book that was especially popular among Boston Unitarians), criticized the materialism of the West, arguing that its preoccupation with activity and work prevented "little time to consider the great questions of regeneration, of personal sanctification, of truth and judgment and of acceptance before God," the audience broke into loud applause.[17] Dharmapala also received a positive response later the same day when he criticized Chris-

5. Eastern delegates on the platform at the parliament: (*left to right*) Virchand Gandhi, Anagarika Dharmapala, Swami Vivekananda

tian missionaries as "intolerant" and "selfish" (WPR II:1093). Such denunciations were greeted not with defensiveness but with tolerance and even warmth. The *Chicago Tribune* referred to the third day of the parliament, when Asian speakers criticized missionary practices in the East, as the "greatest day so far of the parliament," naming it "Oriental day."[18] Christian tolerance thus mediated the conflictual words from the East, not only to evade addressing critiques of missionary work, but also to demonstrate the superiority of Christianity through its benevolence. This explains why the speakers who berated Christianity most vigorously received the warmest applause.

Christianity requires dissent, opposition, and criticism in order to highlight its own tolerance. For a religion that relies on persuasion as a mode of conversion, tolerance is a way of persuading through generosity. So if you cannot convert the "heathen" through doctrine, then you can at least try to do so through kindness. Tolerance also is a valuable way of cohering the different segments of the Protestant community, primarily through a shared belief in the value of Christian charity. At the Parliament of Religions, Christian tolerance united the mainly Protestant audience and also established a bond of sympathy between the audience and the Asian speakers on the stage. The fact that this bond of sympathy should be expressed most intensely when the Asian speakers were at their most vituperative illustrates the lengths to which liberal Christianity would go to embrace opposition in order to preserve its own sense of specialness.

This confused a number of the Asian representatives, especially the Japanese Buddhist layman Hirai Kinzo. Considered the most eloquent of the Buddhist representatives from Japan (perhaps because he was the only one who was fluent in English), Hirai arrived in Chicago with what he knew would be a highly controversial speech entitled "The Real Position of Japan toward Christianity." It was seen as so potentially offensive that Barrows considered preventing Hirai from presenting it (Ketelaar 229). Hirai vilified Christian hypocrisy, racism, and imperialism, listing one offense after another until he proudly declared himself a "heathen":

> When some years ago a Japanese was not allowed to enter a university on the Pacific coast of America because of his being of a different race; when a few months ago the school board in San Francisco enacted a regulation that no Japanese should be allowed to enter the public

school there; when last year the Japanese were driven out in wholesale from one of the territories of the United States; when our business men in San Francisco were compelled by some union not to employ the Japanese assistants or laborers, but the Americans; when there are some in the same city who speak on the platform against those of us who are already here; when there are many men who go in procession hoisting lanterns marked 'Japs must go'; . . . If such be the Christian ethics—well, we are perfectly satisfied to be heathen. (WPR I:448–449)

Hirai's presentation received overwhelming approval. The *Chicago Herald* reported that "loud applause" followed many of his declarations and there were "a thousand cries of 'Shame!' as he pointed out the wrongs . . . of false Christianity." The audience appeared to have disregarded Barrows's ground rules, specifically his recommendation that the audience remain silent. At the conclusion of Hirai's speech, before four thousand people in the Hall of Columbus, "Dr. Barrows grasped his hand, and the Reverend Lloyd Jones threw his arms around his neck, while the audience cheered vociferously and waved hats and handkerchiefs in an excess of enthusiasm."[19] Hirai was rather shocked at this response, as he had expected to be "torn from the platform" before finishing his address. This "excess of enthusiasm" also persuaded Hirai to return to Japan as a "Christian."

In an article written a year after the event, Barrows related what Hirai had told him before embarking for Japan: "I go back a Christian, by which I mean that Christianity is a religion which I shall be glad to see established in Japan. Only let the Christian missionaries not interfere with our national usages and patriotic holidays. I have been delighted with America and especially with its tolerance" ("Results" 141). It seemed that even the most embittered opponents of Christianity, those who most stubbornly retained their "heathenness," could be shown the light through a handshake and a hug. Christian tolerance could convert the "heathen" into a Christian or at the very least a Christian sympathizer, through what Laura Chant, another speaker at the parliament, described as "good manners."

Christian tolerance could be used to persuade the seemingly unpersuadable as well as to reaffirm a sense of Christian community. Pung Kwang Yu, a Chinese diplomat who was stationed in Washington, D.C., ended his speech by reminding his audience about the "honest and law-abiding" nature of Chinese immigrants in the United States: "I have a favor to ask of all the religious people of America and that is that they will treat, hereafter, all my countrymen just as they have treated me" (*WPR* I:439). As an implicit critique of the 1892 Chinese Exclusion Act called the Geary Law, Pung's attack on Christian hypocrisy received loud cheers of support from the audience, and Barrows promised that he would impart the message to the government, adding that he hoped the result would be an end to "the obnoxious Geary law" (Fields 124).

I call this embrace of the vociferous words of Asian critics a "heathen's jeremiad," whereby criticism only served to unite the Protestant audience. Whether denouncing America's domestic policy on immigration or debunking claims to Christian uniqueness, the Asian speakers' words were interpreted by the audience as therapeutic, since they acknowledged and redeemed the audience's sins. The heathen's anger when combined with the audience's self-rebuking shouts of "Shame!" created a balance between lamentation of sins and affirmation of redemption, between crisis and optimism. The jeremiad as a public mode of exhortation was a ritual, according to Sacvan Bercovitch, "designed to join social criticism to spiritual renewal, public to private identity, the shifting 'signs of the times' to certain traditional metaphors, themes, and symbols" (xi). In this period of transition, at a time of growing secularization and the crisis of Christian unity, it only seems appropriate that the jeremiad should surface during the parliament as a way to make sense of these shifting "signs of the times." That the figure of Jeremiah should be an "outsider," and particularly a non-Christian, shows the extent to which the Christian community was refashioning itself to be more inclusive, to be the common ground upon which a global community would develop.

The jeremiad, as a mode of social control, was a way of including the outsider, even the self-confessed "heathen," as already part of the Christian community. As James Ketelaar points out, "the invited 'others' of the Orient were *by their very participation* already constituted by the parliament as representatives who desired to be *included*" (274). The heathen's jeremiad, therefore, was a way for a modernized Christianity to embrace its own internal denominational variety, as well as to include and domesticate religious variety at an international level.

When Jeremiah was an "insider," however, he was decisively rejected. Mohammed [Alexander Russell] Webb, an American Presbyterian convert to Islam, delivered two papers at the parliament. His interest in Islam had begun when he was the U.S. ambassador to the Philippines. After six years of serious study of the religion, he became a leader of an Islamic mission to the United States and edited a New York journal called *The Moslem World*. In 1898 the sultan of the Ottoman Empire appointed Webb an honorary consul to the United States. Webb's talk, "The Spirit of Islam," sought to clarify certain Western misconceptions about Islam, including the controversial topic of polygamy. He adamantly stated that "polygamy never was and is not a part of the Islamic system," but went on to say that in the East some did practice polygamy, which had to be understood in their own cultural terms. He elicited such rage from the audience that Barrows remarked in his collection, "The reading of this paper was an exceptional event in the proceedings ... [with] hisses and cries of 'Shame!'" (*WPR* I:127).[20] On the following day, newspapers included parenthetical references to the cries of disapproval. Because of the controversy of this talk, Barrows omitted Webb's defense of polygamy from his edited collection of the proceedings.

In his coverage of the parliament for the *Methodist Review*, Charles Little explained his objection to this "turbaned American": "An Arab, an East Indian, or a Turk, defending the faith and the practices of his fathers, would have been listened to with patience; but the Koranized American provided a tempest of scorn. The outcry was indeed a protest against polygamy; but it was much more a protest against a flagrant lapse from the Anglo-Saxon ideal and reality of home ... We had not a genuine, but a veneered, Mohammedan ... We heard about Islam, but not from Islam" (208). This passage demonstrates the degree of tolerance awarded to the authentic other, the appropriate Asian, whose words were perceived as the genuine and sincere expression of a people and a place. When this one-to-one correlation between a religious identity and a national one was violated, when the Anglo-Saxon ideal became a "Koranized American," then Jeremiah's words became counterfeit.

Webb was rejected not because he defended polygamy in the East, as Little candidly admitted, but because he personified Christian and Anglo-Saxon anxieties about reversed assimilation. If the recalcitrant Japanese Buddhist could be persuaded to acknowledge the benevolence of Christianity, then the white Christian could also be persuaded by the truths of what were called "ethnic religions." But the "side by side" union that cohered Christian variety could be transgressed only by converting the heathen into a Christian and not the other way around. Ironically, it was not a racial or religious "other" that demarcated the limits of Christian tolerance but an erstwhile Presbyterian who wore a red fez.[21]

As Minnie Andrews Snell's poem suggests, Aunt Hannah's perplexity at the parliament raised the possibility that the West could be Easternized, that the fretting among the Christian denominations made the Eastern faiths more appealing. The theme of deconversion, which was humorously alluded to in Snell's poem, was more literally performed at the end of the parliament after Dharmapala's lecture on Buddhism and theosophy on September 26 in the Athenaeum Building, under the auspices of the Theosophical Society of Chicago. The hall was packed, and as the audience was about to leave, "The announcement came from the platform that an unusual event was about to take place. C. T. Strauss was about to be admitted to the faith of Buddha. The ceremony was simple, yet impressive. Mr. Strauss took his place upon the platform before the priest, Dharmapala pronounced in Sanskrit the formula oath of Buddha. Mr. Strauss repeated it after him. That was all. It was ended in a moment, and Mr. Strauss was an accepted and approved Buddhist of the Maha-Bodhi Samaj" (Fields 129).

Born of Jewish parents and a student of comparative religions and philosophy, Charles Strauss was a twenty-nine-year-old owner of the oldest and largest wholesale lace curtain company in New York City. Newspaper accounts of Strauss's conversion underscore his family's disbelief over their son's "abjuration of the faith of his father" and his move "toward the effete religious mysticism of the East." His housekeeper, however, was not surprised. She told the press that Strauss had been interested in the tenets of Buddhism for some time.[22] In the aftermath of the parliament, an event largely dedicated to persuading the non-Christian delegates that Christianity was the superior world-religion, it is ironic that an American, and specifically a Jewish-American, should convert to Buddhism. This public performance was an implicit rebuke of the parliament's foundational premise of religious and national exceptionalism. It confirmed fears of reversed assimilation, that the West was as potentially impressionable and malleable as its Eastern counterpart. Furthermore, Strauss's conversion demonstrates a point of common identification in that Judaism and Buddhism represent minority faiths vis-à-vis Christianity. While Judaism was marginalized within the

United States (and had little visibility at the parliament), Buddhism was subordinated within the colonial world of the British Empire.

Strauss's conversion, together with Aunt Hannah's religious doubt, also illustrates that the parliament's content could not entirely be controlled. Despite the carefully staged manner of the event, with each speaker occupying a distinct position both physically and spiritually in a "side by side" union on the stage, the unpredictable relation between speaker and audience left open an unstable combination of factors. While for some, listening to critics of Christianity exemplified Christian tolerance, for others, it created religious doubt. For still others, the critical words of the heathen's jeremiad inspired passion, and the boundaries distinguishing the speaker from the audience were transgressed not only vocally with shouts of "Shame!" but even physically, with a crowd of young Victorian ladies storming the stage at one point to kiss Shibata Reiichi, the Japanese "High Priest" of Shintoism.[23] Depicted in the press as a "chaste kiss of brotherhood," the scene of a Japanese priest publicly kissing and embracing several white ladies suggests that the heathen's presence destabilized rather than reinforced the parliament's "side by side" union.

The parliament's organizing principle, unity-in-discreteness, was becoming increasingly indiscreet as Victorian ladies not only climbed over chairs to the stage but also crowded around such charismatic speakers as Dharmapala and Swami Vivekananda asking them to autograph their fans. As the congress progressed, the arrangement of cultures into discrete clusters began to disperse and the Protestant models of cultural contact became increasingly irrelevant. What did emerge were competing models of variety based on fusion or religious syncretism, in which Christian formulations of hybridism contrasted with those articulated by Eastern speakers.

Christian Syncretism

Besides the anti-syncretic model of a side-by-side union, there were alternative ways in which variety and unity were configured. Syncretism or cultural fusion was advocated by Christian and Eastern speakers alike. There were a variety of ways, moreover, to be syncretic. Religious eclecticism did not refer to a fixed and determinate notion of cultural borrowing and blending; rather, it signified an elastic process of synthesis that involved the workings of power and agency. To highlight the different modalities of syncretism, I want to distinguish between syncretism "from above" (hegemonic syncretism) and syncretism "from below" (subaltern syncretism), which represent different axes of authority.[24] First I will focus on syncretism "from above," particularly Christian models of fusion that appeared most definitively in Reverend George Dana Boardman's speech at the parliament, as well as in the post-parliamentary work of two important participants, John Henry Barrows and Crawford Toy. After the parliament, Barrows and Toy went on to defend Christian superiority on the grounds that Christianity could fuse with other religions while retaining its own particularity.

Not surprisingly, "narrow" Christians were suspicious of such syncretic strategies, calling them forms of "melting pantheism." Fusion, according to an orthodox Methodist leader, "effaces distinctions, obscures boundary lines, and betrays the tendency to wipe out every antithesis" (Kuyper, "Part I" 525). To dismantle all boundaries is to extinguish the idea of God. Beliefs require limits. The collapse of boundaries designates not only a crisis of faith but also a loss of subjectivity. Discreteness reflects the Protestant conception of selfhood as independent and autonomous; it is essential to the individuality of "good" character. As Philip Moxom, a Baptist pastor in Boston and a writer on social and economic issues, stated in his lecture at the parliament: "The whole significance of man's existence lies ultimately in its discreteness" (WPR I:467). "The destruction of personality," he continued, "is for man the extinction of being" (468).

Unlike "narrow" Christians who found distinctions, separations, and boundaries essential to the idea of divinity and to selfhood, "broad" Christians understood the transgression of boundaries as necessary for Christian expansion. For Christianity to realize the "very law of its being," to quote Barrows, it had to become a "world-religion" (Barrows, *Christianity* 6, 14). As Reverend Munger pointed out at the parliament: "Christianity is a wide thing and nothing that is human is alien to it" (WPR I:683). To become a "world-religion," Christianity had to package itself as adaptable, accommodating, and culturally elastic. It had to be all things to all people, able to adjust to local beliefs and traditions while at the same time heralding "universal" truths.

At the parliament, the flexibility of Christian doctrine was embodied in the figure of Jesus, who represented the great assimilator, converting others through his chameleon-like ability to adapt endlessly to any locality. He was Christian tolerance personified. In his talk entitled "Christ the Unifier of Mankind," Reverend George Dana Boardman claimed: "Blending in himself all races, ages, sexes, capacities, temperaments, Jesus is the archetypal man, the ideal hero, the consummate incarnation, the symbol of perfected human nature, the sum total of unfolded, fulfilled humanity, the Son of Mankind . . . he is the inhabitant of all lands and of all times" (*WPR* II:1339). As the "archetypal man," Jesus was cast as cosmopolitan and local, Eastern and Western, male and female, young and old, white and not-white. Such an all-encompassing definition, whereby Jesus signified everything, aided in the dissemination of Christianity around the world. Since Jesus knew no boundaries, neither did his missionaries or his potential converts.

By contrast, Eastern religions were inextricably local. "But Buddha and his religion are Asiatic," according to Boardman; "what has Buddha done for the unity of mankind? Why are we not holding our sessions in fragrant Ceylon?" For "broad" Christians, as for "narrow" Christians, Eastern religions served to underscore Christian exceptionalism. Just as the East figured for "narrow" Christians as emblematic of excessive heterogeneity (contrary to the moderation of Protestant denominationalism), so Buddhism was invoked by some "broad" Christians as a sign of localism. Buddha was "ethnic" while Jesus was universal, and Buddha was provincial while Jesus was cosmopolitan.

Three years later John Henry Barrows used a similar comparative strategy to emphasize the universal appeal of Christianity. Speaking to an audience in Calcutta in 1897, Barrows asserted that unlike Buddha and Mohammed, who were inextricably regional, Jesus transcended national limits: "We cannot think of a Western Mohammed. We can hardly think of a Western Buddha, but you discover nothing local or provincial about Jesus Christ" (*Christianity* 97). He contrasted Christian boundlessness with Eastern particularity, implying that the East could be Westernized but the West was immune to reversed assimilation. He went on to censure Hinduism for not having the evangelical and expansionist aims of Christianity. "Hinduism appears to be one of the most exclusive of all faiths. Its followers are forbidden to cross the 'black waters,'— while teaching a comprehensive philosophy, it is pre-eminently an ethnic religion. It does not feel itself constrained to traverse oceans and deserts to tell the life-giving truth to other hearts" (*Christianity* 20).

Eastern religions functioned in Barrows's lecture in a similar way as they did for Boardman: they were considered particular, ethnic, and limited, opposite of the universal boundlessness of Christianity.[25] The universality of Christianity was also evident in its holy texts, in that the Bible signified "universal adaptation": "unlike some other sacred scriptures [the Bible] can be easily translated" (77). Translatability is the textual complement to ideological accessibility and appeal. The Bible, in the spirit of Christianity, was accommodating and flexible.

Also representing "broad" Christianity, Crawford Toy, a professor of Hebrew and Oriental languages at Harvard, argued that cross-cultural contact and the commingling of ideas were vital for religious progress. In an article entitled "Religious Fusion" (1902), Toy attempted to break down the boundaries between religions, so that no single religion could claim originality. As the Christian corollary to Charles Chesnutt's "future American," Toy's model of fusion was predicated on a racial analogy. Just as it was doubtful whether there was a "pure race on the face of the earth," so it was equally implausible to imagine a "pure, unmixed religion on earth." According to Toy, "similar processes of assimilation and union may be discovered in the history of the religions of the world" (31). Whereas Chesnutt used racial fusion to dismantle the dominant category of "whiteness," Toy found in religious fusion a way to maintain the dominance of Christianity. He appropriated the discourse of hybridity for hegemonic means. Although he conceded that fusion characterized all major religions, Toy nonetheless argued that Christians did it better. Buddhism and Christianity established a "moral union of diverse national systems of life," but the latter incorporated a wider range of nations.

For Toy, there were superior and inferior modes of fusion, and Buddhism was inferior precisely because it was local. In a familiar critique, wherein the Eastern other served to highlight Western and Christian exceptionalism, Toy argued that "Buddhism owes its success to a process of religious fusion, but a process of an inferior sort. Guatama created, apparently out of purely Indian material, a faith that was not wholly universal; his absolute ethical system was grafted on a local conception of life" (33). Christianity, in contrast, was the "best example of the genesis of a religion from the union of different faiths," because it combined the ideas of "more than half of the ancient world" (34).

Although "broad" Christians appeared to be more radical than their "narrow" counterparts, there was a sense in which the ends of both groups were the same. Whether it was unity-in-discreteness or unity-in-fusion, both configurations of a heterogeneous union attempted to cast Christianity as the superior religion. Either by showing how Christianity could sustain boundaries (and resist pantheism) or by showing how it could transgress them, "broad" and "narrow" Christians associated Christian variety with national exceptionalism, expansionism, and modernity. Locality, which was dismissed as "ethnic," Eastern, and provincial, was also used to highlight American uniqueness. As Boardman claimed, the parliament took place in "Christianland" and not in "fragrant Ceylon."

The parliament provided the occasion for Christian speakers, and particularly its "broad" participants, to invoke the language of internationalism, universality, and translocalism to promote religious nationalism. Transnationalism was used to reimagine the United States as a Christian nation. As harbingers of modernity, Christianity and the United States became fused as coeval forces trumpeting the arrival of a new millennium. Lilian Whiting's words about the parliament in the *New Orleans Times-Democrat* reflect the ideological success of this event in incorporating religious diversity within a narrative of American exceptionalism: "We are the heirs of all ages and it is in America that the next round of humanity will take place" (Fields 157).

Subaltern Syncretism

Although Christian fusion was the dominant model of syncretism at the parliament, it was by no means the only model. There was also syncretism "from below," from among the religious minorities who represented the "ethnic" other to Christian cosmopolitanism. The Asian delegates enacted a strategy of transvaluation, which used the imperial rhetoric of Christian expansionism and national exceptionalism for dramatically different ends. Similar to African-American writers such as Frances Harper and Charles Chesnutt, who appropriated scientific race theories to underscore the definitive role of African Americans in reformulating a national community, the Asian participants at the parliament used the discourse of religious and national exceptionalism to highlight the cultural authority of the colonized. Syncretism "from below" unsettled Christian claims of superiority by showing that Christianity was not unique, that older world religions had already conveyed its most sacred teachings and values.

Besides underscoring the unoriginality of Christianity, Asian delegates used the same rhetoric of exceptionalism to elevate their own particular faiths. In his speech entitled "Synthetic Religion," Hirai Kinzo claimed that religious syncretism or what he called "Entitism" was uniquely Japanese: "All the religions in the world are synthesized into one religion, or 'Entitism,' which has been the inherent spirit in Japan, and is called Satori, or Hotoke, in Japanese. The apparent contradictions among them are only the different descriptions of the same thing seen from different situations, and different views to be observed in the way to the same termination" (WPR II:1288). Syncretism, in other words, was not a modern, newfangled concept, inaugurated at the World's Parliament of Religions, but was a distinctively Japanese concept, part of a long tradition of diffusing religious conflict by emphasizing commonality.

Swami Vivekananda similarly claimed that Hinduism successfully reconciled unity and variety: "Unity in variety is the plan of nature, and the Hindu has recognized it. Every other religion lays down a certain amount of fixed dogma, and tries to force the whole society through it" (WPR II:976). Hinduism was considered exceptional precisely because of its elastic and accommodating character. Dharmapala, the Sinhalese Buddhist, claimed that syncretism was a distinctively Buddhist tradition: "The grand personality who promulgated the Synthetic Religion is known as BUDDHA" (WPR II:863). In his opening remarks at the parliament, Dharmapala stressed the unoriginality of the event: "When I read the program of this Parliament of Religions I saw it was simply the re-echo of a great consummation which the Indian Buddhists accomplished twenty-four centuries ago" (WPR I:95).

Dharmapala, in particular, promoted fusion from below in order to decenter Christian superiority in a way reminiscent of Chesnutt's deconstruction of whiteness. Dharmapala used the rhetoric of syncretism to argue for the unexceptionalism of Christianity, and to claim that the East was the source of religious inspiration and originality. In doing this, he also articulated modern formulations of religious nationalism, which linked Third World colonies with the greatness of ancient religious traditions in order to challenge imperialist policies and practices.[26] Although the parliament witnessed the reformulation of hegemonic Christian syncretism, it also saw the emergence of a Third World, pan-Asian nationalism that presented religious belief as a source of spiritual and cultural authority. Dharmapala made it clear in his opening remarks that the parliament was an inconvenience, since he had had to interrupt his work of "consolidating the different Buddhist countries" to travel to Chicago (WPR I:95).[27] Rather than static religious icons, the Asian speakers emphasized, their "ancient" religious faiths were living, political practices. In making this point, they undermined the ancient/modern dyad by laying claim to the "modern."

Born in 1864 in Colombo, Ceylon, Dharmapala was originally David Hewivitarne, a member of a long-established Buddhist family. In the tradition of his family, he was expected to study in Buddhist schools, but because of the British government's proliferation of colonial edicts concerning school licensing, Dharmapala instead attended a missionary Christian school. He became a much loved student, delighting his teachers with his knowledge of Christian scripture, and he was expected to dedicate his adult life to the Church. Growing up in a colony where Christianity did not peacefully sit "side by side" with Buddhism, the young Dharmapala was caned at St. Thomas Collegiate School for taking a day off to celebrate Wesak, the full moon day of the Buddha's birth enlightenment.[28]

Never returning to school, David spent his days reading the poetry of Keats and Shelley, as well as Colonel Olcott and Madame Blavatsky's journal *The Theosophist*. When Olcott and Blavatsky arrived in Ceylon in 1880 with the goal of strengthening Buddhism against the imperialist spread of Christianity, Dharmapala joined the Theosophical Buddhists. Later he went to Chicago for the parliament (Figure 6), though Colonel Olcott considered the event a waste of time. In another visit to the United States from 1902 to 1904, Dharmapala visited the Tuskegee and Carlisle training schools because he believed that the key to development for the Sri Lankan people lay in industrial and agricultural education. He lectured around the world throughout his life and eventually established the first Buddhist mission in London. He died in Ceylon in 1933.[29]

Dharmapala's speeches at the parliament illustrate a form of subaltern syncretism in two ways: they fuse Western and Eastern religious traditions under the rubric of a "Synthetic Religion," and they also integrate Buddhism with the efforts of decolonization. A "synthetic religion" was a selective tradition, a *bricolage* of sources that made up a "comprehensive system of ethics." Dharmapala applied this approach to the formation of a national culture, whose "uniqueness" was not claimed on the

6. Anagarika Dharmapala at the World's Parliament of Religions with a Buddha image from Ceylon

grounds of purity but on its ability to collect and synthesize different cultural borrowings. Through his extensive travels abroad, Dharmapala articulated a Third World religious nationalism. What is distinctive about Buddhist Sinhalese culture, reflected in Dharmapala's ideal of a "synthetic religion," is its permeability, its elasticity and openness.

A half-century before independence, Dharmapala took the colonial encounter in Sri Lanka and inverted it so that it became exemplary of the modern nation-state. Just as African Americans claimed racial hybridity as a sign of African-American distinctiveness, so Dharmapala used a strategy in which Sinhalese exceptionalism was based in part on its ability to fuse indigenous and colonial traditions. He described the principle of karma, for instance, through the Christian maxim "What a man sows he must reap" (WPR II:1288). As the anthropologist Jonathan Spencer has noted, the power of Dharmapala was his ability to interpret the East through the language of Western thought (286). His familiarity with Christianity, for example, helped to decenter it: "My own life has been intimately bound up with the Buddhist religion. But I do not come to the West ignorant of Christianity. For twenty years I have been reading and rereading the Christian Bible" (681–682). In contrast to those who sat beside him at the parliament, who more than likely accentuated the exceptionalism and originality of the Bible as the Ur-text of Western civilization, Dharmapala claimed it was derivative, but derivative in a good sense (he was a generous reader). As a textual *bricolage,* the Bible was valuable because it validated the truth-claims of Buddhist ethics.

Dharmapala's syncretic approach to religion was reinforced rhetorically through his lectures that incorporated a wide range of texts. His speeches at the parliament cited Pali stories alongside biblical ones. He brought together Sir Edwin Arnold's popular epic poem "Light of Asia" with the scholarship of European Orientalists such as George Turnour, who first translated Pali Ceylonese history into English, and Eugene Burnouf, who in 1844 wrote the first "scientific" account of Buddhism. In his second speech at the parliament, "The Points of Resemblance and Difference between Buddhism and Christianity," Dharmapala claimed that Jesus' teachings were based in Buddhism and compared various quotes from the Bible and the *Dharmapada* to show their similarity. Whereas Jesus, for example, says "Love your enemies and do good," Buddha says "Let one overcome anger by love" (WPR II:1289). Dharmapala concluded his lecture by quoting R. C. Dutt, a Hindu translator of various legends and histories into English, who argued that "The moral teachings and precepts of Buddhism have so much in common with those of Christianity that some connection between the two systems of religions has long been suspected" (*WPR* II:1290).

By showing that Christianity signified a hybrid tradition, infused with the influences of Asia, Dharmapala reversed the cultural and political flows of colonialism by Easternizing the West. Twenty years after the parliament he continued this critique by asking "What is there in Christianity that is purely Western?" Whereas Barrows localized Buddhism while universalizing Christianity, Dharmapala reversed this logic by insisting that "Christianity is an Asiatic Arabian cult" (464). Christianity was inextricably "ethnic" and particular, while Buddhism was universal. Rather than absorbing the colonized "other," Christianity was itself transformed—and Buddhized—by centuries of colonial encounter.

In Dharmapala's later career he continued hybridizing Christianity, not at the geopolitical site of colonial encounter but within the heart of imperial power, namely in London. Consistent with Du Bois's and Kallen's desire to elevate the partial (subculture) to become determinant of the whole (nation), Dharmapala wanted to see the colonized transform the colonizer. In a 1926 speech in London, he vowed "to convert England to Buddhism," to spread the religion of the subaltern throughout the seat of empire.[30] In this great reversal of imperial power, Dharmapala sought to convert the center of colonial authority by establishing a South East Asian Buddhist mission called the Moha Bodhi Society in the London suburb of Ealey, funded largely through the philanthropic dollars of wealthy American widows. This was the first Buddhist mission in Britain, and Dharmapala was its first missionary. In the same 1926 speech he presented to his English audience his plan for Buddhist conversion, which he framed within the familiar terms of Christian charity: "Instead of hatred, compassion sprang up in my heart to the British people . . . I decided to come over to England and work for the establishment of Buddhism there." In a diary entry the following year he wrote: "Ceylon and England can never again be disunited. I shall therefore work for the welfare of the British people" (665).

Whether Dharmapala's aims were genuine or in jest, or perhaps a bit of both, he insisted on the intermingling of South East Asia and England but in terms that reversed the power relations at the level of culture. His syncretic nationalism was not separatist but paternalistic. In a condescending tone reminiscent of the Christian missionaries at the parliament, Dharmapala presented his counter-imperialist aims as altruistic rather than avaricious, saying that he wanted to export Buddhism to Britain so that the colonizer could adopt "the ethic of forgiving patience."

Dharmapala's model of subaltern syncretism differed dramatically from its hegemonic counterpart in terms of reversing the axis of power as well as in advocating a principle of limits. His "synthetic religion" was not merely a collection of hybrid parts but a selective union structured according to what William James calls "the right scale of subordination." Unlike Barrows and Boardman, whose notions of Christian syncretism were universal and infinite, Dharmapala emphasized the need for boundaries and called for powers of discrimination. In his speech on the eighth day of the parliament, "The World's Debt to Buddha," he defined "synthetic religion" through a principle of exclusion: "All that was good was collected from every source and embodied therein, and all that was bad discarded" (WPR II:863).[31] Buddhism rejected, for instance, Christianity's belief in causation (and creationism), and its temporal configurations of an eternal past and future. It embraced, however, Christianity's ideal of compassion. Dharmapala's synthetic religion illustrates the paradoxical point that although cultures may borrow from one another they must also resist one another at particular points.

Whereas the Japanese Buddhist Shaku Soyen claimed that all religious distinctions were false, Dharmapala maintained the integrity of religious differences.[32] Although the Sinhalese representative challenged Protestantism's "unity-in-discreteness" by showing that Buddhism was itself a contact zone where East and West were joined, he nonetheless sustained a dialectic that resisted the complete collapse of boundaries. Retaining the distinctiveness of Sinhalese culture was an important part of his decolonizing efforts. To claim that the Sinhalese "each-form" had disappeared entirely, that it was fully immersed in Englishness and Christianity, would have been the same as saying that colonialism had succeeded by wiping out a people's memory of itself. By contrast, cultural variety was a sign of subaltern defiance, a sign that "diversities persist," to borrow Kallen's phrase, thus underscoring the resiliency and agency of a colonized culture.

Perhaps this is one reason William James was so drawn to Dharmapala's work. In 1903 James invited Dharmapala to lecture to his advanced students in psychology at Harvard. Years later Dharmapala recounted the experience:

> I tried unobtrusively to reach the back of the lecture-hall to hear the great teacher of psychology, but it is difficult for a man in a yellow robe to be inconspicuous in America. Professor James saw me and motioned for me to come to the front of the hall. He said: "Take my chair, and I shall sit with my students. You are better equipped to lecture on psychology than I am." After I had outlined to his advanced class some elements of Buddhist doctrine, he turned to his students and said, "This is the psychology everybody will be studying twenty-five years from now." (681)

Particularly attracted to Dharmapala's approach to Buddhism as an analytical philosophy that evaluates, selects, and discriminates all information, James saw in Buddhism the psychology of the future, the means to unite religion and science, belief and reason. As Dharmapala stated at the parliament, Buddhism offers a "comprehensive system of ethics," combined with "a sublime psychology," culminating in "spiritual progress" (WPR II:866). Furthermore, Dharmapala's configuration of Buddhism as selective synthesis parallels James's psychological ideal of "healthy-mindedness," which depends on the mind cultivating a principle of selection that determines what matter will be retained and what will be discarded. Without this capacity, which James calls "habits of attention," the mind could degenerate into a "sick soul." Translated into ethics, a belief-system without limits sacrifices truth.

What James found appealing about Dharmapala's "synthetic religion" was that it dramatized at the level of ethics that an equilibrium can be achieved between variety and unity. A system does not need to be entirely hermetic in order to sustain a sense of its own boundaries, nor does it have to be completely accommodating. There can be limits to what is and what is not included within a philosophical or ethical system. The modern element in Dharmapala's thought that appealed to James was the defense of a "synthetic" middle ground between "narrow" provincialism and uncritical acceptance.

"More Diversity Than Harmony"

The *New York Times* headline for the centennial event of the World's Parliament of Religions, held at the Palmer House Hilton Hotel in Chicago in September 1993, was "More Diversity Than Harmony at Religious Assembly." Over six thousand participants attended from all over the world, including such luminaries as the Dalai Lama. (Mother Theresa had been invited but was recovering from a bout of malaria). In contrast to its nineteenth-century counterpart, this commemorative event included representatives from thirty-eight indigenous religions from the United States as well as participants from "tribal religions" in Africa, Guatemala, and New Zealand. Invitations were also extended to goddess worshippers and neo-pagans. Daniel Gómez-Ibáñez, the executive director of the parliament, predicted that it would be "the greatest gathering of religious leaders ever in terms of diversity, breadth and depth of representation."[33]

What further differentiated this event from its predecessor was the changed demographics of Chicago. The fourteen Hindu speakers would find more than a dozen Hindu places of worship in the Chicago area. The Dalai Lama would find twenty-eight distinct Buddhist organizations, ranging from Sri Lankans and Tibetans to Koreans and Japanese. There were also 1,500 American Buddhist converts living in the city, spiritual descendants of Charles Strauss. Muslims, represented in 1893 by the lone Anglican convert Mohammed Webb, now numbered 250,000 in Chicago, with mosques throughout the city and suburbs.

Given this backdrop, one would think that the Asian visitors would have seemed less exotic, blending in, so to speak, with the cosmopolitan heterogeneity of the postmodern city. This was hardly the case. In fact, newspaper accounts of the event exhibited the same fascination with the colorful garb, turbaned heads, and sandaled feet as they had a century earlier. The *Chicago Tribune Magazine* described the lobby of the Palmer House as a "colorful" assortment of saris and "Oriental robes." The *New York Times* referred to the event as a "spiritual bazaar" with a "carnival aura." Audience members were also quoted, as they had been a century before, describing the parliament as "bedlam" and the sessions as "tense and chaotic." The second World's Parliament seemed to be as indeterminate and unpredictable as the original, with its organizational structure yielding to the pressures of the moment.[34]

If the second parliament duplicated the color and bedlam of the original, it also inherited its tensions. The multi-religious congress continued to grapple with the late-nineteenth-century conflict between expressing "distinctive truths" and establishing "a spirit of human brotherhood." But this conflict, together with the structural tensions between discrete presentations (Barrows) and a "diversity of opinion" (Archbishop Freehan), had seemed to intensify during the twentieth century. Now there was no longer even the pretense of playing by a common set of rules. Barrows's request that the presentations be "gentle" and "courteous" would have fallen on deaf ears. In 1993 the Eastern Orthodox Christian participants withdrew from the meeting, angered by the prominence of neo-pagan goddess worshippers. Four local and national Jewish organizations withdrew their sponsorship of the parliament in protest of the inclusion of Louis Farrakhan, head of the Nation of Islam. A Sikh speaker accused the Indian government of repressive actions in Kashmir and was shouted down by others, which led to "a brief flurry of shoving among Parliament participants" (Steinfels).

The organizer Gómez-Ibáñez, who held the same position that Barrows had a century before, tried to account for this hostility at an event dedicated to religious harmony by saying that in contrast to the "mood of optimism" in 1893, there was now "a mood of anxiety all around the world" (Steinfels). What these examples of discord indicate is that the speakers lacked a common ground among the speakers, that when the "diversity of opinion" becomes too inclusive it destroys the possibility of consensus. This, in turn, intensifies the need for commonality.

As a result of these anxieties about boundless diversity, the organizers emphasized the necessity of a common ground far more than their nineteenth-century predecessors had. In fact, they were intent on showing the world that boundless diversity and a common ethics could coexist. This is seen in their ambitious attempt to produce "The Document of Global Ethics," which they predicted would be the legacy of the 1993 event, a legacy that could be discussed and modified in future years. Composing this document, however, was far more difficult than expected. The goal was to extract common values from existing religions. A select group of one hundred religious leaders, who were given the task of writing the document, first listened to various groups who represented concerns such as the AIDS crisis, attacks on Muslims in the former Yugoslavia, and the subjugation of Native Americans. None of these specific concerns made it into the final version. Even the wording was highly contested. The document does not refer, for example, to "God" but to the "Ultimate Reality," so as not to offend Buddhists.

The result was a brief nine-page (5,000-word) document, which mainly consisted of restatements of the ten commandments (do not kill; do not steal), as well a statement condemning abuse, prejudice, pollution, and violence. The Reverend Hans Kung, a Catholic theologian, who had spent more than a year working on the document, said, "I have never worked so many months for so few words." When asked whether the imperative of consensus made the "Declaration" too general, Father Kung simply answered, "We have here a minimum ethic" (Steinfels). But is a "minimum ethic," which includes only the most general values, sufficient? Could not a group of religious leaders devise a more substantial document that actually addressed specific instances of abuse and warfare?

The most valuable lesson of this document is that it could only be written in seclusion. The one hundred leaders had to isolate themselves behind the locked doors of the Arts Institute, a mile away from the Palmer House, in order to create even a "minimum ethic," one that was so general as to be anodyne. The fact that the leaders had to seclude themselves demonstrates that even the most inclusive gesture, such as writing a "global ethics," requires at some point the acknowledgment of boundaries. To reiterate both James and Dharmapala: the key to an ethical system is a process of selective synthesis.

The recognition of limits is precisely what differentiates the late-nineteenth-century parliament from its late-twentieth-century version. The participants in the original parliament were less traumatized by the absence of commonality and the presence of mutually exclusive points of view. They were more comfortable with a bounded sense of variety, with the recognition that there were differences that could not be easily eradicated, despite the efforts of the most persuasive Christian missionaries. Participants, and specifically "broad" Christians, were not made defensive by the late Victorian equivalent of religious identity politics. When Dharmapala claimed that Buddha, and not Jesus, was the originator of the basic principles of Christianity, or when Hirai vilified Western imperialism and missionary efforts, the audience cheered. For other speakers, they booed.

In contrast to the 1993 event, at which speakers' attempts to involve the audience often met with silence, the late Victorians were fully engaged with the content of the speeches. In 1893 the text of each day's speeches appeared in the Chicago dailies replete with parenthetical remarks capturing the audience's reactions. The audience members took sides, conveying their opinions visually (waving handkerchiefs) and vocally (shouting "Shame!"). Without the pressure or even the desire to homogenize all viewpoints into a single position, the late-nineteenth-century participants actually took pleasure in the diversity of opinion that was expressed at the congress. They seemed to listen far better than their late-twentieth-century counterparts, because their event was not structured according to the pursuit of consensus. They could live with disagreement. They acknowledged the limits of persuasion. They accepted the inevitability of a residuum. This is the value of variety.

Afterword

In Defense of Partiality

Throughout this book, my goal has been to trace the variations of Jamesian pluralism through the literary, cultural, and religious debates of the turn into the twentieth century. The case studies I have presented, from regional writing to the urban picturesque, were all responses to a shared challenge, namely to configure variety as the *sine qua non* of U.S. modernity. To address this challenge, various thinkers of the period grappled with the following questions: What is the best way to negotiate the increasing cultural diversity of the nation, and how can this diversity be sustained in an age of standardization and assimilation?

Modern pluralists such as Horace Kallen and W. E. B. Du Bois defined this internal diversity according to competing narratives of ethno-racial exceptionalism, in which Jewishness and blackness, respectively, defined the nation. Regionalists, such as Hamlin Garland, celebrated the diversity of the rural periphery rather than metropolitan centers as the definitive geographical space of the nation. Cosmopolitan *flâneurs,* such as Hutchins Hapgood and Viola Roseboro, considered the ethnic neighborhoods of New York to be the repositories of modern Americanism. The African-American writer Frances Harper championed the internal diversity of the black family as a microcosm of the nation. Finally, certain religious thinkers from the East and West celebrated the variety of religious sects as a product of global development and cosmopolitanism. In all of these instances, modernity was conceived as a process of diversification, which was not anathema to unity but the means toward reimagining modern forms of unity, in which heterogeneity and a common ground were seen as commensurable.

Each chapter represents a counter-narrative of American modernity, which claims that in the midst of the homogenizing forces of incorporation, cultural varieties and individual eccentricities persist. In contrast to the melting pot, which is the classic image of cultural adaptation of this period, I have underscored an alternative cultural pattern, one that holds on to difference and distinctiveness as constitutive elements of modern nationhood. Fusions, hybridities, and cultural borrowings occur, but within specific historical and political parameters, which are dynamic and flexible yet not completely porous. The language of modern variety opposes the all-inclusive conformist unities that flatten out distinctions; instead it acknowledges irreducible differences by insisting that borders cannot be completely melted or fused. This strategy should not be uncritically eulogized. The notion of persistent particularity could be used to support rather dubious projects, ranging from the cultural elitism of the "college-bred" to a defense of variegated whiteness in the urban picturesque. It could also be employed to support various forms of ethno-racial chauvinism. At its best, however, modern variety demonstrates that the language of limits can be part of a truly progressive political vision, one that neither simply rejects nor naively celebrates national diversity.

The lessons of modern variety are twofold. First, it forces us to rethink the familiar narrative of American modernity as a process of standardization and sameness. Moderns also theorized the local, the heterogeneous, and the multiple in ways that teach us that unity and variety are not mutually exclusive. The second lesson of modern variety is the belief that unity, whether it is national unity or universalism, is limited and partisan. Borders function in modern variety to emphasize the inevitability of the "residuum": that nothing can contain everything since something always escapes. They also remind us of the importance of taking sides. This notion of partiality, which links the particular with the universal, continues today when Leonard Harris writes, in Du Boisean fashion, that the "pursuit of universal human liberation always occurs through the struggles of particular communities" (451). This conception of the universal—and the national—is ultimately Hebraic rather than Hellenic in that it represents a contested field of allied and mutually exclusive positions rather than their harmonious synthesis within an all-inclusive union. Throughout this book, I have emphasized this dynamic and conflictual pattern of modern variety, wherein pluralism is structured according to a scale of values that is partisan and situated.

I recover this pattern of variety because it can serve as a modern antidote to our contemporary times. The extreme ends of current formulations of multiculturalism either emphasize multiplicity and incommensurability and refuse any attempt at constructing a common ground or imagine an all-inclusive heterogeneous union without exclusions of any sort. Rather than to adopt either of these extremes, the task at hand, as Chantal Mouffe has argued, is to articulate the "limits of pluralism," which would involve constructing a community through uneven relations of power, where antagonisms are integral to the formation of a common denominator through citizenship.

In a move reminiscent of William James, Mouffe insists on the "constitutive outside," a late-twentieth-century version of the "residuum," through which a partial notion of the "we" is defined. Mouffe goes on to echo second-generation pluralists such as Kallen and Du Bois in claiming that "we've got to impose our conception [of democracy]" (Mouffe 29). Mouffe's use of the collective "we" is unabashedly biased. It addresses a point that James realized through his experience of delivering the Hibbert Lectures, namely that nothing can persuade everyone to a given point of view. The objective of radical democracy is to claim one's position and recognize the fact that there will exist a remainder, or what Mouffe refers to as "an exterior to the community."

In certain left-wing configurations of U.S. multiculturalism, there is a reluctance to acknowledge limits whether in the form of all-inclusivity or in terms of persuasion. Take, for instance, Nancy Fraser's conception of multiculturalism, which offers a model of social justice that reconciles the imperative of economic redistribution with the need for cultural recognition. Her critique of predominant models of multiculturalism is that they supplant class interest with group identity and replace socioeconomic redistribution with cultural recognition. Fraser's goal is to devise a "cultural politics of difference" that can be combined with the "social politics of equality" (20). In delineating strategies for cultural recognition, she recommends that cultural nationalists and feminist culturalists turn to "deconstructive anti-racism" and "deconstructive feminism," respectively. She refers to these processes positively as "de-differentiation" (48). The objective is to undermine "hierarchical racial dichotomies" in order to promote "shifting networks of multiple intersecting differences." This shift from "hierarchy" to "multiplicity" betrays an anxiety of audience.

Fraser's brand of multiculturalism opposes feminist culturalism and black nationalism on the grounds that they may offend or may incite "perverse effects" (48). Women who insist on their "cultural specificity" as women will have "the effect of pouring oil onto the flames of resentment against affirmative action" (37). Likewise, African Americans who insist on their "blackness" risk fueling "the resentment against affirmative action" (38). By contrast, Fraser's brand of "transformative" and "deconstructive" multiculturalism successfully "avoids fanning the flames of resentment" (38, 39). Because it does not incite resentment, "transformative" multiculturalism is inoffensive and therefore more persuasive than particularist models. Fraser's multiculturalism, which is based on the commandment *thou shall not offend,* is symptomatic of the current trend on the multicultural left toward avoiding conflict.

But *who* feels resentful? Fraser prefers to specify those who are inciting resentment rather than those who resent. If women did not assert their particularity and if African Americans did not emphasize their "blackness," then there would not be a backlash against affirmative action. The backlash, according to this argument, is understood as a failure of persuasion. Let me suggest, on the contrary, that the backlash against affirmative action is not the result of subordinated people insisting on their particularity, but the effect of sexism and racism. To focus on curtailing resentment is to blame the victims rather than the agents of this backlash. The Dale Carnegie-ization of the multicultural left, which seeks to make friends and influence people, has come at a price: it shies away from conflict in the name of persuasion. It tries not to offend those with certain views so as to win supporters. This tactic, however, forgets that social change has always depended upon ruffling someone's feathers. If the suffragettes had wanted to avoid male anger, then it is likely that women would not have received the right to vote. If African Americans had feared white rage, then the Civil Rights era would not have happened. It is precisely by "fanning the flames of resentment" that people bring about social change.

Multiculturalists in the twenty-first century must keep pouring oil onto the flames. This is the strategy behind Cornel West's "new cultural politics of difference," which in a Jamesian sense is a "new name for some old ways of thinking." Like Fraser, West employs metaphors of fuel and fire, but toward a significantly different form of political practice, specifically one centered around struggle and partisanism. In the vein of Mouffe's radical democracy as well as in the tradition of Jamesian pluralism, West imagines "intellectual and political freedom fighters with partisan passion, international perspectives, and, thank God, a sense of humor to combat the ever-present absurdity that forever threatens our democratic and libertarian projects and dampens the fire that fuels our will to struggle" ("New Cultural Politics" 23). West's multiculturalism is based metaphorically on fueling the fire rather than dousing it. Furthermore, West's use of such words as "struggle" and "partisan passions" extends and develops the Barthesian imperative to "take sides," to privilege certain interests over others in imagining a future that is "different and better."

West's multicultural vision possesses the spirit and character of modern pluralism, beginning with its Jamesian embrace of partiality and continuing through the Du Boisean stage of linking "subcultures of criticism" with national and international concerns. West is at his most Jamesian when he observes that "openness to others—including the mainstream—does not entail wholesale co-optation, and group autonomy is not group insularity" (22). He sustains James's category of the "some," which creates a space of alliance as well as of non-negotiation between dominant and subordinate groups. West's flexible notion of subcultures provides a dynamic alternative to the classical model of twentieth-century pluralism, which has been traditionally defined according to the either-or formulation of assimilation versus separatism.

West's "new cultural politics of difference" can be seen in two recent examples of what I call "partisan multiculturalism," in which intellectuals and "freedom fighters" nationally and internationally have promoted a democratic notion of a heterogeneous common ground that is united by a shared moral and political vision. The two examples are (1) the recent hunger strike in support of Ethnic Studies at the University of California at Berkeley, and (2) the "First Intercontinental Encounter for Humanity and against Neoliberalism" in Chiapas, Mexico. These two incidents demonstrate the importance of a pluralism structured according to a "scale of values," which recognizes certain limits while challenging others. They also illustrate that social relations and identities are always constructed through asymmetrical forms of power, and that resentment and antagonism are inevitable. Like their early-twentieth-century antecedents, these recent forms of multiculturalism are partial and interested, which is to say that they encourage broad alliances and possess indeterminate dimensions, while at the same time articulating a non-negotiable common ground.

The 1999 hunger strike at UC Berkeley is a national example of partisan multiculturalism. The hunger strikers, five Latino and one white student, with the support of many other students, faculty, and members of the local community, protested cuts to the Ethnic Studies Department. In the past few years the department had lost four or five faculty members who had not been replaced. In addition, there were no full-time tenured professors in Native American Studies, and after 2000 there was to be only one in Chicano Studies. UC Regent Ward Connerly, the same person who had led the successful campaign against affirmative action, initiated an inquiry into the value of Ethnic Studies as a preliminary move toward further cuts and eventual dissolution. To resist this attack, undergraduates reconstituted the Third World Liberation Front (TWLF) in honor of its 1969 victory for Ethnic Studies. On the thirtieth anniversary of the TWLF's founding, police removed forty-six students who had occupied Barrows Hall, the institutional home of Ethnic Studies. The following day, April 15, the entire Ethnic Studies faculty walked out of a meeting with the Executive Vice Chancellor, saying that they would not discuss the matter until the administration dropped charges against the arrested students. When the administration refused, the hunger strike began.

Students demanded full-time tenure-track hires in Ethnic Studies (rather than joint hires with other departments); they also demanded that a multicultural student center be reopened and that a research center be founded to serve community organizations as well as the university. The UC Berkeley chancellor, Robert Berdahl, made the student leaders an offer: seven new faculty hires with the promise of reviewing space allocations available to the department as well as a review of a broad-based proposal for an Institute for Race and Gender Studies. The student negotiators, most of whom were women, decided to reject the chancellor's offer, an offer that seemed reasonable if not adequate to some supporters. This act fueled the flames of resentment among the administration, leading to mass arrests at three A.M. the following day, when police in full riot gear arrested eighty people including five of the hunger strikers. This was, according to the journalist Elizabeth Martínez, the administration's "big mistake" (33). It created widespread support from several sectors of the community, including labor unions such as Local 250 (46,000 health workers) and Local 2850 (6,000 hotel and restaurant workers). Two faculty members joined the fast, and ten promised to get arrested if students were arrested again. City council members also declared their support.

A major rally on May 6 after the mass arrest attracted people from across the community, including high school and middle school students of many nationalities. "That day," writes Martínez, "was unforgettable for the multi-racial, multi-generational unity you could see everywhere" (34). On May 7 Berdahl was forced to settle. The final agreement included eight full-time faculty positions to be filled over five years, more funding so as not to cancel any more classes, a Multicultural Student Center to reopen in the fall of 1999, a $500,000 budget over five years to start an Institute for Race and Gender Studies, a mural in the Ethnic Studies area, and more office space. All criminal charges were also dropped for the more than one hundred arrested students, except for those arrested more than once.[1]

I mention this strike as an instance of partisan multiculturalism for three reasons. First, it is an example of multicultural citizenship, in which specific aims formed the common ground around which a diverse coalition of students, unionists, and community activists rallied. At a time when it is common to see students arrested after killing a number of classmates and teachers, it is refreshing, if not inspiring, to see students arrested for acting as conscientious and engaged citizens. Second, the student organizers possessed a sense of borders, an understanding of which terms were negotiable and which were not. The students confronted the administration, pouring oil onto the flames by refusing to sign an earlier offer that would have satisfied many of their demands. The students' willingness to offend the university—to occupy its property, refuse its initial settlement, and challenge its authority—created a "backlash," most clearly seen in a student editorial in the *Daily Californian* entitled "Ethnic Studies: Good Riddance." More important, the student leaders created alternative alliances that were crucial in drawing public attention to the plight of Ethnic Studies. Their strategy was not to establish a universal community among the students, but rather to link certain student allies with faculty and community groups, including unions and city council members. Finally, the students invoked the pan-nationalist language of the sixties—the Third World Liberation Front—as a way to assert a partisan form of identity politics that was not "deconstructive," as Fraser recommends, but blatantly reconstructive.

Students who belonged to the poorest department of the College of Letters and Sciences insisted on their persistent particularity as a way to "overwhelm" (William James's word) the administrative center of the university. In a strategy reminiscent of Du Bois, students used their particular identities to lay claim to the "human." As one hunger striker said, "I'm not in Ethnic Studies. I'm in Chemical Engineering. But I would never do this for Chemical Engineering. I'm doing it because I am a Chicano. More than that, I am a human being. And Ethnic Studies is about being full human beings" (Martínez 33). The success of this strategy was not lost on the department's chair, L. Ling-Chi Wang, who noted that the students accomplished more in one month than he had through more formal means during the previous ten years.[2]

The second example of partisan multiculturalism, which brings to fruition some of the objectives and strategies of modernist pluralism within an international context, is the "First Intercontinental Encounter for Humanity and against Neoliberalism." The event, which included over 3,000 activists from forty-three countries, was hosted by the Zapatistas (EZLN), who initiated a rebellion against the Mexican government on January 1, 1994, the day NAFTA went into effect. This encounter, held in July 1996 in the remote jungles and mountains of South-eastern Mexico, was in part an international show of support for the EZLN's attack against the fiscal policies of privatization and "free" trade on the American continent. It was also an attempt to begin a dialogue among activists around the world about establishing a common "network of resistance" against the policies of neoliberalism, which the Zapatistas define as the "latest stage of capitalism," in which "capital has all rights and freedom of movement while workers have no right and only the freedom of movement granted to us by the power" ("Gatherings").

The organization of this event—its ability to negotiate the one and the many—is reminiscent of James's pluralistic dynamic between "autonomy" and "connection." The common ground of the event was a discussion centered around a shared opposition to a global order based on market-oriented policies that require austere structural adjustment. From this common ground, the EZLN organizers encouraged autonomous dialogues. Although they organized the event, the EZLN did not intend the conference to be about them or Mexico but rather about international coalition building against neoliberalism. The format of the event was "loose" and "concatenated" (to borrow James's terms), with the participants choosing among five different conversations, ranging from the media to economics, each taking place in a different indigenous community. The openendedness of the conference was reflected in Subcomandante Marcos's opening question: "what happens next?" (qtd. Flood).

The openendedness of the conference was largely derived from indigenous customs of village politics, which depend on observing and listening, rather than on delivering an endless stream of speeches as in modern U.S. and Mexican politics. This indigenous conception of leadership is reflected in a communiqué from the Indigenous Clandestine Revolutionary Committee in 1994: "he who leads obeys if he is true, and he who follows leads through the common heart of true men and women" (qtd. Nash 264). This same "sit and watch" approach to leadership also informed the National Indigenous Forum, organized by the EZLN in January 1996, where all those who attended were invited to speak. The Zapatistas, according to the anthropologist June Nash, who attended the event, "came as listeners and watchers, and except for the opening speeches they maintained an alert audience for what their invited guests said" (Nash 270). The leader's task is not to persuade but to listen, an approach that defines the Zapatistas' understanding of democracy: "not that all think the same, but that all thoughts or the majority of the thoughts seek and arrive at a good agreement" (Nash 261).

The organizational structure of these meetings reflects the high value that the EZLN and its indigenous constituency place on autonomy. The demands of the Zapatistas, since the 1994 uprising, have centered around the necessity of autonomy to gain recognition of the pluricultural and pluriethnic communities within the nation. Since the uprising, the Zapatistas have established six multi-ethnic autonomous regions, each one addressing the immediate problems facing indigenous communities, while at the same time working toward democratizing the Mexican state and international institutions. As Nash has argued, the autonomy of the Zapatistas is not merely that of local rights, but an assertion of the right of local institutions to redefine national policies on land reform and the allocation of funds to rural regions (268). Autonomy is a direct challenge to "presidentialism," in challenging the centralization of government and financial resources in the capital. The call for economic and political access to monetary resources of development is also a challenge to centralized institutions at the global level ranging from the IMF to the World Bank.

Like Jamesian pluralism, Zapatista autonomy is partisan and engaged, not content with merely protecting the local but defining the local as a means toward redefining the state. This strategy of generalizing the particular, whereby autonomous multi-ethnic regions become representative of the new nation, shaped the actual organization of the Intercontinental Encounter as well as the Indigenous Forum six months earlier. In both of these cases, a plurinational state did not merely mean the retention of "folk" practices as innocuous and picturesque elements of ethnic distinctiveness, but the assertion of wide-ranging demands from the right to use indigenous peoples' own language in schools to fair pricing for crops and equal access to electricity, roads, and telephones. Indigenous autonomy serves as an ideal model for refashioning national and even global communities.

Rather than being a strictly economic phenomenon, the indigenous demand for autonomy also includes a cultural dimension, one that recognizes the fundamental diversity of social reality without sacrificing the need for unity. Social and economic equality, in other words, does not necessarily result in cultural sameness. A year before the Intercontinental Encounter, the Zapatistas issued the following statement: "we are all Mexicans, but each lives and feels his or her Mexicanness differently" (qtd. Nash 268). But this celebration of difference does not have to lead to political relativism, in which difference is reified and essentialized as fundamentally benevolent regardless of its content. In a speech at the National Indigenous Forum, Subcomandante Tacho retained a notion of the "good path" in his praise of racial, linguistic, and cultural diversity: "The good path also takes on the word of men and women of white skin and of a different language. In the world that the Zapatistas want, all skin colors fit, all the languages and all the paths. The good world has many ways and many paths. And in those paths there is respect and dignity" (qtd. Nash 269).

To assert the "good path" suggests that not all paths are equally deserving of respect and dignity. In fact, Tacho clearly distinguishes between the "good path" and other paths, which can lead to killing and silencing. The rhetoric of the "good" surfaces frequently in Zapatista writing and speeches as the antithesis of that which elicits suffering and violence. Whereas the "good path" is contrasted with persecution, it is seen as complementary to cultural difference. One can support the rich diversity of cultural practices while retaining a notion of the "good path" or the "good world," which are contemporary versions of William James's "scale of values." The Zapatistas provide a way of acknowledging the value of diversity *and* unity without dismissing the latter as oppressive and homogenizing.

At the Intercontinental Encounter, this indigenous understanding of what I call "partisan plurinationalism" is also seen in one of the most renowned attendees of the event: Eduardo Galeano. The Uruguayan writer, who won the Lannan Prize for Cultural Freedom in 1999, was interviewed about the significance of the event in terms of the diversity of cultures and countries brought together in their shared opposition to neoliberalism. In this interview, Galeano uses the language of variety to link justice and solidarity with a larger sense of material and spiritual well-being, which he calls "happiness" (*"alegría"*). First, he launches a modernist defense of variety as a mainstay against the encroaching uniformity of the world, a uniformity that is the result of the ubiquitous products and brand names of global corporations. Diversity, which is "multiple and contradictory," will save us from boredom: "we do not want to starve but neither do we want to be bored" (*La Jornada*).

In a more recent interview, Galeano elaborates: "We are condemned to accept the global uniformization, a sort of McDonaldization of the entire world... We are practicing each day... a sort of massacre of our capacity to be diverse, to have so many different ways to live life, celebrate, eat, dance, dream, drink, think, and feel. It's like a forbidden rainbow. Now we are being more and more obliged to accept a single way. And this single way is being mainly produced in US factories" (*Progressive* 36). Galeano celebrates diversity, not as an end in itself in the form of an "unoppressive city," nor as a postmodern pastiche, but as a living presence that is constantly under siege by the growing uniformity of the global economy. Defying the McDonaldization of the world is an act of autonomy, an assertion of borders, which opposes and tries to resist the encroaching violence of transnationalism.[3]

Galeano also uses the language of variety to reassert his faith in human unity, defining the "human" in terms reminiscent of Du Bois, as a partial and particular formation articulated against the dehumanizing costs of globalization. Seeing people from different countries, from different cultures and languages, united in their shared opposition to the policies of neoliberalism renews his faith in a common humanity: "the essential unity of the human condition is derived from its own diversity" (*La Jornada*). The international gathering in Chiapas inspired Galeano to address the contemporary crisis of diversity: "The human condition is this way everywhere: it is a rainbow, but we are blind to it. What we share in the human adventure at the end of the century is our blindness to that rainbow, because masks hinder us from seeing it in all of its brilliance and beauty, such masks as racism, which prevents us from recuperating the plenitude of the human condition, or machismo, which has mutilated us reducing us to half, or elitism, or militarism or whatever else that hinders us from regaining the resilient joy of our diversity" (*La Jornada*).[4]

Like indigenous models of partisan plurinationalism, Galeano's notion of diversity is not all-inclusive: it contains borders. It is explicitly defined against racism, sexism, militarism, and elitism. It is also clearly opposed to neoliberalism and corporate power. Galeano insists that within these multiple struggles there is no single model of unity-in-diversity, but such models must develop organically (*"de adentro y de abajo"*) from the specific conditions of distinct places.

This, too, has been the lesson of modern variety. Its multiple and contradictory uses remind us of the importance of context in delineating the historical and political parameters of diversity. But neither Galeano nor the modern architects of variety, such as William James, stop at the local. Their work is far bolder. They demonstrate that contextualization is not synonymous with balkanization, nor are boundaries equivalent to provincialism. To begin with the particular does not mean that one ends there. The key is to reclaim the universal as situated and partisan. This, I suggest, is the most instructive element of modern variety for imagining a multicultural common ground for the twenty-first century. It would create a partisan multiculturalism defined according to a scale of values at a time when human values are subordinated to market values. It would celebrate diversity within an internationalist struggle against dehumanization in its many forms. It would boldly affirm partiality in a world in which we can no longer afford to be impartial.

Notes

Works Cited

Acknowledgments

Index

NOTES

Introduction: Americanizing Variety

1. On Mexican *mestizaje,* see José Vasconcelos, *La Raza Cósmica* (Mexico, 1925); Gloria Anzaldúa, *Borderlands/La Frontera: The New Mestiza* (San Francisco, 1987); Antonio Cornejo Polar, "Mestizaje e hibridez: Los riesgos de las metáforas," *Revista de Crítica Literaria Latinoamericana* 24 (47) (1998): 7–11. For an overview and critique of the Canadian "mosaic," see Richard Day, "Constructing the Official Canadian: A Genealogy of the Mosaic Metaphor in State Policy Discourse," *Topia: Canadian Journal of Cultural Studies* 2 (Spring 1998): 42–66.
2. The study was based on an update of the 1990 census, which involved projecting the figures for 1992. See Richard Morin, "A Distorted Image of Minorities," *Washington Post* (Oct. 8, 1995): A1.
3. Michael Fix and Jeffrey S. Passel, *Immigration and Immigrants: Setting the Record Straight* (Washington: Urban Institute, 1994).
4. "Chronotope" is Mikhail Bakhtin's term to describe how the inseparability of time and space is conveyed representationally. For Bakhtin, a chronotope is primarily, though not exclusively, a literary device of spatial-temporal unity that determines the parameters of plot development, characterization, and action, as well as the formation of literary genres. M. M. Bakhtin, "Forms of Time and Chronotope in the Novel" in *The Dialogic Imagination, Four Essays,* ed. M. Holquist, trans. C. Emerson and M. Holquist (Austin, 1988), 84–258.
5. Bourne's neologism, "Trans-National America," anticipates the "recovery narrative" of our current "nationalist postnationalist" period, when American diversity (rather than "variety") has been invoked to resurrect the familiar story of national exceptionalism within a new global order. See Buell.
6. In the 1950s, David Potter claimed that the distinctive trait of the national character is the belief that abundance will result in democratization and justice: "This American confidence that our abundance will suffice for the attainment of all the goals of social justice is evident throughout the greater

part of our national history" (119). Where Potter's rendition of American abundance is boundless, I underscore the consciousness of limits. American variety, I argue, is a response to an economy of uneven development, an attempt to find the middle ground between excessive abundance and dire poverty. This is seen in James Madison's late-eighteenth-century use of variety, when it figures as a response to the maldistribution of wealth, specifically aimed at diffusing the resentment of renters toward the comparatively small group of property owners.

7. For more on the Lincoln-Douglas debates in terms of race and union, see Wald 56–60.
8. Labor conflicts also increased throughout the United States, from silk mills in New Jersey to Carnegie-owned mines in Colorado. From 1881 to 1905 there were approximately 37,000 labor strikes in the nation, involving over 7 million workers (Freeman 190).
9. Sucheng Chan, "Race, Ethnic Culture, and Gender in the Construction of Identities among Second-Generation Chinese Americans, 1880s to 1930s," *Claiming America: Constructing Chinese American Identities during the Exclusion Era,* ed. K. Scott Wong and Sucheng Chan (Philadelphia, 1998), 158.
10. Van Wyck Brooks, *New England: Indian Summer, 1865–1914* (1940; Chicago, 1978), 31.
11. On pragmatism's critique of Social Darwinism, see Hofstadter, *Social Darwinism,* ch. 7.
12. Raymond Williams, in *The Long Revolution,* describes the term "pattern" as the foundation of cultural analysis, because it refers to a particular organization of life, its interests and activities (63). Williams is careful to present this analytical trope as limited and modest, emphasizing that patterns of culture cannot fully recover life as it was but that they do give a selective sense of a period's structure of feeling.
13. This was certainly not the case for all late Victorian intellectuals. Henry Adams, whom Lears aptly describes as an "antimodern modernist," refuses to distinguish between different formulations of multiplicity, rejecting them all as synonymous with anarchy and chaos. He homogenizes the terms of plurality, showing their uniform ends: "Multiplicity, Diversity, Complexity, Anarchy, Chaos" (455).

1. William James and the Modern Federal Republic

1. If James was the "liberator" of ecclesiastical pluralism, he was also the beneficiary of emergent German formulations of the term within metaphysics. In 1841 the philosopher Rudolph Hermann Lotze was the first to use "pluralism" in its secular sense to describe the composition of the world as a collection of multiple, individual, and "independent" beings. In addition to

Lotze, James appropriated elements from German romanticism, particularly Gottfried von Herder's belief in the benevolence of variety as an essential value. Variety was understood as nature's way of expressing individuality: "No two leaves of any one tree are exactly alike in nature, still less two human faces or two human constitutions" (Herder 282). Herder offered James a notion of "totality" (Herder's term) that sought to capture the dynamic and contingent character of diversity. The lesson that James learned from Lotze and Herder (both of whose work he taught at Harvard) was how to imagine a notion of unity that did not homogenize differences but depended on them. Multiplicity and unity could be mutually compatible if the form of union was flexible and accommodating.
2. Lentricchia, for instance, assumes the benevolence and radicalism of James's pluralism, defining it as a form of "resistance to the imperialist context of his work in the modernist moment" (21). Furthermore, West sees James's "protean pluralism" as a continuation of his "middle-of-the roadism," as occupying, in good pragmatic fashion, the "middle space" between extremes (57). These characterizations of pluralism tell only half of the story. They do not engage with the tensions of his pluralist theory, which has an ambivalent relation to anti-imperialism and the "middle ground," as discussed later in this chapter.
3. Although *Memories and Studies* was published a few months after *A Pluralistic Universe* in late 1909, it mainly consists of reprinted essays. At the time of his death in 1910, James had been composing another philosophical treatise. Realizing that he could not complete it, he gave instructions for its publication, and it appeared in 1911 as *Some Problems in Philosophy,* edited by his son Henry, Horace Kallen, and Ralph Barton Perry.
4. James to Maxwell J. Savage, 4 Jan. 1910; qtd. James, *Selected Unpublished Correspondence* 534.
5. For a different perspective on the relationship between modernism and postmodernism in James, see Livingston. In contrast to my argument, which sees James as a reluctant modernist, Livingston claims that James was a proto-postmodernist, whose pragmatic empiricism established the historical foundations for "modern subjectivity" and "postmodern pluralism."
6. Ellen Rooney argues that pluralism is unable to define its own parameters: "what are the limits of pluralism? Where—and how well guarded—is the border that separates the pluralist from his others?" (21). The inability of a pluralist discourse to answer these questions is due to the fact that it cannot address the principle of exclusion: "exclusion is both a practical and a theoretical problem for pluralism" (21).
7. On the "philosophy of the *via media*" in the context of turn-of-the-century liberalism, see Kloppenberg.
8. Where I find James's use of variety and unity as mutually compatible a re-

freshing move in our contemporary critical climate, in which unity is generally deemed oppressive, Shamoon Zamir considers it a sign of "conservative leanings" (46). For Zamir, James is at his "most radical and creative" when he insists that "the world is a *'plurality,'* not a *'unity'*" (34). As soon as James begins to define the parameters of unity, according to Zamir, he feeds into a "reactionary politics" (46). Zamir's reading of James suffers from a degree of what Terry Eagleton has called, in a different context, postmodern "holophobia," which assumes at its worst that "unity" is *ipso facto* reactionary. This rather rigid defense of heterogeneity, as I note in the Introduction, depends on a staged battle between the Manichean forces of good ("plurality") and evil ("unity"). See Eagleton, *Illusions* 9.

9. I am grateful to Art Efron for bringing this passage to my attention.
10. Jamesian pluralism actually bears a close resemblance to what Ellen Rooney defines as anti-pluralism, which is "the recognition of the irreducibility of the margin in all explanations, the foregrounding of *interests*, with *exclusions* as the inevitable and clearly articulated consequence" (63). Throughout *A Pluralistic Universe,* James acknowledges, however reluctantly, the necessity of emphasis, a principle of exclusion, which is integral in defining the pluralistic universe.
11. James's willingness to resign himself to the impossibility of uniting the different audiences into a single group is another point of differentiation from contemporary pluralism. According to Rooney, contemporary pluralists believe they can persuade all to their way of thinking if their argument is presented clearly and convincingly. "The pluralist critic," writes Rooney, "must exclude no one; he must aim at the persuasion of the entire community, taking each reader as a potential convert" (94). James, in accepting the fact that he will have critics, demonstrates that his modern brand of pluralism is actually, in many respects, a form of contemporary anti-pluralism.
12. Harvard was not the first university to institute an elective system. In 1850 Francis Wayland installed an elective curriculum at Brown, a decision which saw enrollment leap by 40 percent in three years. In 1868 Ezra Cornell and Andrew Dixon White founded a new university in Ithaca, New York, which offered students a variety of ways to realize their career ambitions. Its motto was "Any Student, Any Study." See Keller.
13. On the perception of Harvard's evolution as a reflection of the nation as a whole, see Smith.
14. William James to Mrs. Henry Whitman, 7 June 1899, *Letters of William James*, 2:90.
15. William James to William Dean Howells, 16 Nov. 1900, Howells Papers, Houghton Library, Harvard University; qtd. Cotkin 141.
16. Mabie's distinction between a "heterogeneous collection" and "rounded

personality" can be seen as a late-nineteenth-century variation of the literary distinction between "flat" and "round" characters. According to Deidre Lynch, the privileging of "round" characters as more dimensional and complex than their "flat" counterparts occurred at the turn into the nineteenth century, when novel readers sought to fulfill themselves as "individuals" within an emergent economy of conspicuous consumption. See Lynch, *The Economy of Character: Novels, Market Culture, and the Business of Inner Meaning* (Chicago, 1998).

17. One example of this contemporary tendency to define a power-free multiculturalism is found in Peter Erickson, "What Multiculturalism Means," *Transition* 55 (1992): 113: "The primary criterion for a strong version of multiculturalism is that it not be reducible to a pluralism structured in dominance."

18. James was keenly aware of the intellectual's political weakness at the turn of the century, but he was able to turn his disaffection into engagement. The Dreyfus Affair, for instance, represented to James the potential power of intellectuals as a class. Despite the fact that Alfred Dreyfus, a Jewish army officer in the French army, was wrongly accused of espionage and condemned again in a retrial, James wrote to a friend in 1899: "I don't believe the game is lost." "'Les intellectuels,' thanks to the Republic," he wrote, "are now aggressively militant as they never were before, and will grow stronger and stronger; so we may hope" (*Selected Letters* 175). The Dreyfus Affair was a radicalizing moment for intellectuals because, as Pierre Bourdieu has noted, they intervened politically *as* intellectuals, with "a specific authority grounded on their belonging to the relatively autonomous world of art, science, and literature and on all the values that are associated with this autonomy—virtue, disinterestedness, competence, and so on" (Bourdieu 656).

19. Charles Eliot Norton, a popular fine arts professor at Harvard, addressed the students shortly after the outbreak of the Spanish-American War calling the war criminal and advising them not to enlist. Politicians, journalists, and even clergy condemned his strong public opposition to the war, which ultimately led to his forced resignation from the university.

20. James's vanguard notion of historical progress is seen over two decades earlier in "Great Men and Their Environment." Published in the *Atlantic Monthly* in 1880, this article claims that national greatness depends on "great men" who will initiate an "internal movement" that will "vibrate" throughout the community to establish a great epoch. By the early twentieth century, James includes women within this theory and thus uses the more gender-neutral term "college-bred."

21. Antonio Gramsci, *Selections from the Prison Notebooks*, trans. and ed. Quintin Hoare and Geoffrey Nowell-Smith (London, 1971), 57n.

22. I borrow this phrase from Lentricchia (27).
23. In contrast to a "war of maneuver," which is focused on one front and one moment of struggle, analogous to a military battle, the "war of position" is ultimately more transformative since it is fought on multiple fronts that affect the whole organizational system of a nation beyond the battlefield; it affects, in other words, the structures and institutions of civil society. It is a war of ideological conversion rather than military gain.
24. Letter to *Boston Evening Transcript,* March 4, 1899; qtd. Jordan *Imperial Democracy* 147–148.
25. "Repressive tolerance" is Herbert Marcuse's term for describing the role of the state in neutralizing opposition through condescending benevolence rather than through outright oppression.

2. Identity Culture and Cosmopolitanism

1. *The Crisis* (Feb. 15, 1919).
2. Charles Taylor has defined "recognition" as a vital human need, an extension of the liberal principle of originality: "each of our voices has something unique to say" (78). Recognition represents the distinct identity of an individual or a cultural group in the Herderian sense that cultural groups are valuable in their distinctiveness from one another.
3. Bill Brown briefly uses the phrase "identity culture" to refer primarily to critical perspectives that underscore identity formation as constitutive of a national identity: "Our America is an identity culture definable not by *an* identity but by the fixation *on* identity" ("Identity Culture" 165). I use this phrase—"identity culture"—to refer to "minority" strategies to conserve subcultural particularity while also ethnicizing and racializing the national culture.
4. According to Newfield and Gordon, Kallen's "most lasting contribution to pluralism" is "his strong tilt away from unity" (84). They champion Kallen because he is among the first to anticipate the postmodern trend of differentiating variety from unity. This perspective rehearses the same pattern of contemporary multiculturalism that I address in the Introduction, namely that the privileging of variety as democratic comes at the cost of demonizing its perceived antithesis—unity.
5. The phrase "unharmonizable variety" is Kallen's description of James's pluralistic universe, a quality that he praises and likens to the Hebraic world view of flux and conflict (*Philosophy of William James* 5).
6. Jacobson examines how Jewish thinkers also sustained a mythos of racial distinctiveness. Yiddish writers such as Abraham Cahan as well as Jewish scientists like Maurice Fishberg also promoted a notion of a distinct racial integrity to Jewishness (Jacobson 175).

7. Michael Omi and Howard Winant, in *Racial Formation in the United States* (New York, 1986), foreground the category of race as an understanding of social dynamics within the "racial state." They define "racial formation" as the treatment of race "as a *central axis* of social relations which cannot be subsumed under or reduced to some broader category or conception" (61–62). Furthermore, they problematize the distinction between ethnicity and race, demonstrating that race is also a heterogeneous term, which includes black ethnicities such as Haitian, Jamaican, and Georgian (23).
8. I take my definition of "character" from John Stuart Mill's ideal of authenticity in *On Liberty:* "A person whose desires and impulses are his own—are the expression of his own nature, as it has been developed and modified by his own culture—is said to have a character" (73–74).
9. According to Moses Rischin in *The Promised City: New York's Jews, 1870–1914* (New York, 1962), intermarriage between Jewish and non-Jewish New Yorkers was rare. After 1900 the association of Jewish women and Italian and non-Jewish Russian men in the garment industry led to some marriages. Somewhat less unusual were marriages between uptowners and downtowners (111).
10. Crummell, "The Negro as a Source of Conservative Power," in *Destiny and Race*, 242. The history and the publication date of this piece are unknown.
11. As Hazel Carby has argued in *Race Men*, Crummell continues to figure as the emblematic black intellectual in genealogies of black intellectual thought (5).
12. By the time Kallen published "Democracy versus the Melting-Pot" (1915), Du Bois had largely stopped making biological claims to black distinctiveness. In *The Negro* (1915), he defines race as a "dynamic and not a static conception, and the typical races are continually changing and developing, amalgamating and differentiating" (16). This would continue to characterize his definitions of race after World War I. On Du Bois and race, see Wald, 207–209; Appiah, "Uncompleted Argument."
13. As bell hooks has rightly argued, there is a reason why minorities continue to hold onto essentialist notions: "The unwillingness to critique essentialism on the part of many African-Americans is rooted in the fear that it will cause folks to lose sight of the specific history and experience of African-Americans and the unique sensibilities and culture that arise from that experience" (29).
14. On Kallen's Zionism, see Higham, *Send*, ch. 9; Schmidt, "Zionist Chapter"; Konvitz, *Legacy*. See also Kallen's early work, *Zionism and World Politics* (1921).
15. Gaines argues that black elites replicated the same racist logic that they were criticizing by advocating a value system of bourgeois morality, which was deeply embedded in the troubling assumptions of racial difference (4). I dis-

agree with Gaines in regard to the role of biological racial differences. According to Gaines, black elites used uplift ideology to switch from biology to culture, but as I see it, Du Bois held onto a notion of racial essentialism as well as a cultural and historical understanding of race as part of a dual strategy to affirm a positive identity in a deeply racist society.

16. *The Crisis* (Feb. 1919); qtd. Moses 143.
17. This identification with the position of the indigenous should not be mistaken for a black alliance with Native Americans. Cooper, for instance, juxtaposes the Native American against the African American in order to underscore the superiority of the latter: where the "Indian" has "stood proudly aloof from all their [Anglo] efforts at development," the "Negro," has, by contrast, shown a "perfect amiability of temper and adaptability of mental structure" to the standards of civilization (194).
18. Gordon and Newfield describe the omission of race as a "flaw." Kallen, according to them, "overlooked the importance of racial exclusion and subordination in American life" (86). In fact, as I will demonstrate, Kallen's letters to Wendell regarding the Locke Affair, combined with his debates with Locke about racism, indicate someone who did not merely "overlook" racial exclusion but used it as the starting point from which to theorize pluralism.
19. On Locke's relation to the ideas of Kallen, Du Bois, and James, see Hutchinson; Posnock, *Color.*
20. In an interview, Kallen claimed to have been one of those who did not attend (Sollors, "Pure Pluralism" 269). However, in his memoir, *What I Believe and Why—Maybe,* he states that two "authentically Americans" [sic] refused to attend, but he does not specify if he is referring to himself (173).
21. See, e.g., Du Bois, "Organized Labor" (1912), in *The Seventh Son,* ed. Julius Lester, vol. 2 (New York: Random House, 1971), 301–302.
22. Simon Patten was among the first theorists of working-class consumption, arguing in 1907 that leisure would instill in the laboring classes the discipline of work: their desire for play would make them into obedient factory hands.
23. The phrase "Benetton effect" is borrowed from Chicago Cultural Studies Group, 115. For related discussions, see Robert Stam and Ella Shohat in Goldberg 299.
24. Du Bois seems to have used "inter-nation" inconsistently with varying degrees of emphasis on racial particularity. Posnock has cited a 1933 example in which this term represents a de-racialized ideal: the "Inter-nation, of Humanity, and the disappearance of 'race' from our vocabulary" (*Color* 188).
25. "Cultural affiliations" is Amanda Anderson's phrase. In the contemporary discourse of cosmopolitanism, "affiliation" suggests a degree of detachment that is a preferred alternative to the "extreme allegiances to nation, race, and ethnos" (Anderson 267). Anderson further discredits identity politics

through the phrase the "atomizing effects of identity" (266). She argues for an "inclusionary cosmopolitanism" (as opposed to an "exclusionary cosmopolitanism") that is defined against the "excesses of identity politics" and "partial or false universals." Her brand of cosmopolitanism wants it both ways: to have "ethical ideals" without having to be exclusive or even partial. Furthermore, ethics and ethnos are assumed to be mutually exclusive.

3. The Uneven Development of American Regionalism

1. I use "regionalism" and "local color" interchangeably. Although Judith Fetterley and Marjorie Pryse have claimed that the latter is a touristic mode of representing regions while the former is more empathic, I find June Howard's distinction more pertinent for my purposes. For Howard, local color refers to a specific period, whereas regionalism is a more general movement not confined to the turn of the century.
2. In 1908 Turner writes: "When we look at the underlying forces of economic and social life, and at the distribution of political power in the Union, we find that sectionalism antedated nationalism, that it has endured, though often concealed by our political forms, through the whole of our history, and that it is far from certain that it would pass away though the state should be extinguished; indeed it might gather new vitality and power from such an event" ("Sectionalism" 661–662).
3. The regionalists never fully succeeded in rescuing the term "regional" from its negative connotations, evident in Eudora Welty's acknowledgment that the term is still synonymous with "condescending" and "careless." More recently, the Kenyan writer and activist Ngugi wa Thiong'o has expanded this point for a global context, noting that "local" implies the Third World: "What is Western becomes universal and what is third world becomes local. Locality becomes measured by the degree of its distance from the metropolis of the Western world." "Responses," *Yale Journal of Criticism* 5:2 (1992): 149.
4. The Southern Agrarians' anti-Communist celebration of the "yeoman" ideals of Southern rural life bordered on fascism, with one member, Seward Collins, actually declaring his admiration for Hitler and Mussolini in a 1936 interview with the *New Republic*. F. O. Matthiessen, in his review of American poetry from 1920 to 1940, remarked that "Tate has called himself a 'reactionary,' and some of the less clear minds of the group, taking their stand even against the racial reforms of the New Deal, have drifted dangerously close to native fascism" (qtd. Karanikas 180). On the politics of Southern Agrarianism, see Alexander Karanikas, *Tillers of the Myth* (Madison, WI, 1966).
5. Instrumental to Garland's veritism was the work of Eugène Véron, who

wrote in *Aesthetics* (1878), that "variety" was a sign of individual interpretation according to one's "own genius": "This is the source of the infinite variety in unity—variety of expression in unity of sentiment" (xiv). In his copy of Véron, Garland wrote: "This work influenced me more than any other work on art. It entered into all I thought and spoke and read for many years after it fell into my hands about 1886" (qtd. Holloway 101).

6. William Jennings Bryan similarly claimed in 1896: "the great cities rest upon our broad and fertile prairies. Burn down your cities and leave our farms, and your cities will spring up again as if by magic; but destroy our farms and grass will grow in the streets of every city in the country" (qtd. Bailyn 851).

7. In his earlier work *The Country and the City,* Williams qualifies the type of regional novel that isolates a specific place as an example of "the regional novel at its weakest" (253). However, in "Region and Class in the Novel," Williams describes this same type of regional novel not as the "weakest" form but as its truest form: "the truly regional novel" has "so isolated its region" (61). In his later work there is less insistence on the varieties of regional fiction and greater emphasis on an exemplary type.

8. The land-owning Californios constituted 5 percent of the Mexican population in Alta California in the nineteenth century. They were the major recipients of Mexican government land grants from 1822 to 1848.

9. On Californio *testimonios,* see Sánchez, *Telling Identities.*

10. *Main-Travelled Roads* was first published by the Arena Publishing Company of Boston in 1891; a revised edition appeared in 1899 from the Macmillan Company. *The Souls of Black Folk* was first published in 1903 by A. C. McClurg and Company of Chicago.

11. In *Squatter,* Tom Scott is portrayed as a sympathetic and charismatic figure, the potential savior of San Diego, who is ultimately victimized and consequently dies from despair due to the monopoly conspiracy of the Big Four. According to historical accounts, however, Scott was himself a railroad mogul, who died of a stroke in 1881, according to the Dallas *Daily Herald,* not because of a broken heart but from the "mental strain for a long period as manager of a great enterprise" (V. Taylor 176). Far from the victim that Ruiz de Burton portrays, Scott became the president of the Union Pacific in 1871, then president of the Texas Pacific in 1872 and of the Pennsylvania Railroad in 1874. He built an empire which outstripped those of Cornelius Vanderbilt and James Fisk. He also earned for himself the infamous epithet "the most hated man in Pennsylvania." The battle between the Big Four and Tom Scott was not between Monopoly and the American Public, but rather between two railroad empires.

12. David Luis-Brown claims that the alliance between Californios and South-

erners in Ruiz de Burton's novel demonstrates how both were considered "sectional victims of the corrupt monopolies and the lower classes" (817). What I want to underscore is that the novel is aimed at a northeastern genteel audience, who are both reform-minded and cosmopolitan. Ruiz de Burton's characters visit the various metropolitan and upper-class leisure sites of the Northeast, with only a brief mention of Baltimore, suggesting that the novel is directed more toward the northeastern cosmopolitan elite while still drawing connections with the South.

13. This sense of loyalty to the nation is also expressed at the authorial level. Ruiz de Burton published *Squatter* under the pseudonym "C. Loyal," which refers to "Loyal Citizen" or *"Ciudadano Leal."* This was a common letter-closing convention in correspondence with Mexican government officials in the nineteenth century (Sánchez and Pita 11). Hence, "C. Loyal" could refer to one's loyalty to Mexico as well as to the United States (after all, Mercedes was born on *cinco de mayo* and she marries Clarence on September 16th, Mexican Independence day). In their introduction to *Squatter,* Sánchez and Pita argue that this pseudonym provides an "ironic twist" since the novel is "severely critical of the political structures of American society" (11). The novel is both critical of government corruption, congressional complicity with monopoly interests through bribery schemes, and reverent to U.S. ideals. The novel is ironic and earnest. Through the often tiresome dialogues between government officials, railroad barons, and Ruiz de Burton's protagonists, there is a sense in which the narrative voice is genuinely outraged about government corruption and expects the reader to be as well. By the end of the novel, the pessimism toward government institutions translates into an embrace of the marketplace. Where the government thwarts the entrepreneurial efforts of loyal citizens, the marketplace rewards them through speculation.

14. The Alamars' visit to Mount Vernon is also significant in terms of the novel's faith in speculation. George Washington died one of the wealthiest men in the nation, most of his wealth acquired through land speculation in the West. In a 1903 article on Washington, entitled "The Pioneer Investor," Archer Butler Hulbert remarks that "it is not commonly known that . . . more than half his wealth lay west of the Alleghenies." By the turn of the century, speculation was becoming an accepted part of the national business of money-making, leading to retrospective articles such as this one, which approached the first President not as a great politician or general but as a clever investor. Seen in this light, Clarence, the "lucky investor," is not breaking with the traditions of the past but continuing them in the vein of the founding fathers.

15. In 1894 Garland defined speculation as "getting from some one else a value

which we have not earned. It means living upon someone else" ("Land" 169).
16. See M. Kazin ch. 2.
17. On the populist movement, see Kazin, Goodwyn, McMath, Hicks, and Hofstadter.
18. Michael Kazin in his history of turn-of-the-century populism has noted that even a "tactical alliance with black Southerners was a dangerous, even heroic step at the time," but he adds that despite such gestures the populists continued to assume that the "plain people" meant whites (41). This is certainly true of Garland, in that he racializes Grant McLane's pauperization in "Up the Coulee" through his negroization.
19. In 1915 nearly 90 percent of the black population still lived in the rural South (Kinney 26).
20. This story was in part based upon the author's visit to see his family in Ordway, South Dakota, in July of 1889. A nascent writer teaching in Boston and studying at the Public Library, Garland discovered that his midwest home was in the throes of an agrarian depression that inspired what he called "a sullen rebellion against government and against God" (qtd. Bailyn 855).
21. According to Stilgoe, the "metropolitan corridor" refers to the literal expansion of railroad lines linking a wider spectrum of regions to the city, but it also metaphorically denotes the process of economic and social interdependence and consolidation.
22. Brander Matthews, a well-known literary critic of the period as well as a professor of American literature at Columbia, found this scene highly implausible because of Howard's insensitivity: "the reader wonders whether in ten years the returned prodigal could have forgotten the life of his boyhood so completely as to wear a fancy tennis costume with no thought of its incongruity" (Nagel 43). If Howard did not flaunt his wealth in the first place, or so the logic of Matthews's argument goes, there would not be such fraternal tension. Matthews's point suggests that for many, if not for most, the city/country dichotomy was perceived by the end of the nineteenth century as an unfortunate but permanent characteristic of the national landscape. It could only be placated through humility and consideration.
23. In 1932 Austin defined race as a "pattern of response common to a group of people who have lived together under a given environment long enough" (97).
24. We are also told that Howard's success in New York was largely the result of male mentors, especially Jake Saulsman of Chicago who, according to Howard, "asked me to go to New York with him, and—I don't know why—took a fancy to me some way" (78). Typographical dashes in the dialogue,

we are told earlier, signify moments of hesitation. For instance when Grant's wife pauses before calling Howard to breakfast, the narrator adds that she is "hesitating a little on his name" (69). With this in mind, Howard's hesitation in articulating his relationship to Saulsman further complicates his sexuality.

25. Garland, however, does rescue an impoverished rural family in his 1891 novel and play *Jason Edwards, An Average Man*. Through marital, rather than fraternal, union, the Edwards family, who moved from a Boston ghetto to "Boomtown, USA" to improve their lot, are saved from catastrophe through the marriage of Jason's daughter Alice to a Boston editor, Walter Reeves. Marriage also rescues another of Garland's female protagonists, Agnes Kinney, in "A Branch Road," the story that precedes "Up the Coulee" in *Main-Travelled Roads*. Will Hannan returns from the Southwest to take his childhood sweetheart, Agnes, away from the poverty and hard work of farm life as well as from a bad marriage. Romantic love can save the rural woman, but brotherly love appears to be doomed. Men cannot be rescued from the trials of farm life, unless, like Jason Edwards, they are rescued by a daughter's suitor.

26. In his 1884 study of black southern farm labor, T. Thomas Fortune argues that the social and economic problems of the South are not confined to this specific locality, but are indicative of the nation and the world. Fortune summarizes his main objective: "to show that the social problems in the South are, in the main, the same as those which afflict every civilized country on the globe: and that the future conflict in that section will not be racial or political in character, but between capital on the one hand and labor on the other" (*Black and White* iv).

27. In August 1899 African Americans in Darien, Georgia refused to allow officials to transfer an affluent African American, Henry Delegal, from the local jail, a move, they argued, that would make him vulnerable to lynching. The governor sent in the state militia to disband armed blacks at the local jail; the blacks promised to disband on condition that Delegal would have militia protection to Savannah. A price had to be paid, as Paul Gilje has pointed out, for black audacity. The sheriff arrested Delegal's two sons for allegedly participating in the riot to protect their father. Although Delegal was eventually acquitted of the charge of rape, his sons were given life sentences. In April 1899 Sam Hose, a farmer living outside of Atlanta, shot and killed a white farmer after an altercation over a debt. After Hose was lynched and burned to death, a white mob of over 2,000 men, women, and children fought for pieces of his charred remains as souvenirs (Lewis 226).

28. Du Bois adopts a Dickensian rhetoric of touring, one that Jacob Riis also uses in his study of New York City's "other half," in which the reader is di-

rectly addressed in the second person. But unlike Dickens and Riis, Du Bois uses this intimate form of address within the context of racial segregation, inviting the reader to occupy the position of the racially "other" rather than view African Americans as the "other half": "If you wish to ride with me you must come into the 'Jim Crow Car'" (158).

29. At the start of his novel *The Quest of the Silver Fleece* (1911), Du Bois accentuates the world economy of cotton: "The cry of the naked was sweeping the world. From the peasant toiling in Russia, the lady lolling in London, the chieftain burning in Africa, and the Esquimaux freezing in Alaska; from long lines of hungry men, from patient sad-eyed women, from old folk and creeping children went up the cry, 'Clothes, clothes!'" (54).

30. Garland's partiality to feminist reform movements should also be acknowledged. Bill Brown has opined that part of the reason Garland has returned to canonical stature is his "good" politics. Whether it is Laura McLane in "Up the Coulee" or Alice Edwards in *Jason Edwards,* to name but two examples, Garland frequently portrays rural America as especially oppressive and lonely for young women. The physical drudgery and social isolation of farm life made it a place from which to escape, or at least to imagine an urban alternative.

31. For Williams, the danger of "symmetrical thinking" is the refusal to recognize a process of determination: "For if we come to say that society is composed of a large number of social practices which form a concrete social whole, and if we give to each practice a certain specific recognition, adding only that they interact, relate and combine in very complicated ways, we are at one level much more obviously talking about reality, but we are at another level withdrawing from the claim that there is any process of determination. And this I, for one, would be very unwilling to do" (qtd. Eagleton, "Williams" 169–170).

4. The Urban Picturesque and Americanization

1. Thomas Woodson, "Hawthornesque Shapes: The Picturesque and the Romance," *Studies in the Novel* 23:1 (Spring 1991): 170.
2. Between 1893 and 1897, and then again from 1907 to 1908, industrial unemployment rates soared to 30 percent. From 1881 to 1905 approximately 37,000 labor strikes took place in the United States, involving over 7 million workers (Freeman 120).
3. In *The Urban Sublime in American Literary Naturalism* (1998), Christophe Den Tandt has argued that the turn of the century marked a time of deep ambivalence about modernity, when the metropolis represented a space of

both wonderment and terror. The urban sublime offers a way to understand literary responses to the late-Victorian metropolis that accounts for a degree of pleasure. My work on the urban picturesque is a complement rather than a critique of Den Tandt's argument. It begins with the premise that there are a variety of ways to convey urban pleasure, some of which cannot be classified as sublime. The picturesque represents a more restrained and less dramatic form of urban pleasure.

4. By 1890 one of every three Americans already lived in urban areas (Freeman 13).
5. This association between New York cosmopolitanism and Americanism would be disputed in Ford Madox Ford's 1927 book *New York Is Not America*. The reason Ford loved New York was precisely that it rejected the Puritan spirit that had shaped all other U.S. cities. See Douglas 9–10.
6. See Brand, esp. ch. 2.
7. At the turn of the century approximately 60,000 African Americans lived in New York City, mostly in Manhattan (1000:810). In 1900, for the first time, more than half of the city's black population was born outside the state (53 percent). By 1910 New York City was the second largest African-American urban center in the nation (after Washington, D.C.). See Osofsky.
8. Some exceptions include Du Bois's descriptions of Harlem in *Darkwater* (see Chapter 2) and Howells's *An Imperative Duty* (1891), in which the protagonist, Dr. Olney, strolls through the African-American district of Boston.
9. Although the urban picturesque generally excluded African Americans, there were other cultural forms emerging from the black urban experience that captivated white audiences. According to Richard Newman, minstrelsy in the 1890s was in decline: "Its sentimentality and nostalgia appeared passé and rustic in the more sophisticated and urbanized Gilded Age" (465). Modern forms of black performance included the *fin-de-siècle* craze of ragtime and the cakewalk, which were transforming white middle-class culture from below. The cakewalk craze, which reached its zenith in 1903, fell outside the purview of the picturesque. Given its preference for "daylight" rather than "gaslight," the urban picturesque was more interested in cafés and markets than in nightclubs and dancehalls. See Newman, Woll.
10. Amy Kaplan demonstrates how the "picturesque" provides a familiar discourse of tourism within which the Marches can frame new urban realities: "by viewing New York as a foreign country, the Marches can experience it as familiar. The role of tourist places them in a known relationship to the city and allows them to distance themselves from the surrounding poverty by framing it within the secure lines of the 'picturesque'" (*Social Construction* 49). Although the picturesque was at times not as "secure" as Kaplan here

suggests, as evident in its contradictory use in relation to the Chinese, it did give New Yorkers a vocabulary to express urban experience as pleasurable rather than exclusively fearful.

11. In *Dusk of Dawn* Du Bois recalls that Shaler is the professor who "invited a Southerner, who objected to sitting beside me, out of his class" (581; qtd. Wald 203).

12. Hamilton Cravens has argued in his study of scientific racism in the United States that all immigrants were considered racially other: "it was not simply that whites thought that blacks were a race apart from themselves; so were the Jews, the Catholics—indeed, all immigrants and foreigners—and such racial designations seemed permanent, at least in historical times" (471). Although Nathaniel Shaler's comment certainly supports his claim, I believe Cravens's argument is too sweeping, not taking into account the ways in which liberal cosmopolitans and even conservatives distinguished between immigrant groups. Not all observers lumped all immigrants together, nor did they lump all immigrants with African Americans. During this heyday of social and scientific classification, when new concepts were being invented to depict an increasingly complex society, the category of whiteness was expanded and particularized.

13. Regarding Irish immigrants, Jacobson adds: "No one who has looked into this country's maze of segregation statutes, miscegenation codes, housing covenants, slavery laws, or civil rights debates could ever suppose that being a 'Celt,' say, was tantamount to being some kind of European 'Negro'" (9).

14. On the picturesque in the works of Gilpin, Price, and Knight, see Copley and Garside, Hussey, M. Price, Robinson, and Michasiw.

15. On how Marx and Engels, among others, configured the *Lumpenproletariat* as a racialized nomadic people, or what Peter Stallybrass has described as a "spectacle of heterogeneity," see Stallybrass, "Marx and Heterogeneity: Thinking the Lumpenproletariat," *Representations* 31 (Summer 1990): 69–95.

16. In Stieglitz's magazine *Camera Notes*, his friend Sadakichi Hartmann, an art and photography critic, remarks that the picturesque is emblematic of modernity and urbanism, since it captures the fleeting and transient qualities of the present. It is particularly found in crowd scenes, which contain the variety of "all the classes of society" (93). According to Alan Trachtenberg, the foreigner and the immigrant were for Stieglitz sources of aesthetic pleasure, sincerity, and the epitome of truth itself. See Hartmann; Trachtenberg, *American Photographs* 180–190.

17. According to Benjamin, the midcentury *flâneur* is the model for the "journalist [who] eagerly learns from him" (167). But where the midcentury

flâneur is primarily if not exclusively cast as male, the late-nineteenth-century journalists also included numerous women, urban *flâneuses* such as Viola Roseboro and Alice Harrison. Perhaps as a way to appeal to the largely female readership of commercial magazines such as *Scribner's* and *The Cosmopolitan,* women journalists were often the mediators between the immigrant quarters and the middle-class women readers. In one such tour of downtown New York in 1886, Roseboro observes that just within the past three or four years there has been a "great change" in the number of women on the streets. Although they are still in the minority, more women are seen going to work as "stenographers, type-writers, newspaper writers, engravers" ("Down-town" 222). On women and urban perambulation, see E. Wilson, Walkowitz, Wolff.

18. Howells's observations on the "spectacle of poverty" and its ability to negate the actual reality of poverty by reducing it to an image prefigure Guy Debord's definition of the spectacle as "the *affirmation* of appearance and the affirmation of all human, namely social life, as mere appearance" (10).

19. Ian Munt describes the rhetoric of the new middle-class tourist industry that refers to the client as a "traveller" rather than a tourist and advertises the destinations as "tourist free" or "lesser visited areas" or just as "secrets": "Exclusiveness, uniqueness, romanticism and relative solitude are central to the philosophy of these tour operators" (117).

20. Others who also promoted such a conception of Americanization included progressives such as Jane Addams and George Creel. Addams sought to retain immigrant picturesqueness through a living museum, where immigrant women displayed cottage industries and performed folk traditions. Creel also viewed immigrants as a repository of premodern traditions for the enrichment of modern city dwellers: "The immigrants can be tapped for their rich store of folk-songs, games, and traditional customs so that not only will the native-born be enriched and broadened, but the alien given that absolutely essential sense of belonging" (362).

21. Roseboro's "picturesque" Italians were not as politically apathetic as she suggests. According to Edwin Fenton, many of the immigrants, especially artisans from Northern Italy, were anarchists and socialists already experienced in unionizing. Italian stonemasons, mosaic workers, stone cutters, and brownstone cutters formed their own unions in the late nineteenth century. In the 1880s many Italian immigrants joined the Knights of Labor, when it was under the charismatic leadership of Terence Powderly. Prior to 1900 there were at least seven Italian-language radical newspapers. Even in the mainstream Italian-language press, there were accounts of union meetings and strikes. But most prevalent were articles attacking American unions for discriminating against Italian workers. See Fenton, ch. 5.

22. On Henry James's tour of New York, see Trachtenberg, "Conceivable Aliens."
23. Julian Ralph, "The Bowery," *Century Magazine* 43 (Dec. 1891): 237. David Graham Phillips, "The Bowery at Night," *Harper's Weekly* 35 (Sept. 19, 1891): 710.
24. Variety is also celebrated as a more general sign of modernity. It communicates Dreiser's sense of awe toward the condensation of space and its centralization in New York. Upon the arrival of a transcontinental train, Dreiser exclaims: "The variety of the cars. The variety of their contents. The long distances and differing climates and countries from which they have come—the Canadian snows, the Mexican uplands, Florida, California, Texas and Maine" (*Color* 68).
25. Between 1897 and the publication of *Sister Carrie* in 1900, Dreiser supported himself entirely from his freelance work, turning out almost a piece a week, for which he was paid between $25 and $100 each. This was an extremely good income and the most he would earn until many years after *Sister Carrie*. See Moers, ch 2.
26. Dreiser nevertheless occupied the position of tourist or travel writer when writing about "Little Italy": "you may see such a picture of Italian life and manners as only a visit to Naples and the vine-clad hills of southern Italy would otherwise afford" (*Color* 268). Dreiser's description of the Italians as "pictures" is reminiscent of Amy Kaplan's definition of the picturesque in the context of Howells's *A Hazard of New Fortunes* (*Social Construction* 49).
27. The Geary Law of 1892 renewed the Act of 1882 for another ten years, suspending the entry of Chinese to the United States. It also required all Chinese immigrants to prove through white men's testimony their legal right to be in the United States. By 1902 the suspension of Chinese immigration turned into outright exclusion. See Higham, *Send*, 36.
28. I am grateful to Lisa Botshon for bringing Zhang's essay to my attention. For more on Wong, see Botshon 30–32.
29. In 1880 California lawmakers prohibited marriage between a white person and a "negro, mulatto, or Mongolian." See Megumi Dick Osumi, "Asians and California's Anti-Miscegenation Laws," in Nobuya Tsuchida, ed., *Asian and Pacific American Experiences: Women's Perspectives* (Minneapolis, 1982). Two years earlier, at the California Constitutional Convention, John F. Miller warned: "Were the Chinese to amalgamate at all with our people, it would be the lowest, most vile and degraded of our race, and the result of that amalgamation would be a hybrid of the most despicable, a mongrel of the most detestable that has ever afflicted the earth" (qtd. Takaki, *Different Mirror* 205).
30. See Willa Cather's reports on the Chinese community in Pittsburgh: "Life in

Chinatown," *Pittsburgh Leader* 12 (Feb. 1899): 1; "Chinatown on a Small Scale," *Pittsburgh Leader* 22 (July 1900): 1. Although Cather's articles do not focus on culinary practices, they do include coverage of religious practices as well as of the only Chinese woman living in Pittsburgh, Mrs. Yee Chin, wife of a local tea merchant. I am grateful to Lia Vella for generously sharing with me her research from the University Archives at the University of Nebraska-Lincoln.

31. In 1885 white workers refused to work in the same mine as Chinese workers in Rock Springs, Wyoming. White workers invaded the Chinese section of town and shot Chinese workers as they fled and then burned their buildings. Fifteen Chinese were wounded and twenty-eight murdered. See Takaki, *Iron Cages* 248; Alexander Saxton, *The Indispensable Enemy: Labor and the Anti-Chinese Movement in California* (Berkeley, 1971), 200–213.

32. The New York Race Riots of 1900 were the first serious outbreak of racial violence since the Draft Riots of 1863. In August 1900 a plainclothes policeman named Robert Thorpe approached a black woman, May Enoch (who was waiting for her boyfriend), and charged her with "soliciting." When her boyfriend, Arthur J. Harris, returned from buying cigars, he saw that the policeman had "grabbed my girl. I didn't know who he was and thought he was a citizen like myself." Harris was then clubbed. In self-defense, he took out a knife and "cut him twice." Thorpe died the following day. During the next few days, white mobs randomly attacked African Americans, including the poet Paul Laurence Dunbar. Harris was found guilty of murder in the second degree, and sentenced "at hard labor for the term of his natural life." He died at Sing Sing in 1908. See Osofsky 46–52; Citizens' Protective League, *Story of the Riot,* ed. Frank Moss (New York, 1900).

33. In an interview with the *Pittsburgh Courier* in 1944, Terrell explained that in the 1890s "colored people could dine anywhere in the nation's capital, but near the end of the century, these rights were wrested away from us" (B. Jones 72). Although the anti-discrimination laws of 1872 and 1873 required "all eating-place proprietors to serve any respectable well-behaved person regardless of color," these laws disappeared by the 1890s when the District Code was rewritten. In 1953 Chief Justice William O. Douglas determined that these Reconstruction laws were still valid. See Jones 71–86.

34. Terrell demanded that the social spaces of the nation's capital be desegregated. In 1948, at the age of 85, she led a campaign to end discrimination in the capital's restaurants. She was one of three plaintiffs in an important civil rights case that ended with a Supreme Court decision to uphold the right of all races to equal eating accommodation in Washington. *District of Columbia v. John R. Thompson Co.* (346 U.S. 100, 1953). Food became for Terrell the contested terrain where segregation was challenged and fought.

35. Not all forms of transnationalism deconstruct national boundaries. As Frederick Buell has argued, transnationalism can also reinscribe national borders within a "hyperdeveloped" global economy. Globalization does not make "nationalism go away" nor does it necessarily change national cultures (580). For another challenge to "borderless" versions of transnationalism, see Rouse. For a comparison of transnationalism in the early and late twentieth century, see Foner.
36. Sidney Robinson aptly summarizes the middle-of-the-roadism of this aesthetic: "The Picturesque does not side with radicals any more than it sides with despots" (85).

5. Biracial Fictions and the Mendelist Allegory

1. Despite phenotypical differences, the races of man, according to Darwin, are fundamentally similar, united by a common array of emotions and cultural proclivities. In *The Descent of Man* (1871), he outlines "the close similarity between the men of all races in tastes, dispositions and habits": "This [similarity] is shown by the pleasure which they all take in dancing, rude music, acting, painting, tattooing, and otherwise decorating themselves; in their mutual comprehension of gesture-language, by the same expression in their features, and by the same inarticulate cries, when excited by the same emotions" (536).
2. For Darwin, varieties were constantly being converted into distinct species, thus blurring the line between the two concepts: "every naturalist knows vaguely what he means when he speaks of a species. Generally the term includes the unknown element of a distant act of creation. The term 'variety' is almost equally difficult to define; but here community of descent is almost universally implied, though it can rarely be proved" (38). On Darwin and race, see R. Young, ch. 1.
3. On polygenesis in relation to nineteenth-century imperialism, see R. Young. On Nott's theories in the context of antebellum America, see Fredrickson.
4. George Stocking explains the appeal of polygenesis for late-nineteenth-century anthropology as a way to justify "the white man's imperial dominion" that was becoming greater than ever before (47).
5. Social Darwinism was in large part a misreading of Darwinian evolution, which transformed the indeterminacy of Darwin into a highly teleological and determinant framework of inevitable progress. Social Darwinists also appropriated Darwin's work to corroborate a racist script of Anglo-Saxon domination to justify the subjugation of weaker races in the aftermath of the Spanish American War. Richard Hofstadter in *Social Darwinism in American Thought* showed that the imperialists of 1898 pointed to Darwin's *The Origin*

of Species and specifically its subtitle, which referred to "The Preservation of Favoured Races in the Struggle for Life." Darwin had been talking about pigeons, but the imperialists applied his analysis to colonial subjugation (Hofstadter 171).

6. Shaler, who expelled a white southern student from his classroom for refusing to sit next to Du Bois, was of the generation of New Englanders who supported abolition in their youth and in the case of Shaler actually fought in the Civil War; but during the 1880s and 1890s their sympathies turned to the white South and its racial problems. On Du Bois and Shaler, see Wald 203.

7. I have chosen Jameson's "nationalist allegory" over Abdul JanMohamed's "Manichean Allegory" because the former foregrounds the role of subaltern nationalism. In locating the allegory among the colonized rather than the colonizers, Jameson rethinks the role of nationalism: "a certain nationalism is fundamental in the third world, thus making it legitimate to ask whether it is all that bad in the end" (65). The Mendelist allegory promotes an emergent black nationalism as a way to consolidate the class, color, and regional differences within the black community. JanMohamed's "Manichean allegory," though possessing the either/or binary of the Mendelist allegory, is primarily targeted to the critical analysis of the colonialist text, in which the native is associated with "evil" and the European with moral superiority.

8. The same logic of persistent particularity was used to defend white feminist claims that there are a variety of women-types. The feminist doctor C. W. Saleeby argues that women are just as "variable" as men: "It has long been asserted that woman is less variable than man: but the certainty of that statement has lately lost its edge . . . There is no real reason to suppose that woman is less complex or less variable than man" (66). Saleeby invokes the Mendelian notion of "mutually repellent" factors to make a case that the "brooding instinct" and "intellect" are independent and non-blending attributes. For her, Mendelism is a useful way to explain that not all women are intended to be mothers. Some work with their "brain and mind" (62). Mendelism was appropriated by the "new woman" of the turn of the century to render non-procreative intellectual women as "natural" rather than aberrational.

9. This move from the subculture to the national culture is the literary counterpart to the pluralisms of Kallen and Du Bois, as a means of defending a minority position especially among those who are the most assimilated, ranging from the intellectual in Kallen and Du Bois to the "white Negro" in the Mendelist allegory. Kallen, in particular, invokes a Mendelian logic, as I mentioned in Chapter 2, which insists on the persistence of Jewishness despite Jewish-Gentile intermarriages: "older types persist, and there is noth-

ing to keep them from so continuing on any principle of the relation of heredity to environment that may be applied to them" (*C&D* 177). But where ancestry is for Kallen patrilineal—one cannot change one's grandfather—it is understood in the Mendelian narrative as unequivocally matrilineal.

10. Robert Young explores the relations between white power and white desire for women of color, or as Gayatri Spivak has articulated it, the "relationship between the imperialist subject and the subject of imperialism" (Young 152). Interracial sex, according to Young, was part of the colonial fantasy of conquering otherness.

11. On the diverse ways in which Progressives, including anarchists, feminists, unionists, and socialists, applied eugenics toward reformist ends, see Pickens; Hasian. See also Howard Horwitz's review essay on eugenics, "Always with Us," *American Literary History* 10:2 (Summer 1998): 317–334.

12. Alice Walker's definition of "Womanist" also celebrates the internal diversity of African Americans as an expression of "traditional universalism": "'Mama, why are we brown, pink, and yellow, and our cousins are white, beige, and black?' Ans.: 'Well, you know the colored race is just like a flower garden, with every color flower represented'" (xi). Walker's "womanism" imagines a universalism based on difference, demonstrating that totalities and particularities are not necessarily mutually exclusive.

13. Susan Gillman refers to the term "transculturation" to describe the process of African-American appropriations of the scientific discourses of heredity ("Pauline Hopkins" 64). The term, as Gillman acknowledges, has undergone various transformations. In the 1940s it began as a description of Afro-Cuban culture in the work of the sociologist Fernando Ortiz, then thirty years later it was appropriated for literary studies in the work of Angel Rama (Pratt 228n). More recently, Mary Louise Pratt has used the term to describe the dialectics of colonial encounter in *Imperial Eyes* (5). For my purposes, "transculturation" describes the same process of selection and invention as Stepan and Gilman's term "transvaluation."

14. Gaines argues that theories of heredity were unrecuperable: they pathologized blackness and perpetuated racist stereotypes (81). Reformers, such as Anna Julia Cooper, who did employ biologism "posed a feeble challenge to racial and sexual stereotypes, remaining imprisoned within an anti-black bourgeois morality" (81). I argue that black appropriations of hereditarian theories were more than just "feeble" challenges to racism. They were vehemently anti-racist and were productively used to articulate an ideal of a black community that was unified through its internal diversity.

15. Lamarckianism was the predominant nineteenth-century method for understanding the relationship between the environment and heredity. It

claimed that habits, skills, and expertise developed in one generation could be passed down to future generations. If, for example, one learned how to play the piano, then one's children would have a special aptitude for piano playing. See Stocking; Pfeifer; Ward.

16. My use of Galtonianism versus Mendelism is a variation of George Stocking's distinction between "blending" and "alternating" inheritance. According to Stocking, "Galton's 'law of ancestral heredity' assumed that children tended to 'regress' toward the mean of their ancestors . . . The general effect was a blending of the heredity of parents and ancestors in regular proportions which Galton had calculated. In the simplest form of Mendel's scheme, 'unite characters' were either 'dominant' or 'recessive'—they either appeared or they did not. Inheritance was not a 'blending' of ancestral and parental influences, but an 'alternating' of discontinuous possibilities" (173–174).

17. This notion of "blending inheritance" replaced the early-nineteenth-century preformation theory, which claimed that the embryo grew from a perfectly formed miniature already present in the mother's womb. See Bowler 3.

18. Compare Chesnutt's embrace of hybridity with Anna Julia Cooper's opposition to it in *A Voice from the South* (1892). She writes: "Blending of races in the aggregate is simply an unthinkable thought, and the union of individuals can never fall out by accident or haphazard . . . the average black man in this country is as anxious to preserve his identity and transmit his type as is the average white man. In any case, hybridity is in no sense dependent on sectional or national amity" (221).

19. See Otten; Schrager.

20. At one time or another, 41 of the 50 states or colonies had laws barring interracial marriage. Some laws that were taken off the books by Reconstruction legislatures were put back on by the turn of the century. In the years following the Civil War, 10 new states adopted anti-miscegenation laws (including Missouri and South Carolina, which did not have laws on the books prior to the Civil War). After 1945, 30 states had such laws. I thank Renee Romano for this information. See Romano, "Crossing the Line: Black-White Interracial Marriage in the United States, 1945–1990" (Ph.D. diss., Stanford University, 1996); Byron Curti Martyn, "Racism in the United States: A History of the Anti-Miscegenation Legislation and Litigation" (Ph.D. diss., University of Southern California, 1979); Charles Magnum, *The Legal Status of the Negro* (Chapel Hill, 1940).

21. Noel Ignatiev and John Garvey use the phrase "race traitor" to describe "dissident so-called whites" (13), those who defy the terms of membership in the club of race privilege.

22. One way to explain the different reactions of Tom Driscoll and Lillian Westland is in terms of Ruth Todd's feminism and her black nationalism. When there is anger in Todd's work, it is in the form of revenge and directed exclusively toward white fathers rather than black mothers. In contrast to Twain, who presents Roxy in a sympathetic manner but ultimately as a victim whose "heart was broken," Todd depicts the scorned mulatta mistress as angry and ready to get even. This is another way in which the Mendelist allegory highlights black female agency.

23. In his thematic study of interracial literature, Werner Sollors refers to those narratives that end in Europe as "A World Elsewhere." A variation of the "European theme" used to contrast Old and New Worlds, these narratives represent the American ingenue in search of not history and culture but a safe refuge for an interracial family escaping the prejudice in the United States. See Sollors, *Neither Black* 338–348.

24. My use of "womanism" is taken from Alice Walker's black-inflected definition of feminism. For Walker, "womanist" refers to a black feminist or woman of color who is responsible and serious as well as woman-identified, in that she prefers women's company and culture (Walker xi).

25. The Paris edition of the *New York Herald* (Sept. 6, 1920) published an editorial about *Darkwater* under the title "Black Bolshevism" (Aptheker 154).

26. Black nativism was largely an expression of resentment against European immigrants who were taking jobs in northern cities that would have otherwise gone to African Americans. In 1907 the *Colored American Magazine* warned that "already the day is upon us when the scum of Europe is with us, her paupers, her convicts, her socialists, her anarchists" (qtd. Steinberg 202). See Steinberg, esp. ch. 8. This same strategy of legitimating African Americans *as citizens* by demonizing immigrant groups, particularly Asians, is also seen among Anglo Americans. In Justice Harlan's dissenting opinion in the case of *Plessy v. Ferguson* (1896), a courageous attack on segregation, he slips into a nativist critique of the Chinese: "a Chinaman can ride in the same passenger coach with white citizens of the United States, while citizens of the black race in Louisiana, many of whom, perhaps, risked their lives for the preservation of the Union, who are entitled, by law, to participate in the political control of the States and nation, who are not excluded, by law or by reason of their race, . . . are yet declared to be criminals, liable to imprisonment, if they ride in a public coach occupied by citizens of the white race" (Olsen 119). The racial tensions within American citizenship merit further study. Unfortunately, important textbooks in the field of American pluralism suppress such tensions. For example, Paula S. Rothenberg's classic textbook, *Race, Class, and Gender in the United States* (New York, 1992), excises this passage in the reprint of Judge Harlan's decision.

6. East Meets West at the World's Parliament of Religions

1. Although Barrows would later comment that one of the great successes of the parliament was the improved relations among Catholic and Protestant leaders in the United States, the popular sentiments toward Catholics during this period were less than propitious. The anti-Catholic American Protective Association reached a national level by 1893, expanding from its Midwest base to New York and then Massachusetts. According to John Higham, actual violence against Catholics was not extensive. In 1893 the Association was primarily an ideological campaign trying to incite fears about a Catholic uprising. See Higham, *Strangers* ch. 4; Ziolkowski 143.
2. Keane, one of the most liberal American Catholic leaders, was reproached by the Vatican for participating in the event. Three years later he was removed from his office as the first rector of Catholic University. See Ziolkowski 27.
3. Other auxiliary congresses, besides the Congress on Representative Women, included ones on moral and social reform, education, evolution, and temperance. There were also forums on scientific fields like medicine and engineering, and others on art, music, and literature. See Seager, *World's Parliament* xx.
4. Frederick Douglass made some brief, impromptu remarks defending his decision to privilege "human rights" over "human religions": "If I had not been studying man all my life rather than theology, I should be able to make a speech to you to-day, but I have been studying the great question of human rights instead of human religions" (qtd. Seager 135).
5. See Ursula King, "Rediscovering Women's Voices at the World's Parliament of Religions," Ziolkowski 325–344.
6. As a nationalist corollary to Carus's "broad" Christianity, Theodore Roosevelt's "Broad Americanism," which appeared in an article in *The Forum* the following year, was defined against an "unwholesome parochial spirit." "Broad Americanism" was a secular religion, experienced "in heart and soul, in spirit and purpose" (198). Whereas "broad Christianity" was defined against sectarianism, "Broad Americanism" opposed sectionalism. They were attempts to modernize Christianity and nationalism, respectively, by dislodging an individual's connection to particular and local identities. Both were modern antecedents of contemporary postnationalism, as in David Hollinger's "postethnic America."
7. In 1903 James invited Dharmapala to lecture on Buddhism to his students at Harvard, an encounter I will discuss later. In *The Varieties of Religious Experience,* James refers to Vivekananda's lectures on yoga and the Vedanta philosophy from the 1890s. On the Swami and James, see Prabuddhaprana.

8. Burnham said: "a thousand years hence about all that the world will remember of the fair will be the parliament" (qtd. Barrows, "Results" 136).
9. Dharmapala qtd. in the *Chicago Tribune* (Sept. 23, 1893): 2. Vivekananda, *Selections* 21.
10. The Archbishop wrote to the organizers of the parliament: "the Christian religion is the one religion. I do not understand how that religion can be regarded as a member of a Parliament of Religions without assuming the equality of the other intended members and the parity of their position and claims" (WPR I:20).
11. The following day, *The Daily Inter-Ocean* summarized Schaff's talk on Christian liberalism and George Candlin's lecture on Christian missionaries in China next to a story about mob violence against Chinese immigrants in LaGrande, Oregon. In this incident, Mrs. Winchester, a missionary, protected thirty immigrants who had sought refuge in her home, threatening to shoot the first man to enter the house. "Drive Out Chinese," *Daily Inter-Ocean* (Sept. 26, 1893): 1. This juxtaposition between religious comity and mob violence underlines the wide gap between the liberal theologians at the parliament and the majority of white American Christians.
12. The concept of "nextness" is central for James's pluralistic universe: the term refers to the arrangement of parts in a "loose" confederation that are adjacent and blended with other parts yet still distinct (*PU* 778).
13. *Chicago Times* (Sept. 12, 1893): 1.
14. A sectarian version of Kallen's orchestra, Higginson's pluralistic arrangement of religions reinforced his point that each religion is "partial, limited, unsatisfying; it takes all of them together to represent the *seper, unique et ab omnibus*" (WPR I:784).
15. Vivekananda presented four lectures at the parliament and spoke on six different occasions at auxiliary meetings. See Ziolkowski 226. In a letter to a friend, Vivekananda describes the opening ceremonies: "Imagine a hall below and a huge gallery above, packed with six or seven thousand men and women representing the best culture of the country, and on the platform learned men of all the nations of the earth. And I, who never spoke in public in my life, to address this august assemblage!!" (*Complete Works* 5:20).
16. See Carrie Tirado Bramen, "Christian Maidens and Heathen Monks: Oratorical Seduction at the 1893 World's Parliament of Religions," in *The Puritan Origins of American Sex*, ed. Tracy Fessenden et al. (New York, 2000).
17. P. C. Majumdar, "The Principle of the Brahmo-Somaj," in *The World's Congress of Religions*, ed. J. W. Hanson (Chicago, 1894), 431.
18. *Chicago Tribune* (Sept. 14, 1893): 9.
19. *Chicago Daily Times* (Sept. 14, 1893): 1; qtd. Fields 124–125.
20. Although the audience exclaimed "Shame!" in response to both Hirai and Webb, the meaning of the exclamation changed in relation to context. In re-

gard to Hirai, the audience used "Shame!" as an expression of self-reproach, whereas in relation to Webb's speech, the speaker, rather than the audience, was the target of censure.

21. Another example of the limits of Christian tolerance, which occurred outside the parliament, involved Swami Vivekananda. While touring the United States giving lectures after the parliament, Vivekananda was barred from "several hotels" in Baltimore, because the hotelkeepers thought he was black. An article in the Santa Cruz journal *The Buddhist Ray* (Nov.-Dec. 1894, 11–12) reports this incident and chastises the hotelkeepers not for their racism but for their ignorance about the "Aryan" race: "That speaks well for the education of Baltimore in general, and hotel-keepers in particular: they cannot tell the difference between a negro and an Aryan, though they themselves belong to the latter race." According to this logic, the racist treatment of Vivekananda was an outrage only because it signified a misrecognition of his race. Such a defense of Vivekananda's "brownness" (he-is-actually-Aryan) reinforces the racial order between whites and blacks.

22. "Convert to Buddha," *Chicago Tribune* (Sept. 23, 1893): 2. In Dharmapala's diary he says that his hopes of attending the parliament were diminished due to financial constraints until: "By a strange coincidence my American Buddhist brothers Philangi Dasa, Editor of the Buddhist Ray, Santa Cruz, California, and Mr. Chas. I. Strauss, of Broadway, New York, wrote inviting me to visit America to preach Buddhism, they paying my expenses" (708).

23. Shibata Reiichi was the son of the founder of the Jikko sect of Shinto. "Women from the audience climbed over chairs and tables to pay their compliments to the distinguished oriental . . . Then a loud cheer rent the air and there was a mad rush for the platform . . . The excitement was caused by the High Priest in a spirit of true reciprocity embracing a couple of ladies. It was over in a moment but in that moment they had felt on their cheeks the kiss of the High Priest of Shintoism." *Chicago Tribune* (Sept. 14, 1893): 9. See Ketelaar 276–277.

24. On different forms of syncretism in anthropology, see Peter van der Veer, "Syncretism, Multiculturalism and the Discourse of Tolerance," *Syncretism/Anti-Syncretism: The Politics of Religious Synthesis*. ed. Charles Stewart and Rosalind Shaw (London, 1994), 196–211.

25. The term "ethnic" first appeared in the eighteenth century as a synonym to "pagan" and "heathen." Though this meaning was obsolete by the late nineteenth century, and Barrows never uttered the word "heathen" in his speeches, this earlier usage still informs his critique of "ethnic" religions.

26. On Buddhism and Sinhalese nationalism, see J. Spencer.

27. In 1892 Dharmapala had founded a publication called *Maha Bodhi Journal,* which sought to promote a "united Buddhist World" (Fields 113).

28. On Dharmapala's youthful identity crisis as symptomatic of a Sinhalese

nationalist identity crisis, see Gananath Obeyesekere, "Sinhalese-Buddhist Identity in Ceylon," *Ethnic Identity: Cultural Continuities and Change,* ed. George de Vos and Lola Romanucci-Ross (Chicago, 1982), 231–258.

29. In addition to Tuskegee and Carlisle, Dharmapala visited several industrial training schools in London, Liverpool, Italy, and Denmark. In 1904 he founded an industrial training school in Saranath, India. In 1912 he started the first industrial training school in Ceylon. For more biographical information on Dharmapala, see Fields.

30. Swami Vivekananda had similar fantasies of converting not only the English to Hinduism, but the whole world. In an 1895 letter to a fellow Hindu missionary, he wrote: "We must set the whole world afire . . . In time we shall send preachers in large numbers to all the quarters of the globe" (*Complete Works* 8:353).

31. In 1917 Dharmapala emphasized this same point: Buddhism "is a religion of truths based on analysis. Every idea is subjected to analysis . . . he [the Buddhist] analyses every dogma, rejects the bad and accepts the good" (277). He continued to emphasize the need for conceptual and ethical boundaries in "What Buddhism Is Not," a piece published in 1926 (79–81).

32. In his talk Soyen argued: "We must not make any distinction between race and race, between civilization and civilization, between creed and creed, and faith and faith. We are all sisters and brothers . . . of truth" (*WPR* II:1285).

33. *Chicago Tribune Magazine* (Aug. 29, 1993), 14.

34. One striking difference was the relationship between orator and audience. In 1893 the audience could not keep quiet: people cheered loudly and waved handkerchiefs for Hirai and Dharmapala and shouted "Shame!" when Webb defended polygamy. In 1993 the audience was far more difficult to engage. In the opening ceremony, the Muslim Irfan Khan asked that people raise their hands to ask God's help for the parliament, but some of the "non-Christians kept their hands folded or in their laps." The audience also sat silently when the neo-pagan Lady Olivia Robertson shook a rattle and shouted, "Holy Goddess Isis, mother of all beings, come to thy children!" See Hirsley, "World's Religions."

Afterword: In Defense of Partiality

1. See Robin Wilson, "Berkeley Ends Hunger Strike with Promise to Hire More Ethnic-Studies Professors," *Chronicle of Higher Education* (May 21, 1999): A14. June Jordan, "Good News of Our Own," *The Progressive* (Aug. 1999): 18–19.

2. Patrisia Gonzales and Roberto Rodriguez, "Column of the Americas," http://

www.uexpress.com/ups/opinion/column/cm/text/1999/05/cm9905/42852.html
3. One example of such homogenization is the loss of indigenous languages in the Americas. According to an organization called La Unidad Regional de Culturas Populares, based in Sonoro, Mexico, the fifty indigenous languages of Mexico could disappear completely within ten years. "Medio centenar de lenguas, en peligro de extinción," *Novedades Quintana Roo* (3 Aug. 1999): 2C.
4. All translations are mine.

WORKS CITED

Abbott, Lyman. "Introduction." *Darkness and Daylight, or Lights and Shadows of New York Life: A Woman's Story of Gospel, Temperance Mission, and Rescue Work*, by Mrs. Helen Campbell. Hartford, 1892.

———. "Lessons from the Parliament of Religions." *Christian Thought*, ed. Charles Deems. New York, 1893–1894.

Adams, Henry. *The Education of Henry Adams*. Boston: Houghton Mifflin, 1971.

Ahmad, Aijaz. "Jameson's Rhetoric of Otherness and the 'National Allegory.'" *The Post-Colonial Studies Reader*, ed. Bill Ashcroft et al. New York: Routledge, 1995. 77–84.

Allen, Gay Wilson. *William James: A Biography*. New York: Viking, 1967.

Ames, Robert, and Philip Siegelman, eds. *The Idea of Evolution*. Minneapolis: Dillon Press, 1966.

Ammons, Elizabeth, ed. *Short Fiction by Black Women, 1900–1920*. New York: Oxford UP, 1991.

Anderson, Amanda. "Cosmopolitanism, Universalism, and the Divided Legacies of Modernity." *Cosmopolitics: Thinking and Feeling beyond the Nation*, ed. Pheng Cheah and Bruce Robbins. Minneapolis: U of Minnesota P, 1998. 265–289.

Andrews, Malcolm. "The Metropolitan Picturesque." Copley and Garside 282–298.

Andrews, William L. "Introduction." *The Autobiography of an Ex-Colored Man*, by James Weldon Johnson. New York: Penguin, 1990. vii–xxvii.

Appiah, K. Anthony. "The Multicultural Misunderstanding." *New York Review of Books* (Oct. 9, 1997): 30–36.

———. "The Uncompleted Argument: Du Bois and the Illusion of Race." *Race, Writing, and Difference*, ed. Henry Louis Gates Jr. Chicago: U of Chicago P, 1986. 21–37.

Aptheker, Herbert. *The Literary Legacy of W. E. B. Du Bois*. White Plains, NY: Kraus International Publications, 1989.

Austin, Mary. "Regionalism in American Fiction." *English Journal* 21:2 (Feb. 1932): 97–107.

Bailyn, Bernard, et al. *The Great Republic*. Boston: Little, Brown, 1977.

Baker, Houston, Jr. *Workings of the Spirit: The Poetics of Afro-American Women's Writing.* Chicago: U of Chicago P, 1991.
Balibar, Etienne. "The Nation Form: History and Ideology." *Race, Nation, Class: Ambiguous Identities,* ed. Etienne Balibar and Immanuel Wallerstein. New York: Verso, 1991. 86–106.
Ballantyne, Andrew. "Genealogy of the Picturesque." *British Journal of Aesthetics* 32:4 (Oct. 1992): 320–329.
Barrows, John Henry. *Christianity, The World-Religion.* Madras: Christian Literature Society, 1897.
———. "Results of the Parliament of Religions." Ziolkowski 131–147.
———. ed. *The World's Parliament of Religions.* 2 vols. Chicago: Parliament Publishing Company, 1893.
Barthes, Roland. "Taking Sides." *Critical Essays,* trans. Richard Howard. Evanston: Northwestern UP, 1972. 163–170.
Barzun, Jacques. *A Stroll with William James.* Chicago: U of Chicago P, 1983.
Basu, Sankari Prasad, and Sunil Bihari Ghosh, eds. *Vivekananda in Indian Newspapers, 1893–1902.* Calcutta: Dineshchandra Basu Bhattacharya, 1969.
Bateson, W. *Mendel's Principles of Heredity.* Cambridge: UP, 1913.
Bederman, Gail. *Manliness and Civilization: A Cultural History of Gender and Race in the United States, 1880–1917.* Chicago: U of Chicago P, 1995.
Benjamin, Walter. "On Some Motifs in Baudelaire." *Illuminations,* ed. Hannah Arendt. New York: Schocken, 1969. 155–200.
Bennett, William J. "To Reclaim a Legacy." *American Education* 21:1 (Jan. 1985): 4–15.
Bercovitch, Sacvan. *The American Jeremiad.* Madison: U of Wisconsin P, 1978.
Berlant, Lauren. "The Queen of America Goes to Washington City: Harriet Jacobs, Frances Harper, Anita Hill." *Subjects and Citizens,* ed. Michael Moon and Cathy Davidson. Durham: Duke UP, 1995. 455–480.
Berman, Marshall. *All That Is Solid Melts into Air: The Experience of Modernity.* New York: Simon and Schuster, 1981.
———. *The Politics of Authenticity: Radical Individualism and the Emergence of Modern Society.* New York: Atheneum, 1970.
Bernstein, Richard J. "Introduction." *A Pluralistic Universe* by William James. Cambridge, MA: Harvard UP, 1977. xi–xxix.
Berzon, Judith. *Neither White nor Black: The Mulatto Character in American Fiction.* New York: New York UP, 1978.
Botshon, Lisa. "Cautious Pluralism: Ethnic Women Writers and Early Twentieth Century U.S. Popular Culture." Ph.D. diss., Columbia University, 1997.
Boucicault, Dana. "The Octoroon" (1859). *Representative American Plays,* ed. Arthur Quinn. New York: D. Appleton-Century, 1938. 375–398.
Bourdieu, Pierre. "Universal Corporatism: The Role of Intellectuals in the Modern World." *Poetics Today* 12:4 (Winter 1991): 655–669.

Bourget, Paul. *Outre-Mer: Impressions of America*. New York: Charles Scribner's Sons, 1895.
Bourne, Randolph. "The Jew and Trans-National America." *Menorah Journal* 2 (Dec. 1916): 277–284.
———. "Trans-National America" (1916). *War and the Intellectuals*, ed. Carl Resek. New York: Harper and Row, 1964. 107–123.
Bowlby, Rachel. *Just Looking: Consumer Culture in Dreiser, Gissing and Zola*. London: Methuen, 1985.
Bowler, Peter. *The Mendelian Revolution: The Emergence of Hereditarian Concepts in Modern Science and Society*. Baltimore: Johns Hopkins UP, 1989.
Boxhill, Bernard R. "Du Bois on Cultural Pluralism." *W. E. B Du Bois on Race and Culture*, ed. Bernard Bell et al. New York: Routledge, 1996. 57–85.
Boyd, Melba Joyce. *Discarded Legacy: Politics and Poetics in the Life of Frances E. W. Harper, 1825–1911*. Detroit: Wayne State UP, 1994.
Brand, Dana. *The Spectator and the City in Nineteenth-Century American Literature*. New York: Cambridge UP, 1991.
Brandeis, Louis. "True Americanism" (1915). *Brandeis on Zionism*. Washington: Zionist Organization of America, 1942. 3–11.
Briggs, Charles. "The Alienation of Church and People." *Forum* (Nov. 1893): 366–378.
———. *Whither? A Theological Question for the Times*. New York, 1899.
Brodhead, Richard. *Cultures of Letters*. Chicago: U of Chicago P, 1993.
Brown, Bill. "Identity Culture." *American Literary History* [review essay] (Spring 1998):164–184.
———. "The Popular, the Populist, and the Populace—Locating Hamlin Garland in the Politics of Culture." *Arizona Quarterly* 50:3 (Autumn 1994): 89–110.
Brown, Lois Lamphere. "'To Allow No Tragic End': Defensive Postures in Pauline Hopkins's *Contending Forces*." *The Unruly Voice: Rediscovering Pauline Elizabeth Hopkins*, ed. John Cullen Gruesser. Urbana: U of Illinois P, 1996. 50–70.
Brown, Sterling. "Negro Character as Seen by White Authors" (1933). *Dark Symphony: Negro Literature in America*, ed. James Emanuel and Theodore L. Gross. New York: Free Press, 1968. 139–171.
Bryce, James. *The American Commonwealth*. Vol. 3. London: Macmillan, 1888.
Buck, Paul. *The Road to Reunion, 1865–1900*. Boston: Little, Brown, 1937.
Buell, Frederick. "Nationalist Postnationalism: Globalist Discourse in Contemporary American Culture." *American Quarterly* 50:3 (Sept. 1998): 548–591.
Burke, Mary Louise. *Swami Vivekananda in America, New Discoveries*. Calcutta: Advaita Ashrama, 1958.
Calinescu, Matei. *Five Faces of Modernity*. Durham: Duke UP, 1987.

Camarillo, Albert. *Chicanos in California*. San Francisco: Boyd and Fraser Publishing Company, 1984.
Candlin, George. "Results and Mission of the Parliament of Religions." *The Biblical World* 5 (March 1895): 371–373.
Carby, Hazel. *Race Men*. Cambridge, MA: Harvard UP, 1998.
———. *Reconstructing Womanhood: The Emergence of the Afro-American Woman Novelist*. New York: Oxford UP, 1987.
Carroll, Henry King. "The Methodist Episcopal Church." *The Independent* 52 (Jan. 4, 1900): 37–39.
Carter, George S. *A Hundred Years of Evolution*. London: Sidgwick and Jackson, 1957.
Carter, Paul A. *The Spiritual Crisis of the Gilded Age*. De Kalb: Northern Illinois UP, 1971.
Carus, Paul. "The Dawn of a New Religious Era." *Forum* (Nov. 1893): 388–396.
Chadwick, John. "Universal Religion." *The New World* 3:11 (Sept. 1894): 401–418.
Cheah, Pheng, and Bruce Robbins, eds. *Cosmopolitics: Thinking and Feeling beyond the Nation*. Minneapolis: U of Minnesota P, 1998.
Chesnutt, Charles. "The Future American" (1900). *Theories of Ethnicity: A Classical Reader*, ed. Werner Sollors. New York: New York UP, 1996. 17–33.
———. *The House behind the Cedars* (1900). New York: Penguin, 1993.
———. "A Victim of Heredity." *The Short Fiction of Charles W. Chesnutt*, ed. Sylvia Lyons Render. Washington: Howard UP, 1981. 123–131.
Chetanananda, Swami. *Vivekananda: East Meets West, Pictorial Biography*. St. Louis: Vedanta Society, 1995.
Chicago Cultural Studies Group. "Critical Multiculturalism." Goldberg 114–139.
Chomsky, Noam. *The Common Good*. Monroe, Maine: Common Courage Press, 1998.
Clark, Michael. *Coherent Variety: The Idea of Diversity in British and American Conservative Thought*. Westport, CT: Greenwood Press, 1983.
Coon, Deborah J. "'One Moment in the World's Salvation': Anarchism and the Radicalization of William James." *Journal of American History* 83:1 (June 1996): 70–99.
Cooper, Anna Julia. *A Voice from the South* (1892). New York: Oxford UP, 1988.
Copley, Stephen, and Peter Garside, eds. *The Politics of the Picturesque: Literature, Landscape and Aesthetics since 1770*. Cambridge: Cambridge UP, 1994.
Corbin, John. "The Twentieth Century City." *Scribner's Magazine* 33:3 (March 1903): 259–272.
Cotkin, George. *William James, Public Philosopher*. Baltimore: Johns Hopkins UP, 1990.

Cravens, Hamilton. "Scientific Racism in Modern America, 1870s–1990s." *Prospects* 21 (1996): 471–490.
Creel, George. "The Hopes of the Hyphenated." *The Century* XCI (Jan. 1916): 350–362.
Croce, Paul Jerome. *Science and Religion in the Era of William James: Eclipse of Certainty, 1820–1880*. Vol. 1. Chapel Hill: U of North Carolina P, 1995.
Croly, Herbert. *The Promise of American Life* (1909). New York: E. P. Dutton, 1963.
Crummell, Alexander. *Destiny and Race: Selected Writings, 1840–1898*, ed. Wilson Moses. Amherst: U of Massachusetts P, 1992.
Culler, Jonathan. "Semiotics of Tourism." *American Journal of Semiotics* 1:1–2 (1981): 127–140.
Dainotto, Roberto Maria. "'All the Regions Do Smilingly Revolt': The Literature of Place and Region." *Critical Inquiry* 22 (Spring 1996): 486–505.
Darwin, Charles. *The Origin of Species* (1859) and *The Descent of Man* (1871). New York: Modern Library, 1936.
Debord, Guy. *Society of the Spectacle*. Detroit: Black and Red, 1970.
De Forest, John William. "The Great American Novel." *The Nation* 6 (9 Jan. 1868): 27.
Delany, Martin. *The Origin of Races and Color*. Philadelphia: Harper and Brother, 1879.
Den Tandt, Christophe. *The Urban Sublime in American Literary Naturalism*. Urbana: U of Illinois P, 1998.
Dewey, John. "Americanism and Localism" (1920). *John Dewey: The Middle Years, 1899–1924*, ed. Jo Ann Boydston. Vol. 12. Carbondale: Southern Illinois UP, 1982. 12–16.
Dharmapala, Anagarika. *Return to Righteousness: A Collection of Speeches, Essays and Letters of the Anagarika Dharmapala*, ed. Ananda Guruge. Ceylon: Ministry of Education and Cultural Affairs, 1965.
Douglas, Ann. *Terrible Honesty: Mongrel Manhattan in the 1920s*. New York: Farrar, Straus and Giroux, 1995.
Dreiser, Theodore. "Brandywine, the Picturesque, after One Hundred and Twenty Years." *Selected Magazine Articles of Theodore Dreiser*, ed. Yoshinobu Hakutani. Vol. 2. Rutherford, NJ: Fairleigh Dickinson, 1985. 77–83.
———. *The Color of a Great City*. New York: Boni and Liveright, 1923.
———. *Hey Rub-a-dub-dub, A Book of the Mystery and Wonder and Terror of Life*. New York: Boni and Liveright, 1920.
———. "The Real Howells" (1900). *Selected Magazine Articles of Theodore Dreiser: Life and Art in the American 1890s*, ed. Yoshinobu Hakutani. Vol. 1. Rutherford, NJ: Fairleigh Dickinson, 1985.
———. "Reflections" [A New York Tragedy](1896). *Theodore Dreiser: A Selection of Uncollected Prose*, ed. Donald Pizer. Detroit: Wayne State UP, 1977.

———. "The Sandwich Man." *The Color of a Great City*, 264–269.
Du Bois, William E. B. "The Conservation of Races." *The Oxford W. E. B. Du Bois Reader*, ed. Eric Sundquist. New York: Oxford UP, 1996. 38–47.
———. "Criteria of Negro Art" (1926). *The W. E. B. Du Bois Reader*, ed. Andrew Paschal. New York: Macmillan, 1971. 86–96.
———. *Dark Princess: A Romance* (1928). Millwood, NY: Kraus-Thomson Organization, 1974.
———. *Darkwater* (1920). Sundquist 481–623.
———. "The Lynching Industry." *The Crisis* 9 (Feb. 1915): 196, 198.
———. *The Negro*. New York: Henry Holt, 1915.
———. "The Negro in the Black Belt; Some Social Sketches." U.S. Bureau of Labor *Bulletin* 22 (1899): 401–417.
———. "The Problem of Amusement" (1897). *Writings by W. E. B. Du Bois in Periodicals Edited by Others*, ed. Herbert Aptheker. Vol. 1. Millwood, NY: Kraus-Thomson Organization, 1982. 32–39.
———. *The Quest of the Silver Fleece*. Chicago: A. C. McClurg, 1911.
———. "Race Pride." Paschal 132–133.
———. *The Souls of Black Folk*. Sundquist 97–240.
———. "The Talented Tenth." Paschal 31–51.
———. "The Training of Negroes for Social Power." Sundquist 354–362.
Dwight, H. G. "An Impressionist's New York." *Scribner's* (Nov. 1905): 544–553.
Dyson, Michael Eric. "Essentialism and the Complexities of Racial Identity." Goldberg 218–229.
Eagleton, Terry. "Base and Superstructure in Raymond Williams." *Raymond Williams: Critical Perspectives*, ed. Terry Eagleton. Boston: Northeastern UP, 1989. 165–175.
———. "Enjoy!" [Review of Slavoj Zizek's *Indivisible Remainder*]. *London Review of Books* 19:23 (27 Nov. 1997): 7–9.
———. *The Illusions of Postmodernism*. Oxford: Blackwell, 1996.
———. "Nationalism: Irony and Commitment." *Nationalism, Colonialism and Literature*. Minneapolis: U of Minnesota P, 1990. 23–42.
Eggleston, Edward. *The Hoosier Schoolmaster: A Story of Backwoods Life in Indiana* (1871). New York: Grosset and Dunlap, 1913.
Eiseley, Loren. *Darwin's Century: Evolution and the Men Who Discovered It*. New York: Anchor, 1961.
Fairchild, Henry Pratt. *Immigration: A World Movement and Its American Significance*. New York: Macmillan, 1925.
Fanon, Frantz. "On National Culture." *The Wretched of the Earth*, trans. Constance Farrington. New York: Grove Press, 1963. 206–248.
Fenton, Edwin. *Immigrants and Unions: Italians and American Labor, 1870–1920*. New York: Arno Press, 1975.

Ferguson, SallyAnn. "Charles W. Chesnutt's 'Future American.'" *MELUS* 15:3 (Fall 1988): 95–107.

Fetterley, Judith. "'Not in the Least American': Nineteenth-Century Literary Regionalism." *College English* 56:8 (Dec. 1994): 877–895.

Fetterly, Judith, and Marjorie Pryse. "Introduction." *American Women Regionalists, 1850–1910*. New York: Norton, 1992. xi–xx.

Fields, Rick. *How the Swans Came to the Lake: A Narrative History of Buddhism in America*. Boulder, Colo.: Shambhala, 1981.

Flood, Andrew. "The Story of How We Learnt How to Dream at Reality: A Report on the First Intercontinental Gathering for Humanity and against Neo-Liberalism." hrrp://flag.blackened.net/revolt/andrew/encounter2-report.html

Flournoy, Theodore. *The Philosophy of William James* (1917). Freeport, NY: Books for Libraries Press, 1969.

Foner, Nancy. "What's New about Transnationalism? New York Immigrants Today and at the Turn of the Century." *Diaspora* 6:3 (1997): 355–375.

Forcey, Charles. *The Crossroads of Liberalism: Croly, Weyl, Lippmann, and the Progressive Era, 1900–1925*. New York: Oxford UP, 1961.

Fortune, T. Thomas. *Black and White: Land, Labor and Politics in the South*. (1884). New York: Arno Press, 1968.

———. "The Voteless Citizen." *The Voice of the Negro* (Sept. 1904): 397.

Foster, Frances. *Written by Herself: Literary Production by African American Women, 1746–1892*. Bloomington: Indiana UP, 1993.

Fraser, Nancy. "From Redistribution to Recognition? Dilemmas of Justice in a 'Post-Socialist' Age." Willett 19–49.

Fredrickson, George. *The Black Image in the White Mind: The Debate on Afro-American Character and Destiny, 1817–1914*. New York: Harper and Row, 1971.

Freeman, Joshua, ed., et al. *Who Built America?* (American Social History Project). Vol. 2. New York: Pantheon, 1992.

French, Harold W. *The Swan's Wide Waters*. Port Washington, NY: Kennikat Press, 1974.

Fullerton, William Morton. "America Revisited: The Sensations of an Exile." *Scribner's* (June 1911): 658–664.

Fuss, Diana. *Essentially Speaking: Feminism, Nature and Difference*. New York: Routledge, 1989.

Gaines, Kevin. *Uplifting the Race: Black Leadership, Politics, and Culture in the Twentieth Century*. Chapel Hill: U of North Carolina P, 1996.

Galeano, Eduardo. "Entrevista por Raquel Peguero y Javier Molina." *La Jornada* (29 July 1996); qtd. in http://spin.com.mx/~hvelarde/Uruguay/eduardo.galeano/Chiapas/home.html

———. Interview with David Barsamian. *The Progressive* (July 1999): 35–38.

Galton, Francis. "Hereditary Talent and Character" (1865). *Images of Race*, ed. Michael D. Biddiss. Leicester: Leicester UP, 1979. 55–71.

———. *Natural Inheritance* (1889). New York: AMS Press, 1973.

Gandal, Keith. *The Virtues of the Vicious: Jacob Riis, Stephen Crane, and the Spectacle of the Slum*. New York: Oxford UP, 1997.

Garland, Hamlin. *Crumbling Idols: Twelve Essays on Art Dealing Chiefly with Literature, Painting and the Drama*, ed. Jane Johnson. Cambridge, MA: Harvard UP, 1960.

———. "The Land Question and Its Relation to Art and Literature." *The Arena* 9 (Jan. 1894): 165–175.

———. *Main-Travelled Roads* (1891). New York: Signet Classic, 1962.

———. "Productive Conditions of American Literature." *Forum* 17 (Aug. 1894): 690–698.

———. *A Spoil of Office* (1892). New York: Johnson Reprint, 1969.

"The Gatherings for Humanity and against Neoliberalism." http://www.geocities.com/CapitolHill/3849/gatherdx.html

Giddings, Franklin. "Are We a People?" *Literary Digest* 37 (July 11, 1908): 37–38.

———. *The Elements of Sociology*. New York: Macmillan, 1898.

———. "Sociological Questions." *Forum* 35 (1903–4): 245–255.

Gilje, Paul. *Rioting in America*. Bloomington: Indiana UP, 1996.

Gillman, Susan. "The Mulatto, Tragic or Triumphant? The Nineteenth-Century American Race Melodrama." *The Culture of Sentiment*, ed. Shirley Samuels. New York: Oxford UP, 1992. 221–243.

———. "Pauline Hopkins and the Occult: African-American Revisions of Nineteenth-Century Sciences." *American Literary History* 8:1 (Spring 1996): 57–82.

Gilpin, William. *Three essays: on picturesque beauty; on picturesque travel; and on sketching landscape: to which is added a poem, on landscape painting*. London, 1792.

Gilroy, Paul. *The Black Atlantic: Modernity and Double Consciousness*. Cambridge, MA: Harvard UP, 1994.

Giroux, Henry A. "Consuming Social Change: The United Colors of Benetton." *Disturbing Pleasures: Learning Popular Culture*. New York: Routledge, 1994. 3–24.

———. "Insurgent Multiculturalism and the Promise of Pedagogy." Goldberg 325–343.

Glazener, Nancy. *Reading for Realism*. Durham: Duke UP, 1997.

Goldberg, David Theo, ed. *Multiculturalism: A Critical Reader*. Oxford: Blackwell, 1994.

Goldman, Emma. "Minorities versus Majorities." *Anarchism and Other Essays*. New York: Dover, 1969. 69–78.

Gordon, Avery, and Christopher Newfield, eds. *Mapping Multiculturalism.* Minneapolis: U of Minnesota P, 1996.
Gossett, Thomas. *Race: The History of an Idea in America.* New York: Schocken Books, 1970.
Graham, Maryemma. "Frances Ellen Watkins Harper." *Dictionary of Literary Biography,* vol. 50., ed. Trudier Harris. Detroit: Bruccoli Clark, 1986. 164–173.
Grant, Madison. *The Passing of the Great Race; or, The Racial Basis of European History* (1916). New York: C. Scribner's Sons, 1936.
Grant, Percy Stickney. "American Ideals and Race Mixture." *North American Review* 195 (April 1912): 513–525.
Green, Judith M. "Educational Multiculturalism, Critical Pluralism, and Deep Democracy." Willett 422–448.
Grosz, Elizabeth. "Darwin and Feminism: Preliminary Investigations for a Possible Alliance." *Australian Feminist Studies* 14:29 (1999): 31–45.
Hale, Edward, Jr. "Signs of Life in Literature." *The Dial* 17 (July 1, 1894): 11–13.
Hall, G. Stanley. "Yankee and Jew." *Menorah Journal* 1:2 (April 1915): 87–90.
Hall, Prescott. "New Problems of Immigration." *Forum* 30 (Jan. 1901): 555–567.
Haller, John, Jr. *Outcasts from Evolution: Scientific Attitudes of Racial Inferiority, 1859–1900.* Urbana: U of Illinois P, 1971.
Halloran, S. Michael. "The Rhetoric of Picturesque Scenery: A Nineteenth-Century Epideictic." *Oratorical Culture in Nineteenth-Century America: Transformations in the Theory and Practice of Rhetoric,* ed. Gregory Clark and S. Michael Halloran. Carbondale: Southern Illinois UP, 1993. 226–246.
Halstead, Murat. "The Revival of Sectionalism." *North American Review* CXL (1885): 237–250.
Hampton, Wade. "The Race Problem." *Arena* 8 (July 1890): 132–138.
Hapgood, Hutchins. "The Picturesque Ghetto." *Century Magazine* 94 (July 1917): 469–473.
———. *The Spirit of the Ghetto.* New York: Schocken Books, 1976.
Hapgood, Norman. *The Changing Years: Reminiscences of Norman Hapgood.* New York: Farrar and Rinehart, 1930.
Harding, Sandra. "Is Science Multicultural? Challenges, Resources, Opportunities, Uncertainties." Goldberg 344–370.
Harper, Frances Watkins. *Iola Leroy or Shadows Uplifted* (1892). Ed. Frances Foster. New York: Oxford UP (Schomburg Library), 1988.
Harris, Leonard. "Universal Human Liberation: Community and Multiculturalism." Willett 449–457.
Harrison, Alice. "Chinese Food and Restaurants." *Overland Monthly* 68 (June 1917): 527–532.
Hartmann, Sadakichi. "A Plea for the Picturesqueness of New York." *Camera Notes* 4:2 (Oct. 1900): 91–97.

Hasian, Marouf Arif, Jr. *The Rhetoric of Eugenics in Anglo-American Thought.* Athens: U of Georgia P, 1996.

Herder, Johann Gottfried von. *J. G. Herder on Social and Political Culture.* Ed. F. M. Barnard. Cambridge: Cambridge UP, 1969.

Hicks, John D. *The Populist Revolt: A History of the Farmer's Alliance and the People's Party.* Lincoln: U of Nebraska P, 1961.

Higginson, Thomas Wentworth. "Americanism in Literature." *Atlantic Monthly* 25 (Jan. 1870): 56–63.

Higham, John. *Send These to Me.* Baltimore: Johns Hopkins UP, 1984.

———. *Strangers in the Land: Patterns of American Nativism, 1860–1925.* New York: Atheneum, 1963.

Hirsley, Michael. "Common Cause." *Chicago Tribune Magazine* (Aug. 29, 1993): 14+.

———. "World's Religions Gather to Make Call for Peace." *Chicago Tribune* (Aug. 29, 1993), sec. 2, 3.

Hofstadter, Richard. *The Age of Reform.* New York: Vintage, 1955.

———. *Social Darwinism in American Thought.* Boston: Beacon Press, 1955.

Hoggan, Francis. "The American Negro and Race Blending." *Sociological Review* 2:4 (Oct. 1909): 349–360.

Hollinger, David. "Ethnic Diversity, Cosmopolitanism and the Emergence of the American Liberal Intelligentsia." *American Quarterly* 27:2 (May 1975): 133–151.

———. *Postethnic America: Beyond Multiculturalism.* New York: Basic Books, 1995.

Holloway, Jean. *Hamlin Garland: A Biography.* Austin: U of Texas P, 1960.

hooks, bell. *Yearning: Race, Gender and Cultural Politics.* Boston: South End P, 1991.

Hopkins, Pauline. "Talma Gordon" (1900). Ammons 49–68.

———. *Of One Blood.* In *The Magazine Novels of Pauline Hopkins.* New York: Oxford UP, 1988.

Horwitz, Howard. "Always with Us." *American Literary History* 10:2 (Summer 1998): 317–334.

Howard, June. "Unraveling Regions, Unsettling Periods: Sarah Orne Jewett and American Literary History." *American Literature* 68:2 (June 1996): 365–384.

Howells, William Dean. "Editor's Study." *Harper's Weekly* 83 (Sept. 1891): 638–642.

———. "An Exemplary Citizen." *North American Review* 173 (1901): 280–288.

———. *A Hazard of New Fortunes* (1890). New York: Meridian, 1994.

———. *Impressions and Experiences* (1896). New York: Harper and Brothers, 1909.

———. "Literary Centers." *Harper's Weekly* 72 (Jan. 1886): 324.
Huebner, Grover G. "The Americanization of the Immigrant." *American Academy of Political and Social Science* 27 (1906): 653–675.
Hulbert, Archer Butler. "Washington: The Pioneer Investor." *The Chautaquan* 38 (1903): 43–48.
Hunter, Robert. *Poverty* (1904). New York: Harper and Row, 1965.
Hussey, Christopher. *The Picturesque: Studies in a Point of View.* London: G. P. Putnam's Sons, 1927.
Hutcheson, Robert. "Why the Chinese Should Be Admitted." *Forum* 33 (1902): 59–67.
Hutchinson, George. *The Harlem Renaissance in Black and White.* Cambridge, MA: Harvard UP, 1995.
Ignatiev, Noel, and John Garvey, eds. *Race Traitor.* New York: Routledge, 1996.
Jackson, Carl T. *The Oriental Religions and American Thought: Nineteenth-Century Explorations.* Westport, CT: Greenwood Press, 1981.
Jacobson, Matthew Frye. *Whiteness of a Different Color: European Immigrants and the Alchemy of Race.* Cambridge, MA: Harvard UP, 1998.
Jacoby, Russell. "The Myth of Multiculturalism." *New Left Review* 208 (Nov./Dec. 1994): 121–132.
James, Henry. *The American Scene* (1907). Ed. John F. Sears. New York: Penguin, 1994.
James, W. P. "On the Theory and Practice of Local Color." *The Living Age* 213 (June 12, 1897): 743–748.
James, William. "The Dilemma of Determinism." *The Will to Believe and Other Essays.* New York: Dover, 1956. 145–183.
———. *The Letters of William James.* Ed. Henry James. Vol. 2. Boston: Atlantic Monthly Press, 1920.
———. "The Philippine Tangle." *Boston Evening Transcript* (March 1, 1899). http://www.boondocksnet.com/ailtexts/tangle.html
———. *The Philosophy of William James.* Ed. Horace Kallen. New York: Modern Library, 1925.
———. *A Pluralistic Universe* (1909). *William James: Writings 1902–1910,* ed. Bruce Kuklick. New York: Library of America, 1987.
———. *Pragmatism* (1907). New York: Longmans, Green, 1946.
———. *The Selected Letters of William James.* Ed. Elizabeth Hardwick. New York: Anchor Books, 1993.
———. *The Varieties of Religious Experience.* New York: Mentor, 1958.
———. *William James: Selected Unpublished Correspondence, 1885–1910.* Ed. Frederick J. Down Scott. Columbus: Ohio State UP, 1986.
———. *William James: Writings 1902–1910.* Ed. Bruce Kuklick. New York: Library of America, 1987.

———. *The Will to Believe and Other Essays in Popular Philosophy* (1897). New York: Dover, 1956.

Jameson, Fredric. "Third-World Literature in the Era of Multinational Capitalism." *Social Text* 5 (Fall 1986): 65–87.

JanMohamed, Abdul. "The Economy of Manichean Allegory." *The Post-Colonial Studies Reader,* ed. Bill Ashcroft et al. New York: Routledge, 1995. 18–23.

Johannsen, Robert W., ed. *The Lincoln-Douglas Debates in 1858.* New York: Oxford UP, 1965.

Johnson, Herrick. "The Proposed Parliament of Religions at the World's Fair." *The Independent* 44 (March 24, 1892): 400–401.

Johnson, James Weldon. *The Autobiography of an Ex-Colored Man.* New York: Penguin, 1990.

Johnstone, Paul. "Old Ideals versus New Ideas in Farm Life." *The Shaping of Twentieth Century America,* ed. Richard Abrams and Lawrence Levine. Boston: Little, Brown, 1965.

Jones, Beverly Washington. *Quest for Equality: The Life and Writings of Mary Eliza Church Terrell, 1863–1954.* (*Black Women in United States History,* vol. 13). Ed. Darlene Clark Hine. Brooklyn: Carlson Publishing, 1990.

Jones, Howard Mumford. *The Age of Energy: Varieties of American Experience, 1865–1915.* New York: Viking, 1971.

Jordan, David Starr. "Agricultural Depression and Waste of Time." *Forum* 2 (Oct. 1891): 238–246.

———. *Imperial Democracy.* New York: D. Appleton, 1899.

Kallen, Horace. *Culture and Democracy in the United States.* New York: Boni and Liveright, 1924.

———. "Democracy versus the Melting-Pot." *The Nation* 100 (Feb. 18, 1915): 190–194; (Feb. 25, 1915): 217–220.

———. *Education, the Machine and the Worker: An Essay in the Psychology of Education in Industrial Society.* New York: New Republic, 1925.

———. *Individualism: An American Way of Life.* New York: Liveright, 1933.

———. "Nationality and the Hyphenated American." *Menorah Journal* 1:2 (April 1915): 79–86.

———. "On the Import of 'Universal Judaism.'" *Judaism at Bay: Essays toward the Adjustment of Judaism to Modernity.* New York: Bloch Publishing, 1932. 16–27.

———. ed. *The Philosophy of William James.* New York: Modern Library, 1925.

———. *What I Believe and Why—Maybe.* New York: Horizon Press, 1971.

———. *William James and Henri Bergson: A Study in Contrasting Theories of Life.* Chicago: U of Chicago P, 1914.

———. *Zionism and World Politics.* London: Heinemann, 1921.

Kammen, Michael. "The Problem of American Exceptionalism: A Reconsideration." *American Quarterly* 45:1 (1993): 1–43.

Kaplan, Amy. "Nation, Region, and Empire." *The Columbia History of the American Novel,* ed. Emory Elliott. New York: Columbia UP, 1991. 240–266.

———. *The Social Construction of American Realism.* Chicago: U of Chicago P, 1988.

Kazin, Alfred. *On Native Grounds.* New York: Reynal and Hitchcock, 1942.

Kazin, Michael. *The Populist Persuasion.* New York: Basic Books, 1995.

Keller, Phyllis. *Getting at the Core: Curricular Reform at Harvard.* Cambridge: Harvard UP, 1982.

Kern, Stephen. *The Culture of Time and Space, 1880–1918.* Cambridge, MA: Harvard UP, 1983.

Ketelaar, James. "The Reconvening of Babel: Eastern Buddhism and the 1893 World's Parliament of Religions." Ziolkowski 251–303.

Kevles, Daniel. "Genetics in the United States and Great Britain, 1890–1930." *Isis* 71 (Sept. 1980): 441–455.

———. *In the Name of Eugenics.* New York: Knopf, 1985.

Kinney, James. *Amalgamation! Race, Sex, and Rhetoric in the Nineteenth-Century American Novel.* Westport, CT: Greenwood Press, 1985.

[Kirk, S.]. "Recent Volumes of Short Stories." *Atlantic* (Feb 1881): 281.

Kloppenberg, James T. *Uncertain Victory: Social Democracy and Progressivism in European and American Thought, 1870–1920.* New York: Oxford UP, 1986.

Knadler, Stephen. "Untragic Mulatto: Charles Chesnutt and the Discourse of Whiteness." *American Literary History* 8:3 (Fall 1996): 426–448.

Knight, Richard Payne. *The Landscape, a didactic poem; Addressed to Uvedale Price.* London, 1794.

Konvitz, Milton, ed. *The Legacy of Horace Kallen.* Rutherford, NJ: Fairleigh Dickinson P, 1987.

Kuklick, Bruce. *The Rise of American Philosophy.* New Haven: Yale UP, 1977.

Kuyper, Abraham. "Part I: Pantheism's Destruction of Boundaries." *Methodist Review* 75:4 (July-Aug. 1893): 520–534.

———. "Part II: Pantheism's Destruction of Boundaries." *Methodist Review* 75:5 (Sept.-Oct. 1893): 762–778.

Lasch, Christopher. "The Anti-Imperialist as Racist" (1958). *American Imperialism and Anti-Imperialism,* ed. Thomas G. Paterson. New York: Thomas Y. Crowells, 1973.

———. *The New Radicalism in America, 1889–1963.* New York: Norton, 1965.

Lauter, Paul. "Is Frances Ellen Watkins Harper Good Enough to Teach?" *Legacy: A Journal of American Women Writers* 5:1 (Spring 1988): 27–32.

Lears, Jackson. *Fables of Abundance: A Cultural History of Advertising in America.* New York: Basic Books, 1994.

———. *No Place of Grace*. New York: Pantheon, 1981.

———. "From Salvation to Self-Realization." *The Culture of Consumption: Critical Essays in American History, 1880–1980*. ed. Richard Wightman Fox and T. J. Jackson Lears. New York: Pantheon, 1983. 3–38.

Lentricchia, Frank. "The Return of William James." *Cultural Critique* 4 (Fall 1986): 5–31.

Lerner, Gerda, ed. *Black Women in White America: A Documentary History*. New York: Vintage, 1973.

Levine, Lawrence. *Highbrow/Lowbrow: The Emergence of Cultural Hierarchy in America*. Cambridge, MA: Harvard UP, 1988.

Lewis, David Levering. *W. E. B. Du Bois: A Biography of a Race, 1868–1919*. New York: Henry Holt, 1993.

Limerick, Patricia Nelson. "Region and Reason." *All Over the Map: Rethinking American Regions*, ed. Edward Ayers. Baltimore: Johns Hopkins UP, 1996. 83–104.

Lincoln, Abraham. *The Collected Works of Abraham Lincoln*. Vol. 2. Ed. Roy P. Basler. New Brunswick: Rutgers UP, 1953.

Lingeman, Richard. *Theodore Dreiser: At the Gates of the City, 1871–1907*. New York: G. P. Putnam's Sons, 1986.

Lippard, George. *The Quaker City, Or The Monks of Monk-Hall*. Philadelphia: T. B. Peterson, 1845.

Lippmann, Walter. *A Preface to Politics*. New York: Mitchell Kennerley, 1914.

Little, Charles. "The Chicago Parliament of Religions." *Methodist Review* 76 (March-April 1894): 208–220.

Livingston, James. *Pragmatism and the Political Economy of Cultural Revolution, 1850–1940*. Chapel Hill: U of North Carolina P, 1997.

Lloyd, Henry Demarest. *Wealth against Commonwealth*. New York: Harper and Brothers, 1894.

Lowe, Lisa. *Immigrant Acts*. Durham: Duke UP, 1996.

Luis-Brown, David. "'White Slaves' and the 'Arrogant *Mestiza*': Reconfiguring Whiteness in *The Squatter and the Don* and *Ramona*." *American Literature* 69:4 (Dec. 1997): 813–839.

Madison, James. *The Federalist No. 10. The Norton Anthology of American Literature*, ed. Nina Baym et al., 4th ed., vol. 1. New York: Norton, 1994. 759–763.

Madrid, Arturo. "Diversity and Its Discontents." *Inventing America: Readings in Identity and Culture*, ed. Gabriella Ibieta and Miles Orvell. New York: St. Martin's, 1996. 575–584.

Marcil-Lacoste, Louise. "The Paradoxes of Pluralism." *Dimensions of Radical Democracy*, ed. Chantal Mouffe. London: Verso, 1992. 128–142.

Marcuse, Herbert. "Repressive Tolerance." *A Critique of Pure Tolerance*. Boston: Beacon Press, 1969. 81–123.

Martínez, Elizabeth. "Who's Cleansing Ethnic Studies." *Z Magazine* (June 1999): 31–37.
Matthews, Brander. *Vignettes of Manhattan.* New York: Harper and Brothers, 1894.
Matthews, Victoria Earle. "The Value of Race Literature" (1895). *Massachusetts Review* 27:2 (Summer 1986): 169–191.
Matthiessen, F. O. *Theodore Dreiser.* New York: Sloane, 1951.
McCabe, James. *New York by Sunlight and Gaslight.* New York: Crown, 1984.
McCullough, Joseph. *Hamlin Garland.* Boston: Twayne, 1978.
McDowell, Deborah. "The Changing Same: Generational Connections and Black Women Novelists." *New Literary History* 18 (Winter 1987): 281–302.
McKinley, William. "Inaugural Address" (1897). *Speeches and Addresses of William McKinley, from March 1, 1897 to May 30, 1900.* New York: Doubleday and McClure, 1900.
McLaren, Peter. "Multiculturalism and the Postmodern Critique: Towards a Pedagogy of Resistance and Transformation." *Cultural Studies* 7:1 (Jan. 1993): 118–146.
Mead, Sidney E. *The Lively Experiment: The Shaping of Christianity in America.* New York: Harper and Row, 1963.
Meier, August. *Negro Thought in America, 1880–1915.* Ann Arbor: U of Michigan P, 1970.
Mencke, John G. *Mulattoes and Race Mixture: American Attitudes and Images, 1865–1918.* Ann Arbor: UMI Research Press, 1979.
Mendel, Gregor. *Experiments in Plant Hybridisation.* Ed. J. H. Bennett. Edinburgh and London: Oliver and Boyd, 1965.
Michaels, Walter Benn. *Our America: Nativism, Modernism and Pluralism.* Durham: Duke UP, 1995.
Michasiw, Kim Ian. "Nine Revisionist Theses on the Picturesque." *Representations* 38 (Spring 1992): 76–100.
Mill, John Stuart. *Utilitarianism, On Liberty, Essay on Bentham.* Ed. Mary Warnock. New York: Meridian, 1965.
Miller, Joaquin. *The Destruction of Gotham.* New York: Funk and Wagnalls, 1886.
Miller, Kelly. "Achievements of the Negro Race." *The Voice of the Negro* (Sept. 1905): 612–618.
Moers, Ellen. *Two Dreisers.* New York: Viking, 1969.
Monroy, Douglas. *Thrown among Strangers: The Making of Mexican Culture in Frontier California.* Berkeley: U of California P, 1990.
Morison, Samuel Eliot, ed. *The Development of Harvard University, since the Inauguration of President Eliot, 1869–1929.* Cambridge, MA: Harvard UP, 1930.
Moses, William J. *The Golden Age of Black Nationalism, 1850–1925.* New York: Oxford UP, 1978.

Mouffe, Chantal. "Preface: Democratic Politics Today." *Dimensions of Radical Democracy,* ed. Chantal Mouffe. New York: Verso, 1992. 1–16.

Mullen, Harryette. "Optic White: Blackness and the Production of Whiteness." *Diacritics* (Summer/Fall 1994): 71–89.

Munt, Ian. "The 'Other' Postmodern Tourism: Culture, Travel and the New Middle Classes." *Theory, Culture and Society* 11 (1994): 101–123.

Myers, Gerald. *William James: His Life and Thought.* New Haven: Yale UP, 1986.

Nagel, James, ed. *Critical Essays on Hamlin Garland.* Boston: G. K. Hall, 1982.

Nash, June. "The Fiesta of the Word: The Zapatista Uprising and Radical Democracy in Mexico." *American Anthropologist* 99:2 (1997): 261–274.

Neely, Mary Atwater. "Opinion." *Neely's History of the Parliament of Religions and Religious Congresses of the World's Columbian Exposition,* ed. Walter R. Houghton. Chicago, 1893. 973.

Newfield, Christopher, and Avery F. Gordon. "Multiculturalism's Unfinished Business." Gordon and Newfield 76–115.

Newman, Richard. "'The Brightest Star': Aida Overton Walker in the Age of Ragtime and Cakewalk." *Prospects* 18 (1993): 465–481.

Nicholson, Meredith. "Edward Eggleston." *Atlantic* (Dec. 1902): 804.

Norris, Frank. *Responsibilities of the Novelist.* Cambridge, MA: Walker–de Berry, 1962.

———. "The Third Circle." *The Third Circle, A Deal in Wheat, and Other Stories of the New and Old West.* Vol. 4. Garden City: Doubleday, 1928.

Nott, Josiah, and George Gliddon. *Types of Mankind.* Philadelphia: Lippincott, Grambo, 1854.

Olby, Robert. *Origins of Mendelism.* New York: Schocken Books, 1966.

Olsen, Otto, ed. *The Thin Disguise: Plessy v. Ferguson.* New York: Humanities Press, 1967.

Osofsky, Gilbert. *Harlem: The Making of a Ghetto.* New York: Harper and Row, 1963.

Otten, Thomas J. "Pauline Hopkins and the Hidden Self of Race." *English Literary History* 57 (1992): 227–256.

Palumbo-Liu, David. "Introduction." *The Ethnic Canon: Histories, Institutions, and Interventions,* ed. David Palumbo-Liu. Minneapolis: U of Minnesota P, 1995. 1–27.

Paschal, Andrew, ed. *The W. E. B. Du Bois Reader.* New York: Macmillan, 1971.

Patten, Simon. *The New Basis of Civilization* (1907). Ed. Daniel Fox. Cambridge, MA: Harvard UP, 1968.

Perry, Ralph Barton. *The Thought and Character of William James.* 2 vols. Boston: Little, Brown, 1936.

Peterson, Carla. *"Doers of the Word": African-American Women Speakers and Writers in the North (1830–1880).* New York: Oxford UP, 1995.

———. "'Further Liftings of the Veil': Gender, Class and Labor in Frances Harper." *Listening to Silences,* ed. Elaine Hedges and Shelly Fisher Fishkin. New York: Oxford UP, 1994. 97–112.
Pickens, Donald. *Eugenics and the Progressives.* Nashville: Vanderbilt UP, 1968.
Pitt, Leonard. *Decline of the Californios: A Social History of the Spanish-Speaking Californians, 1846–1890.* Berkeley: U of California P, 1970.
Pittenger, Mark. *American Socialists and Evolutionary Thought, 1870–1920.* Madison: U of Wisconsin P, 1993.
Pizer, Donald. *Hamlin Garland's Early Work and Career.* Berkeley: U of California P, 1960.
———, ed. *Theodore Dreiser: A Selection of Uncollected Prose.* Detroit: Wayne State UP, 1977.
Pfeifer, Edward. "The Genesis of American Neo-Lamarckianism." *Isis* 56:2 (Summer 1965): 156–167.
Posnock, Ross. *Color and Culture: Black Writers and the Making of the Modern Intellectual.* Cambridge, MA: Harvard UP, 1998.
———. "The Politics of Pragmatism and the Fortunes of the Public Intellectual." *American Literary History* 3:3 (Fall 1991): 566–587.
———. *The Trial of Curiosity: Henry James, William James, and the Challenge of Modernity.* New York: Oxford UP, 1991.
Potter, David. *People of Plenty: Economic Abundance and the American Character.* Chicago: U of Chicago P, 1954.
Prabuddhaprana, Pravrajika. "Chicago and Its Impact: Swami Vivekananda's Influence on American Religion and Philosophy." In *Swami Vivekananda: A Hundred Years since Chicago, a Commemorative Volume.* Belur, India: Ramakrishna Math, 1994. 129–139.
Pratt, Mary Louise. *Imperial Eyes: Travel Writing and Transculturation.* New York: Routledge, 1992.
Price, Martin. "The Picturesque Moment." *From Sensibility to Romanticism: Essays Presented to Frederick Pottle,* ed. Frederick Hilles and Harold Bloom. New York: Oxford UP, 1965. 259–292.
Price, Uvedale. *A Dialogue on the Distinct Characters of the Picturesque and the Beautiful.* London, 1801.
———. *Essays on the Picturesque* (1810). Westmead, UK: Gregg International Publishers, 1971.
Punnett, R. C. *Mendelism.* New York: Macmillan, 1915.
Rachman, Stephen. "Reading Cities: Devotional Seeing in the Nineteenth Century." *American Literary History* 9 (Winter 1997): 653–675.
Rajchman, John, ed. *The Identity in Question.* New York: Routledge, 1995.
Ravage, M. E. "Absorbing the Alien." *The Century* 95:1 (Nov. 1917): 26–36.
Riis, Jacob. *How the Other Half Lives* (1890). New York: Dover, 1971.

Ripley, William Z. "The Three European Races" (1899). *This Is Race: An Anthology Selected from the International Literature on the Races of Man,* ed. Earl Court. New York: Henry Schuman, 1950. 194–206.

Robbins, Bruce. "Comparative Cosmopolitans." *Cosmopolitics: Thinking and Feeling beyond the Nation,* ed. Pheng Cheah and Bruce Robbins. Minneapolis: U of Minnesota P, 1998. 246–264.

———. "The Weird Heights: On Cosmopolitanism, Feeling, and Power." *differences* 7:1 (1995): 165–187.

Robinson, Sidney. *Inquiry into the Picturesque.* Chicago: U of Chicago P, 1991.

Romero, Lora. "Vanishing Americans: Gender, Empire, and New Historicism." *Subjects and Citizens,* ed. Michael Moon and Cathy Davidson. Durham: Duke UP, 1995. 87–108.

Rooney, Ellen. *Seductive Reasoning: Pluralism as the Problematic of Contemporary Literary Theory.* Ithaca: Cornell UP, 1989.

Roosevelt, Theodore. "What 'Americanism' Means." *Forum* 17 (1894): 196–206.

Roseboro, Viola. "Down-Town New York." *The Cosmopolitan* 1 (June 1886): 217–223.

———. "The Italians of New York." *The Cosmopolitan* 4 (Jan. 1888): 390–406.

Ross, Dorothy. *The Origins of American Social Science.* New York: Cambridge UP, 1991.

Ross, Edward A. *The Old World in the New.* New York: Century Company, 1914.

———. "The Slavs in America." *Century Magazine* 88 (Aug. 1914): 590–598.

Rouse, Roger. "Thinking through Transnationalism: Notes on the Cultural Politics of Class Relations in the Contemporary United States." *Public Culture* 7 (Winter 1995): 353–402.

Royce, Josiah. *California: A Study of American Character* (1886). New York: Knopf, 1948.

———. *The Philosophy of Loyalty.* Chicago: U of Chicago P, 1968.

———. *Race Questions, Provincialism, and Other American Problems* (1908). Freeport, NY: Books for Libraries Press, 1967.

Ruiz de Burton, María Amparo. *The Squatter and the Don* (1885). Ed. Rosaura Sánchez and Beatrice Pita. Houston: Arte Público Press, 1992.

Russell, Bertrand. "Americanization" [book review]. *Dial* 77 (Aug. 1924): 158–160.

Said, Edward. *Orientalism.* New York: Routledge, 1978.

———. "Traveling Theory." *The World, The Text, and the Critic.* Cambridge: Harvard UP, 1983. 226–247.

Saleeby, C. W. "Mendelism and Womanhood." *Forum* 44 (1910): 60–66.

Sánchez, Rosaura. "Nineteenth-Century Californio Narratives." *Recovering the U.S. Hispanic Literary Heritage,* ed. Ramón Gutiérrez and Genaro Padilla. Houston: Arte Público Press, 1993. 279–292.

———. *Telling Identities: The Californio Testimonios*. Minneapolis: U of Minnesota P, 1995.

Sánchez, Rosaura, and Beatrice Pita. "Introduction." *The Squatter and the Don*, by María Amparo Ruiz de Burton, ed. Sánchez and Pita. Houston: Arte Público Press, 1992. 5–51.

Santayana, George. *Selected Critical Writings of George Santayana*. Ed. Norman Henfrey. 2 vols. Cambridge: Cambridge UP, 1968.

Schlereth, Thomas. *Victorian America: Transformations in Everyday Life, 1876–1915*. New York: HarperCollins, 1992.

Schmidt, Sarah. "Horace M. Kallen and the Americanization of Zionism." Ph.D. diss., University of Maryland, 1973.

———. "Horace M. Kallen: The Zionist Chapter." Konvitz 76–89.

Schrager, Cynthia. "Pauline Hopkins and William James: The New Psychology and the Politics of Race." *The Unruly Voice: Rediscovering Pauline Hopkins*, ed. John Cullen Gruesser. Urbana: U of Illinois P, 1996. 183–209.

Schultz, Alfred. *Race or Mongrel* (1909). New York: Arno, 1977.

Seager, Richard Hughes, ed. *The Dawn of Religious Pluralism: Voices from the World's Parliament of Religions, 1893*. La Salle, IL: Open Court, 1993.

———. *The World's Parliament of Religions: The East/West Encounter, Chicago, 1893*. Bloomington: Indiana UP, 1995.

Senner, Joseph H. "The Immigration Question." *American Academy of Political and Social Science* 10 (July 1897): 1–19.

Shaler, Nathaniel. "Race Prejudices" *Atlantic Monthly* 58 (Oct. 1886): 510–518.

———. "Science and the African Problem." *Atlantic Monthly* 66 (July 1890): 36–45.

———. "The Summing Up of the Story." *The United States of America, a Study of the American Commonwealth*, vol. 2. New York: D. Appleton, 1897. 600–641.

Simmel, George. "The Stranger." *Social Theory*, ed. Charles Lemert. Boulder, CO: Westview Press, 1993. 200–204.

Sinfield, Alan. *Gay and After*. London: Serpent's Tail, 1998.

Smith, Richard Norton. *The Harvard Century: The Making of a University to a Nation*. New York: Simon and Schuster, 1986.

Snell, Minnie Andrews. "Aunt Hannah on the Parliament of Religions." *The Open Court* (Oct. 12, 1893): 3838.

Soja, Edward. *Postmodern Geographies: the Reassertion of Space in Critical Social Theory*. London: Verso, 1989.

Sollors, Werner. *Beyond Ethnicity: Consent and Descent in American Culture*. New York: Oxford UP, 1986.

———. "A Critique of Pure Pluralism." *Reconstructing American Literary History*, ed. Sacvan Bercovitch. Cambridge, MA: Harvard UP, 1986. 250–279.

———. *Neither Black nor White Yet Both*. New York: Oxford UP, 1997.

Speed, John Gilmer. "Food and Foreigners in New York." *Harper's Weekly* 44 (Sept. 8, 1900): 846–847.

———. "The Negro in New York." *Harper's Weekly* 44 (Dec. 22, 1900): 1249–50.

Spencer, Herbert. "Progress: Its Law and Cause." *On Evolution: Selected Writings*, ed. J. D. Y. Peel. Chicago: U of Chicago P, 1972. 38–52.

Spencer, Jonathan. "Writing Within: Anthropology, Nationalism, and Culture in Sri Lanka." *Current Anthropology* 31:3 (June 1990): 283–300.

Sproat, John G. *"The Best Men": Liberal Reformers in the Gilded Age*. New York: Oxford UP, 1968.

Steinberg, Stephen. *The Ethnic Myth: Race, Ethnicity, and Class in America*. Boston: Beacon Press, 1989.

Steinfels, Peter. "More Diversity Than Harmony at Religious Assembly." *New York Times* (Sept. 7, 1993): A14.

Stepan, Nancy Leys, and Sander L. Gilman. "Appropriating the Idioms of Science: The Rejection of Scientific Racism." *The "Racial" Economy of Science: Toward a Democratic Future*, ed. Sandra Harding. Bloomington: U of Indiana P, 1993. 170–200.

Stiehm, Judith. "Diversity's Diversity." Goldberg 140–156.

Stilgoe, John. *Metropolitan Corridor: Railroads and the American Scene*. New Haven: Yale UP, 1983.

Stocking, George, Jr. *Race, Culture, and Evolution: Essays in the History of Anthropology*. New York: Free Press, 1968.

Stone, Alfred Holt. "Is Race Friction between Black and White in the United States Growing and Inevitable?" *American Journal of Sociology* 13:5 (March 1908): 676–697.

Stonequist, Everett. *The Marginal Man: A Study in Personality and Culture Conflict*. New York: Russell and Russell, 1961.

Strong, Josiah. *The New World-Religion*. Garden City, NY: Doubleday, Page, 1915.

———. *Our Country*. Ed. Jurgen Herbst. Cambridge, MA: Harvard UP, 1963.

Stuart, T. McKendree. "A Comparative View of the Ethnic Religions and Christianity." *Methodist Review* 75:1 (Jan.-Feb. 1893): 35–42.

Stuckey, Sterling. *Slave Culture: Nationalist Theory and the Foundations of Black America*. New York: Oxford UP, 1987.

Sundquist, Eric, ed. *The Oxford W. E. B. Du Bois Reader*. New York: Oxford UP, 1996.

———. "Realism and Regionalism." *Columbia Literary History of the United States*, ed. Emory Elliot. New York: Columbia UP, 1987. 501–524.

Takaki, Ronald. *A Different Mirror*. Boston: Little, Brown, 1993.

———. *Iron Cages: Race and Culture in Nineteenth-Century America*. Seattle: U of Washington P, 1979.
Taylor, Charles. *Multiculturalism and "The Politics of Recognition."* Princeton: Princeton UP, 1992.
———. "The Politics of Recognition." Goldberg 75–106.
Taylor, Virginia. *The Franco-Texan Land Company*. Austin: U of Texas P, 1969.
Terrell, Mary Church. "What It Means to Be Colored in the Capital of the United States" (1907). Lerner 378–382.
Todd, Ruth. "The Octoroon's Revenge" (1902). Ammons 135–144.
Toll, William. *The Resurgence of Race*. Philadelphia: Temple UP, 1979.
Toy, Crawford. "The Parliament of Religions." *The New World* 2 (Dec. 1893): 737.
———. "Religious Fusion." *International Quarterly* 6 (Sept. 1902): 29–42.
Trachtenberg, Alan. *The City: American Experience*. New York: Oxford UP, 1971.
———. "Conceivable Aliens." *Yale Review* 82:4 (Oct. 1994): 42–64.
———. *The Incorporation of America*. New York: Hill and Wang, 1982.
———. *Reading American Photographs*. New York: Hill and Wang, 1989.
Trilling, Lionel. *The Liberal Imagination*. New York: Viking, 1950.
———. *Matthew Arnold* (1939). New York: Harcourt Brace Jovanovich, 1977.
Trinh, T. Minh-ha. *Woman, Native, Other*. Bloomington: Indiana UP, 1989.
Trumbull, M. M. "The Parliament of Religions." *The Monist* 4:3 (April 1894): 333–354.
Turner, Frederick Jackson. "Is Sectionalism in America Dying Away?" *American Journal of Sociology* 13:5 (March 1908): 661–675.
———. *The Significance of the Frontier in American History*. Ed. Harold Simonson. New York: Continuum, 1990.
Twain, Mark. *Pudd'nhead Wilson* (1894). New York: Bantam, 1981.
———. "What Paul Bourget Thinks of Us." *North American Review* 160:1 (Jan. 1895): 48–62.
Van Rensselaer, Mariana [Griswold]. "Picturesque New York" (1892). *Gaslight New York: Revisited*, ed. Frank Oppel. Secaucus, NJ: Castle Books, 1989. 311–324.
Véron, Eugène. *Aesthetics*. Trans. W. H. Armstrong. London: Chapman and Hall, 1879.
Vivekananda, Swami. *The Complete Works of Swami Vivekananda*. 8 vols. Calcutta: Advaita Ashrama, 1979.
———. *Selections from Swami Vivekananda*. Calcutta: Advaita Ashrama, 1963.
Wahl, Jean. *The Pluralist Philosophies of England and America*. London: Open Court, 1925.
Wald, Priscilla. *Constituting Americans: Cultural Anxiety and Narrative Form*. Durham: Duke UP, 1995.

Walker, Alice. *In Search of Our Mothers' Gardens: Womanist Prose*. San Diego: Harcourt Brace Jovanovich, 1993.

"Walking Tours." *Harper's Weekly* 48 (Sept. 10, 1904): 1382.

Walkowitz, Judith. *City of Dreadful Delight: Narratives of Sexual Danger in Late-Victorian London*. Chicago: U of Chicago P, 1992.

Wall v. Oyster. *District of Columbia Appeal Cases*, vol. 36 (36 App. D.C. 50). New York: Lawyers Cooperative Publishing Co., 1911. 50–58.

Ward, Lester. "The Transmission of Culture." *Forum* 11 (1891): 312–319.

Warren, Kenneth. *Black and White Strangers: Race and American Literary History*. Chicago: U of Chicago P, 1993.

Washington, Booker T. *The Future of the American Negro* (1899). Chicago: Afro-Am Press, 1969.

———. *Up from Slavery* (1901). New York: Dover, 1995.

Wells, H. G. *The Future in America*. New York: Harper and Brothers, 1906.

———. *New Worlds for Old*. New York: Macmillan, 1908.

Welty, Eudora, "Place in Fiction." *South Atlantic Quarterly* 55 (Jan. 1956): 57–72.

Wendell, Barrett. *Liberty, Union and Democracy*. New York: C. Scribner's Sons, 1906.

Werbner, Pnina. "Essentialising Essentialism, Essentialising Silence: Ambivalence and Multiplicity in the Constructions of Racism and Ethnicity." *Debating Cultural Hybridity: Multi-Cultural Identities and the Politics of Anti-Racism*, ed. Pnina Werbner and Tariq Modood. London: Zed Books, 1997. 226–256.

West, Cornel. *The American Evasion of Philosophy: A Genealogy of Pragmatism*. Madison: U of Wisconsin P, 1989.

———. "The New Cultural Politics of Difference." *Race, Identity, and Representation in Education*, ed. Cameron McCarthy and Warren Crichlow. New York: Routledge, 1993. 11–23.

Wiebe, Robert. *The Search for Order, 1870–1920*. New York: Hill and Wang, 1967.

Willett, Cynthia, ed. *Theorizing Multiculturalism: A Guide to the Current Debate*. Oxford: Blackwell, 1998.

Williams, Fannie Barrier. "Perils of the White Negro." *Colored American Magazine* 13 (Dec. 1907): 421–423.

Williams, Jesse Lynch. "The Walk Up-Town." *Scribner's* 27 (Jan. 1900): 44–59.

Williams, Raymond. "Between Country and City." *Reading Landscape, Country-City-Capital*, ed. Simon Pugh. Manchester, UK: Manchester UP, 1990. 7–18.

———. *The Country and the City*. New York: Oxford UP, 1973.

———. *The Long Revolution* (1961). Harmondsworth: Penguin, 1965.

———. *Marxism and Literature*. Oxford: Oxford UP, 1977.
———. "Region and Class in the Novel." *The Uses of Fiction: Essays on the Modern Novel in Honour of Arnold Kettle,* ed. Douglas Jefferson and Graham Martin. Milton Keynes: Open UP, 1982. 59–68.
Williamson, Joel. *New People: Miscegenation and Mulattoes*. New York: Free Press, 1980.
Wilson, Elizabeth. *The Sphinx in the City: Urban Life, the Control of Disorder, and Women*. Berkeley: U of California P, 1991.
Wilson, Kimberly. "The Function of the 'Fair' Mulatto: Complexion, Audience, and Mediation in Frances Harper's *Iola Leroy.*" *Cimarron Review* 106 (Jan. 1994): 104–114.
Wilson, Rob, and Wimal Dissanayake. "Introduction: Tracking the Global/Local." *Global/Local: Cultural Production and the Transnational Imaginary,* ed. Wilson and Dissanayake. Durham: Duke UP, 1996. 1–18.
Wilson, Woodrow. "The Ideals of America." *Atlantic Monthly* 90 (Dec. 1902): 721–734.
———. "The Making of the Nation." *Atlantic Monthly* 80 (July 1897): 1–14.
———. "The Teacher as Citizen" (1899). *The Papers of Woodrow Wilson,* vol. 11 (1898–1900), ed. Arthur S. Link. Princeton: Princeton UP, 1971. 104–105.
Wolff, Janet. "The Invisible *Flâneuse:* Women and the Literature of Modernity." *Theory, Culture and Society* 2:3 (1985): 37–46.
Woll, Alan. *Black Musical Theatre: From Coontown to Dreamgirls*. Baton Rouge: Louisiana State UP, 1989.
Wong Chin Foo. "The Chinese in New York." *The Cosmopolitan* 5 (1888): 297–311.
———. "Why Am I a Heathen?" *North American Review* 145 (Aug. 1887): 169–179.
The World's Parliament of Religions. Ed. John Henry Barrows. 2 vols. Chicago: Parliament Publishing Co., 1893.
Young, Elizabeth. "Warring Fictions: *Iola Leroy* and the Color of Gender." *American Literature* 64:2 (June 1992): 273–297.
Young, Iris Marion. "The Ideal of Community and the Politics of Difference." *Feminism/Postmodernism,* ed. Linda Nicholson. New York: Routledge, 1990. 300–323.
Young, Robert. *Colonial Desire: Hybridity in Theory, Culture and Race*. London: Routledge, 1995.
Yúdice, George. "We Are *Not* the World." *Social Text* 31/32 (1992): 202–216.
Zamir, Shamoon. *Dark Voices: W. E. B. Du Bois and American Thought, 1888–1903*. Chicago: U of Chicago P, 1995.
Zangwill, Israel. *The Melting-Pot*. New York: Macmillan, 1912.

Zhang, Qingsong (King). "The Origins of the Chinese Americanization Movement: Wong Chin Foo and the Chinese Equal Rights League." *Claiming America: Constructing Chinese American Identities during the Exclusion Era*, ed. K. Scott Wong and Sucheng Chan. Philadelphia: Temple UP, 1998. 41–63.

Ziolkowski, Eric, ed. *A Museum of Faiths: Histories and Legacies of the 1893 World's Parliament of Religions*. Atlanta: Scholars Press, 1993.

ACKNOWLEDGMENTS

I am indebted to the Nanula Drescher Affirmative Action Leave Program for giving me a full year (1998–99) to revise my manuscript. This union-sponsored grant (the United University Professions of New York State) afforded me the time to develop, reorganize, and polish my thoughts. Special thanks to Kerry Grant, the dean of the College of Arts and Sciences at the State University of New York at Buffalo, for supporting my application. Writing a book requires not only the luxury of time but also space. Brian Wells and his crew made sure that the (rented) room of my own in downtown Buffalo was a perfect sanctuary in which to write.

The research for this book began while I was a graduate student in the Modern Thought and Literature Program at Stanford University. The feedback, guidance, and friendship of Ramón Saldívar and Jay Fliegelman informed the project's development and its eventual direction. I am also grateful to George Fredrickson, under whose instruction I first brought together William James, W. E. B. Du Bois, and Horace Kallen. The Dorothy Danforth Compton Foundation and the Chicano Fellows Program at Stanford provided me with funding to complete my dissertation.

While in college at the University of Connecticut, I had the privilege of studying with the poet Jim Scully. He was able to see beyond the impetuous prose and untamed thoughts of an earnest undergraduate to suggest that I pursue a doctorate. His poetry and pedagogy have instilled in me a way of seeing and living in the world, where "the question is not if or whether but when and how."

Since arriving in Buffalo in 1994, I have had the good fortune of belonging to a department that successfully combines rigorous thought with good humor. Despite years of fiscal cuts, intellectual curiosity is still alive and well. From the seminar table to dissertation defenses, conversations with colleagues and students have informed these pages in numerous ways. Mark Shechner and Barbara Bono, who chaired my department during the writing of this book, were unfailingly supportive. Their invaluable assistance continues to be deeply appreciated.

Neil Schmitz has pointed me in the right direction at crucial professional junctures. William Fischer has given me wise counsel and encouragement from the start. For their insightful comments on individual chapters, I thank colleagues both local and national: Tracy Fessenden, Stacy Hubbard, Kathryne Lindberg, and Dennis Tedlock. Conversations with Lisa Botshon and Howard Horwitz were also extremely helpful. Priscilla Wald has always been there to offer generous support and guidance through the various stages of professional hurdles beginning many years ago with doctoral exams. For turning research trips into reunions, I am also grateful to long-time and long-distant friends, Julie Abbruscato, Doug Anderson, Gil Harris, Leslie Harris, and Margaret Pappano. I have also benefited from Alan Sinfield's encouraging words as well as from his scholarship, which has taught me the importance of taking risks and of taking sides. Special thanks to the generous research assistance of Tom Morgan, who gave this project more time than I had any right to expect of him. Marta Valenzuela and Paul Feigenbaum kindly volunteered a summer to track down obscure references. Kevin Grauke assisted me in the painstaking task of indexing. For their patience and assistance, the librarians and staff at the following institutions also deserve special mention: the Buffalo Public Library, Lockwood Library at the University at Buffalo, the libraries at Columbia University, the New York Public Library, including the Schomburg Center for the Study of Black Culture, the Newberry Library, and the Chicago Historical Society. I would also like to thank the department administrators at the University at Buffalo for their warm support and friendship.

At Harvard University Press, I am indebted to the foresight of Lindsay Waters. His genuine love of ideas, combined with his critical intelligence, has made the experience of publishing a first book all the richer. Two anonymous readers offered invaluable suggestions. Camille Smith, my manuscript editor, patiently combed through the pages of this voluminous tome with meticulous care.

On a personal note, I want to thank my parents, Frances Tirado Bramen and Bruce Bramen, for their unconditional support, love, and encouragement. My grandmother, Sylvia Bramen, consistently turned worries into laughter. My brother, Gary, has nobly carried on the duty of all younger siblings, namely not to let the eldest take themselves too seriously. My family from San Jose to Los Angeles offered a patient ear and positive words when they were needed most. On the domestic front, Cecilia and George, our feline refugees, made sure I was regularly awake at the crack of dawn. Their presence every evening sitting by the door was a reminder that home is not where the writing is, as the nineteenth-century novelist Harold Frederic once opined, but where the cats wait.

Most of all, I thank David Schmid, to whom this book is dedicated. He has been my unofficial editor and my most brilliant critic for over a decade. He has also been my source of emotional and intellectual sustenance, who has made the writing of this book a pleasurable and precious memory. This book is in large part a collaborative effort in the sense of intellectual exchange, but more significantly, as the loving expression of the daily routines that nourish and nurture our life together.

Sections of Chapter 4 appear in *American Quarterly* 52:3 (Sept. 2000); parts of Chapter 6 in *The Puritan Origins of American Sex,* ed. Tracy Fessenden et al. (New York: Routledge, 2000). The quotation from Jim Scully's poem "Dropping Out" is from *Raging Beauty* (Washington: Azul Editions, 1994), reprinted by permission of the publisher, Richard Schaaf, and the author, Jim Scully. Permission to reproduce the photograph of Vivekananda and others on the platform of the 1893 World's Parliament of Religions (Figure 5) was granted by the Ramakrishna-Vivekananda Center in New York City. Grateful acknowledgment is made for permission to reprint this material.

Index

Abbott, Lyman, 157
Adams, Henry, 24, 45, 308n13
Addams, Jane, 323n20
Aesthetics, 25; Garland on, 126–127, 129, 141, 153–155, 185; in *Iola Leroy,* 240–241; picturesque, 156, 158–161, 164–169, 175–187, 196–197
Affirmative action, 295–296
Africa, 69, 70, 90–91, 105, 157, 237, 288
African Americans, 7, 69–101, 105–111, 116, 146–152, 192–195, 201–249, 280, 284; and black hair, 109, 165–166; Civil Rights era, 296; commercialism, fear of, 80–81; dialect, 136, 150; and European immigrants, 160–163, 180–184, 195–198; and family, 206, 213, 214, 217, 235–240, 243, 246, 293; farmers, 140, 149–150, 152; feminism, 206, 209, 217, 227, 232, 244–249; and food, 193–195; intellectuals, 80, 88–91, 95, 197, 222; and Jamesian pluralism, 66, 69, 73–75, 80–84, 226–227; and Jewish Americans, 75–78, 238; and Kallen's cultural pluralism, 95–101; middle classes, 89–90, 147, 150, 194–195, 198, 214; migration, 16, 161; and Native Americans, 94, 314n17; and variety, 23, 213, 227, 236–237; women, 197–198, 206–207, 208, 232–236, 238–249; workers, 149, 247, 248–249, 193. *See also* Blackness; Exceptionalism, black; Mendelist allegory; Mulattoes; Nationalism; Race
Aguinaldo, 60–62
American exceptionalism, 1–3, 5, 8, 10–11, 23, 25, 50–51, 85–86, 104; African Americans, 236–238; Jewish Americans, 110; and religion, 254, 257, 280; and the urban picturesque, 176, 195–196

Americanism: African Americans, 18–19, 72, 94–95, 110, 198, 203–204, 207, 227, 248–249; Africanization of, 206, 227; and Christian exceptionalism, 254, 256; cosmopolitanism, 136, 158, 192, 196; and diversity, 3, 5, 8–11, 21; and Hebraism, 93–94; identity culture, 101; and localism, 116; modern, 22, 23, 25, 157, 176, 293; 100 percent, 24, 69; and pluralism, 25, 29, 79, 119; and the urban picturesque, 159, 175, 176, 181, 293; and variety, 9–11, 19, 21–23, 30, 159, 198, 203–204; and whiteness, 17. *See also* Du Bois; Kallen
Americanization, 116, 204; Chinese, 190–191; de-Americanization, 194; as homogenizing force, 69, 75, 79; and urban picturesque, 159, 162, 175–182
Anderson, Amanda, 314–315n25
Andrews, William L., 241
Anti-imperialism. *See* Imperialism, anti-
Anti-Imperialist League, 61
Anti-miscegenation laws, 203, 206, 209–210, 233, 247
Antimodernism, 177–178
Antin, Mary, 79
Anti-picturesque. *See* Picturesque, anti-
Anti-Semitism, 69, 99
Appiah, Anthony, 3–4, 5, 215
Arnold, Sir Edwin, 284
Arnold, Matthew, 54, 89
Ashcan School, 185
Asia, 25, 105, 157, 247, 269, 285
Asian-Americans, 4, 6–7, 187–192
Assimilation, 79, 84, 94, 116, 127, 159, 162, 192, 238, 293, 297; Anglo-Saxonism, 69, 75, 85, 159; anti-, 43, 69, 81, 153–154, 190, 226, 254, 285; in Chesnutt's "Future American," 223–224; in Kallen, 82–83;

365

Assimilation (*continued*)
  religious, 190, 279; reversed, 192, 269, 274, 275, 278
Atlanta, 76, 148
Austin, Mary, 143
The Autobiography of an Ex-Colored Man, 241
Autonomy, 77, 78, 225, 231; in Du Bois, 75, 107–110; intellectual, 39–40, 42, 52, 64–65, 67; in James, 10, 31, 32, 39, 50, 58, 83, 249, 251, 267, 300; in Kallen, 75, 82, 86–87; and the Philippines 59, 62–63; subcultural, 32, 70, 73, 78, 81, 85, 116; and Zapatistas, 301–302

Bacon, Leonard Woosley, 264
Baker, Houston, 233, 240
Balibar, Etienne, 214
Barrows, John Henry, 250, 253, 254, 257, 263–265, 267, 271–274, 277, 278–279, 285, 286, 288–289. *See also* World's Parliament of Religions
Barthes, Roland, 36, 297
Beggar girls, 166–167, 181
"Benetton effect," 105
Benjamin, Walter, 169, 177
Bennett, William, 1–2, 6, 54
Bercovitch, Sacvan, 273. *See also* Heathen's jeremiad
Berdahl, Robert, 298, 299
Berlant, Lauren, 238, 239, 246
Berman, Marshall, 50
Berzon, Judith, 230, 241–244
Bhabha, Homi, 237
Bill of Rights, 93
Biraciality. *See* Mendelist allegory; Mulattoes; "White Negro"
Black Adam, 94–95
Black Belt, 119, 140, 147–152, 210. *See also* Du Bois, "Of the Black Belt"
Blackness: 165, 197, 201, 203, 213, 214–215, 217, 223–224, 227, 228–229, 232, 236, 241, 296; affirmative, 232, 235, 247; in *Iola Leroy*, 243–245; in "The Octoroon's Revenge," 234, 235; in Mary Church Terrell, 194–195; and the urban picturesque, 161–162, 165–166, 183–184, 187, 194, 201; and *Wall v. Oyster*, 211. *See also* Whiteness
Blavatsky, Madame, 282

Blood, 21, 123, 203, 207–217, 244–246; black, 78, 83–84, 210, 212, 214, 217, 219, 227–228, 235, 243; blue, 135, 233, 243; purity of, 15, 17; tragic mulatta, 230, 244; white, 15, 211, 213, 219, 227, 228
Blood, Benjamin Paul, 21
Bloom, Harold, 54
Boardman, George Dana, 277–280, 286
Boas, Franz, 207, 253
Bonney, Charles Frank, 250–251
Boston, 92, 119, 193, 277
Boucicault, Dana, 212
Bourdieu, Pierre, 52, 64–65, 67
Bourget, Paul, 128–129, 171
Bourne, Randolph, 10, 79, 102, 117, 160, 175–176, 190; on transnationalism, 159, 175, 179, 193, 195, 197, 238. *See also* Transnationalism
Bowlby, Rachel, 167
Bowler, Peter, 218
Bradley, Francis H., 43
Brandeis, Louis, 21
Brewster, William, 92
Briggs, Charles, 260, 261
Brodhead, Richard, 121, 123, 124
Brooks, Peter, 229
Brooks, Van Wyck, 16
Brown, Lois Lamphere, 229
Brown, Sterling, 211
Bryan, William Jennings, 170, 179, 316n6
Bryce, Viscount, 117, 118
Buck, Paul, 151
Buddha, 63, 269, 275, 278, 281–286, 290
Buddhism, 25, 252, 263, 278–279, 285, 289; and Christianity, 258, 271, 274, 279, 282–285, 286; James, 287; Judaism, 275–276. *See also* Dharmapala; World's Parliament of Religions
Buell, Frederick, 3, 326n35
Burnham, Daniel, 256–257
Burnouf, Eugene, 284
Burrell, Reverend, 264
Burton, Henry, 133, 137
Butler, Judith, 207

California, 120, 127, 130, 139, 140, 154, 190, 297–300; Los Angeles, 5, 6–7; San Diego, 130, 132–134, 136; San Francisco, 131, 132–133, 191–192, 271–272

Californios, 130–139, 140, 153
Camarillo, Albert, 137–138
Candlin, George, 260–261, 262
Canterbury, Archbishop of, 263
Capitalism, 16–17, 50, 103–104, 121, 133, 137, 300
Carby, Hazel, 88, 90, 236
Carlyle, Thomas, 102
Carnegie, Andrew, 57
Carpenter, Estlin, 257
Carroll, Henry King, 261–262
Carus, Paul, 254, 257, 262, 268, 269
Castelar, Emilio, 265
Cather, Willa, 324–325n30
Catholicism, 128, 138, 177–178, 250–251, 261; attacks against, 250; and Eastern religions, 264–265; and Protestantism, 250–251, 261–262, 264–265
Central Pacific Railroad, 133
Ceylon, 252, 253, 278, 280, 282–285. *See also* Sri Lanka
Chant, Laura, 272
Character: building, 89; "flat," 221, 230–231, 234, 240–241, 245; hereditarian, 204, 211, 216–217, 235, 238, 244; moral, 41, 46, 78, 248–249, 277; national, 238, 248
Chesnutt, Charles, 204–205, 218–220, 280, 281; race fusion, 223–224, 232–233, 235, 248, 249, 279. *Works:* "The Future American," 217, 220, 222–224; *The House behind the Cedars,* 221; *The Marrow of Tradition,* 76; "A Victim of Heredity," 220–221
Chiapas, Mexico, 297, 300–304
Chicago, 15, 70, 105, 183, 288; site of 1893 Columbian Exposition and World's Parliament of Religions, 258, 259, 271, 282, 287, 290
Chicano, 1, 2, 300. *See also* Californios; Latinos
Chicano Studies, 298
China, 22, 108, 181, 188, 190, 193, 252, 253, 260, 263
Chinatown: New York, 169, 187–192; San Francisco, 191–192
Chinese, 16, 106, 160, 187–192, 195, 197, 247, 272; immigration of, 79, 272–273; religion, 22, 263. *See also* Chinatown; Immigrants

Chinese Exclusion Act of 1882, 16, 187. *See also* Geary Law
Christianity, 250–291; "Buddhized," 249, 252; crisis of variety, 260–266; and Eastern religions, 263–264, 268–269, 278–280; exceptionalism, 254, 256, 278–279; in *Iola Leroy,* 240, 243–244, 246; missionaries of, 22, 62–63, 190–191, 258, 259, 263, 270–271, 272, 290; modern Americanism, 254, 256; syncretism, 276–280; as world-religion, 277–280. *See also* Protestantism; World's Parliament of Religions
Christians: "broad," 254, 264, 265, 277–280, 290; "narrow," 254, 262, 277–280
Citizens, 5, 12, 22, 53–54, 58, 79, 207, 248, 299; African Americans as, 94, 194, 197–198, 207, 226, 237, 238, 246–247; immigrants as, 87, 163, 174–175, 178–180; "voteless," 77, 231, 232
Citizenship, 22, 56, 153, 190, 191, 232, 239, 295; African-American, 206–207, 232, 247–248; "dual," 176; and immigrants, 175, 176, 189–190; in *Iola Leroy,* 239–246; multicultural, 299
City: anti-urbanism, 102, 121, 159, 182; and diversity, 4–5, 6–7, 182–183, 151, 157–159, 192–193, 288; in Du Bois, 99–101, 105, 108–109, 150–151; fears of, 19–20, 157–158; industrial, 102; migration from country to, 16, 18, 150–151; and modern Americanism, 157–159, 181, 195–198; as site of culture, 144, 150–151; as site of discrimination, 99–101, 108–109, 192–195; as site of reuniting the black family, 234, 240; uniformity, 117; "unoppressive," 6–7, 17, 102–103, 109, 303; "unreal," 20; urban picturesque, 156–198; "White," 259–260. *See also* City-country division; Immigrants; New York City; Urban picturesque
City-country division, 25, 118, 120–123, 125, 130, 134, 155, 158, 163–164, 167, 181; in Du Bois, 139–140, 148–149, 150–151; in Garland, 139–140, 143–144, 151; lack of distinction between, 117. *See also* Regionalism
Civil War, 15, 16, 41, 54, 56, 117, 152, 202, 239, 244, 264
Class, 52–58, 70, 90, 105–106, 172, 173,

Class (continued)
  196; conflict, 12–13, 101, 142–146, 156–157, 178, 186, 196, 245, 248; and ethnicity, 119–120, 156, 160, 161, 169, 182–187; middle, 6, 54, 89, 103, 106, 122, 147, 158, 159, 167–168, 192, 194–195, 252, 261; patrician, 58, 99, 130–139; and race, 100–101, 106–109, 119–120, 149, 160, 166, 195, 248, 295–296; and region, 121–122; and the urban picturesque, 166–169, 157, 178; working, 54, 56, 103–104, 149, 167, 248. *See also* African Americans; middle classes; Intellectuals; Labor
Clinton, Bill, 3
Columbian Exposition of 1893, 22, 25, 249, 252, 256–260; Midway Plaisance, 256–258, 266; and Orientalism, 257–258. *See also* White City; World's Parliament of Religions
Connerly, Ward, 298
Constitution, U.S., 12–13, 16
Consumers, 4–5, 103–105, 167–168, 179–180, 185, 191, 193–195
Consumption, 6–7, 103–105, 125, 176; African-American, 80, 194–195; "conspicuous," 42, 79; "modern," 167
Coon, Deborah, 59–60
Cooper, Anna Julia, 18–19, 94, 215–216, 220
Corbin, John, 158
Cosmopolitanism, 63–66, 68, 71–73, 85, 101, 108–111, 192–193, 293; and Americanism, 5, 136, 157–158, 181, 192, 196–197; at the World's Parliament of Religions, 252, 253, 256
Cotton, John, 92, 94
Cowan, Michael, 172
Crane, Stephen, 182–183, 184
Crèvecoeur, J. Hector St. John, 11–12, 15, 17–18
Croly, Herbert, 51–52, 103
Crummell, Alexander, 80–81
Culler, Jonathan, 173
Cultural pluralism, 76, 77–79, 84, 86–87, 92, 96–100, 102–105, 109, 110, 117, 118–119, 197, 207, 248; and African Americans, 77, 95–99. *See also* James, William; Kallen; Pluralism
Culture, 10, 20–21, 32, 47, 54–63, 65, 73, 75, 101, 123, 143–144, 151, 178–181, 187–192, 294; Arnoldian, 73, 89; vs. biology, 83–84, 207–209, "good," 53–59, 63, 67, 89; "human," 80, 101, 106–107; vs. Kultur, 79–80; trickle-down, 57, 62, 88–89; university, 24, 39–43, 50–58, 65

Dainotto, Roberto Maria, 124,
Darwin, Charles, 201–204, 206, 215, 218
Declaration of Independence, 93
De Forest, John, 115
Degler, Carl, 209
Delegal Riots, 148
Democracy, 12–13, 14, 29, 59, 108, 136; "deep," 33; "genuine," 78, 207; and hierarchy, 47–48; "industrial," 102, 107; and modern Americanism, 30, 69, 79–80, 91, 198; "radical," 33, 295–296; Zapatista definition of, 301
Dewey, John, 129
Dharmapala, Anagarika, 253, 255, 269, 276, 281–287, 290; critique of Christianity, 258, 270–271, 282; on ethics, 282–284, 287, 290; and James, 255, 286–287; "synthetic religion," 282–284, 287. *See also* Buddhism; World's Parliament of Religions
Difference: conservation of, 80, 85, 86, 122, 176; politics of, 9, 74, 95, 295–297
Discreteness, 25, 206, 212, 248, 251, 277; unity-in-discreteness, 159, 160, 249, 252, 256, 266, 276, 279–280, 286
Dissanayake, Wimal, 130, 196
Diversity: absence of, 117; of African Americans, 213, 226, 293; and American exceptionalism, 1–5, 8, 196, 280; and Americanism, 105, 182, 293–294; and class, 7, 102–106; "cultural," 1–4, 5, 302; -as-discreteness, 108; Filipino, 22; Galeano on, 303–304; immigrant, 17, 157; and individuality, 41; limits of, 8–9, 35; Mill on, 34; and multiculturalism 2, 5–8, 32–33, 63; and a national literature, 115; New York City, 21, 160, 183, 192–193, 196–197; and the politics of hair, 165–166; polygenesis, 202, 204, 215; postmodern politics of, 6–7, 8, 33; and the "race problem," 18–19; regional, 152; religious, 250–252, 261–262, 263, 266–267, 280, 287–291; vs. uniformity, 2, 79, 303;

relation to unity, 33, 79, 251, 266, 302. *See also* Heterogeneity; Variety
Dixon, Thomas, 235
"The Document of Global Ethics," 289–290
Dougherty County, Georgia. *See* Georgia
Douglas, Ann, 157
Douglas, Stephen, 14–15, 17, 18, 19
Dreiser, Theodore, 119, 160, 171, 174, 182–187
Dreyfus Affair, 52, 77, 311n18
Du Bois, W. E. B., 18, 24, 67–111, 119, 120–121, 123, 129, 141, 154, 207, 214, 285, 299–300; and Americanism, 23, 72, 94–95, 101, 106, 110, 116, 120, 198, 207, 256; anti-imperialism, 107–108; black exceptionalism, 248, 285, 293; on the black intellectual, 87–88; on black migration, 16, 161; cosmopolitanism, 72–73, 101–102, 108–109, 110; *The Crisis*, 77, 97, 103, 108; on Alexander Crummell, 80–81; "double consciousness," 229, 241; essentialism, 82–84, 123; on exclusions, 111; and "genuine democracy," 78, 207; humanism, 101, 106–107, 110, 299, 303; "inter-nation," 108, 110–111; and James, 68, 99; Jamesian pluralism, 24, 66, 69–74, 77–78, 80–81, 83–84, 91, 95, 107, 108, 110, 116, 293, 295; masculinity, 89–90; as minority intellectual, 74–75; "Negro college-bred," 88–90, 248; Pan-Africanism, 90–91; populism, 139–140, 141; race pride, 73, 121, 215; regionalism, 127–128, 148–150, 151; and science, 83, 214–215, 221, 222; Talented Tenth, concept of, 100, 141, 194, 207, 248; theory of power, 88–91; and variety, 23, 102, 150–151. *Works:* "Of Beauty and Death," 108; "Of the Black Belt," 130, 139, 146, 148–152; "The Coming of John," 100–101, 108–109; "The Conservation of Races," 80–81, 83, 84, 87, 106, 108, 149, 153, 214, 215, 222, 226; *Dark Princess,* 83; *Darkwater,* 73, 91, 105–109, 149, 248; *The Encyclopedia Africana,* 68; "The Lynching Industry," 77; *The Philadelphia Negro,* 149; "The Problem of Amusement," 151; "Of the Quest of the Golden Fleece," 146, 152; *The Quest of the Silver Fleece,* 237; "Race Pride," 108; *The Souls of Black Folk,* 68, 80, 84, 88, 99–101, 105, 106, 131, 136, 146–152, 214; "The Talented Tenth," 88–89; "The Training of the Negro for Social Power," 88–90; "Of Work and Wealth," 105
Dunbar, Paul Laurence, 238–239, 325n32
Dutt, R. C., 284–285
Dyson, Michael, 213

"Each-form." *See* James, William, "each-form"
Eagleton, Terry, 48, 65, 231, 309–310n8
East St. Louis, 105, 111
Eggleston, Edward, 115, 145
Elective system, 41–42
Eliot, Charles W., 41
Epstein, Jacob, 179–180
Essentialism, 8, 71–73, 82–84, 110–111, 231–232, 236, 247–249; biological, 206–207, 209, 213, 217, 234–235
Ethics, 9, 36, 48–49, 53, 59, 63, 110–111; Christian 272; and Dharmapala, 284, 287, 290; global ethics, 289–300; James, 31, 286–287
Ethnicity, 18, 71, 87, 104, 162; and class, 161, 169; European, 11–12, 15, 16, 17, 19, 96, 222, 187; "fictive," 214; and heterogeneity, 156, 196; modernity, 169, 182; politics of, 231; vs. race, 4–5, 75–77, 98, 161–162, 187, 193; vs. region, 119–120; swarthiness, 161, 166, 169, 185, 187, 196; white, 75–76, 79, 161–163. *See also* Immigrants; Race
Ethnic Studies, 297–299
Eugenics, 204, 205, 214, 216, 217, 218
Europe, 69–70, 83, 94, 96, 105, 156, 157, 161, 175, 196–197, 222–223, 233, 234, 235, 238, 240, 247, 257
Exceptionalism: African-American, 25, 72, 84, 87–88, 214, 227, 232, 236–238, 248, 284; Christian, 254, 256, 271, 273, 278–279; Jewish, 86–87, 97, 110; metropolitan, 193; national, 71, 109, 280; Sinhalese, 284; subcultural, 73, 179. *See also* American exceptionalism
EZLN. *See* Zapatistas

Faction, 12–13
Fairchild, Henry Pratt, 161, 163, 203
Fanon, Frantz, 81, 107

Farrakhan, Louis, 289
"Federal republic." *See* James, William, "federal republic"
Feminism, 205, 206, 208–209, 217, 227, 232, 247–249, 295–296; in *Iola Leroy*, 240–241, 244–247. *See also* African Americans; Mendelist allegory
Ferguson, SallyAnn, 221, 223–224
Fetterley, Judith, 125, 315n1
Field, Eugene, 183
Filipinos, 22, 59–63, 89, 195
Fisk University, 68
Fix, Michael, 4
Flâneur/flâneuse, 6, 18, 100, 109, 122, 169–171, 174, 177, 191, 194, 293. *See also* Walking tours
Food, 158, 189–195
Fortune, T. Thomas, 77, 231, 319n26
Frank, Leo, 76–77,
Fraser, Nancy, 295–296
Freehan, Archbishop, 250–251, 256, 288–289
Fusion, 17, 23, 25, 33, 39, 67, 118, 157, 276, 294; Chesnutt's notion of, 217, 219–224, 232–233, 235, 246, 279; racial, 204–206, 218, 221–224, 228, 236; religious, 252, 256, 279, 281. *See also* Galtonian blending; Race, blending; Syncretism
Fuss, Diana, 208–209

Gaines, Kevin, 89, 213–214
Galeano, Eduardo, 303–304
Galton, Francis, 218–219, 225
Galtonian blending, 216–219, 221, 223–226, 232, 246
Gandal, Keith, 173
Gandhi, Virchand, 255
Garland, Hamlin: aesthetic theory of, 126–127, 129, 141, 153–155, 185; anti-assimilation, 154; asymmetrical regionalism, 152–155; city/country division, 122, 150–151, 293; and diversity 115, 118–119; on partisanism, 129; on the picturesque, 148, 156, 170; populism, 122, 137, 139–141; veritism, 126. *Works: Crumbling Idols*, 120, 126–127, 134, 153; *Jason Edwards, An Average Man*, 319n25; *Main-Travelled Roads*, 131, 145; "The Modern Novel in Germany and America,"

126; *A Spoil of Office*, 140; "Up the Coulee," 130, 139, 142–146, 148
Geary Law, 188, 192, 273. *See also* Chinese Exclusion Act of 1882
Gender: black masculinity, 89–90; effeminacy, 143–144; Institute for Race and Gender Studies, 298; manhood and poverty, 185; women and culture, 55, 144; women and machines, 106; women at the World's Parliament of Religions, 253. *See also* Feminism; Mendelist allegory
George, Henry: Single-Tax League, 140
Georgia, 100, 127, 148; Dougherty County, 25, 130, 147–149, 151
Ghettos, 23, 25, 92, 169, 170, 171, 172, 176, 179, 186. *See also* Slums; Urban picturesque
Giddings, Franklin, 17–18, 19, 20, 22–23, 197
Gillman, Susan, 207–208, 229
Gilman, Charlotte Perkins, 106
Gilman, Sander, 213–214
Gilpin, William, 164, 167, 170
Gilroy, Paul, 72, 90
Giroux, Henry, 33
Glazener, Nancy, 124, 125–126
Globalization, 3, 303–304
Godkin, E. L., 52, 56
Goldberg, David Theo, 7–8, 33
Goldman, Emma, 74–75
Gómez-Ibañez, Daniel, 288, 289
Gordon, Avery, 32, 72, 314n18
Gordon, Reverend, 263
Graham, Maryemma, 241
Gramsci, Antonio, 57, 60
Grant, Madison, 205, 223, 228, 235
Grant, Percy Stickney, 225
Green, Judith, 33
Green, Thomas H., 43
Grosz, Elizabeth, 208–209
Gypsies, 166–167, 181. *See also* Beggar Girls; Immigrants; Rag pickers

Hale, Edward, Jr., 120
Hall, G. Stanley, 109
Halstead, Murat, 117
Hampton, Wade, 224
Hamsun, Knut, 16

Hapgood, Hutchins, 171, 175, 178–179, 182, 194, 197, 293. *See also* Urban picturesque; Walking tours
Harding, Sandra, 216
Harlem. *See* New York City
Harlem Renaissance, 97
Harper, Frances, 23, 197–198, 204, 205, 217, 230, 231, 241, 248, 280, 293. Works: "Duty to Dependent Races," 246; *Iola Leroy*, 217, 226, 229, 233, 238–247, 249
Harris, Leonard, 294
Harrison, Alice, 169, 171, 191–192. *See also* Urban picturesque; Walking tours
Harte, Bret, 191
Harvard, 4, 42, 194, 203, 279; Dharmapala at, 286–287; Du Bois at, 24, 68, 119, 141; the elective system, 40–42; Golden Age of, 37, 40; "inner spiritual," 42, 45, 51, 67, 78, 89, 107–108, 110, 111; James at, 17, 40–42, 45, 54, 65, 68, 97; Kallen at, 24, 91–93, 97, 98; as model of "pluralistic universe," 42–43, 51, 53, 65; philosophy department, 10, 40; Santayana at, 17, 54, 93, 97; "undisciplinables" at, 9, 31, 42, 48, 59, 62, 75; Barrett Wendell at, 92, 93, 98, 99
Hasian, Marouf, 217
Hawthorne, Nathaniel, 156
Haygood, Atticus, 210
Haymarket Affair, 64, 178, 247
"Healthy-mindedness." *See* James, William, "healthy-mindedness"
Heathen's jeremiad, 269–276
Hebraic tradition, 92–93
Hecker, Isaac, 264
Hegemony, 57–58, 209
Herder, Gottfried von, 49–50, 307–308n6
Hereditarianism, 203, 210, 213, 214, 216, 220–221, 227; black appropriations of, 204, 207, 212–217, 220–223, 229, 231–236, 247–248, 249
Heredity, 82, 211, 213, 214, 216–217, 225, 226, 227; "hard," 205, 224, 225, 226, 228; laws of, 212, 213, 215, 220–221; "soft," 205, 218. *See also* Lamarckianism
Heterogeneity: and Americanism, 3, 10, 30, 198; in depictions of Asian culture, 22, 191, 263–264, 268, 278; domestication of, 10, 22; and eclecticism, 19–20;

essentialism of, 7–8, 213, 228; and exclusions, 33–34, 46–48; "heterogeneous personality," 22, 230–231, 244; vs. homogeneity, 7–8, 9, 23, 117–118, 157, 197, 206, 222; and immigrants, 156, 196–197; and modernization, 20; and the metropolis, 9, 19–20, 156–157, 196; "multicultural," 33; pathologizing of, 22; and pluralism, 34, 96; and postmodernism, 21, 33, 288; and progress, 18, 23, 94, 126, 157, 222, 265; and whiteness, 223; and unity, 293. *See also* Diversity; Variety
Hierarchy, 18, 45–49, 65, 118, 123, 155, 187, 205, 295; racial, 135, 160, 162–164, 187, 215
Higginson, Thomas Wentworth, 268
Higham, John, 69, 77, 84, 86
Hinduism, 25, 252, 258, 263, 269, 278; and unity in variety, 281. *See also* Vivekananda; World's Parliament of Religions
Hirai Kinzo, 271–272, 281, 290
Hirsch, E. D., 53–54
Hofstadter, Richard, 216, 326–327n5
Hoggan, Francis, 238
Hollinger, David, 72
Homogeneity, 3–4, 9, 18, 20, 134, 159, 203, 263; and Chesnutt, 224; vs. heterogeneity, 7–8, 9, 23, 117–118, 157, 197, 206, 222; of modernity, 9, 118, 294; and national underdevelopment, 23, 197. *See also* Progress, Spencerian theory of; Standardization; Uniformity
hooks, bell, 313n13
Hopkins, Pauline, 207, 210, 215, 229, 230
Horwitz, Howard, 216
Howard, June, 121, 315n1
Howells, William Dean, 20, 44, 64, 119, 129, 173, 184; and African Americans, 193, 237–239; Dreiser's criticism of, 184, 186. Works: "An Exemplary Citizen," 238–239; *A Hazard of New Fortunes*, 161; *An Imperative Duty*, 193; review of Garland's *Main-Travelled Roads*, 145, 146
Humanism, 101–103, 106, 215, 304; cosmopolitan, 63–64, 71, 73–74; "new," 102–103; radical, 70, 107, 110
Hunter, Robert, 157
Hutcheson, Robert, 79

Hutchinson, George, 207–208
Hybridity, 66, 91–92, 110, 203, 218, 221, 276, 284, 286, 294
Hyphen, 85–86, 119, 136

Identity culture: and cosmopolitanism, 71, 85, 108; and essentialism, 82, 111; and modern Americanism, 88, 101, 104, 227, 248; as a subculture, 81, 88, 107, 110, 248; relation to universalism, 71, 74. *See also* African Americans; Jewish Americans; Subculture
Identity politics, 66, 71–72, 73, 74, 123, 209; critiques of, 110–111. *See also* Essentialism
Ignatiev, Noel, 233, 329n21
Immigrants, 9, 11–12, 16–18, 25, 78; and African Americans, 162, 193, 238, 248; and authenticity, 175–177; as "Caliban type," 16; Caribbean, 16; Catholic, 12, 16, 86, 177–178; Chinese, 16, 106, 160, 187–192, 197, 272–273; European, 12, 16, 17, 96, 144, 160, 161, 162, 163, 174, 179–180, 181, 195, 198, 247, 248, 261; "foreign savor" of, 159, 176, 177, 238; "half-breed," 176–177; Irish, 193; Italian, 158, 161, 167, 171, 175, 176–178, 179, 180, 183, 185, 187, 190; Jewish, 12, 16, 68, 69–101, 103, 109–111, 116, 172, 175, 178–180, 183, 261; radicalism, 178, 179; and the urban picturesque, 158–163, 166–193, 195–198; whiteness, 75–77, 161–163
Imperialism, 69–70, 192, 255, 259, 281, 285, 286; anti-, 58–63, 70, 107, 255; Christian, 271, 282, 290; cultural, 60–62; industrial, 107. *See also* James, William
Incorporation: 10, 16, 25, 61, 69, 84, 116, 159, 160, 175, 294; and McDonaldization, 303–304; and region, 18, 127, 132–133; of subcultures, 237–238; and White City, 259–260
India, 22, 252, 253, 255, 257, 263–264, 289
Individuality, 9, 25, 41, 50, 60, 78, 80, 107–108; "group-individuals," 18, 78; and variety, 13, 14, 24. *See also* James, William, "each-form"
Industry, 102–107, 121–122, 123, 151
Intellectuals, 18, 26, 42, 70, 93, 106; African-American, 66, 73, 80, 83, 88–91, 197; and James, 45, 49–51, 53–58, 63–66, 67, 69; Jewish, 86, 110, 179–180; minority, 52, 74–75, 87
Intermarriage, 4, 84, 162, 202, 215, 228, 233, 236, 247, 248; in *Iola Leroy,* 239–240, 242, 244–245; Kallen on, 79, 82; in *The Squatter and the Don,* 133, 137–138; Wong on, 190, 191. *See also* Chesnutt; Fusion
Islam, 273–275

Jacobson, Matthew Frye, 75, 162
Jacoby, Russell, 4–5
James, Henry, 39, 54, 61, 68, 117, 146–147, 159, 179
James, William, 10, 17, 18, 20, 29–66, 74, 78, 91, 118, 165, 297, 299, 300, 304; anti-imperialism/imperialism, 58–66, 70, 88, 107; on the "college-bred," 50, 53–58, 67, 69, 75, 88–89, 110, 294; cosmopolitanism, 108–111; democracy, 29–30, 44, 47–49, 56–57, 91; and Dharmapala, 286–287, 290, 331n7; on Du Bois, 146–147, 148; "each-form," 24–26, 35, 39, 43, 49, 67, 69, 70, 71, 81–82, 85, 86, 91, 108, 110, 116, 119, 129, 159, 165, 175, 217, 226, 228, 251, 286; on exclusions, 35–36, 39–40, 45–49, 65, 95–96, 111; "federal republic," 49–53, 55, 64, 65, 67, 69, 73, 74, 87, 88, 96, 110, 175, 248; Gifford Lectures, 61; and "good" culture, 53–58, 67; at Harvard, 17, 40–42, 54, 68, 97; "healthy-mindedness," 46, 231, 244, 248, 287; "heterogeneous personality," 22, 230–231, 244; Hibbert Lectures, 36–37, 47, 56, 97, 295; liberal reform, 53–58; on monopolies, 43–44; multiculturalism, 10, 31–36; patrician roots of, 30, 49, 58; Philippines, 58–64, 89, 111; pluralism 10, 24–25, 29–66, 67–71, 73–74, 85, 91, 95–96, 110, 128, 159, 175, 226, 227, 249, 255, 260, 293, 296–297; "pluralistic universe," 12, 25, 34, 35, 38–39, 42, 46, 47, 65, 67, 110, 111, 159, 175, 251, 267; pragmatism, 29–31, 49, 58–59, 92, 104; "residual resistance," 38–39, 69, 70, 116, 127, 152, 192; "residuum," 38, 95–99, 107, 109, 159, 291, 294, 295; "right scale of subordination," 228, 286; "scale of

values," 55, 58, 64–65, 85, 91, 227, 230, 297, 302, 304; and variety, 29, 32, 34, 304. *Works:* "Address on the Philippine Question" 59–61, 63; "Great Men and Their Environment," 46; "The Moral Philosopher and Moral Life," 36, 48; "The Ph.D. Octopus," 37, 42; "The Philippine Tangle" 59–60, 62; "A Pluralistic Mystic," 21; *A Pluralistic Universe,* 29–37, 44–45, 47, 49, 51–53, 55, 58, 62, 69, 70, 85; *Pragmatism,* 31, 37, 40–41; *The Principles of Psychology,* 45–46; "The Social Value of the College-Bred," 47, 53, 62; *Some Problems in Philosophy,* 68; "The True Harvard," 42, 45, 47, 78; *The Varieties of Religious Experience,* 22, 61, 230

Jameson, Fredric, 205, 206
Japan, 252, 263, 271–272, 274, 276, 281
Japanese Americans, 271–272
Jefferson, Thomas, 120–121, 136
Jesus, 277–278, 290
Jewett, Sarah Orne, 125,
Jewish Americans, 16, 17, 66, 69–101, 103, 109–111, 275; and African Americans, 75–78, 90–91, 238; "dangerous" vs. "good," 175–176; as Puritans, 92–94, 101, 110; and socialism, 179–181; Yankee-Jewish bond, 97–99, 109–110. *See also* Bourne; Immigrants; Kallen
Johnson, Herrick, 262
Johnson, James Weldon, 241
Johnstone, Everett, 228
Jones, Reverend Lloyd, 272
Jordan, David Starr, 59, 61, 145
Journalism, 172; and Dreiser, 182–187
Journalists: and urban picturesque, 25, 158, 169, 170, 176, 191, 192; immigrant, 188
Judaism, 82, 93, 253, 275–276

Kallen, Horace, 24, 46, 66, 67–111, 116, 120–121, 146–147, 153, 190, 285, 286; on African Americans, 96–99; Americanism, 70, 87, 91–94, 96, 99, 101, 116, 190, 256; on class, 103–106; "consumptionism," 104–105; cosmopolitanism, 72–73; cultural pluralism, 76–79, 86–87, 92, 95–100, 102–105, 109–110, 117–120, 207; on culture vs. Kultur, 79–80, 207; defense of ethno-racial subcultures, 251, 285, 293; diversity, 286, 293; essentialism, 82–84, 123, 207; on exclusions, 96–99; hyphens, 85–86, 120; on James, 30, 46, 61, 67–68; and Jamesian pluralism, 24, 66, 68, 69–74, 77–80, 82–84, 91, 95–96, 293, 295; Judaism, 91–93; on local color, 118–119, 153; on machines, 101–102; as minority intellectual, 74–75; on modernity, 82, 92, 101, 109; orchestra, 18, 96–97, 99–102, 108, 175, 178, 195; variety, 101–102, 103; on workers, 102–105; Zionism, 86–87, 90. *Works:* "Americanization," 82; "'Americanization' and the Cultural Prospect," 94; *Culture and Democracy,* 79, 92, 96–97, 102–104; "Democracy versus the Melting Pot," 79, 82, 93, 96, 100; *Education, the Machine and the Worker,* 104; "Nationality and the Hyphenated American," 86; *William James and Henri Bergson,* 68

Kammen, Michael, 10
Kaplan, Amy, 20, 123, 124–125, 321–322n10, 324n26
Kazin, Alfred, 126
Keane, Reverend John, 251, 264
Keller, Helen, 68
Kern, Stephen, 16
Ketelaar, James, 253–254, 273
Kloppenberg, John, 56
Knadler, Stephen, 224
Knight, Richard Payne, 164, 166, 171, 173, 175
Knox, Dr. George William, 254
Kohler, Dr. Kaufman, 253
Ku Klux Klan, 70, 76, 77
Kung, Hans, 290
Kuyper, Abraham, 277

Labor, 7, 13, 129, 141, 143, 155, 163, 178–179, 196, 255; division of, 102, 105–106, 121; domestic, 106; Du Bois on, 105–109, 149–152; global, 102, 106–108; Kallen on, 101–105; peonage, 149–150, 152; and race, 105–109, 143, 152, 163, 193–194, 271–272; U.S. Dept. of, 147. *See also* Trade unions; Unions, labor
La Crosse Valley. *See* Wisconsin, La Crosse Valley

374   Index

Lamarckianism, 215, 216, 219–220, 225
Land, 15, 123, 140–141, 148, 150; land-owning class, 139, 149
Lannan Prize for Cultural Freedom, 303
Lasch, Christopher, 52, 59
Latinos, 4, 298
Lauter, Paul, 240
Law of Ancestry, 218. *See also* Galtonian blending
Lears, Jackson, 8, 16, 19–20, 172, 177–178, 231
Lentricchia, Frank, 30, 59
Levine, Lawrence, 54
Lewis, David Levering, 77
Lewis, Sinclair, 242
Liberalism, 24, 41, 73–74, 78, 91; and culture, 47, 54–55, 73, and Du Bois, 74–74, 95; genteel, 17, 19, 56, 58, 95; and James, 29, 42, 54, 56, 58, 95; and Kallen, 73–74, 95, 103; "new," 51; partisan, 73–74, 91, 95; as philosophy of the middle ground, 23, 103; Progressive, 24, 103; and socialism, 56; and variety, 21. *See also* Neoliberalism
Limerick, Patricia Nelson, 119–120
Lincoln, Abraham, 14–15
Lincoln-Douglas Debates, 11, 14–15
Lippard, George, 169
Lippmann, Walter, 29–30, 103–104
Little, Charles, 255, 262, 264, 274
Lloyd, Henry Demarest, 129
Local color, 25, 130, 154, 190; and African Americans, 146–150; and cultural pluralism, 118–121; and essentialism, 123; as hackneyed genre, 120; Kallen on, 118–119, 153; immigrants as, 172, 178, 181; as metropolitan discourse, 123–124; and pluralism, 115; vs. regionalism, 315n1; *The Souls of Black Folk* as, 146–148; and the urban picturesque, 158, 190. *See also* Regionalism
Locke, Alain, 97–99, 207
Longfellow, Henry Wadsworth, 37
Los Angeles. *See* California
Lowe, Lisa, 54
Lowell, James Russell, 37
Loyalty, 116, 232–233, 238–239, 317n13; Josiah Royce's definition of, 245; race, 232–233, 237–238

Luis-Brown, David, 135, 316–317n12
Lynching, 76–77
Lyotard, Jean-François, 21

Mabie, Hamilton Wright, 46–47
Madison, James, 11, 12–13, 18, 33, 51
Madrid, Arturo, 1–2, 6
Magazines, 10, 144, 159–161, 169–170, 176, 182–185, 192; magazine culture, 156. *See also* Periodicals; Walking tours
Majumdar, Protap Chandra, 270
Marcil-Lacoste, Louise, 32
Marcos, Subcomandante, 300
Martin, W. A. P., 263
Martínez, Elizabeth, 298–299
Matthews, Brander, 21, 318n22
Matthews, Victoria Earle, 213, 215, 216
Matthiessen, F. O., 184, 315n4
Mazzini, Giuseppe, 86
McCabe, James, 158–159, 196
McDowell, Deborah, 240
McKinley, William, 14, 61–62, 117–118
Mediation, 232, 236–237, 246
Melting pot, 11, 15, 17, 159, 251, 294; vs. smelting, 17–18, 20. *See also* Giddings; Zangwill
Mencke, John, 228
Mendel, Gregor, 205, 225
Mendelism, 205–206, 217, 221, 225–229, 231, 239, 248
Mendelist allegory, 25, 217, 219, 221, 225–249, 262–263; and asymmetry, 205, 206, 212, 217, 225–226, 230–232; as a black feminist practice, 205–209, 217, 232–236, 245–249; "crisis experience," 234, 241–244; as a defense of essentialism, 206–209, 217, 231–232; as a form of transvaluation, 212–217. *See also* Harper; Todd
Mendes, Henry, 253
Metropolis. *See* City; New York City; Urban picturesque
Mexican American War of 1848, 131
Michaels, Walter Benn, 74, 207–208
Mill, John Stuart, 34, 50, 51, 54, 78
Miller, Joaquin, 157, 158, 182
Miller, Kelly, 214, 221
Minority, 4, 12, 25, 70, 77; cultures, 60, 66, 82, 247; exceptionalism, 85; Emma

Goldman's definition, 74–75; faiths, 275; groups, 71; identities, 206; rights, 67; "sections," 127, 142, 153
Miscegenation. *See* Intermarriage
Missionaries, 22, 62–63, 190–191, 282–283, 285–286, 290; of culture, 55, 59, 67, 88–89
Moderation, 17, 21, 23, 187, 197
Modernism, 9, 21, 34, 155
Modernity: American exceptionalism, 50; anxieties about, 19–20, 45, 156–157; Du Bois on, 100–102, 108–109; and embrace of variety, 20–26; Garland on, 126–127, 142; homogeneity of, 9, 294; James on, 24, 52; Kallen on, 82, 86, 92, 101–102; and liberalism, 21; and national diversity, 5, 293; pluralism, 24; religious, 256, 259; Spencer's notion of, 18; Josiah Strong on, 120–121, 157, 158; and the urban picturesque, 155, 157, 169, 181, 182
Monism, 24, 43–44, 45, 50, 54, 55, 58, 69, 95, 96, 116
Monopoly, 43–44, 48, 121, 130, 133–134, 137, 139, 140, 191
Monroy, Douglas, 137
Moses, Wilson, 214
Mouffe, Chantal, 8–9, 295, 296
Moxom, Philip, 277
Mulattoes: biracial angst, 217, 218, 221, 230, 232–233; black feminist representations of, 226–249; in Chesnutt, 219–224; "fair," 226, 237, 238, 240, 244–245; law of hypodescent, 210; and the "marginal man," 241; and maternal genealogy, 216–217, 232–236, 238–249; as narrative device of mediation, 236–236, 246; "The Octoroon," 211–212; and polygenesis, 201–204, 209–212; tragic mulatta, 209–212, 216, 217, 221, 224, 229–230; untragic mulatta, 204, 224, 229–230, 232–236, 238–244. *See also* Mendelist allegory; "White Negro"
Mullen, Harryette, 213
Multiculturalism, 2–3, 5–8, 24, 124, 191, 193, 257, 295, 304; corporate, 105; and exclusions, 34, 48, 295; Nancy Fraser's conception of, 295–296; "insurgent," 33–35, 36; partisan, 297–304; and pluralism, 10, 32–36, 63, 66, 296, 297, 300;

postmodern, 31–36; Cornel West's conception of, 296–297
Munger, Reverend, 277

NAACP, 69
NAFTA, 300
Nash, June, 301
National Association of Colored Women, 194
Nationalism: American, 72, 74, 81, 86, 88, 91, 180–181, 196; black, 81, 205–206, 213, 214, 226, 232, 239, 243, 244, 246, 247, 280, 295–296; Eagleton on, 231; Jameson on, 205; "New," 51; Pan-Asian, 281–282; post-, 3; and regionalism, 120, 153; religious, 280–281, 284–286
Native Americans, 60, 148, 213, 217, 222, 289, 314n17
Native American Studies, 298
Nativism, 17, 69, 70, 74, 157, 163, 235, 247
Naturalism, 126
Neoliberalism, 297, 300, 303–304
New England, 19, 58, 70, 80, 87, 93, 99, 239, 243; as arbiter of literary taste, 118–119
Newfield, Christopher, 32, 72, 314n18
New York City: African Americans in, 100–101, 108–109, 161, 192–194; and diversity, 21, 157–159, 181, 192–193, 195–198; Dreiser on, 160, 182–187; Du Bois on, 100–101, 108–109; as female hysteric, 157; and food, 192–193; Garland on, 144, 159; Harlem, 73, 91, 109; Hell's Kitchen, 184–185; Howells on, 173; Little Italy, 161, 167–169, 176–178, 187; Lower East Side, 175, 178–180; as model of American modernity, 157–159, 181, 195–198; poverty in, 157, 166–170, 182–187; race riot of 1900, 193, 325n32; rag pickers, 166–170; "Shantytown," 167, 169; as spectacle, 157–158, 160, 175–187; uneven development, 105, 129, 151; and the urban picturesque, 156–191; walking tours of, 159–160, 169–182, 187–192. *See also* City; Immigrants; Urban picturesque
Ngugi wa Thiong'o, 315n3
Nicholson, Meredith, 128
Norris, Frank, 115, 192

Norton, Charles Eliot, 52
Nott, Josiah, 202–203, 215

Olcott, Colonel, 282
Omi, Michael, 76
One drop rule, 206, 210, 212, 215, 217, 223, 226–227, 229, 247

Page, Thomas Nelson, 148
Palumbo-Liu, David, 66, 71
Pan-Africanism, 69; and Zionism, 90–91
Partiality: in James, 38, 39, 48, 297; in regionalism, 128–130, 145, 152–155; significance of, 294, 304; in walking tours, 174
Particularity: ethnic, 18, 69, 104, 134, 175–176; Gilroy on transcending, 72; persistent, 79, 154, 206, 229, 294; and pluralism, 66, 67, 296–297; and progress, 25; racial, 69, 83–84, 90, 101, 108, 226; regional, 116–117; religious, 251, 278; resilient, 24, 111, 153, 237; and subcultures, 85, 109; and universalism, 73, 84, 101, 129, 294; and the urban picturesque, 160
Partisanism, 35–36, 52, 65, 73, 111, 129, 294–297; partisan multiculturalism, 297–304; and partisan plurinationalism, 303–304
Passel, Jeffrey, 4
Periodicals, 158, 159–160, 164, 167, 170–171, 176, 184, 188. *See also* Magazines
Persuasion: limits of, 36, 38, 291, 295–296; and religious conversion, 271–272
Philippines, 22, 31, 53, 58–64, 67, 89, 111, 274
Phillips, David Graham, 181
Philo-semitism, 99
Picturesque: anti-, 165, 187, 192–195; Du Bois on, 148–150; 18th-century, 164–166, 170; and Mendelist allegory, 226; and race, 165–166, 302; and regionalism, 142, 156; spectacle, 267–268; vs. sublime and beautiful, 164, 166, 197; swarthiness, 166–167; tourism, 156, 173–174; traveler, 167–171, 174, 176, 194–195; variety, 158, 165–166; and white supremacy, 165–166. *See also* Aesthetics; Urban picturesque
Pilgrims, 92–95
Pita, Beatrice, 131–132, 133

Pizer, Donald, 126,
Plessy, Homer, 211
Plessy v. Ferguson, 211
Pluralism: and Americanism, 29, 49, 78–79, 119; Christian, 265; Du Bois on, 77–78, 108; as ecclesiastical term, 29; and exclusions, 24, 35–36, 48–49, 65–66; hierarchical nature of, 44–45, 48, 294; Jamesian, 10, 24–25, 29–66, 73–74, 85, 91, 95–96, 105, 110, 128, 159, 175, 226, 227, 249, 255, 260, 293, 296–297; and liberalism, 24, 29, 103; limits of, 8, 36, 38–39, 44–45, 155, 295; and Mendelist allegory, 207, 226–227, 248, 249; and multiculturalism, 10, 32–36, 40, 48, 63, 296, 297; nativist, 74, 82; partisan, 95; postmodern, 35; and pragmatism, 29–31, 49, 58–59, 92, 104; and regionalism, 115–116, 118–121, 128, 155; and the urban picturesque, 159, 175, 197; and variety, 32–34, 158, 165, 256; World's Parliament of Religions, 255, 260, 265. *See also* Cultural pluralism; James, William; Kallen
"Pluralistic universe." *See* James, William, "pluralistic universe"
Polygenesis, 202, 204, 211, 215, 221, 229
Populism, 126, 127, 134, 137, 153, 257–258; in Du Bois, 139–142; in Garland, 139–142; in Ruiz de Burton, 138–139
Posnock, Ross, 58, 71, 84, 95
Pragmatism, 29–37, 49, 58, 92, 104
Price, Uvedale, 164, 165–166, 170, 175, 187, 197. *See also* Picturesque
Professionalism, 37–39, 42, 49, 170, 174, 184
Progress, 2, 19, 21, 25, 88, 124, 126, 134, 197, 223, 258; Chesnutt's theory of, 224; and homogeneity, 224; and imperialism, 258; and national unity, 197; religious, 279; secularization of, 261; Spencerian theory of, 18, 23, 94, 157, 222, 265
Protestantism, 12, 128, 138, 250–253, 286; consolidation of, 261, 264; heterogeneity of, 260–262, 264, 268–269, 271; Methodism as most popular denomination of, 261–262; uniqueness of American, 267; waning authority of, 262. *See also* Christianity; World's Parliament of Religions

Pung, Kwang Yu, 253, 272–273
Puritans, 92–94, 101, 110

Race, 13, 15, 70–84, 87–91, 94–101, 105–111, 210; biological-cultural definition of, 143, 222; blending, 23, 191, 210, 218–219, 232–233, 235, 237, 249; and class, 100–101, 106–109, 119–120, 149, 160, 166, 195, 248, 295–296; and ethnicity, 75–77, 98–99, 161–163, 187, 193; and labor, 105–109, 143, 149, 152, 163, 193–194, 247, 248–249; loyalty, 232–233, 237, 245; melodrama, 229; "pride," 73, 81, 215, 237; "problem," 18–19; "purity," 15, 213, 222, 224, 235; and region, 119–121, 135, 143, 146–152; and religion, 253, 255, 271–272, 279, 280; and science, 83, 201–205, 215–218, 222–229; and segregation, 109; as sociohistorical concept, 215; "suicide," 161; treason, 233; uplift, 205, 213, 217, 224, 227, 233, 238, 240, 241; and the urban picturesque, 161–166, 187–195, 197, 203, 247, 248; and urban space, 194–195; and variety, 14–15, 201–204, 213, 236–238
Race riots, 105, 111, 148, 193
Rachman, Stephen, 169; "devotional seeing," 178, 185
Racism, 15, 69, 70, 84, 111, 149, 165–166, 193, 223, 224, 228, 304; backlash against affirmative action, 296; within black community, 246; the black residuum, 109; Christian, 271; and critiques of identity politics, 208; internalized, 233; and urban picturesque, 161. *See also* White supremacy
Radcliffe College, 47, 55, 89
Radical empiricism, 39
Rag pickers, 166–170
Railroads, 79, 130, 132–134, 147, 259. *See also* Scott, Tom
Ralph, Julian, 181
Ravage, M. E., 172
Realism, 20, 153, 182–183
Regionalism, 18, 21, 25, 111, 115–155, 160, 293; and anti-urbanism, 159; asymmetrical, 152–155; and authenticity, 122, 123, 124, 146–147; literary access, 123; and the metropolis, 123–124, 130, 134, 140; and the middle ground, 118; as a modern genre, 125–128, 158; and a national literature, 115–116, 122, 152–153, 155, 158; native novelist, 122–123, 124, 129; and nostalgia, 124–125; and partisanism, 129, 152–155; pan-patrician, 130–139, 152; and the picturesque, 156; and populism, 139–142. *See also* Garland; Local color
Reiichi, Shibata, 276
Religion, 21, 22, 23, 251, 252, 253, 255, 275, 278, 279, 280; and diversity, 250–252, 266, 276; "ethnic," 253, 256, 274, 278; "synthetic," 281–284, 286, 287; "tribal," 253, 288; "universal," 249, 278–279; and variety, 251, 256, 262, 273, 276, 280, 293
Repressive tolerance, 62
Republicanism, 12, 29, 50–51, 136
"Residual resistance." *See* James, William, "residual resistance"
Residuum, 107, 159, 291; black, 95–97, 109; "unclassified," 95. *See also* James, William
Restaurants, 171, 172, 188, 191–192
Riis, Jacob, 170, 173, 183–184, 187–188, 192
Ripley, William Z., 161, 162, 222–223
Robbins, Bruce, 65
Romero, Lora, 125
Rooney, Ellen, 36, 309n6, 310n10, 310n11
Roosevelt, Theodore, 51, 331n6
Roseboro, Viola, 158, 161, 167, 169, 171, 175, 176–178, 179–180, 182, 185, 194, 293
Ross, Dorothy, 50
Ross, Edward, 16, 109, 117, 161–162
Rouse, Roger, 3
Royce, Josiah, 40, 120, 210, 239, 245
Ruiz de Burton, María Amparo, 127, 129–140, 152–155, 239
Russell, Bertrand, 79

Said, Edward, 164, 258
Sánchez, Rosaura, 131–132, 133
San Diego. *See* California
San Francisco. *See* California
Santayana, George, 17, 54, 58, 93, 97
Schaff, Philip, 265
Schiller, F. C. S., 36–37, 46
Schmidt, Sarah, 93

378   Index

Schultz, Alfred, 228
Science, 10, 83, 95, 201–204, 212, 213, 214–217, 221–223, 228, 287; and multiculturalism, 216. *See also* Hereditarianism; Heredity; Mendelism
Scott, Tom, 133
Sectionalism, 116–118
Senner, Joseph, 195
Shakespeare, 84, 98–99, 129
Shaler, Nathaniel, 161, 162, 203, 204, 213, 236–237
Shibata, Reiichi, 276
Shintoism, 252, 276
Shufelt, Robert, 210
Simmel, Georg, 194–195
Sinfield, Alan, 87
Sinophobia, 191, 192
Slater, Reverend, 263
Slavery, 14–16, 19, 84, 148, 202, 208, 210, 214, 216, 222, 236; debt, 149–150; in *Iola Leroy*, 229, 239, 242, 243; "white slaves," 139
Slumming, 174, 184, 188
Slums, 122, 178, 184–185. *See also* Ghettos
Snell, Minnie Andrews, 256, 257, 260, 269, 275, 276
Social Darwinism, 18, 202–203, 204
Socialism, 56, 157, 179–180, 207, 247
Soja, Edward, 118,
Sollors, Werner, 212
Southern Agrarians, 124
Sovereignty, 14, 15, 24, 75; Filipino national, 59–60; national, 108; subcultural, 78
Soyen, Shaku, 286
Spanish-American War of 1898, 22, 52, 64, 70
Spectatorship: professionalization of, 171–174. *See also* Walking tours
Speculation, 131, 132, 133, 137–138, 317n14
Speed, John Gilmer, 192–194
Spencer, Herbert, 18, 23, 157, 202–203
Spencer, Jonathan, 284
Sproat, John, 56
Squatters, 130–132, 136
Sri Lanka, 252, 284–285. *See also* Ceylon
Standardization, 24–25, 49, 70, 79, 83, 85, 293; of education, 41–44
Stanton, Elizabeth Cady, 253
Stepan, Nancy, 213–214
Stieglitz, Alfred, 167–168

Stiehm, Judith, 6–7
Stilgoe, John, 142; "metropolitan corridor" 133–134, 148
Stoddard, Lothrop, 70, 106
Stone, Alfred Holt, 162
Stonequist, Everett, 241–242
Strauss, Charles T., 275–276, 288
Strong, Josiah, 120–121, 157, 158
Stuart, T. McKendree, 263
Stuckey, Sterling, 81
Subcultures, 6, 23, 24, 70, 74, 78, 79, 119, 129, 179, 180, 188, 190–191, 239, 256; African-American, 87–88, 110, 237–238, 246, 247–248; "of criticism," 23, 87, 297; ethno-racial, 24, 69, 71, 73, 75, 81, 91, 111, 158, 198, 206, 226, 227, 251; intellectual, 25, 45, 52–53, 67
Sublime, 164, 166, 175, 182, 191, 197
Sui Sin Far, 188
Sundquist, Eric, 121, 124
Swarthiness. *See* Ethnicity
Syncretism, 213, 256, 276–280; hegemonic, 277–280, 281, 286; as Japanese concept, 281; subaltern, 277, 280–282, 284–287

Tarkington, Booth, 119
Taussig, Frank William, 141
Taylor, Charles, 70
Terrell, Mary Church, 193–195
Terrell, Robert, 194
Texas Pacific Railroad, 132, 133, 134, 136
Third World, 59, 107, 281, 284
Third World Liberation Front (TWLF), 298–299
Todd, Ruth, 197, 204, 205, 217, 230; "The Octoroon's Revenge," 226, 229, 233–236, 238, 240, 242, 243. *See also* Mendelist allegory
Toll, William, 77
Tolstoy, Leo, 63, 102
Totality, 30, 35
Toy, Crawford, 267, 277, 279
Trachtenberg, Alan, 16, 172, 259–260
Trade unions, 103, 105, 248, 298–299. *See also* Class; Labor
Transnationalism, 3, 25, 72–73, 109, 110, 175, 181, 192, 280, 303; "transnational imaginary," 195–198. *See also* Bourne
Transvaluation, 212–214, 223, 227, 280
Trilling, Lionel, 54

Trinh T. Minh-ha, 190
Trumbull, Matthew, 255
Turner, Frederick Jackson, 120, 127
Turnour, George, 284
Twain, Mark, 122–123, 124, 128–129, 235;
  Pudd'nhead Wilson, 234, 242

Underdevelopment, 23, 133, 146, 147–149, 154
"Undisciplinables." *See* James, William, "undisciplinables"
Uneven development, 25, 105, 111, 125, 130, 133, 140, 142, 145, 152, 259
Uniformity, 2, 9, 67, 79–80, 116–118, 126, 127, 190, 259–260, 303; vs. variety, 14–15, 17, 21, 23, 166, 197
Unions, 13, 20, 82, 138, 166, 197, 202–203, 226, 228, 236; labor, 178, 192, 248, 298, 299; side-by-side, 84, 108, 175, 195, 197, 203, 252, 266–267, 269–270, 274, 276. *See also* Trade unions
Uniqueness: American, 84, 87, 196, 280; Christian, 267, 273; cultural, 179; Jewish, 86; national, 2–3, 87, 282; regional, 156; sectional, 115; Southern, 150; subcultural, 71, 85, 116, 179, 188, 248
Unity: anxieties toward ("halophobia"), 33–34, 309–310n8; Catholic, 264–265; crisis of Christian, 260–266; critique of all-inclusive, 33–36, 43–44, 289–290; -in-discreteness, 159, 160, 249, 252, 256, 266, 276, 279–280, 286; -in-distinctiveness, 116, 118, 119, 175, 197; hierarchical, 44–49; limits of, 33–36, 47–49, 294; national, 1–2, 9, 15–16, 79–80, 116–117, 120, 154, 197, 214; Protestant notion of, 250–252, 266–269; "strung-along" type, 32; and variety, 32–35, 40–41, 116, 118, 119, 154, 165–166, 227, 249,251, 265, 276, 281, 287, 294, 287, 293, 302
Universalism, 25, 65–66, 71, 73–74, 84–85, 101, 129; limits of, 64–66, 294; religious, 266, 279–280
University of California, Berkeley, 297–300
Untragic mulatta. *See* Mulattoes
Urban Institute, 4
Urban picturesque, 21, 25, 155, 156–198, 293; and African Americans, 161, 163, 193–195, 197, 203, 247, 248; and Americanism, 159, 175, 176, 181, 293; and Americanization, 159, 162, 175–182, 190–191, 196; and Chinese immigrants, 187–192; and class, 156–161, 166–169, 172–173, 178, 183–187, 194–196; and Dreiser, 182–187; and European immigrants, 157–163, 166–193, 195, 197, 247, 248; and food, 192–198; and Jamesian pluralism, 159, 175; and local color, 158, 172, 178; and Mendelist allegory, 248; racial limits of, 163, 165, 166–167, 185, 187, 194, 195, 201, 247, 248; ragpickers, 166–170; and swarthiness, 161, 166–169, 182, 185, 187, 196; transnationalism, 158–159, 175–176, 179, 196–198; and variety, 158–161, 163–166, 179, 182–183, 186, 187, 192–193, 195–198, 293; and whiteness, 161–163, 165–166, 194–197, 203. *See also* Picturesque; Walking tours

Van Rensselaer, Mariana, 167, 169
Variety: and Americanism, 3–4, 9–11, 19–21, 197–198, 256, 280, 293; Christian, 260–269, 273, 276; and class, 12–13, 101–106, 183; cosmopolitanism, 6, 74, 196; de-essentializing of, 8; -in-discreteness, 80, 88; Dreiser on, 182–184; Du Bois on, 150–151; essentializing of, 8, 26, 198, 206; ethno-racial, 66, 82, 159–160, 182; "European varieties," 161–163; history of concept, 11–26; interracial sex and, 210; Henry James on, 117; William James on, 29, 32–35, 41, 65; limits of, 23, 25, 155, 166, 195, 291; and Mendelist allegory, 226–227; as moderation, 21–23, 34, 224; and partisanism, 304; "picturesque," 150, 158; postmodern uses of, 6–7, 8, 21, 33, 35; race, 14–15, 18–19, 203, 207, 213, 222, 226, 236–237; regional, 119, 126, 152, 154; religious, 251, 254, 256, 265, 267–268, 273, 274–276, 281, 286; scientific definitions of, 201–204, 206; shows, 104; "unharmonizable," 73, 99; vs. uniformity, 14–15, 294; and unity, 32–36, 70, 78, 102, 265, 281, 294, 303; urban picturesque, 158, 159–160, 165, 179, 192, 195, 196; and whiteness, 17, 70, 161, 163, 165, 203, 223, 227, 249, 251, 265–266, 303, 324; and white supremacy, 15, 165–166. *See also* Diversity; Heterogeneity; Multiculturalism

Veblen, Thorstein, 79
Veritism, 126–127
Véron, Eugene, 315–316n5
Vivekananda, Swami, 253, 255, 258–259, 269–270, 276, 281, 333n21

Wahl, Jean, 40
Walking, 172–173
Walking tours: counter-walking tour, 193–195; intra-urban, 10, 159–160, 169–179, 182–187, 191–194, 197. *See also* Immigrants; Urban picturesque
Wall v. Oyster, 211
Wang, L. Ling-Chi, 300
Ward, Lester, 218–219, 224, 225
Washington, Booker T., 89, 90, 94, 98, 227
Washington, D.C., 132, 134, 194–196, 237
Washington, George, 136, 317n14
Watson, Tom, 77, 210
Webb, Beatrice, 56
Webb, Mohammed [Alexander Russell], 273–275, 288
Weismann, August, 225
Wells, H. G., 56, 171
Welty, Eudora, 315n3
Wendell, Barrett, 92–93, 98–99, 109
Werbner, Pnina, 231
West, Cornel, 23, 49, 87, 296–297; on James, 30, 56, 58–59
Weyl, Walter, 103
White City, 259–260
"White Negro," 205, 206, 217, 221, 226, 228, 229, 231–233, 238, 247; in *Iola Leroy,* 245–246; in "The Octoroon's Revenge," 235–236. *See also* Mendelist allegory
Whiteness: and Americanism, 17–18; Californio, 135–136; and Chesnutt, 222–224, 279, 281; and effeminacy in Garland, 143; in Mendelist allegory, 232, 235; "probationary," 75–76; and the urban picturesque, 161–163, 165–166, 194, 197, 203; variegated, 17; at White City, 259–260; "white light," 265–266. *See also* Blackness; Ethnicity
White supremacy, 14–15, 17, 70, 209, 223, 228–229; relation to variety, 14–15, 165–166
Whiting, Lilian, 280
Whitman, Walt, 35, 153

Wiebe, Robert, 16
Williams, Fannie Barrier, 237, 253
Williams, Jesse Lynch, 174
Williams, Raymond, 11, 21, 121–122, 130, 154, 232
Williamson, Joel, 210
Wilson, Kimberly, 236
Wilson, Rob, 130, 196
Wilson, Woodrow, 22, 85, 117–118
Winant, Howard, 76
Wisconsin, 127, 143, 145; La Crosse valley, 130, 142–143, 145, 151
Wong Chin Foo, 171, 188–192. *See also* Chinatown; Urban picturesque; Walking tours
Working classes, 54, 56, 103–105, 167. *See also* Class; Labor
World War I, 10, 16, 70, 80, 105, 108, 111, 121
World's Congress of Representative Women, 248–249
World's Parliament of Religions, 21, 22, 25, 249, 250–291; African Americans at, 253; Asian delegates at, 253, 255–256, 258–259, 267–276, 280–287; centennial of, 287–291; Christian delegates at, 252–256, 260–269, 276–280; Christian pluralism, 265; vs. the Columbian Exposition, 252, 256–260, 266; cosmopolitanism of, 252–253, 266–269, 291; crisis of Christianity, 260–266; Jamesian pluralism, 251, 255, 260, 267; Protestant audience at, 269–273, 276, 290; Protestant organizers of, 259, 266–267, 269, 276; religious conversion, 252, 254, 269–270; 271, 275–276; 285. *See also* Barrows; Buddhism; Christianity; Dharmapala; Heathen's jeremiad; Hinduism; Syncretism; Vivekananda

Young, Edward Clarke, 70
Young, Elizabeth, 244–245
Young, Iris Marion, 6, 7, 17, 102–103; "unoppressive city," 109, 303
Yúdice, George, 196

Zamir, Shamoon, 309–310n8
Zangwill, Israel, 11, 17
Zapatistas, 300–302.
Zhang, Qingsong, 188, 190–191
Zionism, 86–87; and Pan-Africanism, 90–91